Regional Autonomy, Cultural Diversity and Differentiated Territorial Government

Regional Autonomy, Cultural Diversity and Differentiated Territorial Government assesses the current state of the international theory and practice of autonomy in order to pursue the possibility of regional self-government in Tibet. Initiated by a workshop and roundtable with political representatives from different autonomous regions, including His Holiness the 14th Dalai Lama, this book brings together a group of distinguished international scholars to offer a much-needed enquiry into solutions to the Tibetan quest for 'genuine' autonomy. Examining the Chinese framework of regional self-government, along with key international cases of autonomy in Europe, North America and Asia, the contributors to this volume offer a comprehensive context for the consideration of both Tibetan demands and Chinese worries. Their insights will be invaluable to academics, practitioners, diplomats, civil servants, government representatives, international organisations and NGOs interested in the theory and practice of autonomy, as well as those concerned with the future of Tibet.

Roberto Toniatti and **Jens Woelk** are based at the University of Trento, Italy.

Law, Development and Globalization
Series Editor – Julio Faundez, University of Warwick

During the past decades, a substantial transformation of law and legal institutions in developing countries has taken place. Whether prompted by market-based policies or the international human rights movement, by the relentless advance of the process of globalization or the successive waves of democratization, no area of law has been left untouched. The aim of this series is to promote cross-disciplinary dialogue and cooperation among scholars and development practitioners interested in understanding the theoretical and practical implications of the momentous legal changes taking place in developing countries.

Titles in the series:

Justice Reform and Development: Rethinking Donor Assistance to Developing and Transitional Countries
Linn Hammergren

Law and Society in Latin America
Cesar Rodriguez Garavito

Policing and the Politics of Order-Making
Peter Albrecht and Helene Maria Kyed

Violence Against Women in Legally Plural Settings: Experiences and Lessons from the Andes
Anna Barrera Vivero

Regional Autonomy, Cultural Diversity and Differentiated Territorial Government: The Case of Tibet – Chinese and Comparative Perspectives
Roberto Toniatti and Jens Woelk (eds)

Regional Autonomy, Cultural Diversity and Differentiated Territorial Government

The Case of Tibet – Chinese and Comparative Perspectives

Edited by Roberto Toniatti and Jens Woelk

Routledge
Taylor & Francis Group
LONDON AND NEW YORK

First published 2017 by Routledge

2 Park Square, Milton Park, Abingdon, Oxfordshire OX14 4RN
711 Third Avenue, New York, NY 10017

Routledge is an imprint of the Taylor & Francis Group, an informa business

First issued in paperback 2018

British Library Cataloguing in Publication Data
A catalogue record for this book is available from the British Library

Library of Congress Cataloging in Publication Data
A catalogue record for this book has been requested

ISBN: 978-0-415-52535-0 (hbk)
ISBN: 978-0-367-02416-1 (pbk)

Typeset in Baskerville
by Keystroke, Neville Lodge, Tettenhall, Wolverhampton

Contents

Notes on contributors

Thomas Benedikter, economist and social researcher, Eurac Research, Bolzano/Bozen.

Rafael Bustos Gisbert, Professor of Constitutional Law, University of Salamanca.

Michael C. Davis, Professor of Comparative Constitutional Law and Public International Law, University of Hong Kong.

Jean-François Gaudreault-DesBiens, Professor of Constitutional Law, University of Montréal.

Yash Ghai, Emeritus Professor of Constitutional Law, University of Hong Kong.

Andrew Harding, Professor of Comparative Constitutional Law, National University of Singapore.

John W. Head, Robert W. Wagstaff Distinguished Professor of Law, University of Kansas.

Hans-Joachim Heintze, Associate Professor of International Law, Ruhr University Bochum.

John Morison, Professor of Jurisprudence, Queen's University Belfast.

Roberto Toniatti, Professor of Comparative Constitutional Law, University of Trento.

Michael C. van Walt van Praag, Executive President and co-founder of Kreddha, International Peace Council for States, Peoples and Minorities.

David C. Williams, John S. Hastings Professor of Law, Indiana University, Bloomington.

Jens Woelk, Associate Professor of Comparative Constitutional Law, University of Trento.

Acknowledgements

This edited volume is the result of a collaborative research project that aims to explore the possibilities that the Memorandum on Genuine Autonomy for the Tibetan People may hold in bringing self-government to Tibet. It is about analysing and comparing a number of cases considered good practice in autonomy in order to identify features which may become useful inspiration for innovative solutions. Examining the options offered by the Chinese constitutional and legal situation is possible only by understanding the interests and constraints of both sides. Thus, an attempt to read the Chinese translation and use of concepts, which are familiar to the Western legal tradition and experience, has to be made, as these concepts may have a different meaning and thus operate differently in the Chinese context despite the use of the same terms. This attempt of understanding is the precondition for any attempt to dialogue and to project Tibetan autonomy requests into the Chinese system.

We thank all contributors for having embarked together enthusiastically in this dialogue, which has lasted considerably longer than originally planned and thus made updates of the chapters necessary. We also thank our editors at Routledge (in particular Laura Muir) for their endless patience and continuous support. For careful copy-editing work, we would like to thank Lucia Busatta and Marta Tomasi.

The project has been supported by the Autonomous Province of Trento and organised by the Faculty of Law at the University of Trento (Italy) and Eurac, the European Academy of Bolzano/Bozen (Italy). As such, it benefitted from the strong institutional support of a region that is widely recognised as a successful example of regional autonomy.

Roberto Toniatti and Jens Woelk
Trento, December 2016

Neither panacea, nor Pandora's box

Comparing autonomy with a view on Tibet and China

Jens Woelk

1. Tibet and China: An intractable conflict? 'Genuine autonomy' as the solution?

Since the Dalai Lama fled into exile, in 1959, China has gained formal international recognition of its sovereign claim to Tibet through a combination of physical occupation and *realpolitik*. In parallel, however, over the last decades, a strategy of non-violence and global outreach has created considerable international interest in the human rights situation in Tibet and in the autonomy claims of Tibetans (in exile), reaching a peak after demonstrations, riots and subsequent Chinese crackdown in early 2008, just before the Beijing Olympic Games.

The People's Republic of China (PRC) has long claimed to provide autonomy to Tibet already, dividing the Tibetan settlement areas into a Tibetan Autonomous Region and twelve contiguous autonomous areas. The Dalai Lama and Tibetan exile leaders have long questioned this claim, proposing their own formula for genuine autonomy. After informal contacts between the two sides, this formula was outlined in more detail by the Tibetans in exile in the 2008 'Memorandum on Genuine Autonomy' submitted to the PRC Government.[1] A resolution of the conflicting claims by the parties is not in sight; the Chinese Government has not offered any proposals in response to Tibetan and international concerns. Thus, the question remains open, whether autonomy, as some critics fear, is only the first step on the road to either assimilation or secession, or whether it can be the path to securing basic human rights for the Tibetan people and be a means for preserving and developing their culture.

This volume is about (territorial) autonomy as a means of diversity management enabling culturally diverse populations and sub-national territories to preserve

1 Memorandum on Genuine Autonomy for the Tibetan People (2008) Dharamsala, 16 November 2008. Available at: www.tibetoffice.ch/web/mwa/memorandum/ [Accessed: 14 February 2016]. See in particular Chapters 4 and 5, by Michael C. Davis and Michael van Walt van Praag, in this volume, illustrating the Chinese-Tibetan relations and the contents of the Memorandum.

their diversity,[2] and manage their own affairs as well as a substantial share of public affairs, within the context of a State and its territorial and administrative structures as well as within a globalised and integrated world. The volume is the result of a collaborative research project that aims to explore the potential of the 'Memorandum on Genuine Autonomy for the Tibetan People' from a comparative perspective.

The authors draw on the experiences of autonomous areas around the world confronting them with the Chinese approach to (autonomous) territorial governance with a view to exploring whether there may be a common understanding of autonomy. The larger question is how it is possible to maintain, preserve and develop a distinct identity within the larger context of territorial administration within a State and multinational integration, a challenge many countries have to face in a world where independence and self-determination are a mirage even for those who have formally achieved them.

A comparative overview of good practice in the legal and practical applications of autonomy in Europe, North America and Asia is important for anyone interested in the management of ethnic diversity and conflict around the world. It is especially relevant, however, when applied to the Tibetan case in the wake of the Memorandum on Genuine Autonomy. The Chinese legal system – in theory and practice – is the context in which realistically any future Tibetan autonomy will have to be integrated, as independence does not seem to be an option. Thus, an examination of the Chinese framework of regional self-government, in combination with an analysis of key international cases, promises to open up new perspectives in the exploration of the Tibetan quest for substantial autonomy within China.

2. Territorial autonomy: Not (yet) a positive right, but widely practised

A right to autonomy is not (yet) recognised in international law, despite the increasing number of territorial autonomy arrangements in constitutional law.[3] In fact, contrary to common perception, autonomy is hardly an exception and there

2 According to the focus on diversity management, 'sub-national' refers to 'regional' territorial entities within a State, between municipal and State level, but also understood demographically, i.e. with a population different from the majority of the State in cultural, ethnic, linguistic or religious terms.

3 See SKURBATY, Z. (ed.) (2005) *Beyond a One-Dimensional State: An Emerging Right to Autonomy?* Leiden: Martinus Nijhoff; and ROACH, S.C. (2004) 'Minority Rights and an Emergent International Right to Autonomy: A Historical and Normative Assessment'. *International Journal on Minority and Group Rights*. 11. pp. 411–432. Until the adoption of the UN Declaration on the Rights of Indigenous Peoples (2007), there was no clear international standard by which to evaluate autonomy; however, even this Declaration is not binding. The term 'autonomy' is used differently by scholars; for a broad overview of possible conceptualisations, see TKACIK, M. (2008) 'The Characteristics of Forms of Autonomy'. *International Journal on Minority and Group Rights*. 15(2–3). pp. 369–401.

are numerous autonomy arrangements around the world, as well as growing interest in academic debate.[4]

Territorial autonomy enables a group to form a de facto majority within (a part of) the State, thereby exercising effective control or at least a degree of control on government in this territory. Territorial autonomy ensures that the interests of the members of a minority group are reflected in the linguistic, religious or cultural preferences of that level of government. Therefore, autonomy arrangements directly address the asymmetry of power with the dominant group and a minority's under-representation and weakness in terms of involvement in public and political life, its vulnerability to discriminatory practices and exclusion from effective participation in public life.[5]

In the case of compact settlement of a group, autonomy can be granted to the territory coinciding with that area, creating autonomous territorial entities: in these cases, autonomy is usually realised by means of a sub-national public body (one or more municipalities, a Province or Region, a Member State in a federal system) which often is vested with a wider range of powers. This special status typically requires some form of constitutional or legal entrenchment due to the differentiated status and, by consequence, exceptions from other constitutional rights and values. Entrenchment can take the form of a (Special or Autonomy) Statute or Basic Law, often adopted in a special procedure; the constitutional rank of autonomy (or, at least, its superiority vis-à-vis ordinary legislation) is an important guarantee against subsequent change, which usually requires special procedures.

4 Among the most important contributions to the debate on the topic there are HANNUM, H. (1996) *Autonomy, Sovereignty and Self-Determination – The Accommodation of Conflicting Rights*. Philadelphia, PA: University of Pennsylvania Press; LAPIDOTH, R. (1997) *Autonomy: Flexible Solutions to Ethnic Conflicts*. Washington, DC: US Institute of Peace Press; SUKSI, M. (ed.) (1998) *Autonomy: Applications and Implications*. The Hague: Kluwer Law International; GHAI, Y. (ed.) (2000) *Autonomy and Ethnicity. Negotiating Competing Claims in Multi-Ethnic States*. Cambridge: Cambridge University Press; WELLER, M. and WOLFF, S. (eds) (2005) *Autonomy, Self-Governance and Conflict Resolution. Innovative Approaches to Institutional Design in Divided Societies*. London and New York: Routledge; WELLER, M. and NOBBS, K. (eds) (2010) *Asymmetric Autonomy and the Settlement of Ethnic Conflicts*. Philadelphia, PA and Oxford: University of Pennsylvania Press; SUKSI, M. (2011) *Sub-State Governance through Territorial Autonomy: A Comparative Study in Constitutional Law of Powers, Procedures and Institutions*. Berlin and Heidelberg: Springer; and GHAI, Y. and WOODMAN, S. (2013) *Practising Self-Government. A Comparative Study of Autonomous Regions*. Cambridge: Cambridge University Press. However, few of these take a specifically legal approach, and none addresses the issue of Tibet or of regional self-government in China. An exception is the volume by HENDERS, S.J. (2010) *Territoriality, Asymmetry and Autonomy*. New York: Palgrave MacMillan, which comprises Tibet in a comparative study (together with Catalonia, Corsica and Hong Kong) focusing on asymmetrical autonomy arrangements.

5 It constitutes a power-sharing formula that in effect gives a group the structural and political control from which it may protect itself against the often discriminatory practices of State authorities; see DE VARENNES, F. (2012) 'The Challenges of Globalization for State Sovereignty: International Law, Autonomy and Minority Rights'. In PALERMO, F., POGGESCHI, G., RAUTZ, G. and WOELK, J. (eds) *Globalization, Technologies and Legal Revolution: The Impact of Global Changes on Territorial and Cultural Diversities, on Supranational Integration and Constitutional Theory*. Baden-Baden: Nomos. p. 128.

Allowing for the transformation from minorities into majorities or, at least, into minorities which are numerically stronger and thus more influential, the 'secret' of (territorial) autonomy lies in the exercise of rights and/or self-government within the logic of the majority principle, without challenging it openly, making their operation easier to integrate for the legal systems. In a certain sense, self-government rights replicate or imitate the idea of the nation-state (imagined identity of community and 'its' territory) regarding a part of its territory. It is exactly for this reason that these rights are often (wrongly) associated with the idea of secession.

This is the primary reason for the reluctance of States to recognise such a right at international level: in fact, an express right to autonomy or internal self-determination is still missing in treaty or customary international law. However, some recent international documents and instruments show that the International Community is at least considering self-government options: the UN Declaration of the Rights of Indigenous Peoples; Article 35 of the Copenhagen Declaration on Human Dimension of the Conference on Security and Cooperation in Europe;[6] and the Organization for Security and Co-operation in Europe's (OSCE) Lund Recommendations on Effective Political participation in Public Life of National Minorities. Despite its potential, the majority of States, principal actors at international level, still seem to fear autonomy as a first step on a sliding slope inevitably leading to secession and thus to a change of borders. Empirical evidence seems to tell a different story and several cases, such as the Basque Country, Northern Ireland, Bougainville, Aceh, New Caledonia and Jammu and Kashmir, etc., are proof of the escalation of conflict in case of a refusal to meet the request for a functioning and substantial autonomy system within a State.[7]

Another important reason for the current non-recognition of a right to autonomy at international level is its consequence within the domestic sphere. Territorial autonomy has to be integrated in the structures of territorial government of the State. It not only regards the relationship between individual citizens, the identity groups and the State, but also the composition and powers of the executive, legislative and judicial branches of government and their relationships; in short, it raises questions regarding the institutional structures and the organisation of the State as a whole.[8]

Territorial self-governance alone, allowing for 'internal' self-determination of groups as well as preserving the overall territorial integrity of the State, is often

6 'Appropriate local or autonomous administration as one of the possible means' for the promotion of the 'ethnic, cultural, linguistic, and religious identity of certain minorities'.

7 PALERMO, F. (2009) 'When the Lund Recommendations are Ignored. Effective Participation of National Minorities through Territorial Autonomy'. *International Journal of Minority and Group Rights*. 16. pp. 653–663 ff.

8 These three aspects are highlighted, in different order, by WOLFF, S. (2008) 'Complex Power Sharing as Conflict Resolution'. In WOELK, J., PALERMO, F. and MARKO, J. (eds) *Tolerance Through Law: Self-Governance and Group Rights in South Tyrol*. Leiden and Boston: Martinus Nijhoff. p. 351.

insufficient for a sustainable solution of a conflict. In particular, where minority groups share a territory with parts of the majority population, further mechanisms for the accommodation of ethnic diversity are necessary for guaranteeing a stable and durable settlement of the conflict. Thus, a combination of minority rights and decentralised territorial governance has been discussed above all by political scientists: various theories of conflict resolution have elaborated different approaches for the institutional design in these situations. Among them, power sharing assumes a prominent place, although recently often criticised as too rigid a mechanism.[9] The formula of 'complex power sharing' (Stefan Wolff) is therefore used for characterising 'the result of the implementation of a self-governance regime whose success as a conflict settlement device requires a relatively complex institutional structure that cannot be reduced to autonomy/(ethno)federalism, (traditional) power sharing or power dividing'.[10]

Thus, two different strands can be distinguished when looking at the cases and discussing the option of territorial autonomy: autonomy can be a means for guaranteeing ethnic, linguistic or religious pluralism in minority situations. However, in more general terms, it is also used as an instrument within the system of territorial government for increasing the efficiency of public administration, as well as democratic participation. In the latter dimension, it is intimately linked to sovereign decisions on the State as how to (re-)organise its own institutional and territorial structures.[11] The concrete shape of territorial structures and the room for local and regional self-government usually depends on historical precedents and experiences, but also on economic and demographic considerations. While reference to history and precedents can limit choices (path-dependency, identity issues), territorial government is far from being static as numerous reforms in many countries demonstrate: there is room for choice and change.

In fact, in Europe, after a general trend of strengthening sub-national entities and expanding their sphere of autonomy in the 1990s,[12] notably with the

9 WOLFF (2008), above note 8, summarises the debate between the two different schools on power sharing – consociationalism and integrationism – and the more recent theory on power dividing, pp. 333–338.

10 Definition by WOLFF (2008), above note 8, p. 340.

11 This is, for instance, also recognised by the European Union vis-à-vis the Member States as the respect of their 'national identity' by the EU institutions expressly includes their 'fundamental structures, political and constitutional, inclusive of regional and local self-government', Art. 4.2 TEU (Lisbon Treaty, 2009).

12 The slogan 'Europe of the Regions', coined in this period, emphasised the complementary role of regions in Europe. 'Devolution' in the United Kingdom (1999), constitutional reforms of the regional system in Italy (2001), the continuous reforms in Belgium as well as the reform of the German federal system (2006) are not the only phenomena in the last twenty years. See WEATHERILL, S. (2005) 'The Challenges of the regional Dimension in Europe'. In WEATHERILL, S. and BERNITZ, U. (eds) *The Role of Regions and Sub-National Actors in Europe. Essays in European Law*. Oxford: Hart. pp. 1–35.

introduction of the principle of subsidiarity on different levels of legislation,[13] more recently, since 2008, the economic and financial crisis has triggered a new wave of territorial reforms; these, however, often aim at re-centralising some functions in the name of higher budgetary efficiency.

Partly as a consequence of the trends strengthening local and regional self-government, important progress was possible regarding the solution of some long-lasting conflicts – for example, Northern Ireland.[14] In fact, the recognition of territorial autonomy can contribute to maintaining the unity and territorial integrity of a given State and, at the same time, allow for participation and involvement of minorities through an important role in one level of territorial government in which they are a majority of the population or, at least, a significant portion. In Western Europe, the peaceful solution for contested territories has certainly been favoured by European integration, which softened security concerns and created a general basis for cooperation and a common value system. In this context, cross-border cooperation of sub-national entities offers new potential for developing peripheral border areas economically, but also facilitated maintaining cultural and personal relations with a neighbouring kin State.

Although recently more attention has been dedicated in academic debate to non-territorial forms of autonomy,[15] (the request for) territorial autonomy continues to dominate the scene and therefore the thinking of politicians and their counsellors. Legal systems are generally based upon the territorial criterion – for example, area/scope of application of rules. This holds true in general, but also characterises the organisation of the public administration apparatus in various layers of territorial government and jurisdictions. In consequence, thinking in territorial terms has become the general approach familiar to majorities and minorities alike. Thus, territorial forms of autonomy can be considered the most frequently used means for minority self-government, in particular for groups concentrated in one more or less compact settlement area. A particular feature in these cases is the combination of territorial government with minority rights, on the basis of the territorial principle (specific area of application) and/or the

13 Subsidiarity as a principle for the exercise of powers between different spheres of government strengthens the concept of self-government by means of a bottom-up logic: generally, a task should be fulfilled by the jurisdiction closest to the citizen, provided that there are no efficiency losses in doing so. The principle first appears in the European Charter of Local Self-Government of the Council of Europe (1985). Subsequently, it is used in EU law: 1986 in the European Single Act (related to environmental issues); and 1992 in the Maastricht Treaty establishing the European Union (as a general principle in the field of shared powers).

14 Through the Anglo-Irish Agreement (1985) and the Good Friday/St Andrews Agreement (1998); see the chapter by John Morison in this volume.

15 The debate on Non-Territorial Autonomy (or personal or cultural autonomy) is not new, but has intensified in recent years. See, e.g. ROACH, S.C. (2005) *Cultural Autonomy, Minority Rights and Globalization*. Burlington, VT: Ashgate; and the recent volume by MALLOY, T.H. and PALERMO, F. (eds) (2015) *Minority Accommodation through Territorial and Non-Territorial Autonomy*. Oxford: Oxford University Press.

personal principle (application of specific rules and guarantees for members belonging to a specific group).

3. Combining minority rights and regional self-government: A European or Western model?

The starting point for comparison is the rich experience with regional self-government and territorial autonomy in Europe,[16] which is often combined with minority protection. As the modern (nation-)State is a European invention, it hardly comes as a surprise that territorial solutions guaranteeing the integrity of that State through the accommodation of linguistic, cultural and religious diversity have also been developed in Europe. In fact, the (presumed) homogeneity of the population forming a nation making up a State has, in most cases. rather been a mirage; only few cases of homogenous populations exist in Europe: an exception rather than the rule. Frequent border changes and exchange of territories made it necessary to integrate groups with different characteristics compared to the majority population of the State. These groups were considered 'minorities' vis-à-vis the State-building nation, i.e. smaller in numbers and in a non-dominant position, but having decided to maintain their diversity. Where these groups resided in a compact area, special minority rights could be applied in the linguistic, cultural or religious field and on a territorial basis;[17] self-government of such areas added to these rights in some cases, often based upon international treaties.[18] Thus, 'internal self-determination',[19] i.e. territorial autonomy, became a solution for accommodating self-government claims within a State, where external self-determination would not have been possible or accepted.

16 A comparative analysis and evaluation of different autonomous territories in Europe is provided by the Council of Europe's Chamber of Regions in Recommendation 346(2013) and Explanatory Memorandum 'Regions and Territories with Special Status in Europe', CPR(25)2FINAL, 30 October 2013; both available at: https://wcd.coe.int/ViewDoc.jsp?id=2107887&Site=COE [Accessed: 14 February 2017].

17 The most well-known examples are the territorial compromise regarding religion after the Westphalian Peace and the treaties regarding the population of Poland after the divisions of the country in the eighteenth century.

18 Some treaties on the foundation and guarantee of autonomy regimes go back to the interwar period, such as the establishment of an autonomous regime for the Åland Islands, thus accommodating their Swedish-speaking population in Finland. SUKSI, M. (2007) 'Sub-National Issues: Local Government Reform, Re-Districting of Administrative Jurisdiction, and the Åland Islands in the European Union'. *European Public Law*. 13(3). pp. 379–406; SPILIOPOULOU ÅKERMARK, S. (ed.) (2011) *The Åland Example and Its Components – Relevance for International Conflict Resolution*. Mariehamn: The Åland Islands Peace Institute.

19 SPILIOPOULOU ÅKERMARK, S. (2013) 'Internal Self-Determination and the Role of Territorial Autonomy as a Tool for the Resolution of Ethno-Political Disputes'. *International Journal on Minority and Group Rights*. 20(1). pp. 5–25.

3.1 Minority rights to autonomy in compact settlement areas

History has shown that *international safeguards* for minority rights are often necessary. Thus, the League of Nations established guarantees for various bilateral instruments as well as the possibility of review of individual obligations in order to ensure the effectiveness of the latter.[20] The loss of authority of the League of Nations, lack of a general human rights protection system and strengthening of nationalist spirits throughout Europe in the 1930s led to the failure and dissolution of that early system. However, the 1921 decision on the Åland Islands granting protective instruments for their Swedish-speaking population has survived from this era and still serves as the basis for an advanced and functioning autonomy system.[21]

Despite the general focus on the establishment of a general system of individual Human Rights protection after the Second World War, two important bilateral agreements have been successful in establishing working systems of minority rights and of territorial autonomy, providing empirical proof of the feasibility of sustainable long-term minority rights protection:

- the Bonn-Copenhagen Declaration in 1955, i.e. two unilateral, but interrelated governmental declarations on German and Danish minorities on both sides of the German-Danish border;
- the Gruber-De Gasperi Agreement on South Tyrol (5 September 1946)/ Treaty of Paris (1947).

After 1989, these have become reference points for the creation of new (bilateral and multilateral) instruments. In fact, the main multilateral instruments for minority-protection in Europe were adopted in the *1990s*, as a late reaction to violence and ethnic conflict in the Balkans, the Caucasus and the Baltic Republics: the Council of Europe's (CoE) Framework Convention for National Minorities (FCNM)[22] and the European Charter of Regional or Minority Languages (ECRML)[23] both possess binding character and have been ratified by thirty-nine and twenty-five of the forty-seven Member States, respectively. Complementary to these binding instruments, a growing *body of soft law* illustrates and clarifies the meaning of a number of guarantees. From the mid-1990s, the *OSCE's High Commissioner on National Minorities*, an early warning institution for prevention and

20 HILPOLD, P. (2012) 'Bilateral Protection Agreement(s) in Minority Rights: History, Current Position, and Perspectives'. In PALERMO, F., POGGESCHI, G., RAUTZ, G. and WOELK, J. (eds) *Globalization, Technologies and Legal Revolution: The Impact of Global Changes on Territorial and Cultural Diversities, on Supranational Integration and Constitutional Theory*. Baden-Baden: Nomos. p. 503.

21 See SPILIOPOULOU ÅKERMARK (2011), above note 18.

22 Adopted on 1 February 1995, in force since 1 February 1998 (CETS 157).

23 Adopted on 5 November 1992, in force since 1 March 1998 (CETS 148).

mediation in case of conflict, has released a number of *Expert Recommendations* on various areas relevant to minority protection, such as Education, Linguistic Rights, Political Participation, etc.[24] These instruments shall provide further guidelines of good practice based upon the conviction that dialogue and persuasion of the value of pluralism and minority protection are essential for successful and sustainable solutions (which cannot be guaranteed by unilateral adoption of measures). Some of these instruments include reference to forms of (cultural and territorial) autonomy; the OSCE Bolzano/Bozen Recommendations on National Minorities in Inter-State Relations of 2008 expressly encourages States to conclude bilateral treaties or arrangements for enhancing and developing minority rights (point 18).

In more general terms, in Europe's pluralistic and diverse societies, *territorial ownership has come to be seen as conditioned by minority rights*.[25] However, multilateral standards have to be adapted and refined for guaranteeing the right balances at local level.[26] The complementary role of the three regional organisations – OSCE (security dimension), CoE (democratisation) and European Union (integration) – reinforces the constitutional implementation of guarantees in favour of minorities through monitoring systems and conditionality mechanisms.

3.2 A set of European standards for local and regional self-government

Despite the (historical and present) differences in their systems of territorial government,[27] over the last decades European States have developed a *common legal framework*: a set of common principles regarding sub-national, decentralised territorial government has been recognised and framed in various legal instruments, most of which are in the realm of the Council of Europe.[28] The main documents

24 The most important OSCE Recommendations are the Lund Recommendations on Effective Participation of National Minorities in Public Life (September 1999); Oslo Recommendations on Linguistic Rights of National Minorities (February 1998); The Hague Recommendations on Education Rights of National Minorities (October 1996); and the Bolzano/Bozen Recommendations on National Minorities Inter-State Relations (June 2008); all available on the website of the OSCE High Commissioner: www.osce.org/hcnm/66209 [Accessed: 14 February 2017].

25 This is in line with the Responsibility to Protect (R2P) concept approved by the UN General Assembly in 2005, according to which the primary responsibility to protect the population (including minorities) rests with the State, while opening to a (subsidiary) responsibility of the community of States.

26 In particular, in the case of national minorities, where the role of a (neighbouring) kin State might complicate the picture, a bilateral approach is vital and essential for successfully and sustainably implementing minority rights.

27 With regard to the autonomy of the sub-national level, three main categories of States can be distinguished: States without territorial autonomy or with only administrative decentralisation, States in which (some) sub-national units enjoy legislative or even constitutional autonomy, and federal systems.

28 In particular, through the work of the Congress of Local and Regional Authorities; see Congress website, www.coe.int/t/congress/default_en.asp [Accessed: 14 February 2017].

are the – binding – European Charter of Local Self-Government (ECLSG, 1985), signed and ratified by all CoE Member States, and the – non-binding – Council of Europe Reference Framework for Regional Democracy (2009), containing similar principles for the regional level: in particular, the respect for the rule of law in procedures and institutions as well as equal dignity and mutual respect (as complementary principles) are necessary in horizontal and vertical relations between levels of government.[29]

In the context of regional self-government as part of the system of territorial government of a State, autonomy is seen as an instrument for increasing the efficiency of administrative action and services. An indicator for this approach is the proliferation of the subsidiarity principle, as a legal principle, which provides for decisions to be taken as close as possible to those directly concerned and possibly involving the latter in the same decisions. The subsidiarity principle is part of the ECLSG (Article 4.3).[30] It has been used also in EU law for regulating the exercise of (shared) powers between EU and Member States in a flexible manner, based upon the criteria of necessity and adequateness (Article 5.3, Treaty of the European Union (TEU)). Furthermore, some national Constitutions have recently introduced formal reference to the principle and to similar criteria.[31] EU law is also increasingly taking regional diversity and different systems of territorial government into account.[32]

3.3 The European method: Persuasion through permanent dialogue – at different levels

The development and elaboration of these common principles is characterised by *reciprocal influence* between single models and general standards: while functioning cases contribute to the identification of general rules and principles providing

29 See, for instance, at 1.4.3 Council of Europe Reference Framework for Regional Democracy (para. 25).

30 Art. 4.3 ECLSG: 'Public responsibilities shall generally be exercised, in preference, by those authorities which are closest to the citizen. Allocation of responsibility to another authority should weigh up the extent and nature of the task and requirements of efficiency and economy.'

31 For instance, Art. 118 Italian Constitution (as amended by Const. Law 3/2001) and Art. 5a Swiss Constitution (as amended by constitutional revision of 24 November 2004; in force since 1 January 2008).

32 See the express reference to regional structures of territorial government in Art. 4.4 TEU (2009), as part of the specific 'national identity' of the Member States and their constitutional structures, the European Union has to respect. See TONIATTI, R., PALERMO, F. and DANI, M. (eds) (2004) *An Ever More Complex Union: The Regional Variable as the Missing Link in the EU Constitution?* Baden-Baden: Nomos; BENGOETXEA, J. (2012) 'Autonomous Constitutional Regions in a Federal Europe'. In CLOOTS, E., DE BAERE, G. and SOTTIAUX, S. (eds) *Federalism in the European Union*. Oxford and Portland, OR: Hart Publishing. pp. 230–248; VAN NUFFEL, P. (2012) 'Does EU Decision-Making Take into Account Regional Interests?' In CLOOTS, E., DE BAERE, G. and SOTTIAUX, S. (eds) *Federalism in the European Union*. Oxford and Portland, OR: Hart Publishing. pp. 191–209.

empirical evidence of what works, new standards identifying common trends and convergence on values and principles as well as new institutions also have an impact on the situation in single (conflict) areas, in particular through monitoring and conditionality.[33] This circular, mutually reinforcing approach based upon persuasion and dialogue can be seen as a specifically European method in a geopolitical area characterised by different spheres of political, economic and legal integration.[34]

The intervention of monitoring bodies, such as advisory committees and independent experts, in combination with soft political pressure from an international organisation, facilitate and guarantee a triangular dialogue between the international organisation, the State and the group concerned. Thus, minority protection (and, at least to some extent, territorial governance) is no longer an internal affair of a given State, but an obligation resulting from different domestic and international sources and monitored by international organisations.

The combination of binding law and soft law as well as monitoring requirements and dialogue on different levels, in a context characterised by reliance on the Rule of Law and democratic participation, has created a positive dynamics with a circulation of models and good practices based upon persuasion and consultation rather than imposition by unilateral action. Of course, not all conflicts have been resolved, but the European approach is promising under the aspect of sustainability of solutions, due to the inclusion and participation of those concerned as well as its flexibility allowing for tailor-made solutions.

The majority of States emphasise territorial integrity of the State in their constitutions and does not recognise a right to secession or independence of sub-national entities. However, in recent years, there have been a number of cases of separation and secession in Europe, as well as of respective political claims and movements. Paradoxically, European integration and a peaceful environment appear to favour these claims. However, in a democratic context, respectful of human and minority rights, the right to secession is difficult to qualify as part (or extreme consequence) of the right to democratic participation.[35]

33 Most binding legal instruments of the Council of Europe (including those of the Congress of Local and Regional Authorities, e.g. the ECLSG) provide for monitoring mechanisms, which have been strengthened over time in order to guarantee their effective and sustainable domestic implementation. These monitoring mechanisms are typically based upon a dialogue with State authorities. Conditionality, i.e. (verification of) implementation as a precondition for technical and financial assistance and/or progress in relations with the European Union, in particular regarding preparation of future accession, has added political weight and legal concreteness to the political monitoring process.

34 In particular, through the work of the Congress of Local and Regional Authorities.

35 In the cases of the Basque and Catalan independence movements, the Spanish State refused to address the question of territorial self-determination politically; legal issues and the Constitutional Court played a major role in affirming the principle of territorial integrity. By contrast, the case of the Scottish referendum on independence shows that this fundamental political question may be answered differently in a different constitutional setting and culture. However, the Scottish example

4. Chinese principles and Tibetan expectations: Which potential for autonomy?

On 16 November 2008, the Tibetan Government in exile presented a 'Memorandum on Genuine Autonomy for the Tibetan People' to the PRC Government. The Memorandum had been adopted by a Conference of Tibetans in Exile and represents at present the official position of the Tibetan Government in exile and of the majority of the Tibetan people in exile. The Memorandum 'puts forth [the Tibetan Government in Exile's] position on genuine autonomy and how the specific needs of the Tibetan nationality for autonomy and self-government can be met through application of the principles on autonomy of the Constitution of the People's Republic of China, *as we understand them*' (emphasis added). It was immediately rejected, on a political level, by the PRC.

Taking stock of China's own experiences with differentiated territorial government and taking Chinese worries seriously is the focus of Part I of this volume. The objective is to identify the Chinese view on and implementation of important Western concepts, in particular the rule of law principle, essential for legal certainty and, thus, stability of any autonomy arrangement. The first chapters illustrate the specific Chinese legal culture and the constitutional context of the PRC with the intention to explore the potential of autonomy in that system before analysing the Tibetan expectations and proposals regarding autonomy, in particular the Memorandum.

Based upon Chinese legal history, the first chapter: 'Foreign influence and constitutionalism in the PRC: A Western perspective on change and uncertainty in contemporary Chinese legal culture', by John W. Head, illustrates several related aspects of Chinese constitutionalism. The author examines whether and in which way the current legal system of the PRC corresponds to the concept of constitutionalism and how foreign influences have shaped this concept, before focusing on the 'rule of law' principle and examining the conformity of the amended Constitution of 1982 with this principle. His analysis as well as the observation that different and changing Chinese views on these aspects exist, and thus a fundamental uncertainty, lead the author to warn against the (too) easy

also demonstrates that such a decision cannot be made unilaterally: in case of a positive referendum, negotiation about the details of the way to independence would have been necessary. Comparative experience shows that while political claims cannot be prevented by explicit or implicit rules denying the right to secession, such claims need to be embedded in a procedural context that cannot but include negotiation and agreement by the parties involved. This important lesson, together with the need for pre-established rules and clarity in the referendum procedure, has been learned from the terrible consequences of unilateral referendum decisions leading to the dissolution of Yugoslavia and war; on the issue of the unlawful referendum that took place in Crimea in 2014, see the Venice Commission CDL-AD (2014)002-e. On constitutional issues of secession, see MANCINI, S. (2012) 'Secession and Self-Determination'. In ROSENFELD, M. and SAJÓ, A. (eds) *Oxford Handbook of Comparative Constitutional Law*. Oxford: Oxford University Press. pp. 481–500.

assumption of close correspondence between similar concepts, despite similar terminology: compared to other legal traditions, in particular the Western one, these concepts differ in substantial and fundamental ways in the Chinese context which are not always easy to detect.

In the second of the two chapters he contributes to this volume, 'The rule of law in China: Fundamental uncertainties about "decoding" a fundamental concept' (Chapter 2), John W. Head examines the concept of the 'rule of law', the understanding and implementation of which will be fundamental for any autonomy arrangement for Tibet to be established within the constitutional and legal framework of the PRC. After clarifying its contents in scholarly debate, the author observes that there is a clear commitment to the principle since the Chinese Constitution has been amended in 1999 (including the notion that the government is bound by the law). However, it is highly uncertain whether the Chinese concept translates into a 'thick' version of the rule of law, or whether it is a rather instrumentalist, 'thin' version. According to the author, the Chinese conceptualisation is in any case quite different from the Western one, creating considerable problems for determining the rules governing territorial autonomy within the Chinese constitutional and legal system.

In the third chapter, 'Dilemmas of "Genuine Autonomy" for Tibet', Yash Ghai starts from the observation that the 'current stalemate arises because China has offered autonomy within the constitutional provisions for nationality minorities as set out in the legislation on National Regional Autonomy (NRA) and Tibetans want autonomy under Article 31 (OCTS), which gives considerable discretion to the National People's Congress (NPC) in designing the autonomy'. The chapter examines the two bases of autonomy in order to assess which form would best accommodate the claims of the Tibetans. By contrast with National Regional Autonomy for ethnic minorities, which is regulated in great detail in the constitution and further legislation, in the absence of such legislation, the concrete shape of the OCTS formula fully depends on a basic law adopted by the National People's Congress in order to establish the 'high degree of autonomy'. This corresponds to the necessity of having room for negotiation as OCTS and Article 31 were originally intended as a way for permitting re-unification with Taiwan and only subsequently effectively used for handover of Hong Kong (and Macau). In both cases, the 'purpose of the Basic Law is to retain as much of the economic, social and cultural system of Hong Kong [or Macau] when it was a colony, with the primary focus on its market economy'. However, while China is interested in the market, it feared democracy and has thus resisted the full democratisation of elections. According to the author, the applicability of the OCTS formula to Tibet 'is more a political than a legal issue'. The Hong Kong experience is analysed in detail: an important detail is the mechanism for settling controversies regarding the autonomy, the Committee for the Basic Law to be consulted by the Standing Committee of the NPC before adopting certain important decisions (listed in the Basic Law). Although this is supposed to mean consultation and negotiation, in practice the mechanism has not worked as a true interface. Further weaknesses of Hong Kong's autonomy are illustrated, leading to the conclusion that this path for

Tibetan autonomy would be no more secure, constitutionally and legally, than an autonomy system based upon National Regional Autonomy.

After the Chinese view on minority and regional self-government issues, the two remaining chapters of Part I raise and discuss the decisive question of (which is) the potential for Tibet. While taking into account the different dimensions of the complex situation, the Tibetan demands and their place within existing Chinese law (mainland and Hong Kong) are assessed from a predominantly legal point of view.

The Memorandum is a Tibetan projection of the instrument of autonomy into the Chinese constitutional and legal framework trying to reconcile both. Inspired by the will to find a peaceful and sustainable solution even without external self-determination, this exercise should have signalled to the Chinese side a further attempt to seriously engage in dialogue respecting Chinese concerns. The Memorandum uses the frame of the Chinese system and in particular two of its pillars: the differentiated and asymmetrical system of territorial governance; and the elaborated system of minority protection based upon recognition, special rights and even regional autonomy, which also allows for asymmetrical application. Although reality and implementation are certainly different from the 'law in the books', in particular in the Chinese, post-socialist context, pragmatism and functional solutions also characterise the Chinese system, opening potential room for innovative solutions encouraging Tibetans to look for innovative solutions within that system.

The Memorandum identifies eleven areas as 'the basic needs of Tibetans' to be satisfied in order to realise a 'genuine autonomy' within the PRC and elaborates these further.[36] Comparative research in this volume shall verify whether those eleven areas correspond to internationally – and domestically – consolidated good practices and how they relate to the current constitutional and legal system of the PRC.

Thus, the fourth chapter, 'Chinese policies on regional self-government: The case of Tibet', by Michael C. Davis, considers current Chinese practice and possible alternatives, both from domestic constitutional and international human rights perspectives. The author reconstructs the dynamics in the development of the different positions, with the Chinese Government insisting on its sovereignty claim and the Tibetans in exile initially seeking independence. However, in the 1980s, a policy change took place, when the Dalai Lama repeatedly sought 'genuine autonomy', gathering renewed international attention for the Tibetan issue and earning the Nobel Prize for Peace in 1989. China continued to pretend that there was no Tibetan issue, while repeated unrest in the Tibetan Autonomous

36 The eleven areas of self-government are: (1) Language; (2) Culture; (3) Religion; (4) Education; (5) Environmental Protection; (6) Utilisation of Natural Resources; (7) Economic Development and Trade; (8) Public Health; (9) Public Security; (10) Regulation on Population Migration; and (11) Cultural, Educational and Religious Exchanges with Other Countries.

Region culminated in demonstration and riots, followed by severe reactions of containment by Chinese security authorities. After the March uprising in 2008, there were several informal meetings with the Dalai Lama's representatives in which the latter were asked to outline the Tibetan position under the Chinese Constitution, which led to the adoption of the 'Memorandum on Genuine Autonomy for the Tibetan People' in Dharamsala (India), 16 November 2008. The Memorandum was intended as a starting position for negotiation. It combines two main tracks provided in the PRC Constitution: Article 4, national ethnic autonomy policies; and Article 31, known as the Hong Kong formula ('one country, two systems') and allowing for an exemption of local laws within the scope of autonomy from central government control. Considering history and international practice, the chapter examines the potential of these two tracks which both promise, according to the author, 'a flexible approach tailored to the special needs of the autonomous community'. However, the Chinese Government has offered no accommodation of Tibetan concerns so far, categorically rejecting both approaches – in stark contrast with China's own objectives of a harmonious society.

In the fifth chapter, 'The Memorandum on Genuine Autonomy for the Tibetan People: An explanatory introduction to the Tibetan proposal', Michael C. van Walt van Praag explains the details of the Tibetan proposal for autonomy within the PRC system, as well as the Chinese Government's resultant harsh and critical reactions. The author first looks at the intent of the drafters of the proposal (Memorandum and Explanatory Note), i.e. the Dalai Lama and the leaders of the Tibetan exile community, in order to better understand the form and underlying nature of autonomy they consider 'genuine' (i.e. real, vis-à-vis the current nominal one). Besides meaningful competencies in the field of preservation and development of Tibetan identity and culture with its spiritual and linguistic heritage, as well as environmental protection and questions of migration control, the entrenchment of the autonomy arrangement and dispute resolution are seen as essential for confidence in the faithful implementation of any agreement. Comparison of existing autonomy arrangements underlines the importance of guarantees for the implementation of autonomy and against unilateral change of the arrangement. In the second part of the chapter, the Tibetan requests are put into the wider context of international practice and discourse on autonomy. In particular, China has also supported the adoption of the UN Declaration on the Rights of Indigenous Peoples (2007), which expressly comprises a right to autonomy! The chapter closes with a detailed review of the Chinese Government's reaction to the Tibetan proposal.

5. The comparative approach: Analysing cases of substantial and effective autonomy

Part II compares experiences of regional autonomy and differentiated territorial government by examining their historical experiences, basic foundations, institutional elements and characteristic legal features. It aims to assess the current state of theory and practice regarding autonomy by looking at regions that have been able to establish some measure of meaningful, effective, differentiated territorial government. For this purpose, cases inside Europe – in Spain, the United Kingdom and Italy – as well as outside Europe – Canada (Quebec) and the Asia-Pacific region (Aceh, Burma and Malaysia, as well as in India) – are discussed.

Many of these cases are widely considered good practice, including by those concerned. Some cases present critical or problematic features or are not yet fully implemented. Through comparative analysis with a focus on constitutional law in order to detect the foundations and guarantees of the respective autonomy, common principles and trends shall be identified in order to create the ground for comparison with the Chinese constitutional system. Therefore, in most contributions, the two complementary elements of minority protection and territorial self-governance are at the centre of interest, as well as the analysis of their concrete combination. The way toward autonomy as well as the lessons to be drawn beyond the single cases and with a view to Tibet and China complete the focus chosen for the single chapters.

The analysis of European and Canadian experiences starts with Jens Woelk's chapter 'From compromise to compact: Working autonomy in South Tyrol'. The South Tyrolean autonomy arrangement is widely considered an inspiration and even a 'model' for other situations offering interesting insights regarding the negotiation process leading to the establishment of an autonomy system, as well as issues of implementation over time. In fact, as a system working for decades, it shows the need for constant adaptation to internal as well as external change. The mechanisms of institutionalised dialogue with the central government are illustrated, as well as the power-sharing system for regulating the living-together of groups and their cultural autonomy. The case also shows the potential of autonomy: what used to be a conflict-ridden and extremely poor Alpine region has developed into one of the wealthiest areas of Europe, in which three linguistic groups live together peacefully. Ahead of its time, its experience also inspired more recent instruments on minority protection at European level.

Differentiation based upon historical and current differences is the main focus of Rafael Bustos Gisbert's chapter: 'Asymmetric regionalism in Spain: Catalonia and the Basque Country'. Apart from historical differences, linguistic and cultural diversity, important for justifying differentiated solutions in the Spanish regional system, the author stresses the importance of public security and of economic development and trade relations in the Spanish context (and beyond). In his accounts of the unfolding of the Spanish regional system and, more recently, the self-determination debate regarding the Basque Country and Catalonia, the element of (failed) political negotiations is central, highlighting an important element to be structurally and institutionally considered when establishing an autonomy system.

In the eighth chapter, 'Devolution and devolution plus: Anti-foundationalist foundations for constitutionalism', John Morison presents the complex relationship between the different parts of the United Kingdom resulting from asymmetrical, pragmatic and negotiated 'devolution'. Although certainly a special case, the United Kingdom experience 'demonstrates how a mature democracy can accommodate change, the possibility of a radical re-ordering and even dissolution of some its constituent forms, without undue trauma to the body politic'. In fact, the devolution process has not only affected the three entities, but also transformed the whole country. Central, again, has been negotiation, as is stressed in particular with a view to Scotland (referendum on independence) and to the even more complex situation in Northern Ireland (experience of the peace agreement). With regard to the latter, the potential of ideas of transitional justice and conflict resolution, recognition and power-sharing, and consociationalism to provide an 'anti-foundationalist foundation for new constitutional arrangements' are reviewed and examined, and the compatibility of these features with the constitutional framework is assessed.

'Can Quebec's relative autonomy within Canada be a template for Tibet?' is the question asked by Jean-François Gaudreault-DesBiens in the ninth chapter. It illustrates the autonomous powers and the relative cultural autonomy that Quebec enjoys within the Canadian federation. It also details the mechanisms that ensure its integration and representation at the federal level, inter-communal relations within the Province and the space that is allowed to Quebec in respect of external relations. However, Quebec's progression toward greater autonomy over the years stems from the building of a *rapport de forces* that is grounded in very specific historical circumstances and that stems from the Province's integration within a broader polity that possesses a long-standing democratic political culture. Still, there are hurdles to be avoided in order to facilitate dialogue. Among these, symbolic issues in particular are likely to reinforce nationalism and thus retrenchment, i.e. the reduction of identities and institutional relations to one dimension only, thus continuously stressing the antagonistic elements and deepening existing or perceived cleavages.

Going beyond Europe and Western experiences, not only geographically, a second main focus is (mostly) on Asian experiences in order to verify whether specific Asian approaches exist, different from Western experiences, which are to be considered for the Tibetan autonomy requests vis-à-vis China, as part of a common and more specifically Asian cultural and value context.

In Chapter 10, Hans-Joachim Heintze characterises 'The autonomy of Aceh' as still in the phase of post-conflict rebuilding. In particular, the autonomous powers of the entity have not (yet) been sufficiently used for improving the economic and living conditions of its population. This points to the important fact that the legitimacy of autonomy systems, as that of any territorial entity, is linked to its capacity of efficiently providing services. However, this is not (only) a problem of government. In fact, also according to the author: 'The real challenge is better law enforcement and the development of a civil society.'

David C. Williams raises delicate questions regarding the ways leading to the establishment of an autonomy system. In Chapter 11, 'Sometimes guns are the answer: The path to autonomy in Tibet, Burma and South Sudan', Williams compares the Tibetan situation to that in South Sudan and Burma. While the non-violent approach may mobilise international support, but remain ineffective in terms of results, despite a victory by military means usually being impossible, armed resistance movements have often achieved 'a mutually hurting stalemate . . . conducive to peace settlements', the author provocatively argues.

'Territorial autonomy in India' is at the centre of Chapter 12 by Thomas Benedikter. India's Constitution provides for an asymmetrical federal system and also enshrines some forms of autonomy. While all major linguistic groups have become titular peoples of a federal State during the linguistic reorganisation of the Indian Union in the 1950s and 1960s, minor ethnic groups do not have 'their' State. The chapter illustrates the situation of 'Autonomous District Councils' (ADCs) in districts in the Northeast of India dominated by 'tribal peoples'. The so-called 6th Schedule Autonomy has, however, been insufficient for some peoples, which instead insisted on their quest for 'full federated statehood', some of whom have been accommodated (for example, Naga peoples), while others have not.

Federalism in a complex context is also at the core of Chapter 13 by Andrew Harding: 'Is Malaysian federalism a good example or a warning for solving the China/Tibet issue? A brief inquiry into a half-century experiment in asymmetric federalism'. According to the author, it is an interesting case, because 'despite the lack of enthusiasm . . . it is plausibly the only Asian example of a successful federation' besides India. Highlighting the potential of asymmetrical solutions even within federal frameworks, the author stresses that, under the federal Constitution, two States, Sabah and Sarawak, with a majority of indigenous peoples, enjoy more autonomy than the eleven states of West Malaysia. Consequently, the sustainability 'test is whether the Federal Government can live with state governments of a different political stripe; and whether state governments can in practice operate within the constraints imposed by the Constitution'. Among the examined variables determining balances in a Federation are fiscal relations and party politics ('if a single party holds power at the federal level . . . it can assert overwhelming power and effectively demolish all but the appearance of federalism').

The applicability of the comparative experiences to the Tibetan context, reflections on (territorial) autonomy, its integration in the wider State and international contexts as well as suggestions for the way forward, are discussed in the final conclusions by Roberto Toniatti: 'Concluding observations: One country, *three* systems: The Tibetan quest for genuine autonomy between European experiences and Asian perspectives'. Lessons from the comparative experience are drawn, focusing on power-sharing systems, the implementation and guarantees of autonomy solutions, as well as on specific Asian features of territorial and personal autonomy. Particular attention is paid to the circulation and foreign influence of legal models and best practices in the examined systems.

6. Combining Chinese principles and comparative good practice: It all starts with dialogue ...

The main concern of this book is dialogue. How can dialogue be created and transformed into procedures and institutions in order to guarantee its continuity and consolidation, thus (re-)creating trust and confidence? In a number of cases, dialogue and compromise have helped find and implement solutions for the peaceful living together of different groups and autonomous government of a territory within a State. In the analysed cases, dialogue as well as the autonomy solutions found and applied have been more or less successful depending on the views, interests and, not least, the will of those involved, on the larger context, but also on the specific legal foundations and general cultural environment.

These variables play out differently in the examined cases and there is certainly no standard model for autonomy to be universally applied, nor is there any general road map to be followed for establishing durable and constructive relations on which any autonomy system is necessarily built.[37] Thus, the only way leading to such a system is to create positive incentives for (elites on) both sides, as it is through shared interests that positive dynamics and sustainable solutions can be achieved. The first step on this path is to spell out the respective interests clearly and to discuss them.[38]

Launching the 'Memorandum on Genuine Autonomy for the Tibetan People' some years ago, Tibetans in exile have clarified their positions and expectations by outlining in greater detail than ever before what 'internal self-determination' within the PRC may and shall mean for them. Chinese reactions to these proposals have been far from encouraging. But reliance on a position of strength and power has been the norm rather than the exception in many other cases, too. The same is true for constraints of a political, economic or cultural nature, which are often seen or perceived as insurmountable obstacles.

However, many of the examined cases also demonstrate that dialogue can produce innovative and workable solutions. Taking stock of these experiences is important. Autonomy is the model to which both parties to this dispute have lent their official support – in fact, the PRC has established an Autonomous Region for parts of historic Tibet and autonomy is the model that the Tibetan Memorandum

37 As a decisive common feature, the central importance of guarantees for the implementation of autonomy and against unilateral change of the arrangement has emerged in practically all contributions. An interesting parallel between European and Western systems and the PRC is also the existence of two tracks for justifying territorial autonomy: minority rights and (asymmetrical) decentralisation and regionalism. While in China these seem to be interpreted as alternative ways to regional self-government, in Europe the combination of both is rather common.

38 Various chapters stress the importance of the consultation mechanism for settling controversies regarding the autonomy and its implementation. The Committee for the Hong Kong Basic Law, established with an equal number of members representing the PRC and Hong Kong, reminiscent of the joint commissions in South Tyrol or the Joint Ministerial Committee in the United Kingdom, may be another interesting parallel to explore for an institutional frame of dialogue.

explicitly calls for. This volume focusing on autonomy considering Tibetan demands, Chinese worries and principles as well as comparative experiences from a wider context (both Western and Asian) will hopefully be able to contribute to the important debate in a measured, scholarly and comparative manner, offering support and encouragement to both parties as they attempt to resolve their differences on this issue.

Part I

Differentiated territorial government in China: Potential for Tibet?

Chapter 1

Foreign influence and constitutionalism in the PRC

A Western perspective on change and uncertainty in contemporary Chinese legal culture

John W. Head

1. Introductory observations

1.1 Aims and limitations

My principal aim in this chapter is to help achieve the objective of the volume by offering some general observations about Chinese constitutionalism.[1] I note that the objective of the volume is to verify whether the areas of self-government (enumerated in the 'Memorandum on Genuine Autonomy for the Tibetan People') correspond to internationally and domestically consolidated good practices, as well as to the Chinese constitutional and legal system. Particular attention will be paid to the circulation and foreign influence of legal models and best practices in the examined systems.

I wish to focus my attention on two aspects of this statement of objective: (1) 'the Chinese constitutional and legal system'; and (2) 'foreign influence (in the PRC) of legal models'. In particular, I hope to throw some light on the concept of 'constitutionalism' as it operates in the contemporary legal system of the PRC. In doing so, I shall emphasise that despite a very substantial amount of 'foreign influence', most recently from the West, the Chinese concept of 'constitutionalism' differs importantly from the Western concept – and particularly from the American concept with which I am most familiar.

In a companion chapter to this one – see Chapter 2 – I shall try to illustrate these general points by focusing more detailed attention on how the notion of 'rule of law', as enshrined in the PRC Constitution for about a decade, carries a different meaning in China from the meaning(s) that it carries in the West.

This pair of contributions might be regarded as an exercise in helping to 'decode' certain concepts as they are used in the modern Chinese legal system. My idea of 'decoding' is a process of understanding the differences between the usage

1 I have prepared two chapters for this book, on two distinct but related topics.

of similar or identical terms in radically different cultural contexts. I believe that by appreciating differences in such fundamental legal concepts as 'constitutionalism' (examined in this Chapter 1) and 'rule of law' (examined in Chapter 2), we might better understand differences that might also exist – and that other participants in this Conference have explored – in the meanings of more specific concepts such as self-government, regionalism, decentralisation, autonomy and the like, especially as those concepts might apply in the case of Tibet.

As I shall try to explain in the following pages, I believe there are substantial differences – I might even say dangerous differences – between the 'Western meanings' and the 'Chinese meanings' of such terms as these. Those differences in meaning result from differences in culture and language, which themselves result primarily from differences in history between the West and China.[2] The reason I say they might be *dangerous* differences in meaning is that unless thoughtful and influential people from these two different cultures can understand and use these terms and concepts in a cross-culturally sensitive way, conflict is likely to result. Expressed differently, we are faced with a choice: cross-cultural understanding or cross-cultural conflict. We must strive for the first of these.

I should hasten to acknowledge that I approach this 'decoding' exercise from a predominantly Western perspective myself. That is, my own 'cross-cultural' identity is an assumed one – not obtained at birth, but acquired over time. Nor do I speak or write Chinese, a shortcoming that embarrasses me. On the other hand, I have lived and taught in China and have written several books and articles on Chinese law. In these and other ways I have tried to escape the shackles of my own cultural limitations. I hope these efforts have given me a perspective on China – admittedly a Western perspective, but one that includes a deep respect for China's history and culture – which can help me serve as a 'translator' for some other Westerners who might wish to apply Western terms and concepts to China.

Having said all this, I should also emphasise that, in my view, any attempts at 'translation' – or 'decoding' – of terms and concepts as fundamental as 'constitutionalism', or the more specific terms 'autonomy', 'self-government' and 'decentralisation', can never be fully successful. As linguistic experts know better than I do, there will always be unbridgeable gaps between the meanings ascribed to similar or identical terms as used in *dis*similar cultures and languages. Indeed, I suppose no two people living in the *same* culture have precisely the same understanding of certain fundamental terms – which partly explains why we are unable to offer satisfying definitions of some of the most fundamental words in any language. Expressed differently: ultimately, words are simply not strong enough to carry themselves.

2 By 'the West', I mean principally Western Europe (including Britain) and the countries of the world most heavily influenced by European culture, including my own home country of the United States of America.

1.2 Other definitional considerations

Having identified certain aims and limitations of this undertaking, let me explain a phrase I have used in the subtitle to this chapter. That subtitle is 'A Western perspective on change and uncertainty in contemporary Chinese legal culture'. I have already referred above to my own 'Western perspective'. But what do I mean by 'change and uncertainty in Chinese legal culture'? In researching and writing this chapter, I have drawn from several articles written recently by Chinese legal experts focusing their attention on matters of constitutional law. These views appear in the very valuable journal titled *Frontiers of Law in China*, which since 2006 has provided English translations of important articles written (originally in Chinese) by Chinese law professors.

That journal helps provide 'inside insights' into Chinese legal culture.[3] As I hope will become clear in the pages that follow, those insights indicate that there is significant change and uncertainty among Chinese legal academics on issues relating to constitutionalism.

2. China's receptiveness to foreign influence

Throughout its history, China has been subject to – sometimes buffeted by – foreign influences of various sorts, including foreign legal influences. As I describe in subsection 2.1 below, traditional dynastic China was often extraordinarily successful in either rejecting those foreign influences or absorbing them by 'translating' them in such a way as to make them compatible with Chinese values. In the post-dynastic period (that is, starting after the Qing collapse in the early twentieth century), China has been much more receptive to Western influence – including specifically legal influence – but this receptiveness is evident mainly 'on the surface' and, as explained in subsection 2.2 below, has not reflected as substantial a displacement of fundamental Chinese values as first impressions might suggest.

3 Of particular importance for the paper I prepared for the conference, and therefore for this chapter, are the following articles appearing in various issues of that journal (which I have abbreviated in the following citations as 'FLC'): WEIDONG, C. (2006) The Basic Concepts of Re-Modifying the Criminal Procedure Law. *Frontiers of Law in China*. 1(2). pp. 153–163; JIAHONG, H. (2007) Ten Tendencies of Criminal Justice. *Frontiers of Law in China*. 2(1). pp. 1–22; JIANG, M. (2007) Public Participation and Administrative Rule of Law. *Frontiers of Law in China*. 2(3). pp. 353–377; MA, H. (2006) The Values of Administrative Procedure Law and the Meaning of its Codification in China. *Frontiers of Law in China*. 1(2). pp. 300–310; MA, X. (2007) A Reflection on the History of Chinese Constitutionalism of Last Century. *Frontiers of Law in China*. 2(1). pp. 44–70; WANG, C. (2006) Law-Making Functions of the Chinese Courts: Judicial Activism in a Country of Rapid Social Change. *Frontiers of Law in China*. 1(4). pp. 524–549; WANG, Z. (2007) Democracy, Rule of Law and Human Rights Protection under Gradually Developed Constitutionalism. *Frontiers of Law in China*. 2(3). pp. 335–352; ZHANG, W. (2006) China's Rule of Law in the Globalization Era. *Frontiers of Law in China*. 1(4). pp. 471–485.

2.1 Dynastic China's rejection of challengers[4]

Chinese history reveals many episodes in which serious challenges from outside China were made to the political, ideological, economic or social status quo inside the country. Several such challenges came, for example, in the form of military attack from outside China, especially from the north and west. Other challenges came in the form of new religious and cultural influences, as when Daoism and Buddhism were introduced. Still other challenges appeared in the form of European ideas and economic pressures.

Let us explore a few such episodes in an effort to generalise about how China reacted to these various types of influence and challenge.[5] As we shall see, that reaction typically featured a cluster of elements, including arrogance, ignorance, disinterest, rejection and 'filtering' of foreign influences. In my view, China can be regarded as having enjoyed its long and glorious past partly because of the unusual – I would even say peculiar – way in which it has responded to outside influences.

2.1.1 Military and political challenges

A persistent theme in Chinese history revolves around military challenges from the north and west. To me, the best visual image of this theme comes in the form of a metaphor offered by Nelson Ikon Wu. Although the image Wu offers focuses on cultural influences, the same applies to military attacks:

> The invisible continuity of the Chinese cultural metamorphosis always seems to me like a giant with his two feet firmly planted in the soil somewhere between Ch'ang-an and Loyang in the northern heartland where farther to the east continental Asia meets the Pacific Ocean. Seen from above and

4 This historical account draws on numerous sources, most prominent among them being the following: BODDE, D. & MORRIS, C. (1967), *Law in Imperial China*. Cambridge, MA: Harvard University Press; T'UNG-TSU CH'Ü (1961) *Law and Society in Traditional China*. Paris: Mouton & Co.; FAIRBANK, J.K. & GOLDMAN, M. (1992) *China – A New History*. Cambridge, MA: Belknap Press of Harvard University Press; GELBER, H.G. (2007) *The Dragon and the Foreign Devils: China and the World, 1100 BC to the Present*. London: Bloomsbury; HYUNG I. KIM (1981) *Fundamental Legal Concepts of China and the West: A Comparative Study*. Port Washington, NY: Kennikat Press; MACCORMACK, G. (1996) *The Spirit of Traditional Chinese Law*. Athens, GA: University of Georgia Press; MOTE, F.W. (1999) *Imperial China 900–1800*. Cambridge, MA: Harvard University Press; PYE, L.W. & PYE, M.W. (1991) *China – An Introduction*. 4th Edn. Boston: Little, Brown; ROBERTS, J.A.G. (1999) *A Concise History of China*. Cambridge, MA: Harvard University Press; ROBERTS, J.M. (1995) *A Concise History of the World*. New York: Oxford University Press; SMITH, B. & WENG, W. (1973) *China – A History in Art*. New York: Harper & Row; SULLIVAN, M. (1984) *The Arts of China*. 3rd Edn. Berkley, CA: University of California Press; and various essays in LEE, T.V. (1997) *Basic Concepts of Chinese Law*. New York: Garland.

5 For more details, see HEAD, J.W. (2009) *China's Legal Soul: The Modern Chinese Legal Identity in Historical Context*. Durham, NC: Carolina Academic Press [hereinafter HEAD (2009)], especially pp. 50–58, and other sources cited there.

> judged by the position of his broad shoulders, the giant appears to be facing south-southeast, with his back toward the desert plateau whose western limits border Asia Minor and point to Europe. Rising high over the terrain as he grows, he (. . .) does not enlarge his form in a radial-symmetrical way; [instead,] he moves forward and reaches to the left and to the right. The Himalayan Mountains block him from uniting with India, and *invaders sneak up to enter him from behind.*[6]

Harry Gelber, in his book *The Dragon and the Foreign Devils*, documents the many attacks that invaders have waged on China over the centuries but that the Chinese ultimately repelled or reversed. An abbreviated list of these would include the following:[7]

- the Xiongnu tribal attacks, beginning in the second century BCE and launched from their nomadic ranges in the steppes to the north and northwest of China in an effort to gain access to food sources, especially in winter;
- the Tubo Turks' attacks in the early fourth century CE, resulting in the capture of the city of Loyang and then of the emperor himself;
- the Tibetans' incursions in both the north and the south later in the fourth century CE; and
- the takeover of the northern part of China in the twelfth century CE by the Jin people, forcing the Song dynastic leaders south (thereby starting the so-called 'Southern Song' Dynasty).

Of course, the two most massive external military and political attacks came from the Mongols and the Manchus. These attacks – one occurring in the thirteenth century CE and the other occurring in the seventeenth century CE – resulted in 'alien' control of China for well over half of the last six centuries of its dynastic history.[8] And yet the Chinese culture, and even the core of Chinese political

6 NELSON IKON WU (1973) *Introduction to the Art of China*. In SMITH, B. & WENG, W. (1973) *China – A History in Art*. New York: Harper & Row, p. 13 (emphasis added).

7 See GELBER, H.G. (2007) *The Dragon and the Foreign Devils: China and the World, 1100 BC to the Present*. London: Bloomsbury, pp. 26–28 (Xiongnu, whom the Han emperors fought off and on between about 140 and 51 BCE), 40 (Tubo Turks and Tibetans) and 57 (Jin).

8 For other accounts of the Mongol and Manchu invasions and empires, see HEAD, J.W. & WANG, Y. (2005) *Law Codes in Dynastic China: A Synopsis of Chinese Legal History in the Thirty Centuries from Zhou to Qing*. Durham, NC: Carolina Academic Press, pp. 150–155, 193–196 [hereinafter *LCDC*] and sources cited there. See also the pertinent chapters in FRANKE, H. & TWITCHETT, D.C. (1994) *Cambridge History of China*. Vol. 6. Cambridge: Cambridge University Press, which deals with alien regimes and border states. In a larger sense, attacks and challenges from the north and west also appeared in the form of the Qin state's aggressive conquest of the other warring states in 221 BCE and the Sui people's aggressive reunification of China in 581 CE. These aggressions were not quite as 'alien' or 'external' as were those of the Mongols or Manchus, but they were nearly so.

integrity, may be said to have prevailed throughout those centuries. Why? Because in the first of these cases the foreign control was short-lived and left little imprint, and in the second of these cases the invaders were in a sense 'converted' to Chinese.

As for the Mongols, their Yüan Dynasty faced strong resistance at every attempt to replace Chinese values and institutions with Mongol values and institutions,[9] including attempts to introduce legal enactments inconsistent with the codes that had emerged from the Song, Tang and Sui dynasties that preceded the Yüan. For example, the Yüan legal enactment of 1291 (Treatise of Yüan New Regulations, or *Chih-yüan-hsin-ko*) represented a sharp departure from the pattern of those earlier codes[10] and had to be replaced just forty years later by a legal enactment (the 1331 Treatise of Punishment and Law, or *Hsing-fa chih*) that bore a remarkably close resemblance, both in structure and (especially) in content, to the Tang Code.[11] And of course it should be borne in mind that the Yüan Dynasty, partly for the very reason that it did not adapt well and quickly to many Chinese values and institutions, lasted for less than a century.

As for the Manchus, the fact that they enjoyed a much longer and stronger dynasty (the Qing Dynasty) than did the Mongols (the Yüan Dynasty) surely resulted in large part from the Manchus' careful and thorough adoption of Chinese values and institutions. Indeed, the Manchus seem to have recognised immediately the importance of adopting Chinese culture as their own. Their conscious effort to do so appears in many of their actions just before and during their attempts to supplant Ming rule.

For example, in taking control of Beijing in June 1644, the Manchu leader Dorgon 'rode in the imperial palanquin into the palace grounds' and declared that because the Qing had driven away the rebels responsible for the Ming emperor's suicide, '[n]one in history have ever more properly succeeded to the Mandate [of Heaven]'.[12] He also asserted that 'the empire is a single whole. There are no distinctions between Manchus and Hans'.[13] Similarly, the first Manchu emperor to occupy the capital in Beijing not only 'worked hard to master Chinese', but also 'continued [his uncle] Dorgon's practice of heeding the advice of senior Chinese advisors' and 'pointedly adhered to the institutional structure of the Ming dynasty'.[14] Indeed, he saw to it that the civil service examination system was quickly resumed in 1646.[15]

9 See *LCDC*, above note 8, p. 155, suggesting that Mongol and Chinese forms of government were like oil and water.

10 That 1291 Treatise had a different structure and did not take the form of a predominantly criminal code. See *LCDC*, above note 8, pp. 161–165.

11 See *LCDC*, above note 8, pp. 166–170 (documenting the similarities between the 1331 Treatise and the Tang Code).

12 MOTE, F.W. (1999) *Imperial China 900–1800*. Cambridge, MA: Harvard University Press, p. 819.

13 ROBERTS, J.A.G. (1999) *A Concise History of China*. Cambridge, MA: Harvard University Press, p. 143.

14 Ibid. at p. 823.

15 Ibid. at p. 824. In doing so, the emperor was in fact following the lead of his father, who had adopted the Ming system of examinations (given in the Manchu, Mongol and Chinese languages)

In short, as one historian has remarked: 'It was the Chinese system, Chinese officials, and Chinese ideas that enabled the Manchus to conquer China.'[16]

2.1.2 Religious and intellectual challenges

The same notion of 'conquest by absorption' or 'conquest by translation' also applies to China's response to the religious and intellectual challenges that have faced China over the centuries. For example, the famous Dong Zhongshu – the scholar of the second century BCE who had the ear of the Han emperor Wudi – crafted the rather odd package of 'Imperial Confucianism' that reconciled a cacophony of concepts and influences into a unified theory,[17] thus taking some of the punch out of Daoism and other cosmologies coming from external sources.

Likewise, the teachings of Buddhism, which gained a strong foothold in China in the fourth century CE, were in effect subverted and overcome by traditional Chinese thought and culture.[18] Here is how one scholar has explained how the Chinese language served as a filter for Buddhist doctrine:

> In attempting to transfer or 'translate' their new and alien ideas into terms meaningful for their Chinese audience, the early Buddhist missionaries ran into the problem that has faced all purveyors of foreign ideas in China ever since: how to select certain Chinese terms, written characters already invested with established meanings, and invest them with new significance without letting the foreign ideas be subtly modified, in fact sinified, in the process.[19]

It was perhaps because of this 'sinification' or 'sinicisation'[20] that Buddhism took hold in China. That is, some Buddhist concepts – on the relatively high position

for use in Manchuria even before the Qing gained control over China. SMITH, B. & WENG, W. (1973) *China – A History in Art*. New York: Harper & Row, p. 242.

16 ROBERTS, J.A.G. (1999) *A Concise History of China*. Cambridge, MA: Harvard University Press, p. 140, quoting Franz Michael.

17 See HEAD (2009), above note 5, pp. 22–25. As explained there, these concepts and influences included the concept of the five elements, the organising principle of the three major human relationships (ruler and subject, father and son, husband and wife), the notion of yin and yang, and others.

18 For a brief account of the spread of Buddhism in China, see SMITH, B. & WENG, W. (1973) *China – A History in Art*. New York: Harper & Row, pp. 94–98. They state that the 'first historical mention of a Chinese Buddhist community was recorded in A.D. 65. One hundred years later Buddha was being worshipped along with the Taoist deities. But the ideological fortress of Confucianism, armed with an ethical system governing man's social relations, was not easily penetrated. Not until the collapse of both the social order and the political system (. . .) [in the period of division following the Han dynasty] did Buddhism gain momentum.'

19 FAIRBANK, J.K. & GOLDMAN, M. (1992) *China – A New History*. Cambridge, MA: Belknap Press of Harvard University Press, p. 75. See also ROBERTS, J.M. (1995) *A Concise History of the World*. New York: Oxford University Press, p. 73 (explaining that by the eighth century, 'Buddhist doctrine had become sinicized').

20 The terms 'sinification' and 'sinicisation' may be, and often are, used interchangeably.

that Buddhism gave to women, for example – were simply changed to fit with existing Chinese culture: 'Husband supports wife', for instance, was translated into 'The husband controls his wife'.[21] Thus made culturally appropriate, Buddhism found receptive audiences in both south and north China – making the new religion, according to one author's speculations, perhaps 'China's most important cultural import before the nineteenth century'.[22]

2.1.3 European ideas and economic pressure

One of the most fascinating forms of Chinese contact with foreigners came through trade with people far to the west of China, especially the Europeans. Although ideas and pressures of this sort became especially important beginning in the eighteenth century, they began as early as the time of the Roman Republic[23] – and by 166 CE 'the Romans sent envoys to the Han capital at Loyang'.[24] But the Chinese were hardly enthusiastic about interacting with the Europeans:

> From the beginning the Westerners – traders and others – were highly interested in China and its ways. The Chinese, by contrast, showed no interest in exploration or travel to the far West, as distinct from some trade. Pliny the Elder, for example, noted that 'like savages, the Seres [Chinese] shun the company of others and wait for traders to seek them out.' That contrast between the Europeans' desire for distant exploration and adventure, and the altogether more narrow and domestic focus of China, would continue.[25]

From the European perspective, of course, continued interest in exploration and adventure eventually came to have two related motivating forces: (1) the spread of what the Europeans saw as their own superior civilisation (including Christianity); and (2) profit. Pressure on China to accept European delegations, typically for the purpose of facilitating commercial transactions, grew steadily from the eighteenth

21 FAIRBANK, J.K. & GOLDMAN, M. (1992) *China – A New History*. Cambridge, MA: Belknap Press of Harvard University Press, p. 75.

22 See ROBERTS, J.M. (1995) *A Concise History of the World*. New York: Oxford University Press, p. 215.

23 See GELBER, H.G. (2007) *The Dragon and the Foreign Devils: China and the World, 1100 BC to the Present*. London: Bloomsbury, p. 35 (noting that 'by the fourth century BC the Romans and Greeks began to speak of the "Seres", the silk people').

24 Ibid.

25 Ibid. at p. 36. Gelber offers this explanation of China's 'narrow and domestic focus', and its dismissive attitude more generally toward foreigners: '[Chinese] people and officials continued to assume as self-evident that the Chinese state, headed by the Son of Heaven, could not be merely one state among many. Instead, it was the society of the civilised world, with "China" and "Civilisation" two sides of the same conceptual coin. (. . .) [People] beyond [China's] borders (. . .) were, by definition, "barbarians", in the obvious sense that they were not part of the central civilisation.' Ibid. at p. 33.

century onward. Gelber offers this series of observations about the receptiveness – or rather the non-receptiveness – of the Chinese to such entreaties:[26]

> [I]t hardly occurred to the Chinese ruling classes that – apart from such oddments [as some scientific and astronomical information] – the Europeans might have anything to say that would be of great interest, still less anything that might cause China to amend its political or diplomatic habits.
>
> China's rulers distrusted foreign traders, especially perhaps Western ones, as liable to disturb the empire's domestic peace.
>
> [Reflecting that distrust, starting in the middle of the eighteenth century, all] foreign trade was concentrated at Canton (Guangzhou), which became the filter shielding the [Chinese] population in general, and the official world in particular, from foreign disturbance. Contact was maintained through a selected group of Chinese merchants, known as the Cohong, who operated both as brokers and as superintendents of the foreign traders. (. . .) Communications had to go through the Cohong. They had to be worded as 'petitions' (. . .) The smallest detail of the foreigners' lives and goods were subject to regulation.
>
> [In response to the British trade mission assigned to remove such restrictions, the Chinese made it clear that they] would insist on homage to the emperor taking the normal form of the demonstrative kowtow, which was especially important for domestic consumption. (. . .)
>
> [When the British trade envoy, Lord George Macartney, expressed his unwillingness to perform the kowtow, the Chinese authorities ushered him away with a dismissive imperial edict addressed to King George III, saying:]
>
>> Our dynasty's majestic virtue has penetrated into every country under Heaven, and Kings of all nations have offered their costly tribute by land and sea (. . .). I set no value on objects strange or ingenious, and have no use for your country's manufactures (. . .). It behoves [*sic*] you, O King, to respect my sentiments and to display even greater devotion and loyalty in future (. . .).

This reported combination of ignorance, dismissiveness and arrogance – and particularly the last of these – is even seen by some as the true cause of the Opium War between Britain and China in the 1840s. No less prominent a personage than John Quincy Adams (sixth president of the United States) explained that opium was

> a mere incident to the dispute, but no more the cause of the war than the throwing overboard of tea in Boston harbour was the cause of the American revolution. (. . .) [T]he cause of the war is the kowtow – the arrogant and

26 The following excerpts are drawn from ibid. at pp. 149, 155, 156, 160 and 163–164.

> insupportable pretensions of China that she will hold commercial intercourse with the rest of mankind not upon terms of equal reciprocity, but upon the insulting and degrading forms of the relation between lord and vassal.[27]

However fair or unfair Adams' characterisation might have been, it reflects the deep reluctance and resistance shown by the Chinese government toward European influence. Expressed differently, China proved in this way (as it had in terms of religion and military attacks) to be not only *disinclined* culturally and institutionally to respond to European influence, but strong enough to withstand most such influence – coming in this case in the form of trade.

To summarise: dynastic China exhibited three related features in dealing with literal and figurative 'attacks' (or 'leakage' into China) from outside its borders: (1) an arrogant lack of interest in the ideas that the challengers presented; (2) a rejection of the challengers themselves whenever possible; and (3) a thorough 'filtering' of the foreign influences when they could not be rejected or deflected.

2.2 Contemporary China's response to Western legal influence[28]

Let us shift now from dynastic China to contemporary China, to consider how contemporary China has reacted to foreign influences – especially foreign legal influences – in the dramatic law reform movements of the past three and a half

27 Ibid. at p. 188.

28 This account of certain aspects of contemporary Chinese law draws on numerous sources, most prominent among them being the following: BROWN, R.C. (1997) *Understanding Chinese Courts and Legal Process.* The Hague, Boston: Kluwer Law International; LIANG, B. (2008) *The Changing Chinese Legal System, 1978–Present.* New York: Routledge; CHEN, A.H.Y. (2004) *An Introduction to the Legal System of the People's Republic of China.* 3rd Edn. Hong Kong: LexisNexis; CHOW, D.C.K. (2003) *The Legal System of the People's Republic of China.* St Paul, MN: Thomson/West; CUTSHAW, K.A., BURKE, M.E. & WAGNER, C.A. (2010) *Corporate Counsel's Guide to Doing Business in China.* 2nd Edn. Eagan, MN: West; LIEBERTHAL, K. (1995) *Governing China: From Revolution through Reform.* New York: W.W. Norton; LUBMAN, S.B. (1999) *Bird in a Cage: Legal Reform in China after Mao.* Stanford, CA: Stanford University Press; PEERENBOOM, R. (2002) *China's Long March Toward Rule of Law.* Cambridge: Cambridge University Press; POTTER, P.B. (2001) *The Chinese Legal System: Globalization and Local Legal Culture.* London, New York: Routledge Curzon [hereinafter POTTER (2001)]; VERMEER, E.B. & and D'HOOGHE, I. (eds) (2002) *China's Legal Reforms and Their Political Limits.* Richmond, Surrey: Curzon; WANG, C. & ZHANG, X. (eds) (1997) *Introduction to Chinese Law.* Hong Kong: Sweet & Maxwell Asia; XIN REN (1997) *Tradition of the Law and Law of the Tradition: Law, State, and Social Control in China.* Westport, CT: Greenwood Press; WANG, G. & MO, J. (1999) *Chinese Law.* The Hague, Boston: Kluwer Law International; GUANGHUA YU & MINKANG GU (2001) *Laws Affecting Business Transactions in the PRC.* The Hague, Boston: Kluwer Law International (2001); ZIMMERMAN, J.M. (2005) *China Law Deskbook: A Legal Guide for Foreign-Invested Enterprises.* Chicago, IL: ABA Section of International Law; ZOU KEYUAN (2006) *China's Legal Reform – Towards the Rule*

decades.[29] Numerous observers have painted a rather mixed picture of this. For instance, Professor Wang Guiguo gave the following description in 1999 of how external legal systems and approaches had influenced Chinese law to that point in the PRC's legal reform movement:

> Looking back at the path of China's legal reforms of the last 20 years, China has demonstrated its willingness to learn from the experience of the developed economies in establishing a suitable legal system for strengthening the socialist market economy. China was even prepared to adopt the whole sector of a foreign legal system. In this regard, the tax system (heavily influenced by the US tax system) and the industrial property laws (i.e. patents, designs and trademarks – a copy of the German system) are examples. In most cases, however, *China appeared to be more willing to accept the provisions and concepts of foreign laws than their values and underlying principles.* As a result, China has resisted the notion of 'copying' or 'transplantation' (. . .). [Nonetheless, the] interdependence between China and the rest of the world makes it impossible for China to resist cultural, political and legal influence – including values and beliefs – of foreign countries (. . .) [and therefore in recent years] foreign concepts, values, etc. slowly entered into China and influenced Chinese laws.[30]

Wang and several other colleagues contributing to that same work emphasised the particular influence that other legal systems have had on Chinese law in the area of business and finance, partly in the context of the PRC's accession to the WTO. In these areas, the influence has been very substantial. In areas of law *other* than those relating to business and finance, however, the PRC has been much less receptive to Western influence.[31]

of Law. Leiden, Boston: Martinus Nijhoff Publishers; BEHR, V. (2007) Development of a New Legal System in the People's Republic of China. *Louisiana Law Review*. 67(4). pp. 1161–1180; JIANFU CHEN (2007) The Transformation of Chinese Law – From Formal to Substantial. *Hong Kong Law Journal*. 37(2). p. 689; PEERENBOOM, R. (2003) The X-Files: Past and Present Portrayals of China's Alien 'Legal System'. *Washington University Global Studies Law Review*. 2(1). pp. 37–95; POTTER, P.B. (2003) Globalization and Economic Regulation in China: Selective Adaptation of Globalized Norms and Practices. *Washington University Global Studies Law Review*. 2(1). pp. 119–150 (2003) [hereinafter POTTER (2003)].

29 The year 2014 marked the thirty-five-year anniversary of the initiation in 1979 of a far-reaching legal reform movement in the PRC. For details of that movement, see HEAD, J.W. (2009) *China's Legal Soul: The Modern Chinese Legal Identity in Historical Context*. Durham, NC: Carolina Academic Press, as well as LIEBERTHAL, K. (1995) *Governing China: From Revolution through Reform*. New York: W.W. Norton, p. 133.

30 WANG GUIGUO (1999) The Legal System of China. In WANG, G. & MO, J. (1999) *Chinese Law*. The Hague, Boston: Kluwer Law International, pp. 3–4 (emphasis added).

31 Two of Wang's colleagues, for example, explain that marriage in China 'is different from that in the capitalist states in terms of its meaning, its social foundation and its social consequences. For instance, a marriage is, unlike in common law jurisdictions, not regarded as a contract but rather a crystal of love within the purview of the socialist public family'. LAW, A.M.W. & KWAN, A.W.C.

Another expert, Professor Xin Ren, wrote in her 1997 book *Tradition of the Law and Law of the Tradition* that although 'the current modernisation of law in China emerged as a hybrid of the Chinese imperial legal tradition, Western law, and Soviet socialist law',[32] China has in fact taken its own unique approach to law, the underlying ideology of which does *not* follow a Western model:

> Excited with China's economic reform, many Western observers are watching whether China is going to succumb to the influence of the Western model of law – which often means the separation of law from other political institutions, a professional class of jurists, an independent judiciary, a system of due process, a principle of presumed innocence, and the right to competent legal representation – and eventually to abandon its anti-individualism and nondemocratic legal tradition. (. . .)
>
> Apparently, China's economic openness and privatisation have not changed its authoritarian tradition and lack of democratic voice in state-commanded social control efforts. What is even more puzzling to Western observers is that though China might have created what can be called laws, they are often sidestepped by the government officials. There have been institutions that are called public security, people's procurate, and people's courts, but they seem to have no independent role in resolving the disputes brought before them. There have been defence counsels appointed or hired by the accused, but they have very limited access to the power and privilege that their Western counterparts can enjoy in defending their clients' innocence beyond a reasonable doubt. There has been a constitution that guarantees the rights of free speech, press, and assembly, but its insistence on individuals' obligation to the state and the Communist Party often leaves little room for individuals to exercise their rights.[33]

In another more recent book, Professor Pitman Potter of the University of British Columbia also explores the interplay between external and indigenous influences on Chinese law during the PRC's recent legal reform movement. In the opening passages of his book *The Chinese Legal System – Globalization and Local Legal Culture*, Potter offers this summary:

> Legal reform [in China since 1978] has (. . .) been complicated by (. . .) ambivalence about the introduction of ideals of governance associated with the West. (. . .) *Foreign observers are invited to conclude that Chinese legal reforms express*

(1999) Law of Family, Marriage and Succession. In WANG, G. & MO, J. (1999) *Chinese Law*. The Hague, Boston: Kluwer Law International, p. 418.

32 XIN REN (1997) *Tradition of the Law and Law of the Tradition: Law, State, and Social Control in China*. Westport, CT: Greenwood Press, p. 3.

33 Ibid. at pp. 2–3.

> *an evolving willingness to approach governance in ways that are roughly comparable to or at least compatible with those of the industrialised democracies. These presumptions appear to be supported by the use in China of institutional forms described in the familiar nomenclature of the liberal legal tradition.* Foreign observers are given to understand that Chinese courts, lawyers, and judges are categorically comparable with those of liberal legal systems, and that various categories of substantive and procedural law in China parallel their liberal legal counterparts.
>
> *However, the legal system of the PRC offers students of law a signal lesson in the dangers in uncritical acceptance of such easy comparisons.* (. . .)
>
> (. . .) [Indeed, much] of the story of the PRC's legal reform effort concerns the struggle to adapt international norms to local conditions. Local legal culture refers to the system of Chinese values and practices that informs legally significant behaviour. *Despite the influences exerted by foreign legal norms, Chinese law remains dominated by local legal culture.* The development of the Chinese legal system over the past twenty years has reflected a process of selective adaptation, by which borrowed foreign norms about law and legal institutions have been mediated by local legal culture.[34]

Potter describes various sorts of interaction that have occurred between PRC government officials, including those working at the National People's Congress, and counterparts in Canada, Europe, the United States and elsewhere in the world, particularly on topics relating to such 'institutional' matters as legislative procedure and administrative law.[35] He asserts, however, that in the area of legislative procedure 'foreign influences have been limited to internal procedures and the organisation of legislative organs and have not extended to the broader questions of [Communist] Party dominance',[36] and although the PRC's Administrative Litigation Law 'was heavily influenced by the US Federal Administrative Procedure Act',[37] in fact 'foreign influences have had little effect on the basic normative premise underlying China's administrative law system, namely that administrative law remains an instrument in the service of Party-led governance'.[38]

34 POTTER (2001), above note 28, pp. 1–2 (emphasis added).
35 Ibid. at p. 35.
36 Ibid.
37 Ibid.
38 Ibid. at p. 36. Potter also describes how some specific substantive areas of Chinese law, as adopted or revised in recent years, reflect or resist foreign influence and models. For example, he offers this explanation of property law reform: '[I]n the main Chinese legal specialists working on property rights were compelled to look abroad [including to Japan, Europe, and the Anglo-North-American tradition] for guidance. The adoption of foreign law norms, however, is moderated by local tradition and norms of political and legal culture. In particular, the individualist orientation of liberal property rights regimes conflicts with the collectivist norms in China, while private rights discourses of liberalism conflict with the public law norms of Chinese tradition and PRC policy. The development of property rights in the PRC is largely a process of mediating these conflicts.'

The picture that emerges from the analysis offered by Wang, Ren, Potter and other observers is that the PRC's legal reform effort of the past thirty-five years has exhibited three related characteristics in terms of the significance of external influence. I suggest this synopsis:

- There has been very extensive interest in, and study of, foreign legal systems – their norms, operations and institutions – as China has struggled to create a legal system on a hurry-up basis to accommodate and facilitate the dramatic economic changes that the country's leadership set in motion thirty years ago following the death of Mao and his failed policies.
- From this consideration of foreign legal systems there has emerged a mixed set of reforms, so that (1) in some respects (especially matters of economic law) laws and institutions in today's China bear a resemblance, at least on the surface, to Western laws and institutions,[39] while (2) in other respects (family law, for example), PRC law bears little or no such resemblance to Western counterparts.
- Even in those aspects of the PRC's legal system that do reveal significant external influences, there has been a thorough filtering (or 'screening' or 'translation') of those external influences in an attempt to make the foreign elements compatible with underlying elements of Chinese legal and political culture – and that filtering is sometimes nearly invisible to outsiders unfamiliar with those underlying elements of Chinese legal and political culture.

Here is how Potter expresses some of the ideas I have offered in the above synopsis – especially the idea of 'filtering':

> To a large extent, the development of Chinese legal institutions and practices has reflected the dynamics of local legal culture, and particularly the imperatives of political control for the Chinese Communist Party. While the structures of legislative, administrative and dispute resolution institutions appear quite recognisable to foreign-trained lawyers, the norms and practices of these institutions often depart quite significantly from the expectations of those familiar with liberal legal systems. This reflects the influence of *local legal culture*, which *acts* as *a normative filter through which flow the influences of foreign and international legal models.*[40]

Ibid. at p. 56. See also POTTER (2003), above note 28, pp. 126–127 (further describing the interaction of Western influence and local legal culture in the PRC's reform of property law).

39 It is worth noting that there are substantial differences between various sorts of 'Western laws and institutions', particularly those of the civil law tradition and those of the common law tradition. As a broad generalisation, it can be said that China has been more receptive to the former (especially German law) than to the latter. I am indebted to Lin Miao for emphasising this point.

40 POTTER (2001), above note 28, p. 37 (emphasis added). For a recent discussion of a particularly important way in which (to use Potter's phrase) 'local legal culture [in China] (. . .) acts as a

3. Constitutionalism in contemporary China

I have emphasised in the preceding discussion how erroneous it is to assume, from the 'surface similarity' between legal concepts, labels and institutions in China and legal concepts, labels and institutions in the Western world, that their meanings and operation are fundamentally similar. Instead, according to many sources, the surface similarity can be quite misleading. It can disguise the fact that foreign influences on China's contemporary legal system have in fact been heavily filtered, or rejected outright, in much the same way that foreign influence of various sorts were filtered or rejected in many circumstances during China's long and glorious dynastic period.

Now I wish to shift from these general observations to a more specific focus on the concept of the 'constitutionalism'. An understanding of that concept in the Chinese context bears directly on the subjects at issue in the Conference from which this book emerges, because any assessment of whether the 'Memorandum on Genuine Autonomy for the Tibetan People' does or does not 'correspond to (. . .) the Chinese constitutional and legal system' (quoting from the objective of the conference) rests on an understanding of just what 'constitutionalism' means in contemporary China.

Another contributor to this volume, Professor Michael Davis, has focused close attention on Articles 4 and 31 of the PRC Constitution.[41] Based on his analysis of these two articles, Professor Davis recommends, with regard to Tibet, that there be 'a change of course to establish a more genuine autonomy under Article 31 (. . .) relating to the establishment of special administrative regions', rather than continuing the unsatisfactory discussions under Article 4 (and implementing legislation) regarding China's national minority policy.[42]

I find Professor Davis' assessment compelling. He has undertaken a detailed examination of the pertinent constitutional provisions and found in them what seems to be a workable solution that needs only political will in order to offer real promise of success in creating a new approach – and one that could be mutually acceptable, it would seem, to both the Chinese and the Tibetan interests.

As an additional or complementary aspect of this constitutional analysis, I believe it is important that we consider the underlying significance of the PRC Constitution, and of 'constitutionalism' more generally, in the Chinese legal system. That is what I attempt, in summary form, in the following paragraphs. The central question I wish to address is this: How strong a sense of constitutionalism exists in today's China – or, expressed differently, does China's Constitution lie

normative filter through which flow the influences of foreign and international legal models', see XING LIJUAN (2014) *Behind the Multilateral Trading System: Legal Indigenization and the WTO in Comparative Perspective*. Durham, NC: Carolina Academic Press.

41 See generally DAVIS, M.C. (2008) Establishing a Workable Autonomy in Tibet. *Human Rights Quarterly*. 30. pp. 227–258.

42 Ibid. at p. 227.

close enough to the 'heart' of the Chinese legal system that constitutional arguments will in fact prove persuasive?

3.1 A comparative detour

In order to assess this issue, let us first take a detour and consider what core legal ethic, if any, lies at the heart of the *American* legal system.[43] Although that topic was not directly at issue in the Conference from which this book emerges, giving some attention to it here might provide useful context and contrast to our consideration of Chinese law.

I have expressed the view elsewhere[44] that the core legal ethic in the American system consists of a package of values that I label the 'American Constitutional Ethic'. The main elements in that package would include the following, probably along with several others:

- The substantive and procedural legal protections found in the US Bill of Rights (the first ten amendments to the US Constitution of 1787), and particularly such specific rules as these:
  - freedom of speech;
  - freedom of the press;
  - freedom of assembly and right to petition;
  - freedom of religion, both freedom from having to associate with a state-sponsored religion and freedom to practice the religion of one's choice (if any);
  - freedom from arbitrary arrest and detention;
  - freedom from having private property for public purposes taken without compensation;
  - freedom of movement;
  - the right to have certain 'due process' procedural requirements followed;
  - the right to trial by a jury of one's peers;
  - the freedom from arbitrary search and seizure.
- Other substantive rights that people assume are guaranteed by the US Constitution include:
  - the right to own handguns suitable for killing other humans (I personally deplore this view);
  - the right to privacy;
  - the right to vote in elections for representatives in Congress.

43 I use the term 'American legal system' to refer generally to the US (federal) legal system and the state legal systems.

44 See HEAD (2009), above note 5.

- Other substantive rights that are found primarily in the Declaration of Independence of 1776 (even though many Americans might think they appear in the Constitution) include:
  - the right to equal treatment (on the basis that all people are created equal);
  - the right to 'life, liberty, and the pursuit of happiness';
- freedom from government interference of most types – and, to safeguard that freedom, a guarantee that the government will have only expressly limited powers.

Underlying several of the elements in the 'package' described above are certain popular assumptions – that is, assumptions as to which there is broad consensus across the American population as a whole. These assumptions include: (1) the natural state of persons is a state of freedom;[45] and, relatedly, (2) all powers of the government emanate from the people, in accordance with some form of 'social contract' by which (as Rousseau and Locke asserted) individuals agree (begrudgingly, perhaps) to surrender a limited set of specific rights to a central authority in return for assurances from that central authority that it will provide collective defence, both against external aggression and internal lawlessness. Indeed, the US Constitution itself conveys the sense of a contract in several respects. The opening language enumerates specific purposes for which the people (acting in part through their state governments) have consented to enter into the federal arrangements that the Constitution establishes. These specific purposes include such things as to 'form a more perfect union', to 'provide for the common defence', to 'establish justice', to 'promote the general welfare' and so forth. The Tenth Amendment to the US Constitution, in turn, expressly limits the powers of the federal government by providing that '[t]he powers not delegated to the United States by the Constitution, nor prohibited by it to the states, are reserved to the states respectively, or to the people'.

Much of the US Constitution, of course, addresses structural issues – how the federal government is to be organised and is to function, for example, and what relations (including 'checks and balances') are to be maintained among the three branches of the government. These provisions can likewise be viewed – and, what is more important, *are* viewed by most Americans – as further manifestations of a fundamental organising theme: the government is the servant of the people.

Whether or not this is a *good* theme is entirely beside the point here. I have expressed the various components of what I label the American Constitutional Ethic in terms that I believe reflect how most Americans view them. Ask a 'man on the street' what lies at the very centre of the American legal system, and I think

45 As is well known, the US Constitution originally gave only limited scope to this assumption, especially in its accommodation of slavery.

you will get answers that closely resemble the points I have enumerated above. Objective observers, both inside and outside the United States, will readily point out the many ways in which the reality falls short of the ideal, but the important point for our present purposes is to recognise that there *is* an ideal, that it has developed over many scores of years, and that it constitutes a common popular understanding of how the American legal system should work.

3.2 Constitutionalism as a new and foreign 'ethic' in China

Now let us shift our attention back to China. Does 'constitutionalism' – that is, a strong popular embrace of a package of provisions of the Chinese constitution (or other fundamental legal or policy documents) – serve as a key legal ethic in today's China, in a way that is similar to how I have described the situation in the American legal system? I think the answer must be 'no', for several reasons.

First, the current PRC Constitution is still relatively new, dating only from 1982. It has already undergone four significant amendments.[46] These occurred in 1988 (to define the status of the private sector and the country's policy on private businesses), in 1993 (when the position of democracy was upgraded), in 1999 (when the basic strategy of exercising the rule of law was formulated) and in 2004 (when, among other things, a provision asserting that 'the state respects and protects human rights' was added).[47] Moreover, the current PRC Constitution was preceded by three other constitutions since 1949, and those constitutions show a great deal of discontinuity.

Hence, it would seem that there simply has not been adequate time for the substantive norms set forth in the PRC Constitution to have become internalised by the Chinese people and deeply rooted in the Chinese legal system. The norms themselves have changed too frequently and too dramatically for that.

Perhaps more importantly, the *idea* of constitutionalism – as distinct from the specific norms found in a particular constitution – has almost surely not been internalised by the Chinese people and become deeply rooted into the Chinese legal system. In a fascinating article on Chinese constitutionalism, Ma Xiaohong of Renmin University of China has discussed this issue and offered some comparisons to Western constitutions and constitutionalism:

46 For the text of the PRC Constitution, detailing amendments at the end, see http://english.peopledaily.com.cn/constitution/constitution.html [Accessed: 14 February 2016]. Preceding the 1982 constitution were three earlier constitutions. For a synopsis of those constitutions, as well as the 1982 Constitution and its amendments, see ARJUN SUBRAHMANYAN (2004) Constitutionalism in China: Changing Dynamics in Legal and Political Debates. China Law & Practice. [Online] 1 May 2004. Available at: www.chinalawandpractice.com [Accessed: 14 February 2017].

47 This summary is drawn from WANG, Z. (2007) Democracy, Rule of Law and Human Rights Protection under Gradually Developed Constitutionalism. *Frontiers of Law in China*. 2(3). pp. 335–352, at p. 336. Each of the amendments involved other changes not mentioned here. For further details about the amendments, see HEAD (2009), above note 5, pp. 178–179, 187, 211.

Like other colonial or semi-colonial countries, constitutionalism in modern China did not come from traditions but was passively imported from Western countries. Such passivity means, a colonisation movement, following the heel of the Industrial Revolution, swept across the globe and the entire world was dragged rather than entered into by itself the 'modern path', and China was no exception. (. . .)

Our mistakes began with our misunderstanding of 'what is constitutionalism'. Such misunderstanding is somewhat similar to that of 'rule of law'. (. . .) [However,] [o]ur misconception of constitutionalism is much greater.

As to the origin of Western constitutionalism, no one will deny that it was based on specific traditions. In the works composed by ancient Greek thinkers, we can find the evidence for the checks and balances required by modern constitutionalism and democratic thinking. If we read and compare Plato's *Laws* and Aristotle's *Politics* with Montesquieu's *The Spirit of Laws*, we can readily discern a kind of succession between them. (. . .) Constitutionalism, with the support of traditions and history, acquired a kind of rationality and divinity. To talk about constitutionalism, we first have to mention something about the 'Constitution', which is the text and guiding principle of constitutionalism. Westerners based their knowledge or understanding of the Constitution on traditions. Theoretically speaking, the Constitution is built upon social contracts and it defines citizens' basic rights and obligations in the form of basic law and prescribes the authority of the state's important institutions and their mutual relationship. From the aspect of social contract, the power of the state comes from citizens' authorisation and the Constitution is a contract between the state and its citizens. The state, when exercising its authority, should not harm citizens' rights, and instead, it should try to protect their interests; the purpose of the checks and balances is to prevent power abuse. Such contractual nature will make every citizen feel his personal interest being tied to the Constitution and recognise its indispensability. What is more important and yet ignored by us is that the Constitution in Western countries is regarded as the representation and the essence of their national spirits, civilization and values.

(. . .) *In the past one hundred years, Chinese (. . .) scholars have diligently introduced the types and modes of Western Constitution and constitutionalism. But the connection between constitutionalism and [Chinese] historical traditions and the relationship between Constitution and [Chinese] national values have been overlooked or evaded.* (. . .) What is unfortunate for modern Chinese constitutionalism is that, the constitutionalism arrived in China at a time of national crisis, and even people who truly admired the constitutionalism had no time to leisurely appreciate the historical and cultural elements behind the constitutionalism.

(. . .) *The departure from traditions*, disregard of national feelings and spirits, *and the unrealistic expectation for foreign culture (constitutionalism) were underlying causes [for disappointing results* in efforts to absorb constitutionalism into Chinese culture and society]. As to this, American jurisprudent Pond, as an onlooker, saw most

> clearly. Pond warned: 'the constitutionalism cannot be created in the short term and out of aspiration. A constitutional government must gradually evolve from the native culture and traditional aspiration and is not something that, upon its maturity, can be wilfully transplanted to other countries'.[48]

According to Ma Xiaohong, then, constitutionalism has not succeeded in China, in the sense of providing a central legal ethic for the country. Ma points out that in dynastic times, there *was* such a legal ethic, and it was *lǐ* – that is, the system of proper personal and societal behaviour that developed early in Chinese culture and gained enormous significance with Confucius.[49] Ma offers this explanation of how *lǐ* provided a central legal ethic for China:

> [I]n ancient China, rule by *lǐ* actually had the status and role similar to that of Western constitutions, and moreover, it was closely linked with national feelings. (. . .) Its values and spirits had imprinted an indelible mark upon every native. (. . .) Compared with modern people's indifference to violations

48 MA, X. (2007) A Reflection on the History of Chinese Constitutionalism of Last Century. *Frontiers of Law in China*. 2(1). pp. 44–70, at pp. 48–51 (emphasis added). I see a similarity between (1) Ma's emphasis of China's lack of a tradition of constitutionalism and (2) William Jones' emphasis of the different aims and audience of law in Western culture (especially that most heavily influenced by Roman tradition) as compared with the aims and audience of law in Chinese culture. Here is Jones' explanation of that difference, as evident in the Qing Code (which Jones translated into English): '[T]he [Qing] Code is not much concerned with the disputes of private individuals (. . .) We are accustomed to think that a legal system is primarily a social institution within which "persons" – private individuals, or groups of individuals, or even the state – can make claims against other persons and have these resolved by a neutral trier of fact and law. (. . .) These are all aspects of the legal systems we are familiar with (. . .) [and] they reflect the [fact that much of Western law] was formed by Roman law, (. . .) [which arose] in a very small and predominately agricultural community with a weak government. As a consequence, the legal problems that it dealt with in the formative period [focused on] disputes between private individuals that arose out of torts, simple contracts, and succession. (. . .) The situation in China was radically different. The polity of China consisted of a highly centralised government headed by an absolute ruler who ruled by means of a bureaucracy. The primary obligation of every Chinese was to fulfil the duties assigned to him by the Emperor. All human activities had to be carried on so as to fit into his scheme for directing society. Consequently one would expect the imperial law or Code to take note of human activity only as it was perceived to affect imperial policies.' JONES, W.C. (1994) *The Great Qing Code*. Oxford: Clarendon Press; New York: Oxford University Press, pp. 4–8.

49 For present purposes, a general definition of *lǐ* will suffice: *lǐ* (礼, 豐) amounts to a code of propriety. Although originally confined in meaning to refer to rituals relating to burial and honouring of the dead, the concept of *lǐ* gradually expanded in scope. In Western Zhou times, it referred to proper courtly behaviour of the aristocracy in their dealings among themselves. Confucius broadened the meaning of *lǐ* to refer to proper behaviour generally, based on the place or status of a person within the family or the social and political system. Western analogues to *lǐ* might include such concepts as ritual, chivalry, courtesy, morality and ethical behaviour. (Two Chinese characters for *lǐ* are given above; the first is the modern version, and the second is the older version.) See HEAD (2009), above note 5, p. 11.

> of the [PRC] Constitution, in ancient China, *lǐ* or rule by *lǐ*, once endangered or damaged, people would rush to protect it. (. . .) In ancient China, rule by *lǐ* was not merely an instrument of governance it was also the standard with which people appraised their monarch and officials. It was a belief and a channel connected to various strata and precisely for this reason, *lǐ* and rule by *lǐ* had become the 'basic law' of ancient China. Since the late Qing [Dynasty], the keynote was to relinquish *lǐ* and adopt laws (in its Western sense), and despite some opposition, the westernisation had turned to be irresistible. Yet, in China, the hastily introduced Constitution appeared to be empty talk and, quite embarrassingly, was degraded to an instrument of power struggle.[50]

Another Chinese professor – Wang Zhoujun of Suzhou University – takes a somewhat more cheerful view than Professor Ma does toward the slow movement in developing a strong constitutionalism in China. Noting the common sense involved in 'feeling the stones when crossing the river',[51] Wang applauds 'progressive' or 'gradual' constitutionalism:

> Social development and reform are just like 'crossing the river' and are full of uncertainties, thus constant exploration and continuous choices are necessary. (. . .) Reforms have to be based on specific experience and move along cautiously, that is, have to 'feel the stones'. (. . .) There has to be planning, otherwise 'gradual' progress will become 'blind progress' without any sense of direction. We have to focus all the time on our goal – 'the other side of the river' – a prosperous and powerful, democratic and civilised socialist country.[52]

Then Wang Zhoujun explains that constitutional reform in China 'is different from the constitutional development that is initiated from within the West'. Specifically, he quotes Deng Xiaoping's statement to then-former US President Jimmy Carter in June 1987: 'China's main objective is to develop, shake off

50 MA, X. (2007) A Reflection on the History of Chinese Constitutionalism of Last Century. *Frontiers of Law in China*. 2(1). pp. 44–70, at pp. 66–67. Ma Xiaohong goes on to explain some aspects of that power struggle as exhibited in the development of Chinese constitutions and the degradation of Confucianism. See ibid. at pp. 67–69.

51 See WANG, Z. (2007) Democracy, Rule of Law and Human Rights Protection under Gradually Developed Constitutionalism. *Frontiers of Law in China*. 2(3). pp. 335–352, at p. 347.

52 Ibid. at pp. 347–348. For further development of the notion of 'feeling the stones while crossing the river', and the origin of the phrase, see HEAD, J.W. (2010) Feeling the Stones When Crossing the River: The Rule of Law in China. *Santa Clara Journal of International Law*. 7(2). pp. 25–84; also appearing in Chinese as HEAD, J.W. & LI SONFENG (2013) Crossing the River by Feeling the Stones: The Rule of Law in China. *Journal of Comparative Law*. 126(2). p. 30 – published in Chinese as 摸着石头过河：中国的法治 (*Mozhe Shitou Guo He: Zhongguode Fazhi*), 2 比较法研究 (*Bijiaofa Yanjiu*) (2013).

backwardness, strengthen the nation and gradually raise the standard of living. In order to accomplish this, it is essential to have a stable political environment.'[53] For this reason, Wang asserts, China is conducting 'constitutionalism with stability'.[54]

Moreover, Wang Zhoujun emphasises that this gradualist approach to building a sense of constitutionalism among the Chinese people is to a large extent a *cultural* mandate. That is, China should (Wang says) 'adopt a gradual process of cultural transformation corresponding to that of constitutional evolution' and should avoid 'simply "copying" the constitutional system of the West'.[55] Otherwise China will remain backward and runs the risk of devolution into chaos and continuing to engage in a 'worship of power' and 'clannishness' and the rise of certain 'grass-roots organs of power [that] are not democratic at all but enormously popular'.[56]

Perhaps the gradualist approach that Wang Zhoujun urges is in fact reflected in the slow shift in attitudes about the legal status of the PRC Constitution within the system of justice. In 1955, the Supreme People's Court issued its 'Reply on the Non-Desirability of Referring to the Constitution in the Determination of Crimes and Sentences in Criminal Judgments', which was long regarded as prohibiting courts from relying on constitutional provisions directly in deciding a case – in other words, prescribing that courts can apply only the ordinary legislation (if any) through which the constitution was implemented.[57] Some change in position was indicated in 2001 by the Supreme People's Court in its 'Reply to the Shandong High Court' regarding the case of *Qi Yuling v. Chen Xiaoqi*. That 'Reply' suggested, although rather obliquely, that courts may sometimes refer to and rely on provisions of the Constitution in deciding cases – thereby departing somewhat from the position established on this issue in 1955.[58] This 'Reply', however, prompted some divergence of views and some criticism among Chinese legal academics, partly because the one-paragraph interpretation did not refer to any specific provision of

53 WANG, Z. (2007) Democracy, Rule of Law and Human Rights Protection under Gradually Developed Constitutionalism. *Frontiers of Law in China*. 2(3). pp. 335–352, at p. 348.

54 Ibid.

55 Ibid. at pp. 351–352.

56 Ibid.

57 For a reflection of this view, see CHOW, D.C.K. (2003) *The Legal System of the People's Republic of China*. St Paul, MN: Thomson/West, pp. 71, 78 (explaining that 'it is doubtful (. . .) whether the current PRC Constitution has direct legal effect in the absence of implementing legislation' and that '[m]any scholars in the PRC view the Constitution as [merely] declaratory (. . .) [since] courts in the PRC do not have the power to determine whether a constitutional violation has occurred or to interpret the Constitution').

58 See *Qi Yuling v. Chen Xiaoqi, Case of Infringement of Citizen's Fundamental Rights of Receiving Education under the Protection of the Constitution by Means of Infringing Rights of Name*, 5 *Zuigao Renmin Rayuan Gangbao* [Gazette of the Supreme People's Court of the People's Republic of China] 158 (2001); see also 'Reply of the Supreme People's Court on Whether the Civil Liabilities Shall Be Borne for the Infringement upon a Citizen's Basic Right of Receiving Education Which Is under the Protection of the Constitution by Means of Infringing upon His/Her Right of Personal Name' (adopted at the 1183rd meeting of the Judicial Committee of the Supreme People's Court on 28 June 2001; No. 25 [2001] of the Interpretations of the Supreme People's Court; effective 28 June 2001).

the Constitution and did not expressly state that the Constitution did in fact apply directly to the case at hand. Moreover, a more recent interpretation by the Supreme People's Court seems to mark a departure from the 2001 'Reply': in 2008, the Supreme People's Court published a decision abolishing a number of its earlier interpretations, including the 2001 'Reply'.[59] Given the inconsistency and uncertainty that this series of positions reflects, it can be expected that this issue regarding the precise status of the Constitution in the contemporary legal system of the PRC will evolve further and take some time to solidify.

Before concluding, let me draw attention to a very recent development that might accelerate that evolution and solidification of the status of the Constitution in China's legal system. As part of the efforts by Xi Jinping, the current leader of the Communist Party of China, to fight corruption, new requirements were prescribed in late 2014 intended to raise the profile of the Constitution. An article appearing in *The Economist* offers this description:

> Officials will now have to swear loyalty to China's constitution. There is to be a new 'National Constitution Day'. Schools are to teach its importance. The idea is to make it clear to errant officials that, no matter what they may think of ordinary laws and regulations, there is one big one they cannot ignore. The constitution, for example, enshrines property rights. Of the many thousands of 'mass incidents' of unrest each year in rural China, 65% relate to disputes over the (often illegal) seizure of land by officials. Mr Xi wants to make it clear that their behaviour is not just illegal but also unconstitutional. That sounds scarier.[60]

Naturally, it remains to be seen what long-term effect, if any, this new 'constitutional consciousness-raising' campaign might have. In the short term, perhaps it simply provides some further evidence of how far the Constitution is at this point from the centre of the Chinese legal system.

To sum up: constitutionalism is by no means unimportant in China. At this stage, however, the PRC's Constitution itself is still rather new, and the Chinese people have not yet developed a tradition in which constitutionalism can truly take hold – particularly constitutionalism that follows a Western model, in which a country's constitution can acquire 'a kind of rationality and divinity' and can be

59 See 'Decision on Abolishing the Relevant Judicial Interpretations (the Seventh Batch) Promulgated before the End of Year 2007' (adopted at the 1457th meeting of the Judicial Committee of the Supreme People's Court on 8 December 2008; No. 15 [2008] of the Interpretations of the Supreme People's Court; effective 24 December 2008). I am indebted to my colleague Dr Xing Lijuan for providing me with several of the details discussed above.

60 THE ECONOMIST (2014) *Rule of Law in China: China with Legal Characteristics*. [Online] 1 November 2014. Available at: www.economist.com/node/21629383/print [Accessed: 14 February 2017].

'regarded as the representation and the essence of [the country's] national spirits, civilizations, and values'.[61]

4. Concluding observations

As announced at the beginning of this chapter, my principal aim in this first of my two contributions to the book has been to help achieve its objective by throwing some light on the concept of 'constitutionalism' as it operates in the contemporary legal system of the PRC. In making that attempt, I have emphasised that despite a very substantial amount of 'foreign influence', especially from the West, the Chinese concept of 'constitutionalism' differs importantly from the Western concept – and particularly from the American concept with which I am most familiar. In resisting and 'translating' foreign legal and constitutional influences, China has followed a pattern established many centuries ago during its long dynastic period.

In my view, it is important that we bear in mind these various aspects of uncertainty as we address questions regarding how the Chinese constitutional and legal system handles matters of self-government and 'genuine autonomy', as in the case of China's relationship with the Tibetan people. I regard the underlying structure of constitutionalism in the PRC to be rather shaky – in part because it is still being built as part of a legal reform process that is remarkable both for its speed and for its scope.

61 MA, X. (2007) A Reflection on the History of Chinese Constitutionalism of Last Century. *Frontiers of Law in China*. 2(1). pp. 44–70, at p. 49.

Chapter 2

The rule of law in China

Fundamental uncertainties about 'decoding' a fundamental concept

John W. Head

1. Introduction

We cannot properly understand the concept of 'constitutionalism' in the PRC without first 'decoding' that concept (as I have noted in Chapter 1). Why? Because despite a very substantial amount of foreign influence, most recently from the West, the concept of 'constitutionalism' as it exists in today's China differs importantly from the Western concept. Those differences in meaning result from differences in culture and language, which themselves result primarily from differences in history between the West and China.[1] For that reason, I gave special attention in Chapter 1 to some historical matters – and particularly to (1) China's reaction to outside influences (especially legal influences) and (2) recent developments in China's legal and constitutional system. I asserted that the surface similarity we find between legal concepts, labels and institutions in China and legal concepts, labels and institutions in the Western world can disguise the fact that foreign influences on China's contemporary legal system have in fact been heavily filtered, or rejected outright, in much the same way that foreign influence of various sorts was filtered or rejected in many circumstances during China's long and glorious dynastic period. I then explored just what 'constitutionalism' in China amounts to today. In doing so, I attempted to provide groundwork for an examination by other participants in the Conference of such concepts as self-government, regionalism, decentralisation, autonomy and the like, especially as those concepts might apply in the case of Tibet.

In this Chapter 2, I wish to dig deeper into some of these issues and to provide further illustrations that I consider especially pertinent to the aims of the Conference. In doing so, of course, I operate under the same limitations – and offer the same disclaimers – as those that I identified in the opening pages of Chapter 1. That is, I make no claim that my own views are as objective or as well informed as they should be; a cross-legal-cultural assessment of the type I am

1 As noted in Chapter 1, I use the term 'the West' to mean principally Western Europe (including Britain) and the countries of the world most heavily influenced by European culture, including my own home country of the United States.

attempting is extremely difficult. On the other hand, I am convinced that we need to try. Why? Because any assessment of whether the 'Memorandum on Genuine Autonomy for the Tibetan People' does or does not 'correspond to (. . .) the Chinese constitutional and legal system' (quoting from the objective set for this volume) rests on the assumption that the behaviour of the PRC Government should in fact be faithful to some sort of 'rule of law'. And so, notwithstanding the difficulty of the task, I offer my observations here on the rule of law in contemporary China.[2]

As a final introductory remark, I would draw special attention to the sub-title I have given to this chapter: 'Fundamental uncertainties about "decoding" a fundamental concept'. I consider the notion of 'rule of law' to be a concept that is absolutely fundamental to an understanding of a legal system, and particularly to the integrity and usefulness of that legal system's constitution. Unfortunately, the concept of the 'rule of law' in contemporary China is, in my view, shrouded in fundamental uncertainty and disagreement. As I shall explain in the following paragraphs, that uncertainty and disagreement can be seen not just from a Western perspective, but also in the views of Chinese legal experts who have focused their attention on such matters.

2 My own observations, of course, are informed and influenced heavily by the writings of many other scholars in this area. I would draw special attention to the following sources on which I have relied in formulating my own views: BROWN, R.C. (1997) *Understanding Chinese Courts and Legal Process*. The Hague, Boston: Kluwer Law International; LIANG, B. (2008) *The Changing Chinese Legal System, 1978–Present*. New York: Routledge; CHEN, A.H.Y. (2004) An Introduction to the Legal System of the People's Republic of China. 3rd Edn. Hong Kong: LexisNexis; CHOW, D.C.K. (2003) *The Legal System of the People's Republic of China*. St Paul, MN: Thomson/West; CUTSHAW, K.A. BURKE, M.E. & WAGNER, C.A. (2010) *Corporate Counsel's Guide to Doing Business in China*. 2nd Edn. Eagan, MN: West; LIEBERTHAL, K. (1995) *Governing China: From Revolution through Reform*. New York: W.W. Norton; LUBMAN, S.B. (1999) *Bird in a Cage: Legal Reform in China after Mao*. Stanford, CA: Stanford University Press; PEERENBOOM, R. (2002) *China's Long March Toward Rule of Law*. Cambridge: Cambridge University Press [hereinafter PEERENBOOM (2002)]; PEERENBOOM, R. (2007) *China Modernizes: Threat to the West or Model for the Rest?* Oxford, New York: Oxford University Press [hereinafter PEERENBOOM (2007)]; POTTER, P.B. (2001) *The Chinese Legal System: Globalization and Local Legal Culture*. London, New York: Routledge Curzon; VERMEER, E.B. & and D'HOOGHE, I. (eds) (2002) *China's Legal Reforms and Their Political Limits*. Richmond, Surrey: Curzon; WANG, C. & ZHANG, X. (eds) (1997) *Introduction to Chinese Law*. Hong Kong: Sweet & Maxwell Asia; XIN REN (1997) *Tradition of the Law and Law of the Tradition: Law, State, and Social Control in China*. Westport, CT: Greenwood Press; WANG, G. & MO, J. (1999) *Chinese Law*. The Hague, Boston: Kluwer Law International; GUANGHUA YU & MINKANG GU (2001) *Laws Affecting Business Transactions in the PRC*. The Hague, Boston: Kluwer Law International (2001); ZIMMERMAN, J.M. (2005) *China Law Deskbook: A Legal Guide for Foreign-Invested Enterprises*. Chicago, IL: ABA Section of International Law; BEHR, V. (2007) Development of a New Legal System in the People's Republic of China. *Louisiana Law Review*. 67(4). pp. 1161–1180; CHEN, J. (2007) The Transformation of Chinese Law – From Formal to Substantial. *Hong Kong Law Journal*. 37(2). p. 689; PEERENBOOM, R. (2003) The X-Files: Past and Present Portrayals of China's Alien 'Legal System'. *Washington University Global Studies Law Review*. 2(1). pp. 37–95 [hereinafter PEERENBOOM (2003)]; POTTER, P.B. (2003) Globalization and Economic Regulation in China: Selective Adaptation of Globalized Norms and Practices. *Washington University Global Studies Law Review*. 2(1). pp. 119–150.

2. Contemporary China's official commitment to the rule of law

2.1 Rule of law, rule by law and rule by man

I shall not try to summarise here my views on how the concept of 'rule of law' appears (if at all) in *dynastic* Chinese law, although I have explored that question elsewhere.[3] Instead, let us focus directly on the 'rule of law' in *contemporary* China. In doing so, it will be important to distinguish between three related terms: 'rule of law', 'rule by law' and 'rule by man'.

These three terms, and the concepts they name, can be regarded as describing three different points along a spectrum, with varying degrees of formality in the rules, of discretion exercised by government authorities and (conversely) of the control that law exercises over government. As suggested in Figure 2.1: (1) rule of law (often equated, as described below, with *fǎzhì*) represents a system in which the actions of government authorities are subject entirely to the control of the written law, and the discretion of the authorities to manipulate or circumvent the law is very low; (2) rule by man (*renzhi*) represents a system in which government authorities sit outside the control of the law, and in fact govern not predominantly through law at all, but instead through discretion; and (3) rule *by* law represents a hybrid of the two, under which government officials apply formal, written, perhaps detailed rules, but are not themselves bound by those rules.

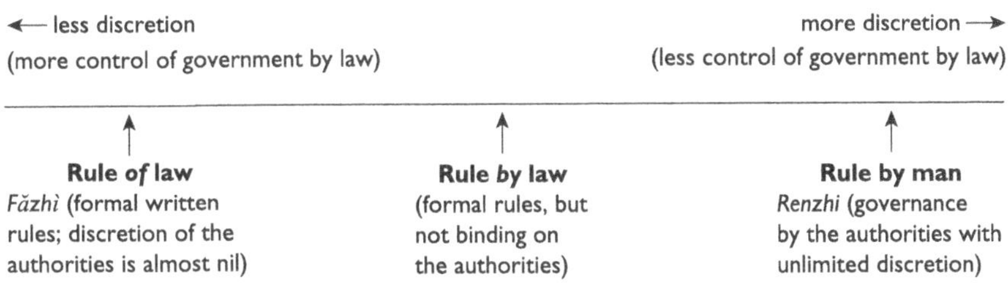

Figure 2.1 Formality, discretion, and control in *fǎzhì*, *renzhi* and rule by law[4]

3 See HEAD, J.W. (2009) *China's Legal Soul: The Modern Chinese Legal Identity in Historical Context*. Durham, NC: Carolina Academic Press [hereinafter HEAD (2009)], esp. pp. 59–63, 109–111.

4 Other elements of the rule of law, beyond the elements of formality, discretion and control, are disregarded for purposes of this simple diagram. For further details on these concepts, see HEAD (2009), above note 3, pp. 107–108, 112–114, and sources cited there. In an appendix to Chapter II of that book, I have enumerated a great many competing concepts of the rule of law, distinguishable from each other in part by the interplay of formality, discretion and control.

2.2 Constitutional provisions on the rule of law

In debating the question of what role law plays in today's China – and in particular whether that country is best characterised now as having 'rule of law', 'rule by law' or 'rule by man' – observers sometimes focus on the actual language of the Constitution of the PRC, and particularly the language appearing in the amendments made in 1999. The pertinent text of those amendments appears in Box 2.1, along with information about varying translations into English.

Box 2.1 Excerpts from 1999 constitutional amendments on 'rule of law'[5]

Amendment Three (approved on 15 March 1999, by the 9th NPC at its 2nd Session)

- The English version of the text of the amendment, as reported on the People's Daily website – http://english.peopledaily.com.cn/constitution/constitution.html – reads as follows:

  One section is added to Article Five of the Constitution as the first section: 'The People's Republic of China practices ruling the country in accordance with the law and building a socialist country of law.'
- The key phrases are examined below – first in *pinyin*, then in Chinese characters, then in English translation using the People's Daily translation as above, then with some alternative translations from various sources.

  - *yifa zhiguo*

    – 依法治国
    – 'ruling the country in accordance with the law' (People's Daily translation shown above)

    or 'governing the nation in accordance with law' (Wikipedia)
    or 'govern the country according to law' (Peerenboom – see below)

  - jianshe shehui zhuyi fǎzhì guojia

    – 建设社会主义法治国家
    – 'building a socialist country of law' (People's Daily translation shown above)

    or 'building a socialist rule of law state' (Wikipedia)
    or 'establish a socialist rule of law country' (Peerenboom – see below)

As noted in Box 2.1, the key language (in *pinyin*) proclaims the policy '*yifa zhiguo, jianshe shehuizhuyi fazhiguo*', which has been translated literally by one (Western) expert – Randall Peerenboom – as 'govern the country according to law, establish a socialist rule of law country'.[6] Peerenboom offers this explanation of that language and suggests that it has been misinterpreted by some commentators who urge that China is not serious about the rule of law:

> [The assumption that a socialist system such as China's] could not be serious about legal reforms and the rule of law (. . .) is evident in the way many Western reporters and some academics translate the phrase *fǎzhì*. This phrase by itself could be translated as either rule of law or rule by law, as there are no prepositions in the Chinese language. However, the phrase is part of a longer *tifa* or official policy statement of *yifa zhiguo, jianshe shehuizhuyi fazhiguo* [as noted above]. The commitment to governing the country according to law reflects the central tenet of rule of law: law is supreme and binds government officials and citizens alike. Indeed, the principle of supremacy of law and the notion that no party or person is above the law is explicitly stated in both the state and Party constitutions. Significantly, an alternative phrase *yifa zhiguo* using a different first character, which means 'use law to govern the country,' was explicitly rejected because it could be interpreted to support an instrumental rule by law rather than rule of law in which all are bound by law. Because the difference between the two phrases had been the subject of much academic debate, the significance of the choice was well known to all. There has also been considerable discussion of the difference between an instrumental rule by law and the rule of law among academics. PRC legal scholars who have given lectures on rule of law to Jiang Zemin and other senior leaders confirm that they understand the distinction between rule by law, in which government actors are not bound by law, and rule of law in which law is supreme. (. . .) Nevertheless, many reporters and some scholars insist on translating *fǎzhì* as rule by law and sometimes even go so far as to translate *yifa zhiguo* as 'relying on law to rule the country' or 'using law to govern' and other such more instrumental renderings. Such translations are not translations in the sense of direct rendering of the ordinary

5 The exact text in Chinese characters of the provision added to Article 5 by the 1999 amendment is beyond any question, of course. The key provisions of that text are shown in Box 2.1. Likewise, the exact text in *pinyin* of the provision added by the amendment is beyond any question. The key provisions of that *pinyin* text also appear in Box 2.1. What is subject to varying opinions is how the Chinese terms (whether in Chinese characters or in *pinyin*) are to be expressed in English. Some alternative translations are offered in Box 2.1.

6 PEERENBOOM (2002), above note 2, pp. 37, 67.

meaning of the words in Chinese. Rather, they are interpretations that reflect the translators' biases or assumptions about the nature of legal reform in China.[7]

By Peerenboom's account, China has officially pledged itself to the rule of law – understood as meaning that the government is bound by the rules of law – as part of its formal constitutional framework. While the Constitution of the PRC is apparently not directly applicable in the same way that the US Constitution is – a matter that I noted near the end of subsection 3.2 of Chapter 1 – the fact remains that China has officially adopted the rule of law as formal legal policy.[8] Indeed, the Communist Party of China congratulated itself in 2008 for implementing that policy so admirably.[9]

2.3 Late-2014 confirmation of a commitment to the rule of law

China's legal system is developing quickly, so it should come as no surprise that the Communist Party recently announced new initiatives regarding its commitment to the rule of law. In the latter part of 2014 – fifteen years since the 1999 constitutional

7 Ibid. at p. 67 (citations omitted).

8 For one authority's detailed account of what was intended at the time of the 1999 amendment of the PRC Constitution, see ZOU KEYUAN (2006) *China's legal Reform – Towards the Rule of Law*. Leiden, Boston: Martinus Nijhoff Publishers, pp. 34–35. Zou quotes from Jiang Zemin's 1997 report to the CPC for this explanation of what Jiang meant by 'rule of law' as called for in what became the 1999 amendment:

> 'The development of democracy must combine the improvement of the legal system so as to govern the country by law. To govern the country with law means to manage the state affairs, economic and social affairs by the people under the leadership of the Party in accordance with the Constitution and law stipulations through various ways and forms. It should be guaranteed that all the work in the state is carried out under the law. Institutionalisation and legalisation of the socialist democracy should be progressively achieved so that the institution and the law will not be changed because of the change of the leadership and because of the change of views and attention of the leadership.'

Zou also explains the earlier views of both Jiang and his predecessor Deng Xiaoping regarding the meaning they ascribed to 'rule of law'. See ibid. at pp. 35–37. For further details on Deng's views, see HEAD (2009), above note 3, p. 118 (explaining that for Deng Xiaoping, it was the 法制 form of *fǎzhì* that China should focus on, not the 法治 form of *fǎzhì*, and that it was not until 1997 that the 法治 form of *fǎzhì* was accepted officially by China).

9 See PRC STATE COUNCIL INFORMATION OFFICE (2008) *China's Efforts and Achievements in Promoting the Rule of Law*. [Online] 28 February 2008. Available at: www.chinadaily.com.cn/china/2008-02/28/content_6494029.htm [Accessed: 14 February 2016]. This February 2008 White Paper, issued by the PRC's State Council, catalogued innumerable ways in which the CPC has, by its own account, delivered to the country an increasingly strong system of law and governance, based on what it calls the rule of law. The White Paper does not, however, actually define the term 'rule of law'.

amendment described above was adopted, and thirty-five years since China began undertaking a dramatic reorientation of its legal system – the Communist Party pledged itself to implement further the rule of law in China.[10]

The build-up to the new initiatives made them sound impressive indeed. A story appearing in the journal *China Daily* a few days before the new initiatives were announced explained that '[t]he Fourth Plenary Session of the 18th CPC Central Committee', scheduled to begin in late October 2014, would 'deliberate on a draft decision of the CPC Central Committee on "major issues concerning comprehensively advancing rule of law"', in the expectation that the new decision would 'set the tone for the CPC to promote rule of law in China in an all-rounded manner under new circumstances'.[11] Moreover, the CCTV website offered this further explanation, also in advance of the pertinent meetings:

> In 2012, the new leadership of the CPC Central Committee envisioned a moderately prosperous society in all respects by 2020, when 'rule of law should be fully implemented as a basic strategy, a law-based government should be basically functional, judicial credibility should be steadily enhanced, and human rights should be fully respected and protected.'

Last month, members of the Political Bureau of the CPC Central Committee echoed that vision (. . .) [and agreed that rule of law] is 'a must' if the country wants to build a prosperous society, rejuvenate the nation, comprehensively deepen reform, and improve socialism with Chinese characteristics and the Party's governance capability.[12]

What emerged from the plenary meetings focusing on 'rule of law' issues in October 2014? The principal elements of the new initiatives – which were expressly designed as components to buttress President Xi Jinping's signature

10 See *CPC Convenes Key Meeting on Rule of Law*. [Online] 20 October 2014. Available at: www.chinadaily.com.cn/china/2014-10/20/content_18769078.htm [Accessed: 14 February 2017]. This 2014 initiative was not the only action taken by the CPC or the government in recent years, of course, to emphasise the rule of law. For instance, a white paper released by the State Council in October 2012 credits the Criminal Procedure Law of 2012 with building a cornerstone of the Chinese legal system to strengthen human rights protection and consolidate the rule of law. See STATE COUNCIL OF THE PRC (2012) *Judicial Reform in China (White Paper)*. [Online]. Available at: www.scio.gov.cn/zfbps/gqbps/2012/Document/1226621/1226621.htm [Accessed: 14 February 2017]. For an excellent survey of the specific ways in which the Criminal Procedure Law of 2012 – amending the 1996 version of that law – manifests the effort by Chinese authorities to give greater emphasis to the rule of law, see XING LIJUAN (2015) The Rhyme of History: A Transition of Legal Culture in China Crowned with the Criminal Procedure Law 2012. *Asia Pacific Law Review*. 23(1). pp. 31–66.

11 Ibid.

12 *CPC Convenes First Plenum on 'Rule of Law' in Reform, Anti-Graft Drive*. [Online] 20 October 2014. Available at: http://english.cntv.cn/2014/10/20/ARTI1413792305484297.shtml [Accessed: 14 February 2017].

anticorruption campaign – called for reforms that would (1) build a more independent and more professionalised judiciary and (2) give greater prominence to the country's Constitution (a matter that I referred to briefly above in Chapter 1).[13]

What did not emerge from the October 2014 plenary meetings was a further definition of rule of law as understood or adopted by the Chinese leadership. Accordingly, as a definitional matter, the rule of law – or, more precisely, the phrase *fǎzhì* – remains grounded in the actual language appearing in the amendments made to the Constitution in 1999.

3. 'Decoding' the concept of the rule of law in contemporary China

Having examined these definitional issues, let us now turn to a key question: if, as seems clear from the above explanation, China has indeed *officially* pledged itself to adhere to the rule of law (defined in general to mean that the government is bound by the rules of law), has China actually pursued this pledge as an *operational* matter? Expressing the same question differently, how are we to understand in practical terms the meaning of the rule of law in the Chinese context – or even more simply, how can we 'decode' the Chinese version of the rule of law and make that term understandable from a cross-cultural perspective?

To address this question, I believe we must focus on two points. First, we should pay attention to the nearly absolute authority of the Communist Party of China (CPC) over China's system of law and governance and the corresponding absence of a genuinely representative legislature reflecting direct influence by society at large. Second, we should consider the distinctions explained most potently by Randall Peerenboom, between a 'thick' and a 'thin' concept of the rule of law.

3.1 The role of the Communist Party of China

Understanding the role of the Communist Party in Chinese law is of absolutely central importance to understanding law in modern China. In his 'nutshell' account of Chinese law, Daniel Chow devotes an entire chapter to this topic. He offers this explanation:

> Given the pervasive role of the Communist Party of China in all facets of the Chinese state and society, any treatment of China's legal system would be

13 For further details on the October 2014 reform announcement, see THE ECONOMIST (2014) *Rule of Law in China: China with Legal Characteristics*. [Online] 1 November 2014. Available at: www.economist.com/node/21629383/print [Accessed: 14 February 2017]; LIAO, R. (2014) The Law of Rule: China's Judiciary after the Fourth Plenum. *Foreign Affairs*. [Online] 26 October 2014. Available at: www.foreignaffairs.com/articles/china/2014-10-26/law-rule [Accessed: 14 February 2017]; HARJANI, A. (2014) *China's Fourth Plenum Tightens Rule of Law*. CNBC. [Online] 24 October 2014. Available at: www.cnbc.com/id/102117814 [Accessed: 14 February 2017].

> wholly inadequate without an examination of the CPC (. . .). The PRC Constitution vests power and authority in the political and administrative structures that form the lawful government of China; the exercise of power through these structures is the legitimate exercise of power (. . .). [T]he CPC (. . .) is a political party and not a governmental entity. A political party is a body of voters formed for the purpose of influencing or controlling the policies and conduct of government through the nomination and election of its candidates for office. By installing its top leaders in leading government positions and its members throughout the PRC government apparatus, the CPC is able to influence and control the PRC government. At certain points, the organs of the PRC government and the CPC appear to be fused or merged together[,] with the CPC exercising effective power through its control of the government organs. When the CPC exercises power through the government apparatus of the PRC as set forth in the Constitution, it exercises legitimate power. If the CPC were to exercise powers directly and not through the filter of government organs, as appeared to be provided for under the 1975 and 1978 Constitutions, there might arise concerns about the legitimacy of its rule as it is not a government entity. *Under the present political system in the PRC, the government structure serves the important purpose of legitimizing the power exercised by the CPC.*[14]

The key point to draw from Chow's explanation is his insistence on the legal legitimacy of the CPC's exercise of power. Such exercise of power is legitimate, he asserts, because the CPC has placed its leaders in government positions in ways that are entirely consistent with the PRC Constitution. Chow asserts that the CPC, while undoubtedly holding absolute power in China, 'is careful to give the appearance of operating within a legal framework', even though 'the political system actually operates quite in reverse of appearances. Decisions are actually made by a small group of Party leaders and then are ratified and rubber-stamped by Party and government organs under the control of a core of Party elites'.[15]

Other observers, echoing Chow's assertion that the CPC exercises absolute authority, emphasise that China is clearly *not* a country in which the great masses of individuals within the society write the rules, either directly or through an elected representative parliament. Indeed, as was recently explained by John Thornton – a professor at Tsinghua University and the former president of

14 CHOW, D.C.K. (2003) *The Legal System of the People's Republic of China*. St Paul, MN: Thomson/West, pp. 115–116 (emphasis added). The literature is full of other similar accounts of the CPC and its relationship with the PRC's political and legal system. See, e.g. ZOU KEYUAN (2006) *China's Legal Reform – Towards the Rule of Law*. Leiden, Boston: Martinus Nijhoff Publishers, ch. 2; CHEN, A.H.Y. (2004) *An Introduction to the Legal System of the People's Republic of China*. 3rd Edn. Hong Kong: LexisNexis, pp. 58–73, 74–94.

15 CHOW, D.C.K. (2003) *The Legal System of the People's Republic of China*. St Paul, MN: Thomson/West, pp. 131–132.

Goldman Sachs – it is only at the village level that Chinese citizens can elect their officials.[16] It is worth noting that the Chinese authorities have given close attention in recent years to the procedures for such village-level elections – with new revisions to such procedures being promulgated in 2010 and 2013 in order to guard against breaches of election laws[17] – but the fact remains that even at the village level the electoral process is designed and implemented in a way that ensures control by the CPC.[18]

Hence, instead of seeing rules of law emanating directly from 'the will of the people carried out through an elected body such as a parliament', as Xin Ren says is the expectation in Western culture,[19] we see law in today's China – like law in dynastic China – written by a very small cadre of officials who have gained power

16 See THORNTON, J.L. (2008) Long Time Coming: The Prospects for Democracy in China. *Foreign Affairs*. 87(1). For details of Thornton's account of 'democratic' elections at various levels of government in China, see HEAD (2009), above note 3, pp. 126–127. For a more recent account, confirming the observations made by Thornton in 2008 about village elections, see HO, B. (2014) *Village Democracy Shrugs in Rural China*. East Asia Forum. [Online] 22 July 2014. Available at: www.eastasiaforum.org/2014/07/22/village-democracy-shrugs-in-rural-china/ [Accessed: 14 February 2017].

17 For instance, amendments were promulgated in 2010 to both the Electoral Law of the National People's Congress and Local People's Congresses of the People's Republic of China and the Organic Law of the Villagers' Committees of the People's Republic of China. In 2013, the Procedure of the People's Republic of China on the Election of Villagers' Committees was promulgated by the Ministry of Civil Affairs. Moreover, according to a government report: 'In 2013 China implemented the principle that everyone is equal as stipulated in the Electoral Law of the People's Republic of China, and adopted [for the first time] the same ratio of deputies to the represented population in the election of [National People's Congress] deputies in both rural and urban areas.' INFORMATION OFFICE OF THE STATE COUNCIL OF THE PEOPLE'S REPUBLIC OF CHINA (2014) *Progress in China's Human Rights in 2013*. White paper. [Online] May 2014. Official English version available at: http://english.gov.cn/archive/white_paper/2014/09/09/content_281474986284512.htm [Accessed: 14 February 2017]. Another official report suggests that these efforts at combatting irregularities and mismanagement of village-level elections have yielded good results. See FEIHANG (2015) *Nearly 200 Cases Involving Breach of Laws and Party Disciplines in the Election at the Village Level Were Investigated and Handled in Shanxi Province*. [Online] 10 January 2015. In Chinese. Available at: www.chinacourt.org/article/detail/2015/01/id/1531270.shtml [Accessed: 14 February 2017]. I am indebted to Dr Xing Lijuan for pointing out these details to me.

18 See HO, B. (2014) *Village Democracy Shrugs in Rural China*. East Asia Forum. [Online] 22 July 2014. Available at: www.eastasiaforum.org/2014/07/22/village-democracy-shrugs-in-rural-china/ [Accessed: 14 February 2017] (noting that 'the prospect of a linear progression to [electoral] democracy' in China evaporated several years ago and that as a practical matter village councils are 'mostly led by the village [CPC] party secretary' – and that as a consequence of this, village 'self rule' takes place 'within the parameters of party-state control' and thus 'the nascent process of democratisation in rural China has come to a standstill'). See also LEVY, R. (2010) *Rural Elections in China – Democracy or Façade?* New Politics. XII(4). [Online] winter 2010. Available at: http://newpol.org/content/village-elections-china-democracy-or-fa%C3%A7ade [Accessed: 14 February 2017] (noting that 'competitive elections are far from institutionalized in China's villages').

19 XIN REN (1997) *Tradition of the Law and Law of the Tradition: Law, State, and Social Control in China*. Westport, CT: Greenwood Press, p. 54.

by birth, through force, or on the basis of their proven apparent fidelity to a favoured ideology. Throughout nearly all of dynastic Chinese history, those officials would have been emperors and the cluster of close advisors, especially Confucian scholars, who surrounded them. In contemporary China, those officials are the most elite of CPC officials – and this remains true today notwithstanding the 1999 amendments to the Chinese Constitution and the new 'rule of law' pronouncements made in October 2014.

3.2 *'Thick' and 'thin' rule of law concepts*

Should we conclude from these observations about CPC control over the political system that there is in fact no rule of law in contemporary China, despite the repeated official endorsements of the rule of law? Should we agree with Pitman Potter, who asserts that as a practical matter today's China still follows 'legal instrumentalism' – that is, rule *by* law – because 'the [Communist] Party retains its authority to determine the content of law'?[20]

Randall Peerenboom has offered some views that would lead us away from such a conclusion. For Peerenboom (whom I quoted above for his explanation of the 'rule of law' language added to the PRC Constitution in 1999), the entire debate over whether today's China aspires to and adheres to a rule of law is plagued by sloppy and biased definitions, some of which he attributes in particular to Ugo Mattei, a comparative law expert at the University of Torino and the University of California at Hastings:

> China seems to be moving toward some form of rule of law, but not the liberal democratic form of rule of law that Mattei implicitly uses as his benchmark (. . .). [S]ome of the traits found in China are hard to reconcile with such a system [that features a liberal democratic form of rule of law]: [those traits include] a hierarchical society, an emphasis on family, different gender roles, different conceptions of rights or at least a different balance between the interests of the individual and group, and different justifications and rationales for those outcomes (. . .). But these features are not at odds with the rule of law per se, just with one particular version.
>
> Mattei (. . .) equates rule of law with Western liberal democracy (. . .) Mattei is not alone [in this respect;] (. . .). For many, 'the rule of law' means a liberal democratic version of rule of law.
>
> The tendency to equate rule of law with liberal democratic rule of law has led some Asian commentators to portray the attempts of Western governments and international organizations such as the World Bank and IMF to promote rule of law in Asian countries as a form of cultural, political, economic, and

20 POTTER, P.B. (2001) *The Chinese Legal System: Globalization and Local Legal Culture*. London, New York: Routledge Curzon, p. 11.

legal hegemony. Critics claim that liberal democratic rule of law is excessively individualist in its orientation and privileges individual autonomy and rights over duties and obligations to others, the interests of society, and social solidarity and harmony.

It may help in sorting out matters to distinguish between thick and thin versions of rule of law. Briefly put, a thin theory stresses the formal or instrumental aspects of rule of law – those features that any legal system allegedly must possess to function effectively as a system of laws, regardless of whether the legal system is part of a democratic or non-democratic society, capitalist or socialists, liberal or theocratic. Although proponents of thin interpretation of rule of law define it in slightly different ways, there is considerable common ground, with many building on or modifying Lon Fuller's influential account that laws be general, public, prospective, clear, consistent, capable of being followed, stable, and enforced.

In contrast to thin versions, thick or substantive conceptions begin with the basic elements of a thin conception, but then incorporate elements of political morality such as particular economic arrangements (free-market capitalism, central planning, etc.), forms of government (democratic, single party socialism, etc.), or conceptions of human rights (liberal, communitarian, collectivist, 'Asian values', etc.).

In China and other Asian countries for that matter, there is little debate about the requirements of a thin theory and the basic principle that rule of law refers to a system in which law is able to impose meaningful restraints on the state and individual members of the ruling elite, as captured in the rhetorically powerful if overly simplistic notions of a government of laws, the supremacy of the law, and equality of all before the law. However, there is considerable debate about competing thick conceptions of rule of law.[21]

I have quoted from Peerenboom at length because I find that his conceptual framework offers a useful way of organising our thoughts on the rule of law in China. Drawing from that framework, I would offer the following hypothesis about contemporary Chinese law: even though China *does* aspire, according to its Constitution, to achieve a 'thin' rule of law – under which the legal system would boast the attributes that Peerenboom draws from Lon Fuller's work (that is, that the laws be general, public, prospective, clear, consistent, capable of being followed, stable and enforced)[22] – China *does not* aspire to the liberal democratic version of a 'thick' rule of law.

21 PEERENBOOM (2003), above note 2, pp. 55–58 (emphasis added). Peerenboom's work, and especially his distinction between 'thin' and 'thick' versions of the rule of law, has been widely cited. See CHEN, A.H.Y. (2004) *An Introduction to the Legal System of the People's Republic of China*. 3rd Edn. LexisNexis, p. 38; CHEN, J. (2007) The Transformation of Chinese Law – From Formal to Substantial. *Hong Kong Law Journal*. 37(2). p. 730.

22 For further explanation of Lon Fuller's views on the 'morality of law', see HEAD (2009), above note 3, pp. 129–131.

If it can be said that China does aspire to *any* thick version of the rule of law, perhaps it is one (or more) of the alternative versions of a 'thick' rule of law that Peerenboom identifies. These include 'statist socialist', 'neo-authoritarian' and 'communitarian' versions of a 'thick' rule of law. Peerenboom briefly defines these various types of 'thick' versions of a rule of law (including the 'Liberal Democratic' version) as follows:

> [T]he Liberal Democratic version of rule of law incorporates free market capitalism (subject to qualifications that would allow various degrees of 'legitimate' government regulation of the market), multiparty democracy in which citizens may choose their representatives at all levels of government, and a liberal interpretation of human rights that gives priority to civil and political rights over economic, social, cultural, and collective or group rights.
>
> Statist Socialists endorse a state-centred socialist rule of law defined by, *inter alia*, a socialist form of economy (which in today's China means an increasingly market-based economy but one in which public ownership still plays a somewhat larger role than in other market economies); a non-democratic system in which the [Communist] Party plays a leading role; and an interpretation of rights that emphasizes stability, collective rights over individual rights, and subsistence as the basic right rather than civil and political rights.
>
> There is also support for various forms of rule of law that fall between the Statist Socialism and the Liberal Democratic version. For example, there is some support for a democratic but non-liberal (New Confucian) Communitarian variant built on market capitalism, perhaps with a somewhat greater degree of government intervention than in the liberal version; some genuine form of multiparty democracy in which citizens choose their representatives at all levels of government; plus a communitarian or collectivist interpretation of rights that attaches relatively greater weight to the interests of the majority and collective rights as opposed to the civil and political rights of individuals.
>
> Another variant is a Neo-authoritarian or Soft Authoritarian form of rule of law that, like the Communitarian version, rejects a liberal interpretation of rights, but unlike its Communitarian cousin, also rejects democracy. Whereas Communitarians adopt a genuine multiparty democracy in which citizens choose their representatives at all levels of government, Neo-authoritarians permit democracy only at lower levels of government or not at all.[23]

23 PEERENBOOM (2003), above note 2, pp. 58–59, n. 76. In considering the conditions of Asia, Peerenboom seems to prefer one of the latter two 'thick' versions of the rule of law listed above – those emphasising communitarian values. In his 2007 book on China, Peerenboom writes this: 'On the whole, I find the arguments in favor of the kind of communitarian or collectivist approach to rights issues found in some Asian countries (. . .) more persuasive, and the results on the whole more attractive, than the liberal approach as practiced particularly in the United States (. . .). To put it

4. Competing views within China about the rule of law

I have hypothesised in the preceding paragraphs that even though China *does* aspire, according to its Constitution, to achieving a 'thin' rule of law – under which the legal system would boast the attributes that Peerenboom draws from Lon Fuller's work – China (or at least its CPC leadership) *does not* aspire to the liberal democratic version of a 'thick' rule of law. Is that hypothesis correct? One way of testing it is to consider a range of views expressed in recent writings by certain Chinese legal scholars from some of the top universities in China.

In Chapter 1, above, I drew from a number of articles appearing in the journal titled Frontiers of Law in China, which since 2006 has provided English translations of important articles written (originally in Chinese) by Chinese law professors. In the following paragraphs, I draw again from articles published in that journal – based on a survey I undertook in preparing for the November 2009 Conference in Trento – in order to provide some 'inside insights' into Chinese legal culture, and especially into the rule of law in China.[24] In particular, I shall summarise some views expressed by experts Wang Zhoujun, Jiang Ming'an, He Jiahong, Ma Huaide and Ma Xiaohong.

4.1 Administrative power and a gradualist approach

Two key themes in Wang Zhoujun's writing on democracy and the rule of law[25] are these: (1) of the various forms of governmental power, it is *administrative* power that increasingly matters in the daily lives of individuals in today's China; and (2) China's contemporary legal system is, and should be, taking a *gradualist* approach to bringing administrative power under the control of the rule of law. As for the second of these points, Wang states that the gradualist approach should resemble the process of 'feeling the stones when crossing the river' in order to avoid falling headlong and drowning in a torrent of uncertainty and risk when making one's

simply, (. . .) liberalism tends to benefit the more talented, smarter, or already well-off individuals in a society at the expense of the vast majority. In contrast, communitarianism benefits the vast majority, albeit at times to the detriment of exceptional individuals.' PEERENBOOM (2007), above note 2, p. ix.

24 Of particular importance for this chapter are the following articles appearing in various issues of that journal: JIAHONG, H. (2007) Ten Tendencies of Criminal Justice. *Frontiers of Law in China*. 2(1). pp. 1–22; JIANG, M. (2007) Public Participation and Administrative Rule of Law. *Frontiers of Law in China*. 2(3). pp. 353–377; MA, H. (2006) The Values of Administrative Procedure Law and the Meaning of Its Codification in China. *Frontiers of Law in China*. 1(2). pp. 300–310; MA, X. (2007) A Reflection on the History of Chinese Constitutionalism of Last Century. *Frontiers of Law in China*. 2(1). pp. 44–70; WANG, Z. (2007) Democracy, Rule of Law and Human Rights Protection under Gradually Developed Constitutionalism. *Frontiers of Law in China*. 2(3). pp. 335–352.

25 See generally WANG, Z. (2007) Democracy, Rule of Law and Human Rights Protection under Gradually Developed Constitutionalism. *Frontiers of Law in China*. 2(3). pp. 335–352.

way to the other shore.[26] Noting that the basic strategy of exercising the 'rule of law' was only officially formulated and adopted in 1999, Wang Zhoujun points to progress that has been made in implementing that strategy, particularly in the area of administrative law.[27]

What Wang Zhoujun (on the law faculty at Suzhou University) does *not* include in the notion of the rule of law – at least as it is pursued in China – is the principle of democracy by majority rule. He claims that China's cultural foundations are ill-suited to that form of democracy because 'China's Confucian traditional culture is a value system of clannishness with the royal authority at its core'.[28]

4.2 Dangers of participatory democracy and unbridled personal rights

Another Chinese legal scholar, Jiang Ming'an of Peking University, also emphasises the importance of (1) enhancing the rule of law in the exercise of administrative power, while (2) taking a cautious and gradual approach to embracing certain aspects of democracy – what Jiang refers to as 'participatory democracy'.[29] For Jiang, 'participatory democracy' can in fact be the enemy of the rule of law, as it was during the Cultural Revolution, 'a period during which China's democracy ran out of control and was distorted, and legal system of destructed [*sic*]'.[30] According to Jiang: 'It is obvious that "mass participation democracy" (or "direct democracy") without a legal system (and rule of law) is horrifying and will drive human beings back to the "natural status" without any safety guarantee.'[31] In view of this danger, Jiang explains, the development of administrative rule of law in China (and the development there of the rule of law and constitutionalism more generally) has followed the path of 'delegate democracy'.[32]

For Jiang, the (administrative) rule of law should *not* entail too much of the substantive freedoms of speech, press and assembly. Jiang asserts that 'various

26 Ibid. at pp. 346–348. For Wang Zhoujun, 'feeling the stones when crossing the river' means that 'in the whole reform process, every step taken has to be very cautious'; and in his view, the other shore of the river is 'a prosperous and powerful, democratic and civilized socialist country'. Ibid. at p. 348. Although Wang Zhoujun does not say so, the phrase 'feeling the stones when crossing the river' is derived from Deng Xiaoping's phrase *mozhe shitou guo he* or 'crossing the river by feeling for stones'. Deng used the phrase in the context of experimenting with economic policies. See GABRIEL, S.J. (1998) Economic Liberalization in Post-Mao China: Crossing the River by Feeling for Stones. *China Essay Series*. [Online] October 1998. Available at: www.mtholyoke.edu/courses/sgabriel/economics/china-essays/7.html [Accessed: 14 February 2017].

27 Ibid. at p. 340.

28 Ibid. at p. 349.

29 See generally JIANG, M. (2007) Public Participation and Administrative Rule of Law. *Frontiers of Law in China*. 2(3). pp. 353–377.

30 Ibid. at p. 356.

31 Ibid.

32 Ibid. at pp. 363–364.

media, especially open discussions over the internet, carry certain risks [that] some people may fabricate rumors and stir up troubles, make libelous, offensive and irresponsible remarks against the government and other people, mislead the public intentionally and create incidents'. Because of these risks, Jiang says, 'on the one hand, the law should protect freedom of speech, and on the other hand, it should regulate the operation of various news media'.[33]

4.3 Administrative procedure and participatory rights

A third Chinese legal scholar, Ma Huaide (Vice President at the China University of Political Science and Law), also focuses on how administrative law, and especially administrative *procedure* law, bears on the rule of law in China.[34] Yet Ma Huaide seems to go further than many other Chinese scholars in embracing what would typically be regarded as liberal democratic political ideology. He asserts that '[a]s the basis of democratic politics, citizen's [*sic*] participation in the management of state affairs and democratic process should be greatly encouraged',[35] and he explains how codifying administrative procedural law can contribute importantly to democratic politics. Such codification can also, Ma points out, 'be conducive to civil rights protection, and human rights promotion, which are the common duties of all countries around the world, and which are also the main aims of bettering rule of law'.[36]

4.4 Rule of law and limitations on government power

He Jiahong, a friend of mine at Renmin University from the time of my Fulbright fellowship to Beijing in 1994, also defines and discusses issues relating to the rule of law.[37] For He Jiahong, the movement toward the rule of law is one of ten key 'tendencies' that he believes will dictate the development of criminal justice (He Jiahong's work focuses on criminal law). He offers this succinct account of what the rule of law is, what it emerged from and why it matters:

> Rule by man is a kind of government for primitive society. In primitive time, since there was no law, rule by man was the only choice, and rulers originally were people with strong body or high prestige (. . .). In modern times, the emerging bourgeois in the western countries turned the 'rule of law' into a banner and instrument for their fight for power, and one of their slogans was

33 Ibid. at p. 370.

34 See generally MA, H. (2006) The Values of Administrative Procedure Law and the Meaning of Its Codification in China. *Frontiers of Law in China*. 1(2). pp. 300–310.

35 Ibid.

36 Ibid.

37 See generally JIAHONG, H. (2007) Ten Tendencies of Criminal Justice. *Frontiers of Law in China*. 2(1). pp. 1–22.

'the King shall not violate the law.' Later, with social development and the accumulation of the experience of social administration, mankind became more and more aware of the superiority and essence of the rule of law. Thus, it is a necessary trend of human society to proceed from rule by man to rule of law.

Currently, the rule of law is in global fashion. Similarly, China should also move along the track of 'rule of law'. The basic aim of the rule of law is to form a law-based stable and benign social order. The basic meaning of the rule of law consists of two focuses and one basic point (. . .). The first 'focus' of the rule of law is to formulate good laws. However, without strict observance, execution and justice, good legislation in itself will not be able to make for a genuine rule of law. The 'non-observance' is equal to the lawlessness (. . .). So, the second focus is to execute laws (. . .). In modern law-ruled nations, social members, especially powerful government officials, must strictly observe laws. Though it is necessary for ordinary people to conform to laws, yet it is more so for officials. Hence the 'basic point' of the rule of law is to restrict officials' power and to adhere to the principle that 'officials shall not violate the law.'[38]

4.5 Rule of law versus rule of *lǐ*

Taking a very different approach, and giving special emphasis to China's traditional dynastic law, is Ma Xiaohong of Renmin University.[39] This legal scholar takes the position that the current enthusiasm, in China and elsewhere, for the rule of law rests on the assumption that the rule of law is superior to the rule by *lǐ*, which Ma Xiaohong defines as 'rites' – 'norms and concepts formed at the beginning of human society, including primitive religions (e.g. sacrificial rites), morals (kindness to tribe members and enmity toward adversaries), and habits (daily conducts and speeches)'.[40] That assumption of superiority, Ma says, is incorrect; it merely reflects biased and racist views by Westerners (he cites the prominent nineteenth-century comparative jurist and legal historian Sir Henry Maine in particular) whose colonisation of the world made them equate might with right.[41] As a result of that colonisation, Ma

38 Ibid. at pp. 9–10.

39 See generally MA, X. (2007) A Reflection on the History of Chinese Constitutionalism of Last Century. *Frontiers of Law in China*. 2(1). pp. 44–70.

40 Ibid. at p. 57. As I explained in Chapter 1 of this volume, the term *lǐ* (礼, 禮) refers to a code of propriety. Although originally confined in meaning to refer to rituals relating to burial and honouring of the dead, the concept of *lǐ* gradually expanded in scope. In Western Zhou times, it referred to proper courtly behaviour of the aristocracy in their dealings among themselves. Confucius broadened the meaning of *lǐ* to refer to proper behaviour generally, based on the place or status of a person within the family or the social and political system. Western analogues to *lǐ* might include such concepts as ritual, chivalry, courtesy, morality and ethical behaviour. (Two Chinese characters for *lǐ* are given above; the first is the modern version, and the second is the older version.) See HEAD (2009), above note 3, p. 11.

41 Ibid.

asserts, 'Western law had become a yardstick for judging whether a country/region's law was "progressive" and "civilized" or "backward" and "barbarous."'[42]

That biased and racist view, Ma Xiaohong implies, should be discarded. Neither one of the two different approaches to law is inferior to the other, he says:

> If we can say that after the lengthy period of the Customary Law, the West, on the basis of their specific economic and social conditions, chose to leave the clanship [that all societies have gone through] for the rule of law, then, China, on the other hand, choose [*sic*] to 'reform the clanship' and enter into the stage of rule by *li*ˇ. The two choices in themselves were not inferior to each other, [but rather] the formation and development of a civilization and a cultural mode [represented by these two different choices] were endowed by the environment and the history and [therefore] no one could be said to be advanced or underdeveloped.[43]

It appears, then, that Ma Xiaohong is issuing a call for China to renounce the 'rule of law' in favour of the 'rule of *li*ˇ'. The former, he indicates, is a foreign element that will never be successfully imposed on Chinese society. The latter, he says, reflects China's deep Confucian traditional values.[44]

4.6 Summary of the diversity

It should be obvious from the survey of views summarised in the preceding paragraphs – and of course numerous other illustrations could also be offered – that Chinese legal scholars bring a wide range of perspectives to the question of whether China aspires to, or should aspire to, a rule of law . . . and if so, what that means. Some scholars do seem to endorse not only the rule of law in its 'thin' version, but also certain aspects of a Western-oriented liberal democratic 'thick' version of the rule of law – including, for example, participatory rights and other procedural safeguards in administrative law, and even certain substantive rights for individuals.[45] Other Chinese scholars take a more gradualist approach, urging caution in China's development of legal changes that could be incompatible with China's current circumstances or long-held values. And some Chinese scholars would apparently have the country return to some of those long-held values, thereby abandoning the efforts made in recent years to adopt any sort of

42 Ibid. This assertion by Ma is echoed, of course, by advocates of many indigenous and other peoples who have found themselves in unfortunate relationships with colonisers from the West.

43 Ibid. at p. 58.

44 Ibid. at pp. 65–69.

45 For Stanley Lubman's assessment on this point – concluding that several leading Chinese legal scholars have 'call[ed] for establishment of the rule of law based on principles familiar in the West' (including a requirement that members of the NPC be elected in public campaigns and that they not provide a 'rubber stamp' for CPC policies) – see LUBMAN, S.B. (1999) *Bird in a Cage: Legal Reform in China after Mao*. Stanford, CA: Stanford University Press, pp. 124–125.

rule of law ideology – including, presumably, even the 'thin' version of the rule of law. That last view, however, would seem to be a minority position, and one that is inconsistent with the 1999 constitutional amendment and with the late-2014 initiatives purporting to confirm the importance of the rule of law in China.

We should hardly find this diversity of views among Chinese scholars surprising. Surely a diversity of views on such an issue would appear in any country, and particularly in one that has experienced such an explosion of legal reform as China has in recent years. Randall Peerenboom offers these observations about that country's varied views on the rule of law and how to achieve it:

> Although one can appreciate the desire for an overall, coherent plan for reforms, no country has ever successfully implemented rule of law in accordance with some preordained theoretical blueprint. Legal reforms are necessarily evolutionary, context-specific and path-dependent. Moreover, China is increasingly pluralistic. As noted, there are important differences in the conceptions of rule of law and the different emphases in the purposes of law among central leaders, local officials, academics, and Chinese citizens, and within these broad categories as well (. . .). Thus, no single view of law or single theory can capture the diversity of perspectives.[46]

5. Concluding observations

I draw three main conclusions from the foregoing discussion. First, China has clearly made an official commitment (enshrined in the 1999 amendments to the Constitution and confirmed since then, including quite recently) to the rule of law, including the notion that the government is bound by the law. Second, although China does aspire to achieve a 'thin' rule of law, China *does not* aspire – either as an official matter or as reflected generally in the writings of the legal scholars I have surveyed – to the liberal democratic version of a 'thick' rule of law. Third, to use Peerenboom's phrase, 'no single view of law or single theory can capture the diversity of perspectives' as to what specific 'thick' rule of law concept (if any) *is* in fact appropriate for contemporary China. Therefore, leaving aside the question of how well China has *delivered* on its constitutional promise to provide a 'rule of law country',[47] it seems clear that substantial uncertainty attaches to exactly what that constitutional promise means.

46 PEERENBOOM (2003), above note 2, p. 94. In another, more general context, Peerenboom asserts that it might even be better to 'avoid reference to "the rule of law," which suggests that there is a single type of rule of law' and instead to 'refer to the *concept* of "the rule of law," for which there are different possible *conceptions*'. PEERENBOOM (2002), above note 2, p. 5 (emphasis in the original).

47 This is obviously a large question to leave aside, for it is clearly important to know not only what China *aspires to* regarding the rule of law, but also what China *adheres to* in that regard. I have explored this question elsewhere. See HEAD (2009), above note 3, pp. 143–149. I point out there that: (1) the PRC now has an impressively comprehensive body of statutory and regulatory law that

Let me now try to place these three conclusions in a larger context. As announced at the beginning of my first contribution (see Chapter 1), my principal aim has been to help achieve the objective of this volume by throwing some light on the concept of 'constitutionalism' as it operates in the contemporary legal system of the PRC. In that first contribution, I emphasised that despite a very substantial amount of 'foreign influence', especially from the West, the Chinese concept of 'constitutionalism' differs importantly from the Western concept. In resisting and 'translating' foreign legal and constitutional influences, China has followed a pattern established many centuries ago during its long dynastic period.

In the present chapter, I have elaborated on those basic views: I have suggested that the notion of 'rule of law', as enshrined in the PRC Constitution now for over fifteen years, carries a different meaning from the meaning(s) that it carries in the West. Indeed, I have gone considerably further than this, by asserting that even though we can be sure that the concept of 'rule of law' in the Chinese context means something different – and definitely not the so-called liberal democratic version of the rule of law – we can*not* be sure just what it *does* mean, and therefore how to 'decode' it. A divergence of views within China, including within the Chinese legal academic community, leaves us with fundamental uncertainty on this point.

In my view, it is important that we bear in mind these various aspects of uncertainty as we address questions regarding how the Chinese constitutional and legal systems address matters of self-government and 'genuine autonomy', as in the case of China's relationship with the Tibetan people.

addresses the whole range of economic issues – contracts, property, tax, labour and employment, government procurement, banking, insurance, consumer protection, intellectual property, trade, securities, insolvency and business associations – as well as civil law, civil procedure, criminal law, criminal procedure, family law, mediation and arbitration, environmental protection and more; and (2) China has also developed a sophisticated array of legal institutions – not just law-making institutions (congresses, standing committees and councils at national level, as well as at the levels of provinces, special municipalities, autonomous regions, etc.), but also a court system, a procuracy system and an increasingly active community of practising lawyers; and (3) these developments have facilitated (for better or for worse) an explosion in the volume of litigation in China in recent years. In the end, I conclude that 'today's China probably *does* possess the minimal attributes required to say that it does adhere to the rule of law – subject, however, to one point of uncertainty' as to whether the rules of law are in fact applicable to all segments of the society, including the government, so as to prevent the government elite from acting arbitrarily. Ibid. at pp. 143–144. I emphasise, however, the 'several aspects of the system that many critics both inside and outside China cite with deep concern', such as the continuing lack of independence (and in some cases inadequate legal training) among members of the judiciary, the unsettling frequency of reports that local officials ignore applicable administrative laws and procedures, and 'the treatment of minorities – Tibetans among them – by a heavy-handed Chinese government prepared to squelch any possible dissent'. Ibid. at pp. 144–145.

Chapter 3

Dilemmas of 'genuine autonomy' for Tibet

Yash Ghai

1. Context[1]

Efforts to find an agreement between the Chinese Government and the Tibetans under the leadership of the Dalai Lama, first attempted in 1951, were resumed in March 1989. Little progress has been made so far. The positions of the two parties have changed significantly. The Tibetan position has softened and the Dalai Lama now accepts that Tibet is part of China, but claims a considerable degree of autonomy, in accordance with the 17-Point Agreement of 1951. This 'agreement' was drafted by China and imposed on the Tibetan negotiators under threat of the military occupation of the entire Tibetan territory (they were already in occupation of a substantive part). It was then repudiated by the Tibetans (the Agreement is reproduced in the Appendix to this chapter). The Chinese Government now rejects that Agreement and offers Tibet a very limited degree of autonomy. There is no consensus either on the scope of the autonomy or its constitutional basis.

This chapter examines the two bases of autonomy to assess which form would best accommodate the claims of the Tibetans, already scaled down from the Dalai Lama's original demands of independence, and described by him as the Middle Way.[2] The Tibetans' original demand was for secession from China, arguing that China had annexed it illegally; China claims that it was always a part of China.[3] The current stalemate arises because China has offered autonomy within the constitutional provisions for nationality minorities as set out in the legislation on National Regional Autonomy (NRA) and Tibetans want autonomy under Article 31 (OCTS), which gives considerable discretion to the National People's Congress (NPC) in designing the autonomy.

1 The discussion on nationality regional autonomy in this chapter draws on GHAI, Y., WOODMAN, S. and LOPER, K. (2010) Is There Scope for Genuine Autonomy for the Tibetans in Tibetan Areas in the PRC System of Nationalities Regional Autonomy. *International Journal on Minority and Group Rights*. 17(1). pp. 137–186. Detailed references are available in that publication.

I thank Kelly Loper for her assistance in the preparation of this chapter.

2 See chapter by VAN WALT VAN PRAAG, M.C. in this volume for the Dalai Lama's proposals for the Middle Way – a compromise between the position of the Tibetans and that of the PRC.

3 See chapter by DAVIS, M. in this volume for a brief history of Tibet's status.

The preamble of the NRA legislation ascribes the autonomy for minorities as an application of Marxism-Leninism. In 1914, Lenin prepared a Bill in which national minorities, including Muslims, would have the right to form autonomous regions with their own government, to promote their national cultures, religions and languages. Under the influence of the Soviet Union, the Chinese Communist Party (CCP) adopted Leninist policies in 1931, promising minorities self-determination and even secession, to enlist their support against the Nationalists.

The current, 1982, Constitution states:

> The People's Republic of China is a unitary multi-national state created jointly by the people of all its nationalities. Socialist relations of equality, unity and mutual assistance have been established among the nationalities and will continue to be strengthened. In the struggle to safeguard unity of the nationalities, it is necessary to combat big-nation chauvinism, mainly Han chauvinism, and to combat local national chauvinism.

The reference to 'Han chauvinism' may have been drawn from Lenin's distinction between the nationalism of the dominant ethnic group and that of minority communities. He considered that the nationalists of a big nation had always perpetrated violence on others – what the Chinese preamble means by the Han chauvinism. Lenin even argued that 'nationalism' was a product of capitalism, to secure control over the market with specified territory. To win over the oppressed nationalities, Lenin came out against the forcible incorporation of a nationality within the boundaries of the state.

This policy served the Chinese Communists extremely well. However, it was soon abandoned, self-determination being downgraded to 'autonomy', within a unitary framework, promoting political integration with cultural diversity. Using labels to decide on the degree of rights to be conferred *à la* Soviet system, China downgraded ethnic groups from 'nations', which would have justified autonomous republics, to 'nationality', entitling it at best to an autonomous region. There is now ample evidence that Mao never intended to honour the earlier commitment, once the party was secure in its hold over power. Mao's decision to cloak his party in the ethno-national garb of the country's dominant element appears out of tune with Lenin's cosmopolitan viewpoints, but it was probably instrumental in its rise to power. The change of policy was probably also due to the impact of foreign powers on China's border regions where most minorities lived.[4] The extract from the preamble shows the ambiguity of China's commitment to autonomy for minorities, in a state overwhelmingly the preserve of the Han.

4 PYE, L.W. (1975) China: Ethnic Minorities and National Security. In GLAZER, N. and MOYNIHAND, D.P. (eds) *Ethnicity: Theory and Experience*. p. 511; and MACKERRAS, C.P. (1994) *China's Minorities: Integration and Modernisation in the Twentieth Century*. Hong Kong: Oxford University Press. p. 72 (hereinafter MACKERRAS (1994)).

2. Types of autonomy

2.1 Nationalities regional autonomy

The Chinese Communist Party's (CCP) understanding of nationality (*minzu*[5]) is an adaptation of Stalin's 1913 definition of nationality: a 'historically constituted, stable community of people, formed on the basis of a common language, territory, economic life, and psychological make-up manifested in a common culture'.[6] This emphasises language and folklore, rather than the deeper springs of ethnic identity, like religious or historical traditions. Both Tibetan Buddhism and Xinjiang Islam provide an alternative world view to that of Chinese Communism, and therefore cannot be easily accommodated within the wider PRC system – which immediately alerts us to the limitations of autonomy, which is not only that there has to be an ethnic claim, validated by the state, to autonomy, but that autonomy stands constantly subordinate to the interests of the state as defined by the central government. Although the CCP, under the influence of the Comintern in 1931, first accepted Lenin's more radical definition of self-determination for ethnic groups in China and assured a right to independence for minority areas, it retracted this promise by 1935 – as well as notions of federalism based on the Soviet model.

The shift away from self-determination and toward autonomy came after the Long March (1934–35) cemented Mao Zedong's status as paramount leader of the Chinese Communist movement.[7] Under Mao, the nationalist and pragmatic orientation of the party brought in a differentiated approach to the various minority groups located on China's periphery, one based on cooperation with certain groups that had been crucial to ensuring the CCP's survival in difficult years.[8] The Chinese Government's 2005 White Paper on ethnic issues states:

> Regional autonomy for ethnic minorities in China means that, under the unified leadership of the state, regional autonomy is practiced in areas where people of ethnic minorities live in compact communities. In these areas, organs of self-government are established for the exercise of autonomy. The

5 This term is now commonly translated into English in official Chinese documents as 'ethnicity' rather than 'nationality'.

6 MACKERRAS (2004), above note 4, p. 2. For a comprehensive analysis of the Chinese ethnic classification system in Yunnan, see MULLANEY, T. (2006) *Coming to Terms with the Nation: Ethnic Classification and Scientific Statecraft in Modern China, 1928–1954*. PhD Dissertation, Columbia University (hereinafter MULLANEY (2006)).

7 For more detail on the CCP's changing policy on self-determination, see XIA CHUNLI (2007) Reappraising the Right of Self-Determination of the People's Republic of China: How Far Can China Go?. *Asia-Pacific Journal on Human Rights and the Law*. 8(2). pp. 1–19.

8 Most notably with the Hui and the Mongols – but the Tibetans were not in this category, with the exception of a few individuals. DREYER, J.T. (1979) *China's Forty Millions: National Minorities and National Integration in the PRC*. Cambridge, MA: Harvard University Press. p. 71. As a reflection of this cooperation, some autonomous areas were set up in areas controlled by the CCP in the early 1940s.

> implementation of this policy is critical to enhancing the relationship of equality, unity and mutual assistance among different ethnic groups, to upholding national unification, and to accelerating the development of places where regional autonomy is practiced and promoting their progress.[9]

After the founding of the PRC, the Chinese version of NRA was gradually articulated and developed, first in the 1949 Common Programme of the Chinese People's Political Consultative Committee (CPPCC), then in the 1952 General Programme for the Implementation of Nationalities Regional Autonomy, and in the 1954 Constitution. Many of the key principles in these documents still inform the current system. Structuring representation of minorities also involved a scholarly 'scientific' dimension, the project of Ethnic Classification (*minzushibie*). In a process that began in the early 1950s and was largely completed by 1956,[10] teams of scholars assessed minority groups for designation as officially recognised nationalities.[11] While 400 ethnic designations were put forward based on self-identification, only fifty-six nationalities (including the Han) were eventually recognised. It is for the government to decide whether a group qualifies as a 'nationality'. Those who are not so accepted are unable to set up institutions or organise communal activities. Those who are recognised have to channel their political and economic activities along predetermined channels, under party supervision and control.

In the early years of the PRC, the CCP cooperated with local elites, including those in ethnic areas, reflecting the broader 'united front' policies, but also its lack of knowledge about, or roots in, most minority areas. Minority elites were recruited into the new structures of power, and fairly liberal policies on matters such as minority languages were adopted. The case of Tibet represented the largest degree of accommodation with the existing political leadership in an autonomous area. As a result of negotiations between the Tibetans and Beijing, the '17-Point Agreement' was signed in May 1951 (see the Appendix). The 'agreement' was imposed on Tibet, with threats of the occupation of all of Tibet by the Chinese army (which already occupied a part of Tibet) and without the opportunity given to the Tibetan delegation to consult the Dalai Lama. Beijing's principal concession to the Tibetans was the guarantee that the 'Central Authorities would not alter the existing political system in Tibet' or the 'established status, functions, and powers of the Dalai Lama'. As a counterbalance, however, the agreement also recognised a rival religious figure, the Panchen Lama.[12] The establishment of a

9 This statement appears in the Preface to the document.

10 KAUP, K.P. (2000) *Creating the Zhuang: Ethnic Politics in China*. Boulder, London: Lynne Rienner. p. 88.

11 Mullaney has demonstrated how Chinese anthropologists adapted the Stalinist classification scheme to fit a consensus among scholars on the basis of ethnicity in China, using language as the primary marker of ethnic distinctions. See MULLANEY (2006), above note 6, pp. 214–215.

12 In fact, the Tibetan Government, as conceived by Beijing, also had a third subdivision: a government formed by secular Tibetans based in Chamdo, Eastern Tibet.

Military and Administrative Bureau in Tibet representing the central government was a contentious issue in the negotiations, which the Tibetans only accepted on the understanding that the Bureau would be headed by the Dalai Lama, and that it would be a temporary arrangement.[13] The agreement reportedly had a 'secret codicil' which specified that very few Chinese troops would be stationed in Tibet.[14] But this agreement was nullified after the 1959 Uprising and was denounced by the Dalai Lama after he fled into exile.

Central Tibet was eventually designated the Tibet Autonomous Region (TAR) in 1965. Other Tibetan regions, Amdo and eastern Kham, had officially been designated nationality autonomous areas – at prefectural and county levels – in the 1950s. This reflected the general preference of the CCP to divide up autonomous areas into several political entities, thus diffusing their political power and securing the principle of central control or democratic centralism.[15] A purpose of this division, which also holds true today, was ensuring security along China's border regions.

The upheaval and radical policies of the Cultural Revolution (1966–76) saw a negation of autonomy policies, as well as extensive cultural destruction and assimilation, particularly in Tibet. In the 1980s, there were attempts to rectify the damage caused by this hard-line, class-struggle approach. In the early 1980s, CCP General Secretary Hu Yaobang visited Tibet and Xinjiang and apologised for the excesses of the Cultural Revolution, ushering in a period of relative liberalism in minority policy. Two CCP documents on Tibet and Xinjiang issued under Hu's leadership reflected a commitment to realising autonomy, with one even stating that the central government would only retain control over foreign affairs, defence and 'veto power'.[16]

During the 1980s, various 'preferential policies' (*youhuizhengce*) were introduced for minorities and autonomous areas. On the individual level, these included efforts to train more minority cadres, lower standards for entry of minority students

13 GOLDSTEIN, M.C., SHERAP, D. and SIEBENSCHUH, W.R. (2004) *A Tibetan Revolutionary: The Political Life and Times of BapaPhüntsoWangye*. Berkley, CA: University of California Press. pp. 150–151 (hereinafter GOLDSTEIN *et al.* (2004)).

14 Ibid. p. 146.

15 See SMITH, W. (2004) *China's Policy on Tibet's Autonomy*. East-West Center Washington, Working Papers, No. 2 October 2004. [Online]. Available at: http://eastwestcenter.org/fileadmin/stored/pdfs/EWCWwp002.pdf [Accessed: 14 February 2017].

16 See GOLDSTEIN *et al.* (2004), above note 13, pp. 287–288. According to Phüntso Wangye, CCP Document No. 31 stated that 'under the unified leadership of the central government, Tibet could exercise true autonomy, including the right to make its own decisions. For example, all central government guidelines, policies, instructions, and regulations could be refused or adapted if they did not conform with the practical conditions in Tibet, although for important cases, Tibet would have to ask permission from the central government'. Document No. 46 went further: '[I]n special nationality areas like Xinjiang and Tibet, the central government would retain authority over only three areas: foreign relations, national defence, and veto power. All other rights belonged to the minority areas.' (The account does not provide dates of these documents.)

into higher education and hiring preferences for minorities in certain types of employment in autonomous areas, as well as more relaxed controls on family planning. In the autonomous areas, levels of economic investment were raised, and special poverty alleviation measures created.[17]

Reflecting these shifts, the 1982 Constitution contained more extensive provisions on NRA. During the drafting process, the idea that China should adopt a federal system was raised – as it had been during the drafting of the 1954 Constitution – but this was not accepted.[18] In a departure from the scheme of the 1954 Constitution, however, the 1982 version accorded all local governments at provincial level the power to enact local legislation, among several changes allowing for a greater degree of self-government. In addition, it was agreed that autonomy should be 'extensive'.[19]

2.1.1 Constitutional provisions on national minorities' autonomy

The general principle of nationalities' autonomy is elaborated in the Constitution. Article 112 prescribes the organs of self-government as people's congresses and people's governments at the regional, prefectural and county levels. If a specified minority exercises autonomy, other minorities in the area should have 'appropriate' representation. Members of minorities exercising autonomy should be appointed as chair or vice-chairs of the relevant people's congress (Article 113), while the head of the government of the autonomous unit must be a citizen of the minority exercising autonomy (Article 114). Autonomous areas have the authority to adapt 'the laws and policies of the state in the light of the existing local situation' (Article 115). The powers of people's congresses in autonomous areas include the making of 'autonomy regulations and other separate regulations in the light of the political, economic and cultural characteristics of the nationality or nationalities in the areas concerned' (Article 116). However, these regulations require higher-level approval. If they are passed by an autonomous region, they have to be submitted to the Standing Committee of the National People's Congress (NPCSC) for approval. If they are passed by lower-level congresses, they are submitted to the congress of the province or region (the term 'region' is used for provinces which have autonomy) for approval; thereafter they are sent to the NPCSC for the 'record'.[20] In general, the autonomous areas have not made much use of their special legislative powers to enact autonomy and special regulations or modification

17 MACKERRAS (2004), above note 4, p. 27.

18 CAIDINGJIAN (2004) *Xianfajingjie* [The Essence of the Constitution]. Beijing: Faluchubanshe. p. 74 (hereinafter CAIDINGJIAN (2004)).

19 Ibid.

20 This wording may suggest that the NPCSC has no further responsibility, but it has a general power to annul local regulations 'that contravene the Constitution, the law or the administrative rules and regulations', Article 67(8).

rules. None of the five autonomous regions has enacted an autonomy regulation or special regulation, although all five have drafted autonomy regulations.[21]

Autonomous areas may administer the finances allocated to them under the state finance system (Article 117) and organise economic development 'under the guidance of state plans' (Article 118). They have greater powers to administer educational, scientific, cultural, public health and physical culture affairs, 'protect and sift through the cultural heritage of the nationalities and work for a vigorous development of their cultures' (Article 119). They may organise local law and order and security, 'in accordance with the approval of the State Council' (Article 120). They may employ local languages 'in common use' in the locality for the work of the organs of self-government (Article 121). Finally, the state should help them in economic and cultural development and in training a 'large number' of cadres and specialised personnel and skilled workers of various professions and trades (Article 122), and take due account of local interests when 'exploiting natural resources and building enterprises in the national autonomous areas' (Article 118).

Under the national minorities' legislation, there is a clear tension between accountability of local governments to their respective LPCs and to the higher-level state administration; Article 110 lists both responsibilities, and does not indicate how they are to be balanced. But the concluding sentence reflects the reality of governance in the PRC: 'Local people's governments (. . .) are state administrative organs under the unified leadership of the State Council and are subordinate to it.' LPCs at the county (rural) and district (urban) levels are directly elected, while the higher-level people's congresses are indirectly elected by those below them (Article 97). LPCs are responsible for ensuring that the Constitution, laws and administrative regulations are followed in their jurisdiction, and they also supervise local government policies and budgets (Article 99).

There is a constant reference to 'socialist development' which must govern the policies and activities of the regional governments. The system of autonomy has to operate within a regime of national laws, policies and institutions which serve to place severe limitations on the discretion of the community or locality. There is no independent mechanism for boundary keeping, so that there are no safeguards against inroads into 'autonomy'. The Communist Party maintains its overall control; and here there is no requirement of local participation or discretion. The current weak status of the rule of law in China, the lack of a democratic political system, as well as state priorities emphasising unity, sovereignty, CCP control and economic development create considerable obstacles for realising genuine

21 GHAI, Y. and WOODMAN, S. (2009) Unused Powers: Contestation over Autonomy Legislation in the PRC. *Pacific Affairs*. 82(1). pp. 29–46. Qin, a minority scholar from Guangxi, noticing the paucity of law-making by autonomous areas, commented that this state of affairs 'is not beneficial to the exercise of autonomy powers by autonomous areas, and affects the development of the economy and culture of nationality autonomous areas' (Qin, 'Lun zhidinh zizhi tiaoli', p. 2). This summary and citation is taken from the article by Ghai and Woodman.

autonomy within the existing system.[22] The preoccupation with sovereignty and centralisation of power fails to provide an effective guarantee of the distribution or sharing of power, reducing 'autonomy' purely to an administrative device.

The promulgation of the 1984 Law on Nationality Regional Autonomy (LRNA) implemented the constitutional provisions on autonomy and expanded them in some key areas. The Law was revised in 2001 after many years of discussion. Following unrest in a number of minority areas – particularly Tibet and Xinjiang – the 1990s saw a tougher approach, abandoning the liberal line of Hu Yaobang to focus on suppressing separatism and fostering economic development as a solution to ethnic unrest. Under this approach, the 'autonomy' aspect of the policy has been played down, while 'modernisation' is seen as the cure for any manifestations of ethno-nationalism. As the 2005 White Paper puts it:

> Regional autonomy for ethnic minorities enables them to bring into full play their regional advantages and promote exchanges and cooperation between ethnic minority areas and other areas, and consequently quickens the pace of modernization both in the minority areas and the country as a whole and helps achieve common development of all regions and prosperity for all ethnic groups.[23]

Similar themes also appear in a 2013 White Paper on Development and Progress of Tibet.[24]

By the late 1990s, the general shift toward marketisation of the Chinese economy and the preferential economic policies granted to certain areas, particularly Special Economic Zones, had resulted in enormous disparities in levels of development and living standards between the coastal provinces and the interior. It had also made the economic benefits that had been given to autonomous areas in the 1980s effectively meaningless. As part of its response, in 1999, the Chinese Government decided to 'upgrade ethnic issues' by improving life in autonomous areas,[25] and in 2000 it launched a campaign to 'Open Up the West'. The strategy is essentially to

22 GHAI, Y. (1999) *Hong Kong's New Constitutional Order: The Resumption of Chinese Sovereignty and the Basic Law*. Hong Kong: HKU Press Law Series. pp. 137–188 (hereinafter GHAI (1999)); GHAI, Y. (2000) Autonomy Regimes in China: Coping with Ethnic and Economic Diversity. In GHAI, Y. (ed.) *Autonomy and Ethnicity: Negotiating Competing Claims in Multi-Ethnic States*. Cambridge: Cambridge University Press. pp. 77–98; and GHAI, Y. (2013) Hong Kong's Autonomy: Dialectics of Powers and Institutions. In GHAI, Y. and WOODMAN, S. (eds) *Practising Self-Government: A Comparative Study of Autonomous Regions*. Cambridge: Cambridge University Press (hereinafter GHAI and WOODMAN (2013)).

23 See White Paper on 'Regional Ethnic Autonomy in Tibet' (hereinafter 'White Paper'), Information Office of the State Council of the PRC, May 2004, Beijing.

24 Information Office of the State Council of the People's Republic of China, October 2013. Available at: http://english.gov.cn/archive/white_paper/2014/08/23/content_281474982986550.htm [Accessed: 14 February 2017].

25 See MACKERRAS (2004), above note 4, p. 38.

further the integration of the interior provinces, including autonomous areas, with the rest of the country, through increasing Han migration, massive infrastructure projects and targeted investment.[26]

Although the overall purpose of the NRA policy has changed over time, certain state objectives have remained dominant, including ensuring security along China's borders, an imperative which has informed the approach of integrating autonomous areas and their populations into the PRC. Autonomy has been a pragmatic device for achieving these related goals. Economic development, as defined by the state, has been the principal method adopted in recent years. The 2013 White Paper explains:

> Developing the economy is an important way to ensure the basic rights of all ethnic groups in Tibet, especially their rights to subsistence and development. The establishment of a modern economy in Tibet and its development has laid a solid material foundation for the progress of various undertakings in the region.

The current emphasis on economic development has eroded autonomy and threatens the way of life of these communities – as the natural resources of their regions are exploited, frequently with the introduction of Han workers, and the environment degraded. Each time the implications of autonomy for restrictions on central policies and initiatives become obvious, autonomy is suppressed – allegedly against the wishes of the local communities.

2.2 'One country two systems' (OCTS)

The second type of autonomy is of more recent origin. It is based on Article 31 of the Constitution, and is usually referred to by the Chinese as 'one country two systems' (OCTS). The Article is very brief:

> The state may establish special administrative regions when necessary. The systems to be instituted in special administrative regions shall be prescribed by law enacted by the National People's Congress in the light of specific conditions.

Unlike the detailed provisions in the Constitution in respect of autonomy for ethnic minorities (as to eligibility and the key elements of the NR autonomy), there is no further elaboration. Nor is there any general legislation on OCTS; instead, the Article leaves it to the NPC to enact a basic law to establish the 'high degree of autonomy'.

26 See, e.g. BECQUELIN, N. (2004) Staged Development in Xinjiang. *The China Quarterly*. 178. pp. 358–378.

The reason for the very broad mandate in Article 31 is the purpose for which it was adopted. The purpose was to bring about the re-unification of Taiwan with the PRC. The pioneer of this approach was the then leader of the PRC, Deng Xiaoping, who abandoned the idea that Taiwan could be coerced to return to the PRC with threats of the use of armed force. He considered that Taiwan could be persuaded to re-join the 'motherland' if it could be granted very substantial autonomy, guaranteeing its economic and social system and 'the way of life'.[27] The open-endedness of the mandate would allow the PRC to negotiate the terms of re-unification, in view of the situation at the time of negotiations. Additionally, the intention was to use the same approach for the re-unification of Hong Kong and Macau: three entities with different degrees of development and cultural and social systems. Deng explained OCTS, in relation to Hong Kong, as that, within the PRC, 'the Mainland would maintain the socialist system, while Hong Kong continues under the capitalist system. The implementation of two systems in one country is the solution for the peaceful reunification of China in accordance with China's realities'.[28]

This was clearly an interesting, innovative idea. As Deng Xiaoping pointed out: 'The notion that a state with socialist system in the main allows other political systems could not be found in classical Marxist texts. However, we boldly proposed such and national reunification would not be possible without such an approach.' The OCTS concept certainly is a breakthrough in the traditional theory that usually only one socio-political system exists in a unified state.[29]

Taiwan showed no interest in the 'return to the motherland' and the PRC seemed to have dropped the idea, at least for the time being. Instead, as Hong Kong's lease to the British was coming to an end and China rejected the British request for an extension or ignored the British claim that a substantial part constituting the colony of Hong Kong had been given to Britain in perpetuity, the Chinese Government made clear to the British that it intended to take Hong Kong back (resuming its sovereignty). It explained to the British and the Portuguese (the latter in respect of Macau) that China would resume sovereignty, but at the same time confer very substantial autonomy so that these territories would retain their current social and economic systems and way of life. As China was not familiar with the details of how these systems worked, Britain prepared lengthy memoranda explaining them – and persuaded China to attach them to the Joint Declaration between the two governments for full implementation of the Basic Law to be

27 DENG, X. (1993) *Deng Xiaoping on the Question of Hong Kong*. Hong Kong: New Horizon Press.

28 See discussion at ibid. pp. 6–9.

29 But it was perhaps not quite as innovative as Deng claimed, for after the First World War, a number of small entities were given a special status under which they could pursue their traditions, culture, religion and languages. However, questions of economic systems did not arise then. For an example – that of the Aland islands in Finland – see SUKSI, M. (2013) Prosperity and Happiness through Autonomy: The Self-Government of the Aland Islands in Finland. In GHAI and WOODMAN (2013), above note 22.

established for Hong Kong.[30] Deng decided to use Article 31 for the return of Hong Kong. So using this Article, China enacted Basic Laws for the return of Hong Kong and Macau, after negotiations with Britain and Portugal respectively, which confer very substantial 'autonomy' to them. Whether the OCTS formula has the potential for Greater China or the rest of the world ascribed to it by Deng is doubtful, for while the substantive powers of Hong Kong are now well understood, the institutional arrangements for their exercise are not. In order to understand the real nature of OCTS, it is helpful to examine the following aspects: the powers transferred to Hong Kong; the institutional arrangements within Hong Kong and their articulation with mainland institutions; the essential purpose of the system; and constitutional guarantees (my discussion is restricted to Hong Kong, but the process and arrangements in Macau are broadly similar). The legal basis for the constitution of the Hong Kong Special Administrative Region (SAR) is a Basic Law enacted by the National People's Congress which came into effect on 1 July 1997.

The purpose of the Basic Law is to retain as much of the economic, social and cultural system of Hong Kong when it was a colony, with the primary focus on its market economy. Accordingly, state powers over all areas except for defence and foreign affairs have been delegated to Hong Kong. Even in the case of foreign affairs, there is a considerable delegation so that Hong Kong can maintain its international trading and other economic relations, enabling it, for example, to keep its membership of international and regional economic and financial institutions and to conclude commercial treaties with other states. The transfer of powers is reinforced by the maintenance of separate systems in Hong Kong, such as its market economic system, currency, fiscal, tax and budgetary system, the common-law-based legal and judicial system, the regime of rights and freedoms, and immigration controls. The laws in force would continue except for those which conflicted with the Basic Law. The assumption was that, having no experience of capitalism, the Chinese would leave Hong Kong to manage its own affairs. China was also particularly concerned that the international business community would not lose confidence in Hong Kong's 'free' market and withdraw their investments. China had another interest in maintaining the market systems in Hong Kong and Macau: it wished to learn at first hand the mechanisms of capitalism, as Deng had by then decided to adopt elements thereof. Consequently, the Basic Law specifies that the executive and legislative authorities would be composed of its permanent residents. Even more importantly, the judiciary would be independent and one judge of the final court would be a distinguished judge from a common-law country. Since most of these were in place before the transfer of sovereignty, OCTS sprang to life instantaneously on 1 July 1997, requiring

30 For a detailed account of the negotiations and the preparation of the Basic Law, see GHAI (1999), above note 22. For Macau, see CARDINAL, P. (2013) Macau: Transformation of an Historic Autonomy. In GHAI and WOODMAN (2013), above note 22.

none of the bureaucratic approvals and delegations that so often delay the implementation of autonomy.

While China is interested in the market, it feared democracy. The Chief Executive is more beholden and accountable to the government in Beijing than to the people or the legislature of Hong Kong. The structure for elections to the office is skewed in favour of the candidate preferred by China. The legislature is elected, but a substantial number of legislators are elected by a few categories of voters, the principal of whom are in the business world, and are careful not to upset China. Consequently, China has resisted the full democratisation of elections, as it had promised to do after 2007. However, Hong Kong has a free (and often critical) press, and academics can write freely, criticising the Hong Kong or Chinese Governments. But there is evidence of China tightening its control, and there are some signs of interference in the judicial process.[31] China seems to have difficulty envisioning a capitalist system operating in a democracy. When presenting the Basic Law to the NPC for its approval, the chairman of the drafting committee explained that the structure of government in Hong Kong 'must facilitate the development of the capitalist economy in the Region'. But overall, Hong Kong people's human rights are well protected and civil society flourishes.

2.2.1 Is Tibet entitled to OCTS autonomy?

It will be clear from the above account that the real purpose of OCTS is not to confer autonomy on the people of Hong Kong, but to devise a framework for managing an alternative type of economy, the market economy, which stood in such sharp contrast to the Chinese planned economy at the time the negotiations for the transfer of sovereignty were conducted. The separation of Hong Kong's systems owes less to respect for its distinct lifestyle as to the perception that they are a necessary adjunct to its economy. It is because the Chinese authorities established Article 31 (OCTS) for this specific purpose that the Communist Party was quick to dismiss the Dalai Lama's request for it, claiming that Tibet had

31 Although the Basic Law guarantees Hong Kong its own legal and judicial system, it gives the Standing Committee of the NPC the right to overrule the Court of Final Appeal on questions of interpretation of the Basic Law (Art. 158). This power was exercised soon after the Chinese resumption of sovereignty when it overruled the CFA on its ruling on the right of children in China of Hong Kong residents having a right of abode in Hong Kong (see for a detailed account CHAN, J., FU, H.L. and GHAI, Y. (eds) (2000) *Hong Kong's Constitutional Debate: Conflict over Interpretation*. Hong Kong: Hong Kong University Press). After this ruling, the NPC became a bit cautious, but it was clear that if it did not really approve of a decision or a likely decision, it would not hesitate to interfere. It did so in 2010, when it openly declared its view in a case concerning Chinese corporations, put pressure on the HK Government, and more or less forced the CFA to secure the interpretation of the issues from the NPC, which was binding on the CFA. For a brief discussion, see GHAI, Y. (2014) ch. 1. In YOUNG, S. and GHAI, Y. (eds) *Hong Kong's Court of Final Appeal: The Development of the Law in China's Hong Kong*. Cambridge: Cambridge University Press. pp. 29–30. Many see this as the demise of Hong Kong's judicial autonomy.

already been integrated into the PRC socialist economy and political system. The PRC position is that Article 31 may only be used for the recovery of regions which were taken away from the 'motherland' and cannot therefore be applied in Tibet.

The 2004 White Paper on Tibet states:

> The situation in Tibet is entirely different from that in Hong Kong and Macau. The Hong Kong and Macau issue was a product of imperialist aggression against China; it was an issue of China's resumption of exercise of its sovereignty (. . .) the Central government has always exercised effective sovereign jurisdiction over the region.

Even though the actual wording of Article 31 does not restrict OCTS to any particular purpose, it is hard to sustain the idea that Article 31 was envisaged as having any broader application than as a solution to the Taiwan question. The provision is clearly linked to the preambular statement: 'Taiwan is part of the sacred territory of the PRC. It is the lofty duty of the entire Chinese people, including our compatriots in Taiwan, to accomplish the great task of reunifying the motherland.'[32]

Caidingjian, however, describes Article 31 as being specifically designed to incorporate into the PRC distinct areas of the country 'where, for historical reasons, socialism had not been practiced' and allow them to continue their existing systems, capitalism in particular.[33] A report from the time cites an NPC deputy as stating that the autonomy of SARs differs from national and ordinary local autonomy.[34] However, the provisions in both the 1951 17-Point Agreement between Tibet and the Central People's Government and the General Programme on the accommodation of different 'systems' can be regarded as the precursors of Article 31 and thus the question of its application in Tibet may be raised.[35] Also, the very fact that the NRA system incorporates autonomous areas at different administrative levels with varying powers indicates that autonomy in the PRC has consistently been asymmetrical, and that a differentiated approach has been taken in which the circumstances of each autonomous area is considered on its own.

32 1982 Constitution, preamble, para. 9.

33 CAIDINGJIAN (2004), above note 18, p. 202.

34 Xinhua, 29 November 1982.

35 That China was willing to negotiate a large measure of autonomy is evident not only from the 17-Point Agreement, but also from the Constitution of the Republic of China/Taiwan, which provides for a special status for Tibet (and Mongolia), but without much detail. See Arts. 91 and 120. When the constitution was adopted, the Taiwan position was no different from that of the PRC. For an interesting account of the changing attitude of Taiwan toward Tibet, from the old rigid Chinese position to substantial autonomy or even independence, see an interesting account by TETHONG, T.N. (2005) Tibet and Taiwan: Past History and Future Prospects. [Online]. Available at: www.mtac.gov.tw/mtacbook/upload/09507/0701/3.pdf [Accessed: 14 February 2017].

The Chinese Government has acknowledged that Tibet has different characteristics from other nationality areas. For example, reference has been made to Tibet's 'four uniques': region, culture, significance and treatment.[36] This could provide justification for special treatment of Tibet within autonomy arrangements. Although the Chinese Government stresses the 'system' of NRA, in fact a differentiated approach to different minority groups has been a feature of this system from its inception. One particular issue here could be to allow Tibetan Party members to practise their religion, if they so desire, and to allow religious believers to join the party.

Whether Tibet would be entitled to rely on Article 31 is more a political than a legal issue. Even in the disputed 17-Point Agreement, Tibet's special status and its distinctive concerns are recognised, which prompted distinct treatment of Tibetans compared with other minorities. In addition, it seems evident that the idea of tolerating 'different systems' within the PRC that is expressed in Article 31 originated in NRA as conceived in the years immediately after 1949. It is clear that the needs and legitimate aspirations of Tibetans are distinctive in several respects, and if genuine autonomy is to be exercised in Tibet, the framework of NRA as it has operated in the reform era will be inadequate.

What would be Tibet's position under the Dalai Lama's Middle Way? The Middle Way has a close resemblance to the 17-Point Agreement, as the Dalai Lama recognises. The Middle Way consists of the acceptance by the Tibetans that Tibet is part of China (the Chinese position) and the acceptance by China of 'genuine autonomy for all Tibetans living in the three traditional provinces of Tibet'.[37] In the division of powers, China would be responsible for foreign affairs and defence, and presumably Tibet for the rest, under a fully democratic and peaceful system. This is consistent with a statement of Deng that if Chinese sovereignty was accepted, it could have authority over all internal matters.

The Tibetan people do not accept the present status of Tibet under the People's Republic of China. At the same time, they do not seek independence for Tibet, which is a historical fact. A way between these two paths lies, within the framework of the PRC, in the means to achieve genuine autonomy for all Tibetans living in the three traditional provinces of Tibet. The Dalai Lama describes the Middle Way approach 'as a non-partisan and moderate position that safeguards the vital interests of all concerned parties – for Tibetans: the protection and preservation of their culture, religion and national identity; for the Chinese: the security and territorial integrity of the motherland; and for neighbours and other third parties: peaceful borders and international relations', with Tibet 'transformed into a zone of peace and non-violence'.

36 SAUTMAN, B. (2002) Resolving the Tibet Question: Problems and Prospects. *Journal of Contemporary China*. 11(30). pp. 77–107, at p. 103.

37 OFFICE OF HIS HOLINESS THE DALAI LAMA. *His Holiness's Middle Way approach for Resolving the Issue of Tibet*. [Online] Available at: www.dalailama.com/messages/middle-way-approach [Accessed: 14 February 2017].

He went on to say:

> Irrespective of population size, economy or military strength, the equality of nationalities means that all nationalities can co-exist on an equal footing, without any discrimination based on one nationality being superior or better than the other. As such, it is an indispensable criterion for ensuring unity among the nationalities. If the Tibetan and Chinese peoples can co-exist on an equal footing, this will serve as the basis for guaranteeing the unity of nationalities, social stability and territorial integrity of the People's Republic of China, which are of paramount importance to China. Therefore, the special characteristic of the Middle-Way Approach is that it can achieve peace through non-violence, mutual benefit, unity of nationalities and social stability.
>
> It is doubtful if this grand vision of China would have the same appeal to the Chinese authorities. Past negotiations between Tibet and China show that China is unlikely to move from its own conception of autonomy for Tibet.[38]

However, it is clear that if China were to agree, the arrangements would have to be established under Article 31. Political and constitutional rules governing NRA cannot accommodate the kind of autonomy proposed by the Dalai Lama. Article 31 autonomy, suitably framed, would be in Tibet's interests. Tibet may not need the same degree of autonomy as in Hong Kong – for example, of monetary or fiscal systems, international trade or the legal system, but the freedom of religion, freedom to pursue language policies, the development of a distinct political system based on genuine local representation and participation, and relations between Tibetans and non-Tibetans living in Tibet, necessary to the vision Tibetans have for their region, could be accommodated under Article 31.

2.2.2 If Tibet gets OCTS autonomy, what then?

It is obvious from the experience of OCTS autonomy in Hong Kong and Macau that OCTS might be no more secure, constitutionally and legally, than NRA. Drawing from the Hong Kong experience, I illustrate the weaknesses of its autonomy. This analysis would, I hope, also guide Tibetans as they begin, yet again, negotiations with the Chinese Government. But I begin with a short discussion of the factors that heighten possibilities of an effective, successful autonomy, drawn from comparative experience. One of the most interesting developments in constitutional law is the emergence of 'autonomy' as a solution to national problems. From small to large states (India at one end and the Solomon Islands at the other) there have been demands for autonomous areas to

38 As this chapter was being written, the Chinese President declared categorically that no special autonomy would be given to Tibetans (reported in the *South China Morning Post*, 5 September 2015).

accommodate the concerns of minorities.[39] In my study of a large number of autonomous areas, I identified a number of factors which affect the success of autonomy.

ISSUE OF SOVEREIGNTY

In several countries the issues of the nature and extent of autonomous powers have been complicated by considerations of sovereignty – in terms of the powers devolved or the international relations and engagement of the autonomous area. Many states have found it easy to concede considerable powers to small regions, power they would hesitate to grant to larger entities (Hong Kong has been given extensive powers, but few have been given to Tibet, whose original territory was as large as China itself). The notion or 'concept' of sovereignty has played a peculiar role in China, in its relations to outside powers or parts of China. In the former case, it has tended to invoke the sharp 'Western' concept, whereas in the latter it has been more flexible and accommodating. However, there is considerable ambiguity in relation to Hong Kong and Macau: which one is it? The continued practice of 'one country two systems' in Hong Kong requires us to proceed from the fundamental objectives of maintaining China's sovereignty, security and development interests and maintaining the long-term stability and prosperity of Hong Kong. The preamble to the Basic Law talks of the resumption of 'the exercise of sovereignty over Hong Kong' from 1 July 1997. Similarly, Deng told the Dalai Lama that the Tibetans could have whatever powers they wanted provided they acknowledged Chinese sovereignty.

What does sovereignty mean in this case, and in Hong Kong's? If autonomy is seen as a favour from the centre, it gives the impression that autonomy in Tibet or Hong Kong is a gift from 'China' and can be withdrawn at will. This seems to be the message of the 2014 White Paper on Hong Kong, which says that the high degree of autonomy is subject to the authority of Beijing.

INTERNATIONAL INVOLVEMENT IN THE DESIGN AND SUPPORT OF AUTONOMY

When foreign, regional or international groups or organisations become involved in negotiations, they can exert pressure for autonomy, especially in cases of conflict (as has happened in several instances, in times past and present). At times, as in relation to Bosnia-Herzegovina, the international community not only drafted the constitution, but underwrote it – its persistence is largely the result of the EU involvement in its working. Although China had no option but to negotiate with Britain, and then Portugal, in respect of Hong Kong and Macau, it has shown

39 See GHAI, Y. (2013) Introduction: Nature and Origins of Autonomy. In GHAI and WOODMAN (2013), above note 22.

marked hostility to any 'foreign' involvement in the negotiations on Tibet – to the extent of excluding Tibet's foreign legal advisers. Britain was expected to ensure that China observed the terms (and spirit?) of the Joint Declaration on Hong Kong (in part under pressure from the British Parliament). But this role turned out to be incompatible with British commercial interests on the mainland; Britain has done little to hold China to the Declaration. It does still present a six-monthly report to Parliament on developments in Hong Kong (sometimes mildly critical of China), but little attention is paid to it. There is no public evidence of remonstrance to the Chinese Government. Given China's economic development and generally its new, major role in the world, it is unlikely that either other states or international organisations will criticise China or China will pay any attention to criticism.

LOCAL PARTICIPATION

Another factor that may be relevant to the implementation of and respect for autonomy is the degree of the involvement of the community seeking autonomy. If there have been serious discussions, with each side sensitive to the concerns of others (and not coerced by external 'facilitators'), it is likely that the autonomy will be respected. Ironically, in the negotiations regarding extensive autonomy for Hong Kong and Macau, the local inhabitants had no say whatsoever, and were not even told of the framework and details of the OCTS that China was negotiating with the colonial power (although local representatives participated in the drafting of the Basic Laws). There are examples of successful autonomy when the community had no part in designing it (Aland in Finland), and failure when it was not involved (Bosnia-Herzegovina) and when it was (South Sudan).

Past experience regarding Tibet shows that China not only kept foreign participants out, but that it coerced the Tibetan delegates to accept Chinese proposals, under the threat of the total invasion of Tibetan territory.

3. Rules for amendment of laws on autonomy

I now turn to the aspects of the autonomy itself. A key factor is the degree of protection of the laws on the autonomy, particularly the entrenchment in the constitution. An autonomy well entrenched is reassuring to the minority of the persistence of autonomy, and when differences arise between it and the national government, serious efforts are likely to be made to resolve it amicably. If they cannot agree, the dispute would be resolved by an independent judiciary. I have already attempted to show that there is no such protection under Article 31 (everything is left to the NPC – which effectively means the Chinese Government (the executive)). Article 159 of the Basic Law attempts to regulate the procedure for the amendment of the Basic Law. Amendments can be proposed by the Chinese Government as well as by Hong Kong, but the procedure to be followed by the latter is complex, effectively giving a veto to the Chinese Government. No formula is prescribed for the voting in the NPC; presumably a simple majority suffices. There are thus few barriers for the Chinese Government in amending the Basic Law, but many exist for groups, including legislators, in Hong Kong. At a late stage in the drafting of the Basic Law an attempt was made to give some protection to the autonomy by specifying that 'No amendment to this Law shall contravene the established basic policies of the People's Republic of China regarding Hong Kong' – this would cover most areas of autonomy. The effectiveness of this has not been put to the test. However, whether or not a basic policy has been violated is a matter for the Standing Committee of the NPC (for which read the Chinese Government). But the reality is that China does not need to invoke this procedure, for no one can effectively challenge its breaches of the Basic Law. So, to conclude, the formula for amendment gives no assurance to the 'minority' and does not constitute a barrier to the Chinese Government.

3.1 Settling of disputes between the national government and the government of the autonomous region

It is inevitable that there will be differences of views between the central government and the government of the autonomous region/units on their powers and functions, and other aspects of their relationship. There are often problems in setting up new institutions and the transfer of functions and resources. It is usual to have mechanisms for discussion and resolution of differences. There are no such mechanisms in the schemes of autonomy in Hong Kong and Macau (but see later a consultative committee – the Committee on the Basic Law). And Beijing acts very much as if it were the master and the autonomous area its vassal. In practice, the Hong Kong Government, under the Chief Executive – who is effectively chosen by Beijing, has generally carried out the instructions of the government regardless of compliance with the law. China was careful in the early days to follow the law relatively strictly (except for setting up a provisional legislative council in breach of the Basic Law), but gradually this changed. It is fortunate that the Basic Law conformed with the then system of economy, civil society, public service, judiciary, etc., as this meant there were no problems in setting up the system.

The establishment of a Tibetan autonomous region will undoubtedly pose difficulties, and differences between the Tibetan Government and the Chinese Government. Without a mechanism for discussion and, if necessary, to give instructions on how to resolve them, Tibet would have to defer to China.

3.2 Rule of law and independent judiciary

In most federal or autonomous systems disputes about the respective powers and authority of national and autonomous government and other legal issues are ultimately resolved by the judiciary, which is competent and independent. Courts have played a critical role in maintaining the integrity of federal and autonomous areas, clarifying points of law, and protecting the rights and powers of states and autonomous areas. There is unfortunately no such reliable mechanism in Hong Kong and Macau.

A particular difficulty in the accommodation of Hong Kong's autonomy to Chinese sovereignty lies in the different systems of law. The Hong Kong courts, in the tradition of the common law, have jurisdictions over issues arising from the Basic Law and to make final decisions and orders. The judiciary is competent and highly respected – in the Court of Final Appeal (CFA), in every case, a distinguished foreign judge sits. There are considerable difficulties in the relationship between the CFA and the Standing Committee of the NPC (NPCSC) (the highest body for purposes of the interpretation of the Basic Law). The style and modes of legal reasoning, the independence of the adjudicating body and the deference to the law are strikingly different. In China, the interpretation of the law is mostly driven by the need to achieve a political objective – and the final decisions are made by a political body, the NPC; while in the common law, there is great deference to the law (although political or social factors might influence some decisions when the law is ambiguous). If an issue concerns the relationship of Hong Kong with China or China's authority over Hong Kong, the CFA has to refer the issue to the NPC. In the relations between China and Hong Kong, the final interpretation is that of the NPCSC for interpretation (Article 158). And on at least four occasions the NPCSC has overturned the CFA.[40] As I have stated: 'The power of interpretation is deeply intertwined in the relationship between Beijing and Hong Kong; it is not simply about the meaning of laws but about power relationships.'[41]

3.3 Traditions of democracy

Autonomy has undoubtedly been most successful in states that already operate within a liberal framework, because the established traditions and institutions reflect the values of democracy in their formation and functioning. These values include the rule of law and pluralism, and respect for decisions commonly arrived at. There is respect for cultural and religious differences. Autonomy arrangements require give and take; they depend on frequent negotiations for adjustments of relationships and the impartial application of the law. Political parties may operate at both the central and autonomous levels, acting as a powerful political link between administrations at the two levels. And the party which dominates at the central level may be in the minority at the federal or autonomous level – thus requiring different parties to cooperate as well creating a balance in the state. And because a party which is in power at the central level may be defeated in the next elections, but win at the autonomous level, it has an interest in maintaining the balance between the two levels. Critical is respect for the constitution – the underlying basis of the state.

Unfortunately, China's one-party system dominates the centre, and is not used to negotiating with other political parties or groups. The party also dominates

40 LO, P.Y. (2011) *The Hong Kong Basic Law*. Hong Kong: LexisNexis. pp. 817–826.

41 GHAI, Y. Hong Kong's Autonomy: Dialects of Powers and Institutions. In GHAI and WOODMAN (2013), above note 22, p. 345.

the state at the national level, and is in a powerful position to dictate to the autonomous area.

3.4 Institutions

Institutions play a critical role in the operation of autonomy at both the autonomous and the central levels in two important aspects. The first is the efficacy of institutions at the autonomous level and the commitment to protect the autonomy, and the other is the relationship between the autonomous government with the central government. Unfortunately, the real weakness of Hong Kong's OCTS lies in the weakness of both. A close analysis of institutional arrangements makes it abundantly clear that China wanted to retain effective control over Hong Kong affairs, notwithstanding its slogan of 'Hong Kong people ruling Hong Kong'.

The internal political system is heavily weighted in favour of the Chief Executive, the head of the government, who has firm control over the legislative process through vetoes not only over bills, but also over the introduction of legislative proposals. The Chief Executive is appointed by the Chinese Government and cannot be dismissed by the Legislative Council, even on impeachment, except with Chinese approval. On the other hand, the Chief Executive has limited powers of dismissal of the legislature in the eventuality that they are in conflict. The weakness of the legislature is compounded by its partially non-democratic character. A majority of its members are elected through narrow functional constituencies or a special committee which privilege business and conservative interests, who are in turn committed in their support of China. Consequently, the Executive is both unable and unwilling to stand up to the Chinese Government, and the more autonomy-minded members of the legislature are unable to hold the government accountable or to secure Hong Kong's autonomy. Although genuine autonomy is not possible without democracy, China was able to devise OCTS only because of the lack of democracy in Hong Kong. A democratic Hong Kong would not fit into 'one country', as China is finding in relation to Taiwan. But this very fact imposes and defines the restrictive scope of OCTS autonomy.

The Chinese authorities interact not only with the Hong Kong Executive, but also its legislature and judiciary. The National People's Congress reviews Hong Kong legislation and has the power of veto over laws which its Standing Committee deems to violate Basic Law provisions regarding responsibilities vested in the Chinese authorities. It also has the power to interpret the Basic Law, overriding decisions made by Hong Kong's highest court. These powers are very wide and can also be used to change the Law (this view of its powers has been endorsed by Hong Kong's Court of Final Appeal, as explained above). It has become clear now that the Hong Kong judiciary is incapable of protecting autonomy. For other reasons, too, the autonomy is without any reliable safeguards. The prevailing orthodoxy is that the relationship of the Chinese authorities with Hong Kong is determined not only by the Basic Law – despite Article 159 governing its amendment, which aims to restrict the powers of the Chinese authorities (which would have provided some safeguard) – but also by the PRC Constitution, which places no limits on the powers of the National People's Congress and, effectively, the State Council.

Although the Basic Law defines in detail the relationship between Hong Kong and mainland institutions, with a view to ensuring Hong Kong's autonomy, it has been difficult in practice to fully ensure that autonomy. The Central Authorities are frequently referred to as the 'sovereign'; the Chief Executive of Hong Kong is essentially an appointee of the Central People's Government, and being the most important official in Hong Kong, serves to implement directives he or she receives from Beijing. The lack of democracy in political institutions in Hong Kong and China means that decisions are made bureaucratically, without people's participation, and the autonomy of the people is thereby weakened. Doubts remain as to the exact scope of the application of the PRC Constitution (contrary perhaps to the intention that the Law under Article 31 would establish a self-standing constitutional order). And then there is the transitional nature of Hong Kong's autonomy; it is valid only for fifty years from July 1997.

Somewhat surprisingly, China agreed to a mechanism to assist in the settlement of its differences with Hong Kong, the Committee for the Basic Law (CBL). The Standing Committee of the NPC is to consult the CBL before it makes a number of decisions, as follows: declaring Hong Kong law invalid due to inconsistency with the Basic Law; the application of a Chinese law in Hong Kong (in the area of defence and foreign affairs, as well as 'other matters outside the limits of the autonomy of the Region as specified under the Basic Law'); the NPC interprets the Basic Law; and before the NPC amends the Basic Law. There are twelve members of the CBL: six from China and six from Hong Kong (the Hong Kong members are to be nominated jointly by the Chief Executive, the President of the Hong Kong legislature and the Chief Justice). The idea of such a committee seems to have been derived from the Nordic autonomies. But it has worked very differently from there. Typically, China has ensured that the CBL's advice would be in accordance with China's position; Hong Kong members seem to be chosen for their 'loyalty' to the mainland ('patriots'); meetings are held on the mainland, and the agenda is distributed the night before the meeting, with a clear indication of China's preference.[42] There is no consultation with the relevant Hong Kong authorities before China goes on to make its decision.

Effectively, therefore, China has a free hand in altering or disregarding the Basic Law. There are several instances of this, most recently in the reforms of the rules on the election of the head of the Hong Kong Government.[43] That China believes

42 This assessment is based in part on discussions with some Hong Kong members of the CBL. See GHAI, Y. (2001) Resolution of Disputes between the Central and Regional Governments: Models in Autonomous Regions. *Journal of Chinese and Comparative Law* 5(1). pp. 1–20.

43 DAVIS, M. (2015) The Basic Law, Universal Suffrage, and the Rule of Law in Hong Kong. *Hastings International and Comparative Law Review*. 28(2). pp. 275–298.

that it has the right to do so is amply demonstrated in a White Paper on Hong Kong issued by the Chinese Government in 2014. The context of the Paper seems to be an imminent decision on the reformed system for the election of the Chief Executive and the attempt on the Chinese side to de-legitimise those arguing for recognisable 'free and fair elections' in accordance with Article 25 of the International Covenant on Civil and Political Rights and other international instruments – and a readiness for mass action if this was not accepted. The Paper was as much for the benefit of other states as for Hong Kong (it was published in seven languages). In doing this, China set out its understanding of the Basic Law and the doctrine of OCTS.

The underlying assumption of China is well captured in the following quotation from the White Paper:

> As a unitary state, China's central government has comprehensive jurisdiction over all local administrative regions, including the HKSAR. The high degree of autonomy of HKSAR is not an inherent power, but one that comes solely from the authorisation by the central leadership. The high degree of autonomy of the HKSAR is not full autonomy, nor a decentralised power. It is the power to run local affairs as authorised by the central leadership. The high degree of autonomy of HKSAR is subject to the level of the central leadership's authorisation. There is no such thing called 'residual power'. With China's Constitution stipulating in clear-cut terms that the country follows a fundamental system of socialism, the basic system, core leadership and guiding thought of the 'one country' have been explicitly provided for. The most important thing to do in upholding the 'one country' principle is to maintain China's sovereignty, security and development interests, and respect the country's fundamental system and other systems and principles.

With this statement, China shattered the myth of 'high degree of autonomy', 'Hong Kong people ruling Hong Kong'. China's sovereignty over Hong Kong is comprehensive and, with it, it can do what it likes. China can, for example, decide who is qualified for public office (including judges, who must be 'patriots' as defined by party bosses in Beijing). Autonomy and sovereignty do not sit easily with one another; 'sovereignty' in the broad sense used by China (at least in the Basic Law) is a negation of autonomy.

4. Constitution of the Chinese Communist Party

In discussing China's constitutional order, there is a tendency among lawyers to concentrate on the state constitution and to overlook a more relevant and telling instrument – the Constitution of the Chinese Communist Party. The point I want to raise – the importance of party organisation as opposed to state organisation – is very well put by Albert Chen. Comparing the perceptions of law in liberal and Communist states, he refers to Marx's view of law as merely reflecting social forces rather than driving social change. Chen notes that:

> In Communist states the moral authority of the law is questioned as law is only an instrument of the ruling class for dictatorship and control of the whole society. Post-revolutionary USSR and China have both attempted to re-establish the authority of law by reference to the concept of 'socialist legality'. It is argued that in a socialist state, the law embodies the will of the people. However, a tension exists between the authority of law and that of the Communist Party. The party had led the masses to victory in the revolution, and in the new socialist society the party continues to be the sole interpreter and guardian of the interests of the people and the nation. The supremacy of the party means that the Constitution and the law may not be supreme, particularly if there is conflict between the decisions and actions of the top party leadership and the requirements and procedures prescribed by law.[44]

In such a system, safeguards of the liberal constitution such as the separation of powers or the rule of law mean little, since all key state organs are under the control of the Communist Party, and civil society is weak and under constant threat from the state. As Chen notes, 'all these factors tend to lower the relevance of the constitution as a device to contain, structure or direct the operation of political forces'.

The Constitution of the Communist Party is a better guide to the sources and structure of power – but no more than a guide.[45] The current constitution (after the 1992, 1997 and 2002 amendments) institutionalises the concept of 'socialism with Chinese characteristics', with an emphasis on increase in economic productivity. State ownership is relaxed and replaced by 'an ownership structure with multiple co-existing economic forms'. There is indeed considerable flexibility as China ventures into capitalist-style legal forms and capitalist/commercial practices, including, of course, stock markets and closer engagement with the global capitalist economy. As with the structures of the state, despite an elaborate style, power resides with a small group, the Central Committee of the party, carefully avoiding democratic processes and decision-making. The state institutions, representing in practice key party leaders, are subordinated to those of the party. As Chen summarises:

> As regards the general nature of the political system in mainland China, some of the salient characteristics are that ordinary people or even ordinary CPC members have no control over the selection of political leaders; there is not as yet a civil society consisting of independently minded and privately operated

44 CHEN, A.H.L. (2004) *An Introduction to the Legal System of the People's Republic of China*. Hong Kong: LexisNexis. p. 40.

45 A clear and reliable account of the Communist Party Constitution and its implications for politics and the economy is to be found in CHEN (2004), above note 44, pp. 81–94.

plural interest groups, trade unions, student unions or churches (not to say competing political parties which can exert pressure on the party-state apparatus (. . .)).[46]

5. Conclusion

In this system, autonomy cannot function. The high hopes that Hong Kong and to some extent Macau will show Chinese leaders how a democratic market system works have long been shattered. Even the international agreements that China made with Britain and Portugal have not deterred the PRC from violating their Basic Laws or these agreements. Anyway, Tibetans should, if the opportunity arises, negotiate for a democratic system within Tibet, defining the elements of that democracy. Before negotiations start, they should present a draft Basic Law, as the basis of substantive discussions on the nature and scope of autonomy. It should include mechanisms for consultation and negotiations as differences arise in its operation, on matters that intersect the two jurisdictions. On matters which are purely national, Tibetans should insist on a rule which requires the Tibetan Government to be informed and consulted if these matters impact on Tibet. For these purposes, a consultative committee representing the two sides should be established. The Basic Law should be entrenched; amendments can only be made if both sides agree. There is considerable international experience of these matters; Tibet should negotiate for such devices as have worked elsewhere.

46 Ibid. p. 93.

Chapter 4

Chinese policies on regional self-government

The case of Tibet

Michael C. Davis

1. Introduction: The rocky road to the present impasse

The March 2008 Tibetan uprising and the subsequent Chinese crackdown raised considerable international concern about Chinese policies and human rights practices in Tibet.[1] While Chinese officials were angered by the riots in Tibet and by the international protests that followed the Olympic torch, they faced considerable international pressure to meet with the Dalai Lama and resolve this long-standing dispute. With the 2008 Beijing Olympics approaching, China immediately moved into the damage-control mode, though it appears without any intention to seriously address the underlying issues. They quickly held an informal meeting with the Dalai Lama's representatives in Shenzhen near Hong Kong in May of 2008 and scheduled the seventh and eighth rounds in their ongoing formal discussions in July and October.

In these meetings, the Chinese side showed little interest in discussing substantive concerns and appeared to set roadblocks. They merely reiterated their long-standing position that the 'contacts and dialogues were about the Dalai Lama's personal future, and not so-called "China-Tibet negotiation" or "dialogue between Han and Tibetan people".'[2] They insisted on three 'stops' and four 'non-supports'. The Dalai Lama's representatives were told to 'stop activities aimed at splitting China, stop plotting and inciting violence and stop disrupting and sabotaging the Beijing Olympic Games'. Later, this was refined to include 'four non-supports': 'not to support activities to disturb the upcoming Beijing Olympic Games, not to support plots to fan violent criminal activities, not to support and concretely curb the violent terrorist activities of the "Tibetan Youth Congress" and not to support any argument and activity to seek "Tibet independence" and split the region from

1 An earlier version of portions of this analysis, subsequently revised and updated, was published in Orbis. DAVIS, M.C. (2012) Tibet and China's National Minority Policies. *Orbis*. 56(3). pp. 429–446.
2 (2008) Chinese Official Urges Dalai Lama to Respond with Sincerity after Recent Contact. *Xinhua*. 6 July.

the country'.[3] The Tibetan side has long met all the conditions stated by the Chinese Government, though they would surely contest Chinese accusations of terrorist activities by the Tibetan Youth Congress. In a crude display of disdain for the Tibetan cause, Chinese officials and supporting experts went so far as to challenge the Dalai Lama's credentials to represent the Tibetan people, insisting that he must speak to the central government as a 'common person'.[4] Further dampening the spirit of discussion, throughout the weeks and months following the March 2008 uprising Chinese leaders launched vociferous personal attacks on the Dalai Lama, labelling him a 'wolf in monk's robes', lumping together all branches of the exile Tibetan community as the 'Dalai clique'.[5]

In response to a request at the July Sino-Tibetan meeting that the Tibetans outline their position under the Chinese Constitution, the Tibetan side prepared a 'Memorandum on Genuine Autonomy for the Tibetan People'.[6] The Tibetan Memorandum elaborates Tibetan 'aspirations' for autonomy in eleven policy areas, including language, culture, religion, education, environmental protection, utilisation of natural resources, economic development and trade, public health, public security, population migration and cultural, educational, and religious exchanges with other countries. As discussed below, all of these are covered by existing unfulfilled national ethnic autonomy policies enacted under Article 4 of the PRC Constitution, except those relating to public security, migration and external exchanges, which appear instead to track the Article 31 'one country two systems' Hong Kong formula. Similar to Hong Kong, their proposal includes a specification that local laws within the scope of autonomy not be subject to central approval – as is now required in minority areas – and that the terms of their agreement with the Central Government not be subject to the Central Government's unilateral amendment. They sought Hong-Kong-style control over immigration into the Tibetan areas and control over local public security, as well as control over external relations in non-sensitive commercial and cultural areas. They further proposed to unify contiguous Tibetan areas. While Chinese officials frequently emphasise that this would constitute one-quarter of the landmass of the present-day PRC, these large, mostly mountainous, and often arid areas are in fact

3 Ibid.

4 (2006) Expert Calls for Dialogue on Tibet within China's Constitutional Framework. *Xinhua*. 18 July. This view was further supported by Dong Yunhu, the Director General of the State Council Information Office, who stated: 'The Central Government will never discuss the future of Tibet with the Dalai Lama', as 'he has lost all right to negotiate on the future of Tibet'. (2008) China Unwilling to Broach Tibet with Dalai. *Indo-Asian News Service*. 15 July.

5 DAVIS, M.C. (2008) For Talks to Succeed China Must Admit to a Tibet Problem. *Yale Global Online*. [Online] 16 May. Available at: http://yaleglobal.yale.edu/content/talks-succeed-china-must-admit-tibet-problem [Accessed:14 February 2017].

6 'Memorandum on Genuine Autonomy for the Tibetan People', Issued During the Seventh Sino-Tibetan Meeting, 4 November 2008 (hereinafter 'Tibetan Memorandum'). See also 'Summary of the Memorandum on Genuine Autonomy for the Tibetan People', Dharamsala, India, 16 November 2008.

already designated as Tibetan autonomous areas by the PRC – being divided into thirteen contiguous areas instead of one. This proposal, like all others, was presented as a starting position over which the Tibetans are willing to negotiate.

The Chinese position hardened even further in response to this Tibetan memorandum. In early November, in an extraordinary press conference hosted by the Chinese State Council, Mr Zhu Weiqun of the United Front Works Department issued a stinging attack on the Tibetan position.[7] In the printed State Council Address that accompanied the press conference, the Tibetan request for 'genuine autonomy' is treated as a request for 'a high degree of autonomy', as is promised to Hong Kong. In seeking such 'high degree of autonomy', the Tibetans are accused of seeking 'half-independence' and 'covert independence'. No explanation is given as to why the exact same language applied to Hong Kong means only autonomy. The State Council Address further accuses the exile Tibetans of continuing to 'collude with such dregs as "democracy activists", "falunkun (falungong) elements" and "Eastern Turkistan terrorists"', though no evidence of this is given. In seeking control over Chinese migration into Tibet, the Dalai Lama is accused of 'ethnic cleansing'. The exile government is characterised as a 'small group of splittists'.

The State Council Address makes clear that the Chinese Government had no intention to discuss substantive issues. The meetings are said to be designed to persuade the Dalai Lama to 'give up his splitting activities'. The State Council Address declared, "We never discussed the so-called 'Tibet issue' and will 'never make a concession.'" In January 2009, China demonstrated even greater indifference and insensitivity to the Tibetan cause by creating a new holiday they have labelled 'Serfs Emancipation Day', to celebrate their 'liberation' of Tibet.[8] Despite China's dismissive attitude, at a large mid-November Tibetan exile meeting in Dharamsala, Indian participants decided to continue efforts at achieving genuine autonomy. The participants determined to suspend this fruitless series of talks and find more effective non-violent strategies to promote their cause. The Tibetans have seemingly given up on expecting any goodwill from the current regime, but hold out hope that a future reformed democratic China will offer Tibetans some form of genuine autonomy.[9]

Since China seized Tibet in 1950, world leaders have raised questions about both the legitimacy and the quality of the Chinese occupation. Was the original Chinese occupation a violation of the sovereignty of an independent state? Has the Chinese Government fulfilled its human rights obligations to the Tibetan people? Is China obliged, either morally or legally, to provide genuine autonomy

7 Address at the Press Conference by the State Council Office, Beijing, 10 November 2008 (hereinafter 'State Council Address') (address given by Mr Zhu Weiqun, Executive Vice-Minister of the United Front Work Department of the CPC Central Committee).

8 (2009) Tibet Sets 'Serfs Emancipation Day'. *Xinhua*. [Online] 19 January. Available at: www.chinadaily.com.cn/china/2009-01/19/content_7410293.htm [Accessed: 14 February 2017].

9 (2008) China's Communist Regime Losing Ground. *Agencies*. 16 January.

for Tibet? China's obligations concerning Tibet are best understood through the lens of these questions and any current efforts to achieve a solution. The 2008 discussions were not just a product of the uprising that year, but actually began several years earlier. After five decades of impasse, discussions between Beijing officials and representatives of the Dalai Lama began anew in 2002. Throughout these discussions, the Tibetan leaders in exile endeavoured to build a 'conducive atmosphere' by limiting public displays of resistance to Chinese rule, while the Chinese side has shown little seriousness and has offered no concessions.

Chinese anxieties over Tibetan intentions have blocked all efforts at finding a solution to this seemingly solvable problem. At least rhetorically, the parties' stated positions appear to reveal an overlapping consensus supporting autonomy under Chinese sovereignty.[10] The Chinese Government has, however, offered no concessions regarding the character of autonomy, claiming only that autonomy is provided under existing national minority laws – which some would say is no autonomy at all.[11] The Tibetan representatives in these discussions have conceded to Chinese demands regarding sovereignty, while insisting on what they call 'genuine autonomy' under a formula they have labelled the 'middle way' approach.[12] In asking for 'genuine autonomy', the Tibetan exile leaders clearly appreciate the role of political autonomy as an essential step for participation in cultural, social, economic and political life, promoting both democracy and human rights in Tibet.[13] If mutual accommodation in line with current Tibetan autonomy proposals is to be achieved, it seems that some agreement on the character of such autonomy arrangement should become the focus of Sino-Tibetan discussions.

To understand fundamental challenges implicated in this dispute, it is helpful to begin with basic demographics. Though Tibetan areas represent a quarter of the contemporary Chinese-held territory, the Tibetan population of 5.5 million

10 Warren Smith expresses scepticism about the potential for agreement, arguing that the central issue for Tibetans is the maintenance of Tibetan national identity and for the Chinese is to extinguish it. SMITH Jr., W.W. (2008) *China's Tibet: Autonomy or Assimilation*. Boulder, CO: Rowman and Littlefield. p. 279.

11 The Chinese position is described in their White Paper on Tibet. White Paper on 'Regional Ethnic Autonomy in Tibet' (hereinafter 'White Paper'), Information Office of the State Council of the PRC, May 2004, Beijing. Interviews with Chinese officials tend to bear out this hard line. Interview with Liu Hongji (and Wang Xiaobin), Tibetology Research Centre, Beijing, 25 August 2006.

12 His Holiness the Dalai Lama began to modify his position in speech in the 1980s before the US Congress and before the European Parliament. Address to Members of the United States Congress: Five Point Peace Plan for Tibet, 21 September 1987; Address to Members of the European Parliament by His Holiness the Dalai Lama, 15 June 1988. These original positions have been amended in response to Chinese requirements to make clear that he is not seeking independence nor imposing any conditions for discussions. See Autonomy and the Tibetan Perspective, Tibetan Parliamentary & Policy Research Centre, 2005; The Middle-Way Approach, A Framework for Resolving the Issue of Tibet, Department of Information and Public Relations, CTA Dharamsala, 2006.

13 Interview with His Holiness the Dalai Lama, Dharamsala, India, 9 August 2006.

represents only a fraction of the Chinese national population of 1.3 billion.[14] About 130,000 Tibetans live in exile, mostly in India. The dominant Han Chinese ethnic group in fact makes up 92 per cent of China's national population and the remaining fifty-five recognised national minorities only 8 per cent. In what appears like a divide-and-conquer strategy, the area occupied by Tibetans has been divided into thirteen contiguous autonomous areas. The Tibetan Autonomous Region (TAR) constitutes about half of this area, while twelve contiguous lesser autonomous prefectures and counties are in adjoining Yunnan, Qinghai, and Szechuan provinces. Demographic data within the Tibetan areas is disputed, as Tibetans in exile worry that China, as part of a policy of assimilation, intends to eventually swamp the region with Chinese migrants. The building of a new railway into the region has enhanced this concern. The Chinese census data projects the Chinese population in these areas at about 1.5 million compared to 5.5 million Tibetans. The Chinese figures for only the TAR is approximately 2.5 million Tibetans and 160,000 Chinese. The Chinese census data appears to leave out significant numbers of temporary residents, including members of the People's Liberation Army (PLA) and unregistered temporary Chinese traders and workers in Tibet. Chinese policies to encourage Chinese to 'go west' to migrate to minority regions are seen as reflecting Chinese aims to dominate the urban sector and assimilate minorities. Some conclude that the Chinese have already swamped the Tibetans in the larger urban areas of Lhasa and Xigaze, where Chinese are now thought to be in the majority.[15] To appreciate Tibetan concerns with being swamped, it is helpful to consider what has happened to two comparable ethnic nationalities on China's western borders: in Xinjiang, the Uyghur population of 8.3 million represents only 45 per cent as compared to 40 per cent Chinese; while in Inner Mongolia, the Mongols are at 17 per cent compared to 80 per cent Chinese.

This chapter will offer a context for assessing China's various claims about its national minority policies and the Tibetan response by considering: first, the current practice under China's national minority policies; second, historical patterns of Sino-Tibetan relations as a suggestion of the nature of this long-standing relationship; third, international legal practice regarding autonomy for territory-based indigenous national ethnic groups; and fourth, the best constitutional practice for meeting China's historical and international obligations. A more careful consideration of the foundations of the Sino-Tibetan relationship may point the way forward to mutual accommodation. China's current policies

14 Tabulations on Nationalities of 2000 Population Census of China, Beijing: Nationalities Publishing House (2003).

15 See DREYER, J.T. (2006) Economic Development in Tibet under the People's Republic of China. In SAUTMAN, B. and DREYER, J.T. (eds) *Contemporary Tibet: Politics, Development and Society in a Disputed Region*. London: M.E. Sharpe. pp. 129–151, 139; BLONDEAU, A.-M. and BUFFETRILLE, K. (eds) (2008) *Authenticating Tibet, Answers to China's 100 Questions*. Berkeley, CA: University of California Press (comments by Andrew M. Fischer). pp. 144–151.

are neither consistent with historical commitments and practices, nor with international standards. Because of both parties' expressed interest in autonomy as the goal of the current discussions, the question of independence is set aside in the analysis that follows. Whether a lack of progress in Sino-Tibetan discussions will push that issue to the fore again is hard to predict.

2. Tibetan national minority autonomy under Chinese rule

China's current national minority policies offer very little autonomy and have left the Tibetan people with a weak voice in their own affairs, as well as very little security for basic human rights. The current national minority autonomy policies were promulgated in articles on national regional autonomy in the 1982 PRC Constitution[16] and in the Law on Regional National Autonomy (LRNA) passed in 1984, as revised in 2001.[17] PRC Constitution Article 4 provides that: 'Regional autonomy is practiced in areas where people of minority nationalities live in concentrated communities.' Article 15 of the LRNA provides that autonomous areas carry out their role 'under the unified leadership of the State Council and shall be subordinate to it'. The LRNA expressly provides protections for national minorities in the areas of language, education, political representation, administrative appointments, local economic and financial policies, and the use of local natural resources. How effectively minorities can exercise the powers the law purportedly gives them is in doubt. Article 4 and its associated laws have served as the basis for substantial intrusions of central control and the national political system into local affairs. This intrusion contrasts dramatically with the broad and flexible provision for the establishment of special administrative regions under Article 31 of the PRC Constitution, as applied in Hong Kong. National minority autonomy has been more of a vehicle for asserting central control than a vehicle for genuine autonomy. A close look at the national minority laws serves to illustrate such limitation.

Under the liberalising influence of China's then emerging open policy, the 1982 PRC Constitution appeared to aim at allowing a degree of local control under China's national minority policies. This expressly included the power, subject to higher approval, to enact 'regulations on the exercise of autonomy (*zizhi tiaoli*) and other separate regulations (*danxing tiaoli*) in light of the political, economic and cultural characteristics'.[18] The LRNA repeats this same language, allowing for the enactment of 'regulations on the exercise of autonomy and other separate regulations', and specifying the need for approval from the next higher level of

16 PRC Constitution (1982), Arts. 4, 59, 65, 89, and 112–122.

17 Law of the People's Republic of China on Regional National Autonomy (hereinafter LRNA), 1984, revised 2001.

18 PRC Constitution (1982), Art. 116.

government.[19] 'Regulations on the exercise of autonomy' are expected to have the status of a sub-constitution or basic law and it is typically expected that only one such regulation will be enacted in each autonomous area.[20] For autonomous regions, the highest-level autonomous areas, such approval must come directly from the Central Government, while for lesser autonomous areas at the prefecture and county levels such approval must come from the higher provincial government. The PRC has five autonomous regions, which include Tibet, Xinjiang, Inner Mongolia, Guangxi, and Ningxia. None of these regions has received approval for such basic regulation on the exercise of autonomy. The one attempt at enacting a basic regulation on the exercise of autonomy in the TAR went through fifteen drafts and was eventually abandoned.[21] Lesser autonomous areas at the prefecture and county level have received approval from provincial governments for basic autonomy laws that largely track the LRNA. Autonomous regions and areas have enacted many 'separate regulations', the second category specified in the authorising provisions.[22] A third category would be ordinary laws unrelated to autonomy, which do not require such higher approval, though they are bound to conform to national constitutional and legislative requirements.[23]

The system of Communist Party rule in China imposes even greater top-down control. Chinese Communist Party (CCP) control over the legislative drafting processes involves oversight and approval at every step in the legislative drafting process. There is very little legislative discretion available at the local level. Chunli Xia identifies a complex system of CCP oversight of the legislative drafting process as follows: first, the Party Committee of the Local People's Congress (LPC) sets up a legislative group made up of people from the LPC Party Committee, the LPC Standing Committee, and the local government; second, a draft is circulated and submitted by the LPC Standing Committee to the Party Committee of the autonomous area; third, after approval by the Party Committee of the autonomous area, it is then submitted to a higher party committee for further review; fourth, when the Party Committee of the autonomous area receives approval it submits the draft to the LPC Standing Committee Party Committee to be submitted to the LPC for passage.[24] According to Xia, this process has been followed especially

19 LRNA Art. 19. Such provision is repeated in Art. 66 of the Legislative Law.

20 Ibid. at 10.

21 GHAI, Y. (2005) China's Constitutional and Legal Framework for Autonomy, Limitations and Possibilities for Negotiations. Draft paper, 18 June 2005, at 19 (available from the author).

22 Separate regulations (translated by Xia as 'singular regulations') are regulations made by autonomous legislative bodies on specific topics such as language, marriage, family planning, etc. See CHUNLI XIA, Autonomous Legislative Power in Regional Ethnic Autonomy of the People's Republic of China: The Law and the Reality, presented in Conference on 'One Country, Two Systems, Three Legal Orders – Perspectives on Evolution', Macau, February 2007 (citing Organic Law of the People's Republic of China, Article 7 and the Legislative Law, Article 63) at 11.

23 Ibid.

24 Ibid. at 19–20.

since the 2001 revisions of the LRNA.[25] After such party approval and legislative passage, the legislation is still subject to the above-noted higher-level official approval. Given the centre's control over the CCP and the fact that Chinese party officials from the centre have always occupied top local party positions, there is little room for local legislative initiative by autonomous communities. The tight approval processes both in the formal government structure and the CCP drafting process leaves local autonomous regions with very little legislative autonomy.[26]

There is much more to this story than is revealed by technical legal analysis. To such legal impediments the national minority policy adds at least two structural and conceptual impediments that pose a particular challenge to the realisation of national minority autonomy. First, the fact that national minority policies replicate the national political structures in minority areas renders minority areas especially susceptible to top-down central administrative control. The highly centralised people's congress system, with CCP domination, is replicated in minority areas, as is evident in the above-described legislative processes. Minority areas are not allowed a distinct structure of indigenous government suitable to local self-rule. The 17-Point Agreement in respect of Tibet promised a distinctive form of minority autonomy, though it was ultimately not delivered. The only local system available today for delivering such distinctive local self-rule arises in Hong Kong and Macau, under Article 31 of the PRC Constitution relating to special administrative regions.

Second, Marxist doctrines deny the essential character of China's policies in Tibet. These Marxist doctrines see the 1950s occupation of Tibet as 'liberation' and the institution of CCP rule in Tibet as 'democratic reform'. According to this Marxist logic, colonialism is a product of capitalist exploitation and does not arise in a non-capitalist environment. Since China had not reached the stage of full capitalist development, it could not have colonised Tibet. Under this theory, the exploited classes of Tibet were to be joined under a Chinese internal multinational system, in a 'common program' of local autonomous rule.[27] Under this policy, any autonomy regime is merely a temporary solution on the path to ultimate assimilation of minority nationalities into the dominant multinational Han Chinese state.[28] Statements to the contrary, such as the 17-Point Agreement, were temporary in their vision. The 17-Point Agreement promised: 'Central Authorities would not alter the existing political system in Tibet.' But, as the subsequent record of pervasive CCP intrusion suggests, it clearly envisioned that the liberated Tibetans would seek 'reform' and embrace the CCP's vision of

25 Ibid. at 21.

26 See BLONDEAU and BUFFETRILLE, above note 15, pp. 191–196.

27 Common Program of the Chinese People's Political Consultative Committee (1949).

28 SMITH, above note 10, p. 233. When Chinese officials from the Tibetology Research Centre are confronted with the discrepancy between the current version of autonomy and the looser indirect imperial version, they cite advanced technology and modern communications. Interview with Liu Hongji, above note 11.

minority autonomy. Such system was in fact imposed after the 1959 uprising, when the Dalai Lama fled.

In Tibet, especially after the 1959 Uprising, all forms of traditional political structure were progressively eliminated. This purging of traditional political forms was especially radical during the Cultural Revolution (1966–1976), which was a period of hard-line class struggle and massive cultural destruction across China. After the Cultural Revolution, Chinese Premier Hu Yaobang observed especially dire conditions in Tibet. A somewhat remorseful China pursued a brief period of liberalisation in the early 1980s, but this was followed by greater repression and even martial law later that decade. Policies restricting the use of Han cadres in Tibet in the early 1980s were followed by greater central control by the end of the decade. In the most recent decade, a policy of cracking down on political support for the exiled Dalai Lama and so-called patriotic education has been combined with greater emphasis on economic development under which free Chinese immigration has been favoured.[29] Massive Chinese economic investments in Tibet have done little to assuage Tibetan concerns and resentment. Only those Tibetans willing to collaborate with Chinese rule have been given some role in the Chinese structure of regional control. The CCP still dominates Tibet and Han Chinese still dominate CCP leadership.

Over the years, Chinese repression has included military occupation and crackdowns, the sacking and razing of Buddhist monasteries during the Cultural Revolution, suppression of religion, coerced 're-education' of monks and nuns in monasteries, imprisonment of dissidents, and the forced relocation of rural dwellers and herders to more populated areas. Monks and nuns thought to be most supportive of the Dalai Lama have especially been targeted and have been asked to renounce him.[30] Popular dissent and rebellion famously arose in 1959, 1989 and 2008. More often, resistance by monks, nuns, and others against Chinese rule and its methods has taken place on a smaller scale, as monks and nuns in the monasteries resist attempts at 'patriotic education' and Chinese attempts to control religious doctrines and decisions. Ordinary Tibetans may quietly express their resistance through sending their children over the Himalayan Mountains to Tibetan schools in India. Chinese distrust of Tibetan people and their intentions has become evident.

A number of studies and reports have appeared on both sides of this debate. On the Chinese side, the May 2004 official White Paper on Regional Ethnic Autonomy in Tibet highlights favourable statistics on Tibetan participation in autonomous

29 SMITH Jr., W.W. (2004) China's Policy on Tibetan Autonomy. *East-West Center Washington Working Papers*. No. 2, October.

30 Interview with President, Gu Chu Sun Movement of Tibet (Association of former Political Prisoners), Dharamsala, 3 August 2006; Interview of 'Singing Nun' Renchen Choeky, Dharamsala, 4 August 2006 (after refusing to denounce the Dalai Lama in re-education meetings in their nunnery, sentenced to prison for demonstrating in protest in Lhasa; and sentenced again while in prison when eighteen nuns produced a singing recording that was smuggled out).

governance, including: very favourable data on Tibetan participation in the local people's congresses and local government; a 93 per cent voter turnout rate for county level elections; Tibetan and other ethnic minority deputies in excess of 80 per cent at both the regional and city levels; and a claim of generally over 80 per cent Tibetan occupation of the top positions of various autonomous governments and standing committees.[31] It is reported that, at the time of the report, twelve of the nineteen deputies from the TAR to the National People's Congress were Tibetan. The report states that the Tibetan language is taught in the schools and widely used along with Chinese language – though critics worry this is mostly at the primary level.[32] The report also highlights the wide promotion of Tibetan religion, noting that there are 46,000 resident monks and nuns. The White Paper brags about the Chinese Government's official involvement in the process of selecting high reincarnate lamas, including the 11th Panchen Lama and the 17th Karmapa. The report fails to note that the 11th Panchen Lama earlier designated by the Dalai Lama has disappeared and that the Karmapa nurtured by the Chinese Government has fled into exile.

The Chinese White Paper and many other Chinese statements seek to highlight China's contribution to Tibet's economic development. While economic circumstances are certainly better than they were in the 1950s and before, when both Tibet and China were impoverished, critics have worried that China's earlier collectivisation policy destroyed the traditional basis of the Tibetan economy and that current growth-oriented policies tend to benefit Chinese more than Tibetans.[33] Andrew M. Fischer worries that the current policy of large public subsidies tends to benefit Chinese officials and large Chinese construction companies, while creating dependency and the need for more subsidies for Tibet – what he calls the boomerang effect.[34]

Outside reports have highlighted statistics that tend to show a lack of local autonomy in areas where it most counts. In a 1997 report, the International Commission of Jurists (ICJ) noted that while 'Tibetans are in positions of nominal authority, they are often shadowed by more powerful Chinese officials' and 'every local organ is shadowed by a CCP committee or "leading group".'[35] The ICJ report describes the above-noted repression and the relatively poor economic development of Tibet compared to other regions of China.[36]

A 2007 report prepared jointly by Minority Rights Group International and Human Rights in China describes more generally the deficiencies in China's

31 White Paper, above note 11.

32 See BLONDEAU and BUFFETRILLE (2008), above note 15, p. 235.

33 Ibid. (comments by Andrew M. Fischer), at 250–277. Fischer sees greater agriculture productivity if Tibetans are left alone in the traditional mixed system of herding and farming. Ibid. at 275.

34 Ibid. at 269.

35 *Tibet: Human Rights and the Rule of Law* (Geneva: International Commission of Jurists, 1997), 14–21.

36 DREYER (2006), above note 15, pp. 129–151.

national minority policies.[37] It notes that the centralisation of power in the top leadership of the CCP impedes popular empowerment across the country, even for the Han majority. The above concerns with the law-making process, including the lack of approval for basic autonomy laws, Chinese dominance of CCP leadership in minority areas, and the lack of real power at the local level are noted. The report raises doubt about the power of minorities, noting: 'Minority leaders are therefore typically viewed as "puppets" who, despite holding fairly high positions such as chief of a government department, are usually "assisted" by a Han deputy who, along with the local Party leadership, controls actual policy formulation.' Of particular concern for the deeply religious Tibetan nationality is a CCP rule that bars party members from practicing Tibetan Buddhism, a rule certain to undermine Tibetan participation.[38] This imposition was increased for Tibetan cadres after the 2008 Uprising by adding a requirement that they must withdraw their children from Tibetan schools in India if they are to retain their jobs.[39] Added to these specific limitations are the usual problems in China of severe restrictions on freedom of speech, press, and association. Such restrictions weigh heavily on minority groups by closing off channels of complaint and oversight.

3. History

Chinese officials are fond of arguing: 'Since Ancient times Tibet has been an inseparable part of Chinese territory.'[40] A closer look at Sino-Tibetan history reveals a more nuanced story and hardly one that would justify such claim.[41] There is little agreement among Chinese officials and Tibetan exiles over how to interpret their shared past.[42] Chinese efforts at imperial conquest have met with Tibetan resistance for nearly a thousand years. Imperial conquest as a justification for sovereign claims would clearly meet with present-day scepticism. In the face of such scepticism, it is doubtful that this historical record proves anything compelling to support current claims for Chinese sovereignty. This historical record does highlight the special character of the historical Sino-Tibetan relationship and offers a yardstick by which to assess current autonomy policy and shape a future autonomy relationship.

It is widely agreed that in the imperial age China generally aimed to contain external threats by subordinating and eventually incorporating its neighbours.

37 Human Rights in China and Minority Rights Group International, *China: Exclusion, Marginalization and Rising Tension* (Minority Rights Group International, 2007).

38 GHAI (2005), above note 21, p. 21.

39 KWOK, K. (2006) Officials to be Sacked for Sending Their Children to 'Dalai Lama Schools'. *South China Morning Post*. 18 July.

40 White Paper, above note 11.

41 SPERLING, E. (2004) *The Tibet-China Conflict: History and Polemics*. Washington, DC: East-West Center, Policies Studies 7.

42 Ibid.

Though Tibet was certainly a target of such efforts, Chinese success was limited. After Tibet's own imperial age during the Chinese Tang Dynasty, Tibet was sufficiently remote and non-threatening that it was never fully assimilated into the Chinese Empire.[43] Loose imperial association usually involved indirect rule through the Tibetan ruling religious elites, though during the last Chinese imperial dynasty, the Qing – in the eighteenth and nineteenth centuries – this sometimes involved military invasion and degrees of imperial occupation and control. Tibet was treated essentially as a vassal state.[44] Eliot Sperling points out that China's current claim that Tibet was always an inseparable part of China is a late-twentieth-century idea.[45]

Present-day Chinese accounts usually date China's claimed incorporation of Tibet to the Mongol-ruled Yuan Dynasty (1270–1368). The Tibetan abbot Sakya Pandita is reported to have subordinated Tibet to the emerging Mongol Empire in 1247 AD. With some initial Tibetan resistance, the Mongols invaded and established administrative control in 1267. It was subsequent to this in 1270 that the Mongol King, Kubilai Khan, proclaimed the Yuan Dynasty in China. China was administered separately from Tibet among the Mongol's conquest.[46]

Warren Smith describes a rather carefully calibrated diplomatic relationship from the Yuan Dynasty forward between China's emperors and Tibetan lamas. China's imperial attempts at subordination would be matched with Tibetan resistance.[47] In the Yuan Dynasty, leading Tibetan lamas served in a religious advisory role for the Mongol emperors – a role characterised by the Tibetans as a *Cho-yon* or patron-priest relationship.[48] This state of affairs persisted in the succeeding Chinese Ming Dynasty (1368–1644), though the Ming court seemed to value Tibetan lamas more for their intermediary role in dealing with the still threatening Mongols than for their religious role.

The succeeding Manchu-dominated Qing Dynasty (1636–1910) featured the highest level of Chinese intervention in Tibet, which in the eighteenth century sometimes involved imperial conquest. The Qing considered Tibet a special case and pursued the same chess game of diplomacy. Visits to Beijing by the fourth and fifth Dalai Lama and their successors were carefully choreographed around various

43 For discussion of this earlier Tibetan imperial period, see BECKWITH, C.I. (1987) *Tibetan Empire in Central Asia. A History of the Struggle for Great Power among Tibetans, Turks, Arabs, and Chinese During the Early Middle Ages*. Princeton, NJ: Princeton University Press. pp. 24, 167.

44 CROSSLEY, P.K. (1999) *A Translucent Mirror: History and Identity in Qing Imperial Ideology*. Berkeley/Los Angeles, CA: University of California. pp. 327–336; SPERLING (2004), above note 41, pp. 28–30. Both Crossley and Sperling note that these areas fell not under the Qing civil government, but under the Court of Colonial Affairs (lifan yuan).

45 Ibid. at 28.

46 SMITH Jr., W.W. (1996) *Tibetan Nation: A History of Tibetan Nationalism and Sino-Tibetan Relations*. Boulder, CO: Westview. pp. 83–100.

47 Ibid.

48 In his assessment of the historical record, Sperling points out that this relationship did not exclude political domination. SPERLING (2004), above note 41, pp. 30–31.

ceremonies and the conferring of imperial titles. Complex interplay and protocol would offer the emperor's support for rule in Tibet by the Gelugpa Buddhist sect under the Dalai Lama.[49] As the Qing Empire expanded in the eighteenth century, it intruded more and more on Tibetan autonomy. By 1720, under the Emperor Kang Hsi, the Qing occupied and ruled Tibet, though the Qing garrison was withdrawn when he died in 1722. Such occupation was restored later and off and on in the decades to follow. During its occupations, to advance its efforts at indirect rule the Qing set in place a permanent government under a Tibetan Kashag or council. The Qing was also represented in Lhasa by its Amban. Though Qing control would vary over time, reaching its height in the late eighteenth century, it always involved some form of indirect imperial rule. Tibet was considered part of the Qing Dynasty's 'exterior empire', though the Eastern Tibetan provinces of Kham and Amdo were sometimes under direct Qing control.[50] By the late nineteenth century, the declining Qing was less able to exercise control in Tibet.

From 1911 until the PRC invasion in 1950, Tibet enjoyed *de facto* independence. Chinese officials are fond of depicting Tibet during this period as hopelessly feudal and savage, as a way to justify their invasion and occupation.[51] There is little evidence to show that Tibet suffered from any worse conditions than those that prevailed throughout much of the surrounding Asian region at that time. Commentators have contested recent Chinese characterisations of systematic savagery during this period or even Chinese characterisations of commoners in Tibet as serfs.[52] While accepting the characterisation of feudal serfdom, even Melvyn Goldstein, whose characterisations China sometimes cites, notes that Tibetan serfs 'were not necessarily downtrodden'.[53] In general, it seemed that Tibet had a traditional land-based economy with hierarchical social structures that are not uncommon in such traditional systems.[54] It would be difficult to argue in the modern world that one country should be privileged to invade and occupy another because of poverty.

During this time, Tibet also began the first stages of political modernisation. Tibetan political institutions began to show more capacity for modern forms of self-governance. There had been a council or cabinet called the Kashag since the

49 Ibid. at 111–112. Chinese officials have long tried to gain some political advantage by claiming that China had in fact created the position and the word Dalai Lama. Even an official Chinese booklet purporting to answer 100 questions about Tibet has acknowledged that this title was introduced during the Ming Dynasty by Mongol leader Altan Khan in an exchange with Sonam Gyatso, the abbot of the Drepung monastery who then became the third Dalai Lama. BLONDEAU and BUFFETRILLE (2008), above note 15, pp. 35–36. The word Dalai comes from the Mongolian word *Tale*, for oceans.

50 SMITH (1996), above note 46, pp. 121, 134–138, 145, 151.

51 Tibet White Paper, above note 11.

52 See BLONDEAU and BUFFETRILLE (2008), above note 15, pp. 81–84.

53 GOLDSTEIN, M.C. (1989) *A History of Modern Tibet, 1913–1951. The Demise of the Lamaist State.* Berkeley/Los Angeles, CA: University of California Press. p. 5.

54 BLONDEAU and BUFFETRILLE (2008), above note 15, pp. 293–298.

late Qing Dynasty and Tibetans had in the 1860s introduced a national assembly or *Tshongdu*, which included representatives of Lhasa's monasteries and secular officials.[55] The promise of these nascent constitutional developments has been borne out in recent Tibetan exile. A form of liberal constitutional democracy has been instituted that includes universal suffrage in the exile community, a directly elected prime minister served by a cabinet or Kashag, a Supreme Justice Commission, and an elected Assembly of Tibetan People's Deputies.[56] The Dalai Lama and the exile government have included liberal democracy, human rights, and rule of law commitments, including the Dalai Lama's withdrawal from temporal rule in exile, in proposals for the same in respect of future autonomy in Tibet under the 'middle way' approach.[57]

It was also during this period that the language of modern statehood and sovereignty was first introduced into the Tibet debate. In negotiations with Tibet and British India, Republican Chinese officials began to articulate in modern state terms the character of their claims to Tibet. While claiming Tibet as their own, Chinese leaders generally acknowledged that Tibet had a special status with only Chinese indirect rule. In negotiations at Simla, India in 1913, the British advanced a notion, similar to that China had agreed for Mongolia, of inner and outer Tibet. This would distinguish a largely independent central Tibet under Chinese suzerainty from a subordinate Eastern Tibet under Chinese sovereignty. In various negotiations, first with Britain and China at Simla and then directly with China in the 1930s, China acknowledged Tibet's high degree of autonomy under nominal Chinese rule. All parties actually initialled the Simla Convention accepting this view, though the Chinese ultimately did not ratify it, as they were dissatisfied with the stipulated boundary between inner and outer Tibet.[58] British reluctance to recognise full Tibetan sovereignty appeared to be the only thing that held Tibet back in securing its own *de jure* independence. Concerned about its own imperial ambitions in Central Asia, Britain characterised Chinese feudal imperial territorial claims as suzerainty.[59]

When the Chinese People's Liberation Army (PLA) invaded Tibet in 1951, the Dalai Lama faced an offer he could not refuse to join the PRC.[60] With weak international support to do otherwise, that year he accepted a 17-Point Agreement

55 Ibid. at 10–31.

56 SANGAY, L. (2003) Tibet: Exiles Journey. *Journal of Democracy*. 14(3). pp. 119–130. Lobsang Sangay is the current elected prime minister.

57 Guidelines for Future Tibet's Polity and the Basic Features of the Constitution, 26 February 1992; The Middle-Way Approach, above note 12.

58 GOLDSTEIN (1989), above note 53, pp. 68–80, 832–841.

59 '[A] distinctive element of the feudal suzerainty relationship is that the suzerain holds the source of the governmental authority of the vassal state whose ruler he grants the right to exercise the authority autonomously.' VAN WALT VAN PRAAG, M.C. (1987) *The Status of Tibet*. Boulder, CO: Westview Press. pp. 105–106.

60 DALAI LAMA (1991) *Freedom in Exile, The Autobiography of the Dalai Lama*. San Francisco, CA: Harper Collins Publishers. p. 64; GOLDSTEIN (1989), above note 53, pp. 798–803.

on 'measures for the peaceful liberation of Tibet'.[61] The PRC claimed to be 'liberating' Tibet, presumably from foreign influences such as those of British India. It seems that the Chinese were more concerned with imperialism on their southern flank than they were with saving Tibetans from feudal poverty. The 17-Point Agreement, presented by a much more confident China that had the upper hand in the situation, still acknowledged the special status of Tibet. It is noteworthy that this is the only treaty-like agreement into which the PRC has entered with any of its purported national minorities. As a clear sign that China understood the special character of its historical relationship with Tibet, the agreement promised Tibetan autonomy and local self-rule under its existing system of governance. In implementing its so-called reform policies, China failed to keep these special commitments. A state of popular rebellion ensued and the Dalai Lama fled Tibet in 1959.[62] This brought to an end the centuries of Tibetan self-rule.

After the Dalai Lama's departure, on 28 March 1959 China dismissed the local government of Tibet and established direct Chinese rule. The Preparatory Committee for the Tibet Autonomous Region (PCTAR), which had been established under the Dalai Lama's earlier formal chairmanship, was designated as the official governing body of Tibet.[63] In September 1965, the TAR was proclaimed under the first People's Congress of the TAR. Since the Dalai Lama's departure in 1959, China has exercised direct rule, currently under its national minority law. Tibet no longer enjoys any special status, being lumped together with fifty-five designated 'national minorities' under China's Constitution and national minority law. The refusal of the Dalai Lama to accept another sanitised version of history promoted by China has been a major sticking point in its relations with him.[64]

4. International practice

Beyond history, China has made great efforts to justify its Tibet policies on the basis of international law. It has sought to legitimate its original invasion based on an international law claim of historical title and its current policies as part of its sovereign prerogative. There is cause for doubts about both China's historical-title-based claim of sovereignty and the legitimacy of its current policies. Regardless of these doubts, China has forcefully maintained effective control over Tibet for several decades, to the point where its sovereignty claims have gained international recognition. The uncertain status of both autonomy and indigenous rights in

61 Agreement of the Central People's Government and the Local Government of Tibet on Measures for the Peaceful Liberation of Tibet, 23 May 1951 (hereinafter '17-Point Agreement'). See GOLDSTEIN (1989), above note 53, pp. 759–772.

62 Dalai Lama, above note 60, p. 136.

63 Preparatory Committee for the Tibetan Autonomous Region (PCTAR), established in April 1956.

64 SPERLING (2004), above note 41.

international law has also been a factor in the reluctance to directly challenge China's policies. Human rights violations and questionable Chinese autonomy policies have, nevertheless, attracted considerable disapproval and criticism. The exiled Tibetan Government has faced even greater difficulties. While seemingly having a just basis in international law to challenge Chinese sovereignty, it has lacked sufficient resources to do so. It has to take a more accommodating approach if it wants to reach a reasonable and internationally recognised settlement.

The above historical narrative offers little support for China's claim that Tibet was an integral part of China. It appears to have been at most a vassal state during limited periods of the Yuan and Qing dynasties.[65] But such vassal state status would offer little justification for China's claim of historical title. It appears that imperial China long both defended against and had designs on neighbouring countries and kingdoms in Central and North Asia. These neighbouring polities likewise formed their own alliances of resistance and conquest. The Tibetan narrative of security was especially entangled in that of the Mongols. The only substantial claim China laid to central Tibet before the eighteenth century was that engendered in this Mongol relationship, a claim that became Chinese in the Mongol-ruled Yuan Dynasty. A patron-priest and sometimes a full vassal state relationship largely prevailed until the end of the Chinese dynastic period.[66] China's most direct intervention came in the eighteenth century with occasional military invasions and some active indirect rule. Such invasions were more frequent and sustained in Eastern Tibet, encompassing some Tibetan regions now outside the TAR in adjoining provinces.

Without more, the above-described imperial claims would not today justify a claim of sovereignty based on historical title. In an anti-colonial age, such imperial claims are generally viewed with suspicion. In this particular case, such imperial claims are particularly weak, given their weak empirical foundation and the fact that they appeared to end completely as the Qing dynasty collapsed. Added to these difficulties associated with China's imperial past is the general weakness of historical title as a basis for sovereign claims. In the *Western Sahara* case, the ICJ judged such claims as a rather weak basis for claiming territory held by neighbouring national groups.[67] Such claims usually cannot be sustained except by brute force.

Actual control, especially by a major power, may pose an equally difficult challenge. Tibetans have had to live with five decades of Chinese occupation and direct rule in Tibet. The Chinese regime clearly sees the retention of control over Tibet as a matter of vital national interest and has worked aggressively to gain

65 Ibid. at 28–30. Sperling points out that the Chinese need to recast Tibet as an historically internal part of China came up only under CCP rule in the last half of the twentieth century in order to justify occupation of Tibet.

66 Ibid. at 30.

67 *Western Sahara* [1975] *ICJ* 4.

international acceptance of this *fait accompli*. *Fait accompli* and *realpolitik* appear to have left Tibetans with little hope of independence. In such circumstances, is there a strong argument for a heightened security in international law for internal self-determination and autonomy?

The notion of self-determination was conceived in the UN Charter and various UN declarations. International law generally distinguishes between an external and internal right of self-determination.[68] The external right of self-determination is generally thought to include a right of secession. The internal right is concerned with minority rights of self-governance within a sovereign state. Common article (1) of both the International Covenant on Civil and Political Rights (ICCPR) and the International Covenant on Economic, Social and Cultural Rights (ICESCR) provides 'all peoples' with the right to 'freely determine their political status and freely pursue their economic, social and cultural rights', but these clauses offer little guidance on who such peoples are and how the right is to be exercised.[69] Such ambiguity has often left international law on the sidelines in efforts to seek a solution to this and similar conflicts.[70]

The Supreme Court of Canada offers some guidance in this regard. In *Reference re Secession of Quebec*, the Supreme Court concluded:

> The international law right to self-determination only generates, at best, a right to external self-determination in situations of former colonies; where a people is oppressed, as for example under foreign military occupation; or where a definable group is denied meaningful access to government to pursue their political, economic, social or cultural development.[71]

One could argue that Tibet satisfied both of these criteria, that they were formerly either independent or a vassal state and that they are now 'denied meaningful access to government to pursue their political, economic, social or cultural development'. Three UN General Assembly resolutions passed after the Dalai Lama's 1959 departure in 1959, 1961, and 1965 appeared to say as much.[72] After

68 See Declaration on the Granting of Independence to Colonial Countries and Peoples, 1960 UNGA Resolution 1514 (XV), 15 UN GAOR, Supp. (No. 16), UN Doc. A/4684 (1960), at 66; Declarations on Principles of International Law Concerning Friendly Relations and Cooperation Among States, 1970 UNGA Resolution 2625 (XXV), Annex, 25 UN GAOR, Supp. (No. 28), UN Doc. A/5217 (1970), at 121.

69 International Covenant on Civil and Political Rights, 16 December 1966, 999 UNTS 171; International Covenant on Economic, Social and Cultural Rights, 16 December 1966, 993 UNTS 3.

70 See, generally, HANNUM, H. (1996) *Autonomy, Sovereignty, and Self-Determination, The Accommodation of Conflicting Rights, Revised Edition*. Philadelphia, PA: University of Pennsylvania Press.

71 Reference re Secession of Quebec, (1998) 161 DLR (4th) 385, para. 135, Supreme Court of Canada.

72 For a discussion of the three UNGA Resolutions condemning China's human rights record in Tibet (1959, 1961, 1965), see SMITH (1996), above note 46, pp. 492–532.

the Dalai Lama fled Tibet, his exiled government's claims for self-determination were grounded in the above noted character of the Sino-Tibetan relationship and four decades of de facto Tibetan independence after the end of the Qing Dynasty. While the three UN resolutions did not contest Chinese sovereignty and demand withdrawal, they did condemn China severely for human rights violations and effective denial of self-determination.

Guarantees of internal autonomy have generally not been well secured by international law.[73] It may be argued, however, that in two circumstances autonomy becomes effectively internationalised: (1) when it is the consequence of treaty arrangements transferring or surrendering sovereignty; or (2) when it arises out of the denial of rights of self-determination, especially those of indigenous people. The Tibet case implicates both possibilities. It experienced a treaty arrangement in the 17-Point Agreement and Tibetans can be argued to be indigenous people. In the court of public opinion, Tibet has attracted a degree of scrutiny in this regard, though there is little hope of strictly enforcing such right.

These evolving standards of human rights and self-determination have now gained greater international traction in the new UN Declaration on the Rights of Indigenous Peoples. The Declaration, passed by the UN General Assembly on 13 September 2007, provides a more comprehensive account of established international standards.[74] It gives new salience to the notion of internal autonomy and suggests its substantive content. UN declarations are usually considered soft law and are not considered legally binding. But declarations passed with unanimity or ones that purport to merely declare existing customary law may be taken as binding. In this regard, the new UN Declaration on the Rights of Indigenous Peoples has some qualities that recommend it, including its nearly unanimous passage 143 to 4, with 11 abstentions.[75] It also appears to interpret existing international legal requirements embodied in the UN Charter and other international human rights treaties.[76] The Chinese Government voted for the resolution

73 SANDERS, D. (1986) Is Autonomy a Principle of International Law? *Nordic Journal of International Law*. 55. p. 17; KIRGIS, F.L. (1994) The Degrees of Self-Determination in the UN Era. *American Journal of International Law*. 88. p. 310; HEINTZE, H.-J. (2007) Autonomy and Federalism: Which Evolution?. In Conference on 'One Country, Two Systems, Three Legal Orders – Perspectives of Evolution', Macau, PRC, 5–7 February (available from the author).

74 UN Declaration on the Rights of Indigenous Peoples (hereinafter 'Indigenous People's Declaration'), www.un.org/esa/socdev/unpfii/documents/DRIPS_en.pdf [Accessed: 14 February 2017].

75 Ibid. The four opposing the Declaration were the United States, Canada, New Zealand, and Australia. The eleven abstaining were Azerbaijan, Bangladesh, Bhutan, Burundi, Columbia, Georgia, Kenya, Nigeria, Russian Federation, Samoa, and Ukraine.

76 Declarations that purport to lay down or interpret existing international legal obligations may be viewed as a reflection of customary international law. The opening preliminary phrase added to the draft at its final stage before passage indicates that the General Assembly was '[g]uided by the purposes and principles of the Charter of the United Nations, and good faith in the fulfillment of the obligations assumed by States in accordance with the Charter'. The Declaration in other preliminary clauses invokes treaty obligations regarding the right to self-determination and

adopting this declaration both in the UN Human Rights Council and the General Assembly. Unfortunately, China maintains its consistent position that there are no indigenous peoples in China,[77] claiming that for 5,000 years the Chinese were always united with minorities living on their own lands.[78] Given Tibet's unique status, as recognised in the 17-Point Agreement, there is room for considerable doubt as to extending such claims to Tibet.

The UN Declaration does not define 'indigenous peoples'. It does specify that covered indigenous communities exist throughout the world and are seemingly not confined to former victims of European colonialism in the Americas.[79] A 1986 UN study defined indigenous peoples as follows:

> Indigenous communities, peoples and nations are those which, having a historical continuity with pre-invasion and pre-colonial societies that developed on their territories, consider themselves distinct from other sectors of the societies now prevailing in those territories or parts of them. They form at present non-dominant sectors of society and are determined to preserve, further develop and transmit to future generations their ancestral territories, and their ethnic identity, as the basis of their continued existence as peoples, in accordance with their own cultural patterns, social institutions and legal systems . . .[80]

The Tibetan people clearly satisfy these criteria. They were forcefully invaded in 1950, consider themselves distinct from other sectors of society, form a present non-dominant sector of society, and seem determined to preserve their ethnic identity. Whatever the legal status of this declaration, it can clearly serve as a useful guide for the treatment of indigenous or similarly situated peoples.

respecting human rights, ultimately invoking the Declaration's role 'as a standard of achievement to be pursued in a spirit of partnership and mutual respect'. Article 1 then makes clear this existing international legal status, providing: 'Indigenous peoples have the right to the full enjoyment, as a collective or as individuals, of all human rights and fundamental freedoms as recognized in the Charter of the United Nations, the Universal Declaration of Human Rights and international human rights law.'

77 China Concerned with Protection of Indigenous Peoples' Rights, Embassy of the People's Republic of China in Switzerland. [Online] 1 April 1997. Available at: www.chinamission.be/eng/zt/rqwt/t72327.htm [Accessed: 14 February 2017].

78 Speech of Chinese Representative Group Deputy Tong Zhihwa, Human Rights Council, 1st Meeting, 11th Drafting Session.

79 The UN Working Group A 1986 UN study of indigenous populations included several Asian countries in the study: Bangladesh, Burma, India, Indonesia, Japan, Laos, the Philippines, and Sri Lanka. United Nations Economic and Social Council, UN Sub-Commission on the Prevention of Discrimination and Protection of Minorities, Jose Martinez Coho, Study of the Problem of Discrimination Against Indigenous Populations, UN Doc. E/CN.4/Sub.2/1983/21/Add.8. (hereinafter 'UN Working Group Report'). There are thought to be over 370 million indigenous people worldwide. UN Adopts Declaration on Rights for Indigenous Peoples Worldwide, *International Herald Tribune*, 13 September 2007.

80 UN Working Group Report, above note 79.

China's above noted current policies clearly fall short of the standards articulated in the Declaration on the Rights of Indigenous Peoples. The preliminary articles of the Declaration emphasise demilitarisation of indigenous lands; the right of indigenous people to freely determine their relationship with states; that treaties, agreements, and constructive arrangements with states are matters of international concern; 'the fundamental importance of the right of self-determination of all peoples, by virtue of which they freely determine their political status and freely pursue their economic, social and cultural development'; and that the right to exercise self-determination in conformity with international law shall not be denied.

The operative articles of the Declaration guarantee indigenous peoples the following rights: the right of self-determination;[81] the right to autonomy or self-government in matters relating to their internal and local affairs;[82] the right to manifest, practise, develop, and teach their spiritual and religious traditions, customs, and ceremonies, including access in privacy to their religious and cultural sites and control of their ceremonial objects;[83] the right to participate in decision-making in matters which would affect their rights, through representatives chosen by themselves in accordance with their own procedures;[84] the right to be consulted and prior consent through their own representative institutions before implementing state legislative and administrative measures;[85] and the right to recognition, observance, and enforcement of treaties, agreements, and other constructive arrangements. At the same time, they are guaranteed the rights protected by the various human rights treaties and covenants. China's treatment of Tibetan people under its national minority laws has clearly fallen considerably short of these requirements. China's long-stated preference to promote a harmonious society would surely be advanced by embracing these standards.

International legal recognition of autonomous rights of democratic self-governance may be the first step toward providing greater security for such rights under domestic autonomy arrangements. For internal national groups, such international solicitude may offer an avenue to group security and protection of rights short of full independence. For a host country, such international legal security for such internal autonomy and its democratic guarantees, through a treaty or otherwise, may allow the country to offer a secure autonomy arrangement short of full secession. Such approach would also go a long way toward reducing the tendency to convert autonomy into the first step toward independence,[86] a fear clearly driving Beijing's hard-line approach to the Tibet issue. The international

81 Indigenous People's Declaration, above note 74, Art. 3.

82 Ibid. Art. 4.

83 Ibid. Art. 12.

84 Ibid. Art. 18.

85 Ibid. Art. 19.

86 HANNUM, H. (2004) Territorial Autonomy: Permanent Solution or Step Toward Secession? In WIMMER, A., GOLDSTONE, R.J., HOROWITZ, D.L., JORAS, U., and SCHETTER, C. (eds) *Facing Ethnic Conflicts: Toward a New Realism*. Lanham, MD: Rowman & Littlefield Publishers.

treaty and global solicitude that underlie the Hong Kong arrangement have clearly rendered that arrangement more reliable for all concerned. A similar approach to Tibet would allow China to achieve full international support for its autonomy policy in Tibet.

5. Achieving autonomy for Tibet

China appears to face a choice of pursuing its existing national minority policy with the strict constraints that such course entails or considering a more open-ended flexible approach. The latter can be achieved either under the 'one country two systems' approach in Article 31 or by applying its national minority laws in a more flexible way that recognises Tibet's unique status. Both the national minority laws and Article 31 promise a flexible approach tailored to the special needs of the autonomous community. Unfortunately, there has been little sign of such flexibility under a national minority law that seems aimed at assimilation of the targeted minority. Article 31 appears to allow greater autonomy, providing that: 'The state may establish special administrative regions when necessary. The systems to be instituted in special administrative regions shall be prescribed by law enacted by the National People's Congress in light of the specific conditions.' This flexible approach, now employed in Hong Kong and Macau, contrasts with the above pattern of central intrusion upon and domination of Tibetan affairs. Such approach would clearly offer a better constitutional fit than current efforts to address the issue under national minority principles. Whichever approach is taken, the goal should be to offer a more flexible approach tailored to Tibet's special circumstances.

In its 2004 White Paper on Tibet, China credited its refusal to apply Article 31 in Tibet to a lack of 'imperialist aggression' and contestation over 'effective sovereignty':

> The situation in Tibet is entirely different from that in Hong Kong and Macao. The Hong Kong and Macao issue was a product of imperialist aggression against China; it was an issue of China's resumption of exercise of its sovereignty. Since Ancient times Tibet has been an inseparable part of Chinese territory, where the Central Government has always exercised effective sovereign jurisdiction over the region. So the issue of resuming exercise of sovereignty does not exist. With the peaceful liberation of Tibet in 1951, Tibet had fundamentally extricated itself from the fetters of imperialism. Later, through the Democratic Reform, the abolition of the feudal serfdom under theocracy and the establishment of the Tibet Autonomous Region, the socialist system has been steadily consolidated . . . So the possibility of implementing another social system does not exist either. . . . Any act aimed at undermining and changing the regional ethnic autonomy in Tibet is in violation of the Constitution and law . . .[87]

87 White Paper, above note 11.

Because of this statement, Tibetan negotiators began to put their case under PRC Constitution Article 4 and laws governing national minorities. They have argued that the Chinese Government has not fulfilled its constitutional requirements toward national minorities, which promise local autonomy and a flexible approach tailored to specific minority interests.[88] But Chinese officials have rejected this move as well, arguing that the contents of the 'middle way' approach offered by Tibetan representatives are 'tantamount to not recognizing the Central Government, not recognizing ethnic autonomy, and not recognizing the socialist system'.[89] The Chinese stress that the Dalai Lama must: (1) recognise Tibet as part of China; (2) recognise that Taiwan is a Chinese province; (3) give up all activities toward independence; and (4) recognise the leadership of the CCP.[90] As noted above, in discussions leading up to the Beijing Olympics, they appeared to ratchet up these demands, adding specifications respecting support of the Beijing Olympics and effectively rejecting Tibetan claims that they had met such demands.[91] It sometimes appears from Chinese statements that China will enter serious discussions with the Tibetan side only if the Tibetans admit there is nothing to discuss.[92] Because of the above categorical rejection of the Article 31 approach and the effective rejection of Tibetan efforts to put their case under the national minority provisions in Article 4, the Chinese Government has effectively offered no accommodation of Tibetan concerns.

If Chinese officials are reluctant to take a flexible approach under China's national minority regime, then the Article 31 route to resolving this long-festering problem is a realistic constitutional option. Such approach would allow Beijing to treat Tibet as the distinctive case that it has always been. The above claim that Article 31 only applies under circumstances that are a 'product of imperialist aggression against China' or involve 'an issue of China's resumption of the exercise of its sovereignty' is not evident in the text of Article 31. It is not evident that Taiwan, to which Article 31 applies by design, would meet such requirement. China generally takes the view that the ruling elites in Taiwan are Chinese nationals. Even if dispute as to sovereignty were required as a precondition for application of Article 31, the same White Paper in the next sentence appears to raise precisely that issue in speaking of Tibet being extricated from the 'fetters of imperialism'. The further claim in the above White Paper excerpt that Tibet has already undergone democratic reform is not credible. Beijing's rejection of such consensual approach appears to be a question of policy, not constitutional law.

If this constitutional issue could be resolved, then the discussions might address the more serious question concerning the form of democratic institutions to be

88 Interview with then Kalon Tripa (Chair of the Kashag or elected Prime Minister) Samdhong Rinpoche, Dharamsala, India, 3 August 2006.

89 Interview with Liu Hongji, above note 11.

90 Ibid.

91 The numerous Tibetan efforts to concede to China's demands have been viewed with suspicion and rejected. YUAN, Z. (2008) Independence in Disguise. *China Security*. 4(2). pp. 38–45.

92 SMITH (1996), above note 46, p. 256.

employed in an autonomous Tibet. Chinese scholar Li Xiong Wang has suggested that Beijing's anxiety might be better allayed by some form of indirect democracy. He argues for a model which, while providing genuine choice at the local level, employs a structure somewhat like the people's congress system, having a pyramid structure where locally elected assemblies elect representatives to the next higher county, prefecture, and regional assemblies.[93] To be more democratic than the current system, such model could include multi-party competitive elections with associational freedoms at the base of the system. Wang argues that the Chinese Government will be reassured only if the Dalai Lama's plan can be modified to make the separation of Tibet impossible. Wang feels by shifting politics more down to the village level there will be less grandstanding and more moderation. This is just one among many possibilities.

Chinese officials involved in the Tibet issue have remained suspicious and have refused to move the discussions forward. They accuse the Dalai Lama and his supporters of 'splittist' activities.[94] A leading Tibetan Communist retired official, the late Phuntso Wangye,[95] expressed rare dissent from within. In three letters to then Chinese President Hu Jintao, he argued that hawks have thrived on their opposition to the return of the Dalai Lama:

> They make a living, are promoted and become rich by opposing splittism. . . . If the Dalai Lama and the central government reconcile, these people will be in a state of trepidation, feel nervous and could lose their jobs. . . . Any notion of delaying the problem until after the 14th Dalai Lama dies a natural death is not only naïve, it is also unwise and especially tactically wrong (fearing the radicalization of young Tibetans).[96]

He argued that China's objectives of a harmonious society would be advanced by welcoming the Dalai Lama and thousands of Tibetans home. A policy that genuinely respects Tibetan autonomy and treasures Tibet as a valued national constituent of the Chinese multinational state may offer a more appropriate path to resolution of this issue. The current Dalai Lama could be a reliable and efficacious partner in resolving these issues.

93 XIONG WANG, L. (2006) Indirect Representation vs. a Democratic System: Relative Advantages for Resolving the Tibet Dispute. In SAUTMAN and DREYER, above note 15, pp. 107–128.

94 YEDOR, 'On the "Middle Way" of the Dalai Lama'. *China Tibet Information Centre*. (The name 'Yedor' is given for this lengthy critique of the Dalai Lama, though it is generally understood that this is not a real person.)

95 Phuntso Wangye reportedly helped lead Chinese advanced troops into his homeland in the 1950s and served as a translator in negotiations with the Dalai Lama in 1954.

96 KANG LIM, B. (2007) Tibetan Says Hawks Blocking Dalai Lama's Return. *Reuters*. 7 March. It is interesting that Chinese officials accuse the Tibetan Government in exile of the same thing, saying they 'live on independence; they eat political rice'. Interview with Liu Hongji, above note 11.

Chapter 5

The Memorandum on Genuine Autonomy for the Tibetan People

An explanatory introduction to the Tibetan proposal

Michael C. van Walt van Praag

1. Introduction

The Memorandum on Genuine Autonomy for the Tibetan People (hereinafter the 'Memorandum on Genuine Autonomy' or simply the 'Memorandum') and the Note on the Memorandum on Genuine Autonomy for the Tibetan People (hereinafter simply the 'Note'),[1] taken together, represent the view of the Fourteenth Dalai Lama and the Tibetan political leadership today on how the long-standing conflict between the Tibetan people and the Chinese Government can be resolved.

The Memorandum was presented to Minister Du Qinglin and Vice Minister Zhu Weiqun[2] of the central government of the People's Republic of China (PRC) by the Envoys of His Holiness the Dalai Lama, Lodi Gyaltsen Gyari and Kelsang Gyaltsen, on 31 October 2008. A little more than a year later, on 26 January 2010, the Tibetan envoys gave their counterparts the Note, before the start of the ninth round of talks in Beijing. The Note was prepared by the Tibetans in order to respond to some of the Chinese Government's comments and reactions to the Memorandum and to remove any misinterpretation and misconception, as well as to 'offer some constructive suggestions for a way forward in the dialogue process'.[3]

1 The full texts of the Memorandum and the Note can be found in *Middle Way Policy and All Recent Related Documents*, DIIR Publications (3rd Edn, New Delhi 2012) and on www.Tibet.net [Accessed: 14 February 2016], the official website of the Central Tibetan Administration.

2 Du Qinglin is Minister and Head of the United Front Work Department and Deputy Chairman of the Chinese People's Political Consultative Conference, and Zhu Weiqun is Vice Minister and Executive Deputy Head of the United Front Work Department of the Chinese Communist Party (CPC) Central Committee. They headed the delegation of the Central Government of the PRC in the dialogue with the Dalai Lama's delegation. In this chapter, reference is made to the central government or Chinese Government positions and views on the understanding that these are reflected in the statements of these senior officials.

3 'Issues Raised by Envoys of H.H. The Dalai Lama During the Ninth Round of Dialogue with Representatives of the Chinese Leadership, March 2010', and (2010) Statement by Special Envoy

The proposals contained in the Memorandum were rejected by the Chinese Government in public statements delivered only days after the receipt of the Tibetan document, brushing the Tibetan demands aside as tantamount to independence or 'independence in disguise' and contrary to the principles of a unitary state.[4]

The Memorandum and Note have been discussed in a number of international conferences and other fora, including at a hearing of the Foreign Affairs Committee of the European Parliament,[5] a roundtable at the University of Hong Kong[6] and an international conference of legal experts in Trento[7] in the autonomous region of Trentino-Alto Adige/Südtirol, a living example of a successful tailor-made autonomy.

This chapter is intended principally as an explanation of the Tibetan proposal and an examination of the Chinese Government's response to and criticism of it. I first examine the intent of the Memorandum and Note and the nature of the autonomy proposed by the Dalai Lama and the Tibetan political leadership. I briefly touch on international practice in the field of autonomy before reviewing the Chinese Government's reaction to the proposal. It is hoped that this chapter will increase our understanding of the Tibetan proposal both in the context of the international discourse on autonomy and its potential for resolving the seemingly intractable conflict between the Chinese Government and the Tibetan people.

2. The intent of the Memorandum

The Memorandum on Genuine Autonomy is intended to be a transparent proposal without a hidden agenda and is an expression of the 'middle way' approach

of His Holiness the Dalai Lama, Kasur Lodi Gyari, head of the delegation which visited China in January 2010. [Online] 2 February. Available at: www.Tibet.net.

4 Press conference of the State Council for Information Office, Beijing, 10 November 2008. The full text of the statement by Vice Minister Zhu Weiqun was reported in *China Daily*, 11 November 2008. An English translation of a number of these were published in *China's Tibet* (2009), 20(1), pp. 7–10. Some commentary also appeared in the Chinese public media reflecting the government's view. See, e.g. Yiduo (2008) On the 'Memorandum' of the Dalai Clique. [Online] 21 November. Available at: www.chinaview.cn, reproduced at http://news.xinhuanet.com/english/2008-11/21/content_10391968.htm [Accessed: 14 February 2017]. See also (2008) China Refutes Dalai's So-Called 'Middle Way', [Online] 10 November. Available at: www.chinadaily.com.cn/china/2008-11/10/content_7190996.htm [Accessed: 14 February 2017]; (2008) China Says Serious Differences in Talks with Private Envoys of the Dalai Lama. [Online] 10 November. Available at: www.china-un.org/eng/zt/xzwt/t521742.htm [Accessed: 14 February 2017].

5 European Parliament, Committee on Foreign Affairs. Hearing Tibet: An update on the current situation, 31 March 2009.

6 Roundtable on Regional Autonomy and Central-Local Relations in China, Law Faculty, University of Hong Kong, 29–30 July 2009.

7 Roundtable on Regional Self-Government, Cultural Identity and Multinational Integration: Comparative Experience for Tibet, Autonomous Province of Trento in cooperation with the Department of Legal Sciences, University of Trento and the European Academy Bolzano/Bozen, Trento, Italy, 16–17 November 2009.

espoused by the Dalai Lama since the 1970s.[8] As the Dalai Lama stated in his address to the European Parliament in 2008, 'the essence of my Middle Way Approach is to secure genuine autonomy for the Tibetan people within the scope of the Constitution of the PRC'.[9] Stated differently, the 'middle way' policy means that 'Tibetans will not seek restoration of independence, and the Chinese government will respect the distinctive character of the Tibetan people, thereby making it possible for the Tibetan people to enjoy genuine regional autonomy'.[10]

The Tibetan leadership holds the position that Tibet was an independent country before its invasion by Communist China in 1950/51 and that the Tibetan people ultimately have the right to decide on their own future.[11] At the same time, the Dalai Lama's view that the basic needs and aspirations of the Tibetan people can be met through a negotiated extensive autonomy within the PRC is by now well established as the policy of the Tibetan leadership. It has prevailed in discussions among representatives of the exile community,[12] although there continues to be a significant opposition to the policy, especially among the younger Tibetans, many of whom are in favour of struggling for full

8 Memorandum, section VII. See also Kalon Tripa Prof. Samdhong Rinpoche, paper presented in the roundtable on Regional Self-Government, Cultural Identity, and Multinational Integration: Comparative Experiences for Tibet, Trento University, 16 November 2009; *Middle Way Policy*, above note 1, pp. 1–19.

9 The Dalai Lama, Address to the plenary session of the European Parliament, 4 December 2008, reproduced in (2009) A Compilation of the Memorandum on Genuine Autonomy for the Tibetan People, His Holiness the Dalai Lama's Brussels Statement of 4 December 2008, and the Chinese State Council's Press Briefing of 10 November 2008. DIIR Publications. See also Kelsang Gyaltsen, Statement presented at the European Parliament Committee on Foreign Affairs, Hearing on Tibet: An update on the current situation after the breakdown of negotiations with China, Brussels, 31 March 2009.

10 GYARI, L. (2007) Statement: Hearing before the Committee on Foreign Affairs, House of Representatives, Tibet: Status of Sino-Tibetan Dialogue. [Online] 13 March. Available at: www.foreignaffairs.house.gov [Accessed: 14 February 2017].

11 The Dalai Lama, Address, 4 December 2008, above note 9. The Dalai Lama does not demand that China accept the Tibetan view on its history and past independence, instead believing that the conflicting PRC and Tibetan views on Tibetan history should not be allowed to impede the achievement of a political solution that, under the circumstances, cannot easily be derived from past history. Note on the Memorandum on Genuine Autonomy for the Tibetan People, Section 1. See Statement by H.H. the Dalai Lama on the 47th Anniversary of the Tibetan National Uprising Day, 10 March 2006. Available at: www.tibet.net and www.dalailama.com. See also GYARI, L. (2008) Tibet at a Crossroads: The Current Status of Discussions between His Holiness the Dalai Lama and the Government of the People's Republic of China. [Online] 8 October. Available at: www.unpo.org/article/8774 Accessed: 14 February 2017].

12 A Special Meeting of the Tibetans in exile, 17–22 November 2008, called by the Dalai Lama and involving some 600 community leaders, endorsed the continuations of the dialogue with the PRC on the basis of the Dalai Lama's 'middle way' approach. Recommendations of the First Special General Meeting Convened under Article 59 of the Charter. Available at: http://tibet.net/2008/11/23/recommendations-of-the-first-special-general-meeting-on-tibet/ [Accessed: 14 February 2017].

independence.[13] Thus, the current political leadership of the Central Tibetan Administration – that is the Sikyong (the elected chief executive and chairman of the council of ministers, also referred to as prime minister), the Kashag (council of ministers) and the Tibetan Parliament in Exile – also follow the 'middle way' policy of dialogue with the Chinese Government on the basis of the demand for genuine autonomy for all Tibetan areas within the PRC.[14]

The Memorandum and the Note set out the features of an autonomy that the Tibetan leadership considers could be acceptable to Tibetans and reiterates the Dalai Lama's 'firm commitment not to seek separation or independence'[15] and to fully respect the territorial integrity of the PRC.[16]

The autonomy proposed is referred to as 'genuine' (Tibetan *ming thon tsung pa*, literally meaning 'the name/term corresponding to the reality', i.e. real autonomy[17]) to distinguish it from the current nominal ('being such in name only') autonomy bestowed by the PRC on the Tibetan regions. Under the Constitution and laws of the PRC, the authorities of the areas designated as 'Tibet Autonomous Region', 'Tibetan autonomous prefectures', 'Tibetan autonomous districts' and 'Tibetan autonomous counties' have what Yu Xingzhong characterises as 'limited administrative autonomy',[18] namely, limited delegated powers to administer

13 See, e.g. www.tibetanyouthcongress.org [Accessed: 14 February 2017]; Members of the Tibetan Youth Congress pledge 'to struggle for the total independence of Tibet even at the cost of one's life'. Available at: http://tibetanyouthcongress.org/about-tyc/ [Accessed: 14 February 2017].

14 Since the Dalai Lama's formal handing over of his political power and responsibilities to an elected leadership on 29 May 2011, it is the directly elected Sikyong who represents the highest political authority in exile, while the Dalai Lama may, under the Charter, remain 'engaged in the efforts to reach a satisfactory solution to the question of Tibet and to accomplish the cherished goals of the Tibetan people'. Charter of the Tibetans in Exile, amended Article 1 (30 May 2011). Available at: http://www.phayul.com/news/article.aspx?id=29582 [Accessed: 14 February 2017]. The current Sikyong has confir-med his commitment to continuing the 'middle way' approach of the Dalai Lama in seeking genuine autonomy. See (2011) Inaugural Speech of Kalon Tripa Dr Lobsang Sangay. [Online] 8 August 2011. Available at: www.tibetan.fr/?INAUGURAL-SPEECH-OF-KALON-TRIPA-DR [Accessed: 14 February 2017] (delivered on the occasion of his swearing in as the Kalon Tripa of the Central Tibetan Administration and Statement by Kalon Tripa following the Task Force meeting, Press Release, Dharamsala, 12 October 2011, available at: www.tibet.net).

15 Memorandum, section I. Although not stated explicitly in the Memorandum, it stands to reason that this commitment should be considered as conditional on reaching mutually acceptable settlement on the issue of genuine autonomy.

16 Memorandum, section III. The Tibetan intent not to separate from the PRC and to respect the state's territorial integrity is broadly acknowledged by governments following the issue. See, e.g. (2011) US Department of State (2011). Available at: http://2001-2009.state.gov/documents/organization/88264.pdf [Accessed: 14 February 2017], p. 2.

17 The official version of the Memorandum was prepared in Tibetan language, after which it was translated into English and Chinese. The Chinese term used is *mingfu qi shi*, which is a literal translation of the Tibetan original.

18 YU XINGZHONG, *Ethnic Regional Autonomy in the People's Republic of China*, International Conference on Comparative National Experiences of Autonomy: Purposes, Structures and Institutions, Centre for Comparative and Public Law, The University of Hong Kong, 10 April 2005, p. 14.

decisions made in Beijing by the Chinese Communist Party or the central government. The autonomy of these areas does not include decision-making authority, because there is no clear allocation of powers between the central government and the autonomous government. Nor are there reserved matters, such as culture or religion, that are the exclusive competency of the autonomous region and other matters in which the central and autonomous authorities share power. Rather, the autonomous authorities are subordinate in every respect to central authority, and the essential features of autonomy as this is generally understood are consequently missing.[19]

The core needs of Tibetans, as articulated by the Dalai Lama and the Central Tibetan Administration, are the preservation and development of the Tibetan identity and culture with its spiritual and linguistic heritage and the values that these represent, as well as the protection of the fragile Tibetan environment.[20] The means to realise these objectives, the Tibetans argue, is territorially based political autonomy, enabling the Tibetan people living in the Tibetan areas within the PRC to make their own choices and decisions by governing themselves and by doing so under one administration. Once the central role of culture, language and religion in Tibetan society is understood, as well as the people's connection to the unique Tibetan environment, they maintain, it becomes clear why territorial self-governance is needed.[21]

19 GHAI, Y., WOODMAN, S. and LOPER, K. (2010) Is There Space for 'Genuine Autonomy' for Tibetan Areas in the PRC's System of Nationalities Regional Autonomy? *International Journal on Minority and Group Rights*. 17(1). pp. 139, 156–157. The supremacy of the CCP and the central government is unmistakably articulated in the Law of the People's Republic of China on Regional National Autonomy, 1984 (sometimes also referred to as the Law on National Regional Autonomy or Law on Regional Ethnic Autonomy, 'LRNA'), revised 2001. This is the legislation that gives effect to Article 4 of the Constitution of the People's Republic of China, which provides that: 'Regional autonomy is practiced in areas where people of minority nationalities live in concentrated communities.' See GHAI et al. (2010), above, pp. 152–153. Due to the way in which the Tibet Autonomous Region is ruled today, it has been described as 'the "least autonomous" place in China'. ZHENG, G. (2010) *Towards Cultural Autonomy in Tibet*. Berkeley Electronic Press. [Online]. Available at: http://works.bepress.com/george_zheng/1/ [Accessed: 14 February 2017], p. 41.

20 It has been articulated in these terms for a long time. See, e.g. Statement of H.H. the Dalai Lama on the 44th Anniversary of the Tibetan National Uprising Day, 10 March 2003. See also Address of Kalon Tripa Prof. Samdhong Rinpoche at the 4th World Parliamentarians' Convention on Tibet, Edinburgh, 18 November 2005; H.H. THE DALAI LAMA (2008) Appeal to the Chinese People. [Online] 27 March. Available at: www.dalailama.com [Accessed: 14 February 2017]. See also US Department of State, above note 16, p. 2 for a reflection of that.

21 The Tibetan proposals should not be confused with demands for 'cultural autonomy', as some scholars suggest. See, e.g. WOMACK, B. (2007) Resolving Asymmetric Stalemates: The Case of the Tibet Question. *Journal of Contemporary China*. 16, n. 52, p. 444; ZHENG (2010), above note 19, pp. 46, 65. The emphasis on the core objectives to be realised through autonomy in terms of culture, linguistic, spiritual and environmental values does not amount to a demand for 'cultural autonomy'. See BENEDIKTER, T. (2007) *The World's Working Regional Autonomies: An Introduction and Comparative Analysis*. London: Anthem Press, pp. 43–44 for a discussion of cultural autonomy. To be sure, the Memorandum contains features of cultural autonomy, but it goes well beyond that to propose territorial and political autonomy in order to achieve those objectives.

3. The nature of the proposed autonomy

The autonomy proposed by the Dalai Lama and the Central Tibetan Administration is extensive. It envisages considerable powers of independent decision-making, involving legislative and executive authority in fields ranging from Tibetan culture, religion, language and education to local environmental protection, economic development and internal public security. Tibetan authorities would be permitted to regulate the migration and settlement of non-Tibetans into the confines of the autonomous region, they would be involved in decision-making on extraction and utilisation of Tibet's natural resources and would be permitted to conduct border trade with neighbouring states. The PRC central government, on the other hand, would retain its competencies with respect to foreign policy and defence. Since nothing is stated in the Memorandum on matters of fiscal and monetary policy, national transport and communications, postal services and a number of other areas of primary interest to the state as a whole, these competencies would probably also be considered central government responsibilities. The Memorandum envisages that in some areas, such as trade, utilisation of natural resources and economic policy, the central government and the autonomous government would share authority in ways that would be mutually beneficial.[22]

The autonomy envisaged in the Memorandum would apply to the whole people and consequently to all contiguous 'Tibetan autonomous areas', as these are currently designated in the PRC, and not only to the 'Tibet Autonomous Region', which makes up less than half of the territory and of the population of the Tibetan areas in the PRC. To this end, all the currently designated 'Tibetan autonomous' prefectures and counties contiguous to the Tibet Autonomous Region would be included in the settlement and in the administrative area to be vested with the new autonomy.[23] This is a critical issue for the Tibetans. Most of the Tibetan population lives in compact communities in the Tibetan areas contiguous to the Tibet Autonomous Region and the Tibetan leadership believes that in order to be able to ensure the survival and development of the Tibetan culture, spiritual values and identity, it is essential for these communities to be governed under the same policies and institutions, and by one set of laws and regulations, and one educational system.[24] Tibetans argue that solutions that have been crafted for the Tibet Autonomous Region alone, thus excluding the majority of Tibetans, as the 17-Point Agreement did in 1951, have had disastrous results. This has been amply demonstrated by the uprisings in the Eastern Tibetan regions in the 1950s and by the intensity of Tibetan protests in some of those same regions in recent years.[25]

22 See Memorandum, section IV, and Note, section 5.

23 Memorandum, section V; Note, section 5(e). It should be noted that the Chinese Government publication *China's Tibet* (*Zhongguo Xizang*) covers all Tibetan areas referred to here, suggesting that it uses an equally broad definition of the term 'Tibet'.

24 Memorandum, sections II and V; Note, section 5(e).

25 See GYARI (2007), above note 10. Reference is to the Agreement of the Central People's Government and the Local Government of Tibet on Measures for the Peaceful Liberation of

Despite the existence of regional differences, Tibetans in all Tibetan areas share a common language, ethnicity, culture, spiritual beliefs and traditions and today have a strong sense of common identity and culture. They view their political struggle largely from that perspective. Given the importance of this cultural and religious identity to Tibetans, as well as their connection to their distinct natural environment on the Tibetan plateau, it is hard for them to conceive of an effective way to preserve and advance those core aspects of their common life while they are being kept administratively divided. This is particularly pertinent since so many Tibetans belong to communities that, under the present administrative demarcations, constitute a minority – sometimes an insignificant minority – in the provinces that rule them. In those areas, the level of self-government would of necessity remain much inferior to what would be exercised in a genuinely autonomous Tibet Autonomous Region.[26]

The principal features of the autonomy would be entrenched in the Constitution of the PRC such that these could not be easily and unilaterally altered. The institutions appropriate for such an exercise of autonomy would have to be created or appropriately modified. And, finally, a process of consultation or appropriate institutional mechanism should exist to resolve disputes that may arise regarding the scope and exercise of the agreed-upon autonomy.[27] Both the entrenchment and the dispute resolution aspects of autonomous arrangements are essential to provide the confidence that the agreement can be faithfully implemented. In principle, this benefits all parties to such agreements, but it is particularly important for the 'weaker' party in asymmetric relationships, especially where other guarantees are absent.

Tibet, 23 May 1951 (full text in English can be found in VAN WALT VAN PRAAG, M. (1987) *The Status of Tibet: History, Rights, and Prospects in International Law*. Boulder, CO: Westview Press, pp. 337–340. In 2008, protests and uprisings took place in all Tibetan areas. SHAKYA, T. (2008) Tibetan Questions. *New Left Review*, No. 51; SMITH Jr., W.W. (2010) *Tibet's Last Stand? The Tibetan Uprising of 2008 and China's Response*. Plymouth: Rowman & Littlefield, pp. 11–39 and map opposite p. 1. More recently, repeated clashes between Tibetan protesters and Chinese security forces occurred in the Tibetan areas in Qinghai (Amdo in Tibetan) and Tibetan Autonomous Prefectures and counties in Sichuan. See WONG, G. (2012) Clashes Spread in Tibetan Region in China. *Associated Press*. 25 January; BARRIAUX, M. (2012) Unrest Spreads in Tibetan Areas of China. *AFP*. 25 January; BEECH, H. (2012) As Another Tibetan Monk Self-Immolates, China Declares 'War' on Tibetan Protesters. *Time*. [Online] 10 February. Available at: http://world.time.com/2012/02/10/as-another-tibetan-monk-self-immolates-china-declares-war-on-tibetan-protestors/ [Accessed: 14 February 2017]. A map showing the spread of the 2012 protests is accessible at www.tibetnetwork.org [Accessed: 14 February 2017]. The vast majority of self-immolations by Tibetans, which have taken place in the past two years in protest at Chinese policies, have occurred in the Tibetan areas outside the Tibet Autonomous Region. See International Campaign for Tibet (ICT) report: *Storm in the Grasslands: Self-Immolations in Tibet and Chinese Policy* (London, Washington, DC, 2012).

26 See Memorandum, section V; Note, section 5(e). It will be noted that the Tibetan side has not argued the issue on historical grounds, as is often mistakenly assumed and suggested by the Chinese Government.

27 See Memorandum, section VI; Note, section 4.

4. International practice and the Memorandum

Autonomy, as this is generally understood and practised in various parts of the world, is increasingly recognised as an effective way to resolve intrastate conflicts of the kind that exists between the Chinese Government and the Tibetan people. The United Nations and the Organization for Security and Co-operation in Europe (OSCE) have developed standards with respect to governance in situations involving indigenous and minority peoples that are of particular relevance to the nature of the autonomy proposed by the Tibetans.

Of particular interest in this regard is the UN Declaration on the Rights of Indigenous Peoples. It was adopted by the UN General Assembly in 2007 with the vote of an overwhelming majority of member states, including China,[28] and represents the most recent expression of international consensus on the existence of an entitlement to autonomy covering virtually all the issues addressed in the Memorandum. The 1992 UN Declaration on the Rights of Minorities,[29] the Lund Recommendations on the Effective Participation in Public Life,[30] as well as the constructive arrangements involving national minorities considered by the UN Independent Expert on Minority Issues and the OSCE High Commissioner on National Minorities,[31] are all also highly relevant to the Tibetan proposal, and they support the kinds of demands contained in the Memorandum.

Although the autonomy envisaged by the Dalai Lama and the Central Tibetan Administration is unique in that it is designed to respond to the specific needs of the Tibetan people and those of the Chinese state, it is of a kind that is prevalent throughout the world.

Well-established autonomies such as those of South Tyrol/Alto Adige (in Italy), Catalonia (in Spain), Faroe and Greenland (in Denmark), Zanzibar (in Tanzania), Cordillera (in the Philippines), Sarawak (in Malaysia), Azores and Madeira (in Portugal), Mizoram (in India), the Autonomous Region of the North Atlantic (in Nicaragua), Åland (in Finland), New Caledonia (France), Tatarstan (in the Russian Federation), Scotland (in the United Kingdom), Gagauzia (in Moldova), Nunavut (in Canada), Kuna Yala (in Panama) and Hong Kong and Macao (in the PRC) serve as excellent examples to draw from when designing an autonomous arrangement. New autonomies, such as those in Bougainville (Papua New Guinea), Aceh and Papua (Indonesia) and Kurdistan (Iraq) are equally useful to study. Many of these are discussed in some detail by scholars elsewhere.[32]

28 UNGA Res. 61/295, 13 September 2007 adopted by 143 votes to 4, with 11 abstentions.

29 UNGA Res. 47/135, 18 December 1992.

30 *Lund Recommendations on the Effective Participation in Public Life*, published by the OSCE High Commissioner on National Minorities (The Hague, September 1999).

31 See generally, *Report of the Independent Expert on Minority Issues*, UNGA Doc. A HCR/13/23, 7 January 2010; VAN DER STOEL, M. (2005) Prologomenon. In SKURBATY, Z. (ed.), *Beyond a One-Dimensional State: An Emerging Right to Autonomy?* Leiden/Boston: Brill. p. xix.

32 For a concise discussion of the elements of autonomy that contribute to stability and good functioning of such arrangements, see LAPIDOTH, R. (2001) *Elements of Stable Regional Autonomy*

The features of autonomy proposed in the Memorandum are already found in these existing autonomies and incorporated in different ways in their specific arrangements.[33] They also correspond to the international standards relevant to such autonomy arrangements mentioned above.

One issue that has proven to be of great importance to the functioning of autonomies is the provision of security, sometimes in the form of guarantees, for the fulfilment of agreements reached and for the protection against unilateral changes to important provisions of autonomy arrangements. The importance of this issue cannot be overstated, given the poor record of implementation of autonomy agreements and the resulting scepticism this often provokes among parties.[34]

Some autonomous arrangements have their source in international agreements, as is the case for the autonomies of the Åland Islands, of South Tyrol/Alto Adige and of Hong Kong.[35] These agreements, which serve as international guarantees, are as good as the political will of the states that provide them. Thus, whereas in the Åland and South Tyrol/Alto Adige cases the international basis for the autonomy arrangements has proved to be very important to their continued full implementation, the British Government does not appear to play a role in ensuring China's full respect for Hong Kong's autonomy. In fact, it is Hong Kong's economic importance as an international centre of commerce that provides the best security for the preservation of its autonomy. But all of these autonomies also have a basis in domestic law for their status, and the entrenchment of autonomy agreements, or essential provisions thereof, in constitutional documents provides an essential form of security for most autonomies.[36]

Arrangements. Working Paper. Munich: Centrum für angewandte Politikforschung. A number of relevant case studies can be found in HANNUM, H. (1990) *Autonomy, Sovereignty, and Self-Determination: The Accommodation of Conflicting Rights.* Philadelphia, PA: University of Pennsylvania Press; BENEDIKTER (2007), above note 21; and BENEDIKTER, T. (ed.) (2009) *Solving Ethnic Conflicts through Self-Government: A Short Guide to Autonomy in Europe and South Asia.* Bozen: EURAC. See also GHAI, Y. (ed.) (2000) *Autonomy and Ethnicity; Negotiating Competing Claims in Multi-ethnic States.* Cambridge: Cambridge University Press.

33 These models served as inspiration to the drafters of the Memorandum and as examples to draw from in conceptualising an appropriate autonomy arrangement for Tibet within the PRC. A number of experts were invited already in the 1990s to share their knowledge and assist in the examination of forms and experiences of autonomy. See, e.g. TIBETAN PARLIAMENTARY POLICY AND RESEARCH CENTRE (2000) *Tibetan Autonomy and Self-Government, Myth or Reality?* New Delhi.

34 BOLTJES, M. (2011) The Implementation Challenge in Intrastate Peace Processes: An Analysis and DE VARENNE, F. (2011) Recurrent Challenges to the Implementation of Intrastate Peace Agreements: The Resistance of State Authorities. Both in BOLTJES, M. (ed.) *Implementing Negotiated Agreements: The Real Challenge to Intrastate Peace.* The Hague: TMC Asser Press.

35 See HANNUM (1990), above note 32, pp. 371–375; WOELK, J. (2011) From Compromise to Process: The Implementation of the South Tyrolean Autonomy. In BOLTJES, above note 34, pp. 157–176. The Sino-British Joint Declaration. 19 December 1984. Text available on the Hong Kong Government's official website, at www.legislation.gov/hk/.

36 GHAI (2000), above note 32, pp. 21–23.

A useful example of entrenchment is provided by the Bougainville autonomy. The negotiators of the Bougainville Peace Agreement of 2001 provided for a double entrenchment of the autonomy arrangement.[37] It is entrenched in the Papua New Guinea Constitution, which now provides that Bougainville's autonomy cannot be amended by the national parliament acting on its own. Any change requires the support of a simple majority of all members of the Bougainville legislature and two-thirds of all the members if it concerns the provisions on the referendum on the future status of Bougainville contained in the peace agreement. In addition, the Constitution of the Autonomous Region of Bougainville (a sub-national constitution) can be amended only in accordance with its own terms and not by the PNG Parliament. A requirement for prior consultation also promotes the development of common positions on such important matters.[38]

5. The Chinese Government's reactions to the proposals

The PRC's publicly articulated position on the Memorandum is best reflected in the exceptional 2008 and 2010 press statements made by Vice Minister Zhu Weiqun, in response to the Tibetan proposals. The background to the Chinese position can also be understood from a number of White Papers published by the PRC Government in past years, detailing its positions, policies and achievements.

Within days of the presentation of the Memorandum by the Tibetan envoys, the Chinese Government publicly rejected the document in surprisingly harsh terms, insisting that it proved the Dalai Lama's separatist ambitions. Zhu Weiqun reiterated in a press statement that the Dalai Lama must give up those ambitions and 'ask the forgiveness of the central government and also the forgiveness of the people all over the nation'.[39] He spelled out the conditions to further talks, which included that 'the Dalai Lama and his clique (. . .) must not only make public recognition of Tibet as but one part of the inalienable territory of China (. . .), they must publicly accept that the People's Republic of China is the only legal government of China'.[40] The Chinese Government rejected the specifics of the proposals because they entailed extensive degrees of self-governance and,

37 Bougainville Peace Agreement, 30 August 2001, full text accessible at www.usip.org/sites/default/files/file/resources/collections/peace_agreements/bougain_20010830.pdf [Accessed: 14 February 2017]. See A. REGAN (2010), *Light Intervention: Lessons from Bougainville*. Washington, DC.

38 REGAN (2010), above note 37.

39 Zhu Weiqun, Press conference, 10 November 2008, above note 4. Zhu later characterised the Dalai Lama's autonomy proposals as an attempt to 'restore the theocratic, feudalist slavery that was practiced in Old Tibet and to resume the supreme power and position of the Dalai Lama'. He also argued that 'the true nature of his "middle way approach" is indeed "Tibetan independence"'. Interview with Zhu Weiqun, Beijing, 9 September 2009, by *Focus Magazine* and published in (2010) 21 *China's Tibet*, No. 1, p. 7.

40 Ibid.

therefore, considerable devolution of power from the central government to an autonomous one, as well as because the proposals would require an adjustment of administrative boundaries to bring all Tibetan "autonomous" areas under one administration. In the PRC's view, such ideas 'obviously violate the PRC's Constitution'.[41]

The basic premise of the PRC's position, repeated on many occasions, is that 'Tibet is an inseparable part of China', and that the Tibetan people are a member of 'the big family of the Chinese nation',[42] a position it bases on its interpretation of history.[43] When China's People's Liberation Army entered Tibet in 1950, it did so to 'liberate it and expel imperialists from it'.[44] In doing so, the PRC claims it asserted its existing sovereignty over Tibet. The Chinese Government has repeatedly demanded that the Dalai Lama explicitly recognise that Tibet is an inalienable part of China as a precondition to substantive negotiations.[45]

41 Minister Du Qinglin summarised his government's response as follows: 'If the 14th Dalai Lama does wish to see progress made during the talks and improved relations with the Central Government, he should respect history, face up to reality and go with the times, and make a thorough self-examination of his words and deeds and radically correct his political positions.' Press conference of the PRC State Council Information Office, Beijing, 2 February 2010, reproduced in Xinhua News Agency, Beijing, 11 February 2010.

42 Information Office of the State Council of the People's Republic of China, Protection and Development of Tibetan Culture (White Paper, Beijing, September 2008), p. 1. The PRC Government view is that Tibetans and Han peoples have interacted since ancient times and Tibet was 'formally incorporated into the territory of China's Yuan Dynasty' in the mid thirteenth century and has, ever since, 'remained under the jurisdiction of the central government of China'. Information Office of the State Council of the People's Republic of China, Tibet – Its Ownership and Human Rights Situation (White Paper, Beijing, September 1992), p. 1.

43 See JIAWEI, W. and GYAINCAIN, N. (1997) *The Historical Status of China's Tibet.* Beijing: China Intercontinental Press. Chinese historians, according to Martin Jacques, 'generally describe the process of Chinese territorial expansion as one of "unification" rather than conquest, with expansion being seen as a progressive evolution towards a preordained and inevitable unity. Territory once taken, has been regarded as immutably Chinese.' JACQUES, M. (2009) *When China Rules the World: The rise of the Middle Kingdom and the End of the Western World.* London: Penguin. p. 237.

44 Information Office of the State Council of the People's Republic of China, Sixty Years Since Peaceful Liberation of Tibet (White Paper, Beijing, June 2011), section I-3. See JING WEI (ed.) (1991) *'Is Tibet an 'Independent State'? – On Van Praag's 'The Status of Tibet'.* Beijing: New Star Publishers; JIAWEI and GYAINCAIN (1997), above note 43, pp. 191–193.

45 PRC Prime Minister Wen Jiabao stated that if the Dalai Lama 'recognizes that Tibet is an inalienable part of Chinese territory', then 'we are willing to carry out consultations and dialogue on his personal future'. KWOK, K. (2007) Dalai Lama Must Give Up Secession, Says Premier. *South China Morning Post.* 17 March. p. A6. President Jiang Zemin, at a joint press conference with President Bill Clinton in June 1998, had made the same condition, adding the requirement that the Dalai Lama also recognise that Taiwan is part of China. Embassy of the People's Republic of China in the United States of America, *Jiang, Clinton Have Frank Exchange of Views at Press Conference*, President Clinton's State Visit to China. [Online]. Available at: http://www.china-embassy.org/eng/zmgx/zysj/kldfh/t36236.htm [Accessed: 14 February 2017]. Although the dialogue is always framed in terms of the Dalai Lama's personal future, discussions between the parties so far have not in fact focused on this.

As far as the government system is concerned, the 'persistence of the leadership of the Communist Party of China'[46] within a system of 'democratic centralism' in which all authority is subject to that of the central government of the PRC is the core principle from which no deviation is tolerated.[47]

Within this framework, Tibetans, as one of China's 'minority nationalities', are governed according to the regional nationality or national (*minzu*, currently often translated as 'ethnic') autonomy system, which Zhu Weiqun describes as 'the successful and precise integration of ethnic autonomy and regional autonomy'.[48] The scholar Zeng Ge characterises the Chinese approach as an 'integrationist solution to ethnic and cultural diversity'[49] and explains that for the 'founding fathers' of the PRC, the basic principles underlying regional nationality autonomy were that of 'equal citizenship of all Chinese people, regardless of their nationalities' and the presumed voluntary union of all nationalities in the PRC.[50]

Zhu Weiqun acknowledges the international practice with respect to autonomy, but emphasises that the PRC's system provides for a different autonomy from that exercised elsewhere in the world because China's centralised government structure is unique: although the word 'autonomy' means the same everywhere, 'each country has different national conditions and may conceptualise this word in a different way'.[51] Zhu points out that regional nationality autonomy is also 'clearly different from the "one country two systems" approach in place in both Hong Kong and Macao'.[52] Hong Kong and Macao enjoy a special autonomy under Article 31 of the PRC Constitution, which enabled China to recover its sovereignty over those territories, but this regime would not be applicable to Tibet.[53] The Law

46 Press conference, 10 November 2008, above note 4.

47 See GHAI et al. (2010), above note 19, pp. 143, 146.

48 Press conference, 10 November 2008, above note 4. See for detailed statements of policy Information Office of the State Council, Regional Ethnic Autonomy in Tibet (White Paper, Beijing, May 2004) and Information Office of the State Council, Regional Autonomy for Ethnic Minorities (White Paper, Beijing, February 2005).

49 ZHENG (2010), above note 19, p. 9. See also MACKERRAS, C. (1994) *China's Minorities; Integration and Modernization in the Twentieth Century*. Oxford: Oxford University Press. pp.145, 165.

50 Ibid., p. 11.

51 Zhu Weiqun, Interview by *Focus Magazine*, above note 39, p. 5. Ghai, Woodman and Loper, in their study of the PRC regional national autonomy system, conclude: 'it is clear both from the law and practice that the concept of 'autonomy' in China is fundamentally different from increasingly accepted understandings of autonomy standards'. GHAI et al. (2010), above note 19, p. 156.

52 Press conference, 10 November 2008, above note 4.

53 This position is consistent with earlier statements, notably the 2004 White Paper on Regional Nationality Autonomy in Tibet, which clarified that Article 31 could only be used for the recovery of regions previously taken from China by imperialist aggression. 'The situation in Tibet is entirely different from that in Hong Kong and Macau. The Hong Kong and Macau issue was a product of imperialist aggression against China; it was an issue of China's resumption of exercise of its sovereignty. Since ancient times Tibet has been an inseparable part of Chinese territory, where the Central government has always exercised effective sovereign jurisdiction over the region. So

on Regional National Autonomy, which does apply to Tibet, specifies in its Article 15 that autonomous areas carry out their role 'under the unified leadership of the State Council and shall be subordinate to it'.[54]

From Chinese Government statements and White Papers it is clear that the maintenance of the PRC's unity and securing sovereignty are high priorities of the central government and protection against the loss of a portion of territory from China is a serious concern.[55] The PRC's highly centralised control structure as well as its regional nationality autonomy system are, at least in part, a means to safeguard these needs. They also form the cornerstone of the government's policy toward minority nationalities, which is of special importance with respect to the large ethnic groups, such as the Tibetans, Uighurs and Mongols living on the PRC's vast border regions. The regional nationality autonomy system is thus designed to cement China's unity and stability and protects its borders by not only integrating such groups into the political and economic fabric of the 'nation', but also by assimilating them.[56] The Chinese leadership's response to the Tibetan proposal for genuine autonomy, which characterises it as a demand for semi-independence or 'covert independence' intended to 'deliberately promote secession and sabotage national unity',[57] should be read in this light.

At the same time, it is very important to note that the Chinese Government acknowledges that the Tibetan proposal represents a compromise between its own position and that of independence for Tibet. In his press conference, Vice Minister Zhu Weiqun admitted that the adoption by the Dalai Lama of the middle-way approach in the 1980s 'literally means that the Dalai Lama and his clique have dropped the demand for "Tibetan independence"'.[58] He affirmed that the Memorandum on Genuine Autonomy was a clear and precise expression of the Dalai Lama's middle-way approach and explained that Tibetans 'chose to seek a trade-off scheme between the two positions'.[59]

the issue of resuming exercise of sovereignty does not exist.' Information Office of the State Council, above note 48, p. 9. For discussion, see GHAI et al. (2010), above note 19, p. 158.

54 Law on Regional National Autonomy, Art. 15.

55 For a detailed analysis, see CARLSON, A. (2005) *Unifying China, Integrating with the World; Securing Chinese Sovereignty in the Reform Era.* Stanford, CA: NUS Press. For the section specifically relating to China's Tibet policy, see in particular pp. 91–123.

56 Warren Smith shows that PRC explanations on the nature of autonomy reveal that to Beijing any form of autonomy is merely 'a temporary expedient until ultimate integration and assimilation could be achieved'. SMITH Jr., W.W. (2008) *China's Tibet? Autonomy or Assimilation.* Lanham, MD: Rowman & Littlefield. p. 233. See also GHAI et al. (2010), above note 19, p. 139. In a recent article, Zhu Weiqun argues in favour of removing ethnic differentiation and privileges for minorities in the PRC and promoting assimilation for the sake of 'national cohesion'. (2012) *South China Morning Post,* 15 February, reported by M. Chan.

57 Press conference, 10 November 2008, above note 4. Also characterised by Zhu, in the same press conference, as a 'roundabout way to pursue to independence'.

58 Ibid.

59 Ibid.

Equally important is the Chinese Government's realisation that implementation of genuine or 'higher' autonomy would require the transfer of significant powers of decision-making to the autonomous level of government, and this it does not want. Its analysis of the proposal appears to be that, if implemented, it would 'subvert, deny and therefore weaken the authority and power of the central government'.[60]

The demand that all Tibetan areas within the PRC be united as one administrative autonomous region was rejected by the government primarily on the grounds that these areas were not historically under the administration of the government in Lhasa.[61] The other reason given for rejecting the administrative unification of these areas is the sheer size of the territory in question.[62]

The PRC Government also reacted to other specific points contained in the Memorandum, such as the allocation of powers of internal security (police) to the autonomous authorities, the demand that Tibetan be the principal official language in Tibet and that the future settlement of non-Tibetans in the autonomous region be regulated. Curiously, rather than responding to those proposals on their merits, in the course of their talks with the Tibetan envoys Chinese officials reacted to them only on the basis of earlier Tibetan statements and proposals, extraneous to and replaced by the Memorandum. Some of these arguments had already been made in a general way in Zhu Weiqun's 2008 press statement.[63]

Perhaps the most puzzling and disturbing part of the Chinese response to the Memorandum is Zhu's disclosure that his government's objective in the dialogue with the Dalai Lama's representatives (which had been going on for six years at that point) was solely to ascertain whether the Dalai Lama had changed his position in line with Chinese Government demands. It was emphatically not to discuss the issues raised in the Memorandum, on which the government had no intention of changing its position.[64] This is puzzling not only because in the same statement Zhu admits that these issues have in fact been discussed with Tibetan representatives for a long time,[65] but also because the Memorandum was prepared specifically in response to the invitation extended to the Dalai Lama to present his views on these matters, to Zhu himself and Minister Du Qinglin at the seventh

60 Ibid.

61 Ibid.; GYARI (2007), above note 10.

62 GYARI (2007), above note 10. It should be noted, however, that provincial and autonomous region boundary changes have been made a number of times with respect to Jilin province (1954); the bifurcation of Xikang province with one part allocated to the Tibet Autonomous Region and the other to Sichuan province (1955); and more recently the creation of Hainan province out of a portion of Guangdong province (1988).

63 Press conference, 10 November 2008, above note 4.

64 Ibid.

65 Ibid. This is confirmed by the head of the Tibetan delegation, Lodi Gyari. GYARI, L. (2010) The Way Forward on Tibet: The Status of Discussions between His Holiness the Dalai Lama and the Government of the People's Republic of China. [Online] 25 November. Available at: http://csis.org/files/attachments/100305_csis_gyari.pdf [Last accessed: 14 February 2017].

round of talks, in July 2008. Instead of welcoming the submission by the Tibetan side of concrete and detailed proposals that might enable the parties to get down to the business of truly negotiating a settlement, Zhu's statement exudes frustration at the apparent inability of the Tibetan side to comprehend and accept that his predecessors' rejection of Tibetan demands for 'a "high degree of autonomy" [and] a "greater Tibetan-inhabited autonomous region"' twenty years earlier had not settled the matter once and for all.[66]

6. Concluding remark

A first public sign of a Chinese Government willingness to enter into a dialogue with Tibetan leaders was President Jiang Zemin's unexpected reference to Tibet at the joint press conference with President Bill Clinton on 27 June 1998. He volunteered to inform the public that: 'Just now President Clinton also mentioned the Tibetan issue and urged dialogue with the Dalai Lama.' He then stated that: 'As long as the Dalai Lama can make public the statement and commitment that Tibet is an inalienable part of China and recognise Taiwan as a province of China, then the door to our negotiation is open.'[67]

The Dalai Lama's envoys and the Chinese Communist Party's United Front Work Department leaders met for the first round of talks in September 2002, after which another eight rounds of talks were held between them over a period of a little over seven years.[68]

In 2007 and 2008, an atmosphere of optimism surrounded the talks, despite the tensions surrounding the Tibetan protests related to China's hosting of the Olympic Games. The Tibetan envoy, Lodi Gyari, expressed the feeling that the two sides had 'now reached the stage where if there is the political will on both sides, we have an opportunity to finally resolve this issue'.[69] This optimism seemed justified when, at the seventh round, in July 2008, the Chinese delegation extended an invitation to the Dalai Lama to present his views on the degree or form of autonomy he was seeking.[70] To this invitation the Tibetan side responded eagerly by preparing the Memorandum, which they handed to the Chinese delegation in October of the same year.

66 Ibid. The government had earlier warned that 'any act aimed at undermining and changing the regional ethnic autonomy in Tibet is in violation of the Constitution and law, and it is unacceptable to the entire Chinese people, including the broad masses of the Tibetan people'. Information Office of the State Council, above note 48, p. 9. This sweeping statement would seem to preclude discussion of any kind of change.

67 Embassy of the People's Republic of China in the United States of America, Jiang, Clinton Have Frank Exchange of Views at Press Conference. [Online]. Available at: www.china-embassy.org/eng/zmgx/zysj/kldfh/t36236.htm [Accessed: 14 February 2017].

68 See for details the statements issued following each round of talks by the Special Envoy of the Dalai Lama, to be found on www.tibet.net and www.savetibet.org [Accessed: 14 February 2017].

69 GYARI (2007), above note 10. See also for a discussion HE, B. and SAUTMAN, B. (2005–06) The Politics of the Dalai Lama's New Initiative for Autonomy. *Pacific Affairs*. 78(4). pp. 601 ff.

70 The invitation was extended by Du Qinglin and Zhu Weiqun.

The Tibetan proposals, which could be implemented within the framework of China's Constitution, provide an opportunity for the parties to negotiate an appropriate autonomy arrangement capable of satisfying the essential needs of both sides. It is disappointing that the Chinese Central Government rejects those proposals outright and appears unprepared to engage in discussions on *any* form of real autonomy. This represents a missed opportunity.

Part II

Practice of regional autonomy: Experiences compared

Chapter 6

From compromise to compact?

Working autonomy in South Tyrol

Jens Woelk

Today, the situation in the Autonomous Province of Bolzano, South Tyrol is generally seen as a success. What used to be a conflict-ridden and extremely poor Alpine region has developed into one of the wealthiest areas of Europe, in which three linguistic groups live together peacefully. Its system of territorial autonomy is widely considered an inspiration for other situations and even as a 'model' for other situations.[1]

1. Interest in South Tyrol: Decades of experience in working autonomy

Apart from the Åland Islands in the Baltic Sea,[2] South Tyrol is Europe's oldest working territorial autonomy. It can thus offer valuable insights into problems of implementation and long-term implications of autonomy arrangements. By contrast with the Åland Islands, it is neither isolated, nor does it present a homogenous situation in demographic terms. Instead, it is placed in a strategically important position in the Alps, on the main route between Italy and Austria/Germany, and its population of roughly half a million inhabitants is composed of three linguistic groups: approximately two-thirds German speakers, one-quarter

1 Appreciation is increasingly shared by local politicians, who frequently receive delegations from abroad and explain the South Tyrolean 'model'. Most recently, in May 2015, the former President of the Province, Luis Durnwalder, travelled to the area of Donetsk in Ukraine in order to discuss the South Tyrolean experience with secessionist leaders, while Senator Francesco Palermo, elected in the Province, has been consulted by Ukraine's constitutional commission in Kiev on the same issue. See for a profound analysis of the South Tyrolean 'model' and its fundamental elements: WOELK, J., PALERMO, F. and MARKO, J. (eds) (2008) *Tolerance through Law. Self-Governance and Group Rights in South Tyrol*. Leiden, Boston: Martinus Nijhoff.

2 See on the situation of the Åland Islands (with a population of 95 per cent Swedish speakers), e.g. ACKRÉN, M. (2011) *Successful Examples of Minority Governance – The Cases of the Åland Islands and South Tyrol*. Reports from the Åland Islands Peace Institute No. 1-2011 [Online]. Available at: www.peace.ax/images/stories/publications/rapport_1-2011_webb.pdf [Accessed: 14 February 2017] and SPILIOPOULOU ÅKERMARK, S. (ed.) (2011) The Åland Example and its Components – Relevance for International Conflict Resolution. Mariehamn: The Åland Islands Peace Institute.

Italian speakers and the small group of Ladins.[3] These and other characteristics, such as the mountainous environment, make South Tyrol an interesting subject of comparison, also for Tibet.[4]

Austrian territory and part of the 'crown land' Tyrol until the annexation by Italy in 1919, the evolution toward today's situation mirrors all important developments of the twentieth century in miniature, in particular war, nationalism and politics of domination of one linguistic group over the other. However, in the end, assimilation has not been realised as the vicious circle of domination of one group over the other has been broken through compromise, starting with a bilateral treaty between Austria and Italy in 1946 (the Gruber-Degasperi Agreement). As its implementation was considered flawed by the German speakers, protest rose and even became violent: in the 1960s there was a series of bombing attacks and some ambushes, as well as Italian counter-terrorist action. However, negotiation was chosen in time as the method for solving the conflict and by this method today's solid autonomy could be established as a compromise. Through a system of permanent negotiation, it has been successfully implemented and consolidated.

Despite overall success, South Tyrol's autonomy is a solution designed in the 1960s, originally based upon a dominant logic of separation of the groups in order to create security (which later should permit the building up of trust). Today, the challenge is to adapt the autonomy system to globalisation, European integration and the reforms of the Italian State preserving the special characteristics of the territory. Also, a process of 'normalisation' between the linguistic groups can be observed due to more relaxed relations between them within the Province. While this process has created support for 'internal self-determination' within all groups, it has also shifted the legitimacy of the autonomy arrangement toward the quality of services provided for (all) citizens, from protection of one group to joint management for all residents. On the one hand, the relaxation of inter-group relations increasingly raises questions regarding the rigidity of some core principles of minority protection, such as the quota system in the public administration or separation in the educational sector. On the other hand, with the crisis of the Italian political and economic system after 2008, calls for external self-determination have recently re-emerged from the nationalist German-speaking opposition parties.

3 According to the last census in 2011, the exact figures for the three language groups are: German speakers (69 per cent), Italian speakers (26 per cent) and Ladin speakers (4.5 per cent). For data in detail, see: PROVINCIAL STATISTICS INSTITUTE ASTAT (2016) *South Tyrol in Figures 2016*. [Online]. Available at: http://astat.provinz.bz.it/downloads/Siz_2016-eng.pdf [Accessed: 14 February 2017].

4 In a beautiful photo book, South Tyrolean and Tibetan, Alpine and Himalayan living conditions and contexts are confronted with each other in amazing pictures (BERNHART, U. and LANER, J.B. (2002) *Leben die sich gleichen. Bergklöster aus Alpen und Himalaya*. Zürich: Offizin Verlag). The Dalai Lama has been to Bolzano three times since 1997; a study group within the Tibetan Government in Exile has intensively dealt with the South Tyrolean and other autonomy arrangements in order to draw lessons from comparison and to prepare a dialogue with the Chinese Government. The 'Memorandum on Genuine Autonomy' is an outcome of these comparative studies.

This chapter analyses the main features of the South Tyrolean autonomy system in an evolutionary perspective. The objective is to show its innovative and asymmetrical characteristics, which laid the basis for 'internal self-determination' gradually accepted by both, the majority of the population in the Province across all linguistic groups, as well as the Italian Government. A system of guarantees and permanent negotiation in a democratic State was key to success, as well as the political will to make the autonomy arrangement function. Political unity of German speakers combined with soft external intervention in critical moments by kin State Austria, as well as the wider context of European integration, were important favourable conditions.

The illustration and analysis of South Tyrol's complex autonomy system distinguishes between issues regarding negotiation – at the beginning, for reaching compromise, and as a permanent principle for implementation and beyond – and the peculiar and innovative solutions found within the Italian context, minority rights, territorial governance and elements of complex power sharing. As South Tyrol has been a working autonomy for decades, a look at its dynamic evolution and the adaptation of the system to new challenges will conclude the chapter.

2. From conflict to compromise: Negotiation as the fundamental principle

After the First World War, the 1919 Peace Treaty of Saint Germain[5] provided for the annexation of South Tyrol and Trentino by the Italian State, despite the contrast with President Wilson's declaration on the principle of self-determination, as the overwhelming majority of inhabitants were German-speaking South Tyrolese. In the following decades, the Italian Government under Mussolini subjected the German speakers of South Tyrol to forced Italianisation, repressing German-speakers in all spheres of cultural, economic and political life, and prohibiting schools, political parties and even names in the German language.[6] In order to create a homogenous population, after Austria's annexation by the German Reich in 1938, Hitler and Mussolini agreed on an 'Option' for German speakers: they were offered German citizenship under the condition of emigration

5 HANNUM, H. (1996) *Autonomy, Sovereignty and Self-Determination – The Accommodation of Conflicting Rights*. Philadelphia, PA: University of Pennsylvania Press. pp. 432–441.

6 This policy of forced assimilation not only created a deep-rooted historical trauma and distrust in all future Italian policies and motives, but also increased German nationalism. See, for a historical overview, in English, LANTSCHNER, E. (2008) History of the South Tyrol Conflict and Its Settlement. In WOELK et al., above note 1, pp. 3–15; STEININGER, R. (2003) *South Tyrol: A Minority Conflict of the Twentieth Century*. New Brunswick, NJ: Transaction Publishers; and ALCOCK, A.E. (2001) *The South Tyrol Autonomy: A Short Introduction*. Paper. County Londonderry, Bozen/Bolzano, May 2001. [Online]. Available at: www.buergernetz.bz.it/en/downloads/South-Tyrol-Autonomy.pdf [Accessed: 14 February 2017].

and (re-)settlement in the German Reich; the alternative was remaining and accepting the Italian assimilation policy.[7]

2.1 From 'first' to 'second autonomy': Renegotiation supported by kin State Austria

After the Second World War, when Allies insisted on autonomy for South Tyrol at the Paris Peace Conference, a complicated triangular relationship of negotiation developed: Austria became involved in bilateral negotiations with Italy for finding an autonomy arrangement and in turn asked the South Tyrolean People's Party (*Südtiroler Volkspartei* – SVP)[8] to send three representatives as advisers. The outcome of the bilateral negotiations was the 1946 De Gasperi-Gruber Agreement, which constitutes the international legal basis and obligation for the negotiations on autonomy.[9] It also justified kin State Austria's monitoring role regarding fulfilment of the agreement (Article 3: 'in consultation with the Austrian Government')[10] without expressly containing Austrian renunciation of South Tyrol. Thus, from the Italian perspective, territorial stability had not been finally recognised. As Italian speakers were a numerical minority in the Province, 'the result was an Autonomy Statute restrictively interpretive of the Paris-Agreement, and restrictively applied'.[11]

As the larger Autonomous Region of Trentino, South Tyrol, established in 1948, included also the Italian-speaking province of Trentino, German speakers in South Tyrol found themselves outnumbered by Italian speakers in the regional government, which controlled regional political and economic matters. Moreover, the massive influx of Italian workers continued. As the autonomy was considered to be inadequate, protests and public rallies began; in the early 1960s bombing attacks on power lines marked a new dimension in the struggle of German speakers for a satisfactory autonomous arrangement.[12]

7 Eighty-five per cent chose to resettle in Germany, but only about one-third actually left during the war and many of those returned after 1945. The decision left a deep scar between the two different factions ('*Optanten*' and '*Dableiber*') within the German group. For an excellent description, see ALCOCK, A.E. (1970) *The History of the South Tyrol Question*. Geneva: University Genève.

8 Today, the SVP continues to be the overall representation of German speakers in South Tyrol, still maintaining the absolute majority of seats in the Provincial Assembly, despite a trend of growing support for German-speaking, right-wing opposition parties.

9 This agreement between Austria and Italy, bearing the names of the two Foreign Ministers, Alcide De Gasperi and Karl Gruber, was signed in Paris on 5 September 1946 (and is also known as the 'Paris Treaty'), and it subsequently became Annex IV to the Treaty of Peace with Italy, signed in Paris-St Germain on 10 February 1947 (49 UNTS 3).

10 Including eventual intervention as the German speakers' 'protecting power' ('*Schutzmacht*').

11 ALCOCK (2001), above note 6, p. 6.

12 There is controversial debate among historians on whether these bombings actually helped in changing the Italian Government's attitude or whether they were rather counterproductive. Initially, the targets were mostly power lines, as electricity had become a State monopoly in Italy and hydroelectric facilities in South Tyrol were seen as symbols of the State depriving the area of its natural resources without compensation.

Austria's involvement as a kin State was responsible and moderate, although there is no direct reciprocity in the relations between Austria and Italy regarding minorities, by contrast with the Danish-German, Italian-Slovene or Austrian-Slovene situation with respective groups in both States. After both world wars, Austria had to recognise that external self-determination for South Tyrolean German speakers was not feasible. Thus, it insisted on territorial and legislative autonomy as well as on minority protection, which can be considered the price for the guarantee of Italy's territorial claims. It was the bilateral De Gasperi-Gruber Agreement that created a real obligation for Italy vis-à-vis Austria.[13]

Austria's attempts of support for the implementation of the principles laid out in the De Gasperi-Gruber Agreement were rejected by Italy, which insisted on these issues being a domestic matter.[14] However, Austria succeeded in bringing the dispute to the attention of the UN General Assembly, which adopted two resolutions,[15] calling both parties to resume negotiations and to resolve all differences regarding the implementation of the Paris Treaty, thereby establishing that this was not solely an internal Italian affair. But the implementation of the autonomy agreement was an Italian obligation regarding its domestic sphere leaving Austria with a monitoring role. Once the negotiations had begun, the 'soft' pressure from the 'protecting power' Austria certainly contributed to keeping Italy's interests in the fulfilment of its obligations alive.[16] However, formal insistence on the international character of the autonomy did more harm than good: only when both Italy and Austria became more flexible and pragmatic in their respective positions did success, i.e. a well-working autonomy in South Tyrol, become possible.

The internationalisation before the UNGA and the subsequent bilateral (Italy–Austria) and triangular relations (plus consultations with the South Tyrolese) distinguish the South Tyrolean case from the Tibetan one, despite some resemblance to the '17-Point Agreement' and its unsatisfactory implementation.[17] In fact, after

13 Subsequently included in an annex to the multilateral Peace Treaty with Italy. See, for the international character and the bilateralisation of the conflict, the contributions by GEHLER, M. (1992) Vollendung der Bilateralisierung als diplomatisch-juristisches Kunststück. p. 17; HILPOLD, P. (1992) Der Südtiroler Weg völkerrechtlicher Stufenlösung im europäischen Vergleich. pp. 109 ff. Both in CLEMENTI, S. and WOELK, J. (eds) *Ende eines Streits. Zehn Jahre Streitbeilegung im Südtirolkonflikt zwischen Italien und Österreich*. Baden-Baden: Nomos.

14 In May 1955, the occupation of Austria ended and with the State Treaty concluded with the Allied Powers it became fully independent within the frontiers of 1 January 1938, which were guaranteed by the Allied Powers. This guarantee removed any doubt regarding South Tyrol, which would definitively remain with Italy.

15 VII Resolution 1497 (XV), 31 October 1960 and Resolution 1661 (XVI), 28 November 1961.

16 In its declaration on conflict settlement (5 June 1992), the Austrian Parliament underlined once again Austria's continuous monitoring role as well as the possibility of submitting future disputes to the International Court of Justice in case of gross violations.

17 The similarities exist, in fact, only at first sight: both are bilateral agreements, but apart from the pressure of an agreement signed in a moment of occupation and China not being a democratic

having to acknowledge that the 'first autonomy' was not accepted by the local population, Italy and Austria began looking for a renewed compromise, on the basis of the principles of the original agreement.[18] The Italian Government now directly involved also the local population: in 1961, it established a commission of 19 members (11 Italians, seven South Tyrolean German speakers and one Ladin speaker) in order to conduct an inquiry and draw up proposals for a solution. The commission's report, released in 1964, became the basis for subsequent negotiations on various levels: between the Governments of Austria and Italy, within the Italian Government, between the Italian Government and representatives from the Region and the Province, etc. These negotiations benefitted from the more tolerant political climate in Italy with centre-left governments (in particular under Aldo Moro) and ultimately resulted in the adoption of a compromise in 1969.

Known as 'the Package of measures in favour of the population of South Tyrol', the compromise consists of 137 administrative and legislative measures to be adopted in order to reform and to expand South Tyrolean autonomy. Ninety-seven of these measures concerned amendments to the Autonomy Statute of 1948, transforming its substance into a 'new' or 'Second' Autonomy Statute. A road map, an 18-stage 'operational calendar' was added, setting a time line for implementation measures. And once the Package would be fully implemented, Austria was to formally declare the end of the dispute before the United Nations. Apart from Austria's involvement, at local level the approval by South People's Tyrolean Party, representing the majority of the population and close to all German speakers, made the compromise possible.[19] This is important as it guaranteed the necessary local support without a referendum, which would have most probably split the population (and created dividing lines even within the groups).

The basic innovative principles of the Package are: (1) the creation of two autonomous Provinces (South Tyrol and Trentino) within the Autonomous Region of Trentino, South Tyrol with broad legislative and administrative powers previously reserved to the State or the Region transferred to the Provinces; (2) the principles of ethnic proportionality and linguistic parity to be applied to employment in all State and semi-State bodies in the autonomous Province of South Tyrol, with the exception of the military and the national police forces.

State, Tibetans lack a kin State which could have supported their claims and position in the international arena. Instead of a legal document becoming the international anchoring and core of the autonomy, like in the South Tyrolean case, the '17-Point Agreement' is rather political in character and – due to the flaws in implementation – disappointing in the result.

18 Although their (positive or negative) influence is still controversial (see note 12), the terrorist bombings in South Tyrol in the early 1960s created rising pressure and an urgent need for finding a solution.

19 Both Package and operational calendar were approved by the Parliaments of Italy (4 December 1969) and Austria (16 December 1969). Before this (on 22 November 1969), a narrow 53.4 per cent majority had already supported the compromise during an extraordinary Congress of the South Tyrolean People's Party in Meran/Merano.

It is difficult to qualify the nature of the Package: in legal terms, it is not an international treaty itself. In fact, Italy insisted that its international obligations regarding the South Tyrolean autonomy had already been fulfilled with the (unsatisfying) implementation of the De Gasperi-Gruber Agreement. Keeping any further concession strictly within its domestic legal sphere, any intervention from the Austrian side was to be excluded, even in case of future amendments. Understandably, Austria disagreed, but nevertheless participated in the adoption of a – political – compromise. Thus, ambiguity and controversy remained. However, the compromise is much more than a mere gentlemen's agreement: Italy expected Austria to stop any activity at the international level after the compromise and to wait (and trust) the fulfilment of all measures. According to the *estoppel* principle, a party, which has gained from the advantages of trust-based behaviour of another party, cannot justify different behaviour with the absence of a true obligation under international law.[20]

Future disputes on the implementation of the Package between Italy and Austria can be submitted to the jurisdiction of the International Court of Justice (ICJ) in The Hague because of the respective formulation in the UN Resolution of 1960, which expressly recommends the consideration of such a submission in case of unsatisfactory results of negotiations.[21] However, despite the long duration needed for full implementation (20 years, until 1992), not a single case has been taken to the ICJ.[22] This proves that negotiation, compromise and trust-building measures had achieved the effect of providing a sound basis for the elaboration of the details of implementation.

To a considerable extent, success depended also on the wider context: a compromise had not been actively sought during the 1950s and 1960s due to the Cold War and because of Italian domestic politics. It is also no coincidence that the reform of the Autonomy Statute took place in 1972, in the context of general decentralisation and fully unfolding regionalisation of Italy. At that time, the 15 ordinary regions were effectively established, thus completing the regional system as designed in Italy's Constitution of 1948.[23] Another positive influence was the progress in European integration: the democratisation of Central and Eastern

20 HILPOLD, P. (2003) Der Südtiroler Weg völkerrechtlicher Stufenlösung im europäischen Vergleich. In CLEMENTI and WOELK (1992), above note 13, pp. 109–117 (pp. 110 ff.). Of course, a violation of this principle is much more difficult to prove than a violation of a clearly formulated obligation in an international treaty.

21 VII Resolution 1497 (XV), 31 October 1960 (point 2).

22 The two countries also agreed to conclude an Austrian–Italian treaty of friendship and cooperation of a general nature, i.e. going beyond the issue of South Tyrolean autonomy: see Article 18 of the operational calendar. In the end, such a treaty was never concluded; today, both parties being Member States of the European Union, it is probably no longer necessary.

23 See, for the interrelations between the evolution of South Tyrolean autonomy and Italian regionalism, WOELK, J. (2013) South Tyrol Is (Not) Italy: A Special Case in a (De)federalizing System. *L'Europe en formation, Revue d'études sur la construction européenne et le fédéralisme/Journal of Studies on European Integration and Federalism*. 3. pp. 126–137.

Europe gave a new and final momentum to the solution of the conflict by completely changing its security dimension. The prospect of Austria's EU membership at the beginning of the 1990s accelerated the final conclusion of the implementation of the 'Package': in 1992, Austria and Italy declared their conflict formally settled by handing over a declaration to the UN Secretary General; in 1995, Austria joined the European Union.[24]

2.2 *Bilateral negotiation as a permanent principle for implementation and beyond*

In order to keep a constructive dialogue alive during the implementation phase, thus building up trust and confidence, the implementation process innovatively relies on procedures for bilateral negotiations between State and Province(s). Peculiar institutions have been created, in which the representatives of the State and the Province as well as the major linguistic groups have equal number and standing in order to avoid dominance by one side or one group.[25]

The most important functional elements are two joint commissions formed specifically for consultation on the details of implementation of the autonomy statute (i.e. a basic law with constitutional rank). Article 107 of the Autonomy Statute of 1972 (ASt) provides for its implementation by legislative decree; elaborated by the government and adopted in the form of a Presidential Decree. Bypassing Parliament and the ordinary political process, two consultative bodies, the joint commissions, are involved in the process of drafting these decrees: the so-called Commissions of Six (for the Autonomous Province of Bolzano/South Tyrol, only) and of Twelve (where powers of the Region are involved). Although similar joint commissions exist in all five Autonomous Regions of Italy, only in Trentino, South Tyrol have they become the pivotal institutions of the whole autonomy system, in terms of numbers of adopted decrees, as well as going beyond their consultative mandate acting *de facto* as a forum of negotiation between State and Region/Province.[26]

Their pivotal role is due to their peculiar composition: besides the Commission (of Six) acting as a joint organ of State and Province, it also represents both major linguistic groups in the Province: the Commission of Six is composed of three members nominated by the State (including at least one German member) and

24 See in particular CLEMENTI and WOELK (1992), above note 13.

25 Consultative bodies are a recent and frequent phenomenon in the field of minority protection: in particular, Councils of National Minorities have been established in nearly all Central and South-Eastern European States for representing the interests of groups vis-à-vis authorities.

26 Autonomy Statute of Trentino-South Tyrol, Art. 107. Cf. Arts 43 ASt (Autonomy Statute) Sicily, 56 ASt Sardinia, 65 ASt Friuli-Venezia Giulia and 48 *bis* ASt of Aosta-Valley. Whereas in the XIII legislature the Italian Government has adopted twenty-three enactment decrees for the Autonomous Region Trentino-South Tyrol and the autonomous province of Bolzano/South Tyrol, respectively, it has adopted only six for Friuli-Venezia Giulia, four for Sardinia and three for Sicily.

three members nominated by the Province (including at least one Italian speaker; Article 107 paragraph 2). This provision can only be considered as recognition of the ethnically plural character of both, State and Province, in conformity with the Constitution (Articles 6 and 116) and the constitutional rank of the Autonomy Statute and its Article 2.[27]

In practice, this procedure is very similar to international diplomatic negotiations where, despite all differences among them in the real world, States are formally put on the same level. Of course, differences in position, power, resources and economic strength do exist between the parties and this will influence the negotiations. However, during the negotiations the legal fiction of equal standing of both delegations is maintained, favouring the joint search for compromise and agreement and excluding unilateral imposition of a solution; this peculiar arrangement has been characterised as a 'quasi-federal' element distinguishing the special autonomy from the other, ordinary regions in Italy.[28]

Although formally established as a consultative body of the Italian Government and designed to be of a technical nature, the South Tyrolean Commission of Six gradually transformed into an autonomous political body for bilateral negotiations between State and Province.[29] In practice, the Commission of Six has gradually taken on the role of drafting the enactment decrees, which are subsequently adopted by the government in the form of presidential and/or legislative decrees. This important development and the special nature of the enactment decrees (as a 'negotiated source of law') have been confirmed in various decisions by the Italian Constitutional Court.[30]

3. Innovative solutions: Treating different situations differently

Differentiation is at the same time recognition of the diversity of a peculiar situation requiring specific reactions as well as an instrument for its integration into

27 Art. 2 Autonomy Statute of Trentino-South Tyrol: 'In the region, all citizens are granted equal rights regardless of the linguistic group to which they belong, and their respective ethnic and cultural characteristics are safeguarded.'

28 PALERMO, F. (2012) Italy: a Federal Country Without Federalism? In BURGESS, M. and TARR, G.A. (eds), *Constitutional Dynamics in Federal Systems – Sub-national Perspectives*. Montreal & Kingston, London, Ithaca, NY: McGill-Queen's University Press. pp. 237–254.

29 The members representing the Province are nominated by the Provincial Assembly, in which the South Tyrolean People's Party occupies more than a simple majority of the seats. The fact that the Commission's members include lawyers, prominent local politicians and even members of the Italian Parliament strengthened the Commission's political legitimacy in negotiations and thus its political role and weight as the central institution for coordination and negotiation between State and Province. Moreover, the active involvement of its representatives made it increasingly difficult for the Italian Government to treat the outcome of negotiations as mere non-binding opinions.

30 See the references in PALERMO, F. (2008) South Tyrol's Special Status within the Italian Constitution. In WOELK et al., above note 1, pp. 33–49.

the wider context. Differentiated treatment of Trentino, South Tyrol compared to other situations and regions in Italy has been another important feature for success. Particularly innovative were, at the time of the compromise in the late 1960s, the peculiar tripolar and asymmetrical institutional structure and the specific mix of (territorial and personal) principles for the protection of minorities.

In 1972, the implementation of the 'Package' elevated the two Provinces, South Tyrol and Trentino, to the rank of autonomous Provinces, transferring nearly all important legislative and administrative powers of the Autonomous Region of Trentino, South Tyrol to them. This institutional innovation left the Region as a mere 'roof structure' and transformed the Provinces into the main institutional actors which – gradually – came to exercise all substantial powers, autonomously transforming the German speakers finally into a local majority able to determine the exercise of the autonomous powers. The adoption of the 'new' or 'second' Autonomy Statute in 1972 can therefore be considered a 'second constituent moment'.[31]

The current structure is both symmetrical and asymmetrical at the same time. It is asymmetrical as there are no other autonomous Provinces in Italy (and these are not even foreseen in the Constitution itself).[32] It is innovative and symmetrical, in substantial terms, because Trentino and South Tyrol can be considered in many respects as equal to (autonomous) Regions, as in Italy only Regions are vested with legislative powers. Symmetry also applies as both autonomous Provinces have the same legislative and executive powers. Beyond the powers of territorial governance, the institutional structure within the Region is again asymmetrical, as special provisions regarding minority protection and the relations between the linguistic groups only apply to South Tyrol, thereby establishing a system of consociational democracy (or power sharing) in accordance with the principles of cultural autonomy, linguistic parity and ethnic proportionality.[33]

Of course, this different use of symmetrical and asymmetrical features has been favoured by Italy's two-track regional system, which from its origins in 1948 foresees a distinction in status and powers between five autonomous or 'special' Regions and ordinary Regions (Article 116).[34] Differentiation and asymmetry have

31 In reality, although formally no new Statute had been adopted, so many provisions of the 'first' one of 1948 had been amended that in terms of substantial change the Statute is 'new' (which was important for obvious political reasons); among the 137 measures of the 'Package', more than eighty concerned amendments to the autonomy statute.

32 The legal basis for the establishment of autonomous Provinces is the specific act of legislation, the Autonomy Statute which has constitutional rank and can therefore derogate from other legislation, including the Constitution.

33 See WOELK, J. (2002) *Reconciliation Impossible or (Only) Undesirable? South Tyrolean Experiences.* Austrian Ministry for Education, Science and Culture Peace Project: *Universities Researching for Society: Peace and the Avoidance of Violence.* [Online] November 2002. Available at: www.alexanderlanger.org/it/178/936 [Accessed:14 February 2017].

34 Reminiscent to some extent of the People's Republic of China's system of differentiated territorial governance.

later been confirmed also concerning the minority-protection regime: Act 482/1999 'on the protection of historical linguistic minorities' provides for a common set of rights, but applies differently to different territories, according to the needs and preferences expressed and activated by the local population.[35] Creating different situations and levels of protection as well as of autonomy in territorial governance is thus a general characteristic feature of the Italian constitutional system in terms of cultural and territorial pluralism. However, only the innovative element of pragmatically creating two autonomous Provinces as 'sub-regions' has made a solution of the historical conflict possible.

4. Complex power sharing in South Tyrol: Anticipating the Common European Framework for the living together of groups and territorial government

The system of 'complex power sharing'[36] in South Tyrol is characterised by a combination of minority rights based upon the personal principle – for the protection of persons and linguistic groups – and the territorial principle (i.e. related to the self-government of an area in which specific rules apply). This has led to a unique institutional mix and balance of different principles. Its main elements are the three categories of rights – equality, minority rights, territorial governance and powers – as well as power sharing related to the territorial governance of the area (integrated in Italy's regional system). The system of minority protection based upon the 'Package' compromise and established in 1972 through amendments to the Autonomy Statute has anticipated many elements of the European system created in the 1990s,[37] as a reaction to the Balkan wars and the situation in the

35 Act No. 482 of 15 December 1999 'on the protection of historical linguistic minorities' (text available in English from: www.usenglishfoundation.org/view/336 [Accessed: 14 February 2017]), for comments, see, e.g. ANDEVA, M. (2013) Accommodating Minority Groups: The Politics of Minorities' Protection in Italy. *New Balkan Politics*. [Online]. pp. 111–125. Available at: www.newbalkanpolitics.org.mk/item/Accommodating-minority-groups:the-politics-of-minorities%E2%80%99-protection-in-Italy#.VsCwd_nhDIU [Accessed: 14 February 2017]. Art. 18 of Act 482/1999 provides that the Act does not apply to Autonomous Regions and Provinces, at least where a higher level of protection is provided by the respective Autonomy Statutes or specific principles are implemented by special enactment decrees.

36 The term has been used, in relation to South Tyrol, by WOLFF, S. (2008) Complex Power Sharing as Conflict Resolution. In WOELK et al., above note 1, pp. 329–370 (definition of 'Complex Power Sharing' and further references, p. 330, note 3).

37 Europe's multi-level framework of provisions on minority protection consists of various interrelated layers which influence each other: at European level, within the Council of Europe, there are the Framework Convention on National Minorities (FCNM, 1995) and the European Charter on Regional and Minority Languages (ECRL, 1992), as well as some provisions of the European Convention on Human Rights which can be useful for minority groups, such as freedom of thought and non-discrimination. At the national level, most Member States of the Council of Europe have specific legislation regarding minority groups in force, complemented by even more specific

Baltic Republics. Subsequently, the principles established at European level have, in turn, strongly influenced the domestic systems of the ratifying States leading to the adoption of progressive legislation,[38] even where compliance with these rules was not required as a precondition for obtaining something else, i.e. conditionality for advancing toward European integration in the pre-accession process.

Despite a general trend toward decentralisation and devolution,[39] the same convergence cannot yet be observed with regard to regional autonomy in Europe. Territorial governance remains one of the important domains of State sovereignty and the great variety of different solutions demonstrates this clearly. This is particularly true for regional government. However, starting from the level of local government, the Congress of Local and Regional Authorities in Europe has, amongst other actors, created a framework of commonly accepted, legally binding principles exerting influence (although admittedly weaker in the field of regional democracy).[40]

The European multilateral instruments on minority protection and local and regional self-government have been adopted long after the compromise in the South Tyrolean case had been reached.[41] In the following paragraphs, the essential elements of the South Tyrolean autonomy system shall be examined, confronting them with the current situation under the multilateral instruments.

regulations at regional and/or local level. From general principles and widely framed provisions, these rules usually become more detailed and concrete the closer the level of government is to the concerned groups and the areas of their residence.

38 An interesting example is Italy itself which ratified the FCNM in 1998 and only then adopted legislation 'on the protection of historical linguistic minorities' (Act 482/1999) for the whole country, thus finally implementing, with a delay of nearly five decades, Art. 6 of the Italian Constitution which calls, since 1948, for 'appropriate measures [to be taken] to safeguard linguistic minorities'.

39 As it is immediately clear looking at the processes which have transformed Spain, Belgium and the United Kingdom, as well as, to a minor extent, other European States over the last decades; see the chapters on Spain and the United Kingdom in this volume.

40 In 1985, the European Charter of Local Self-Government (ECLSG, ETS 142) was adopted as a multilateral, binding treaty; it is nowadays ratified by all forty-seven Member States of the Council of Europe and can thus be considered a common denominator. See the brief overview by HIMSWORTH, C.M.G. (2011) Treaty-Making for Standards of Local Government: The European Charter of Local Self-Government and Its Possible Application Beyond Europe. University of Edinburgh School of Law Working Paper No. 2011/24. 4 October 2011. [Online]. Available at: http://papers.ssrn.com/sol3/papers.cfm?abstract_id=1938255 [Accessed: 14 February 2017], and the website of the Congress (www.coe.int/t/congress/default_en.asp). The planned adoption, based upon the experience of the ECLSG and drawing from its principles, of a similar Charter of Regional Self-Government did not succeed, however, and only a soft law instrument was adopted in 2009: 'The Reference Framework for Regional Democracy'. Available at: https://wcd.coe.int/ViewDoc.jsp?id=1962521&Site=COE [Accessed: 14 February 2017].

41 In fact, the ECRML was adopted in 1992, the FCNM in 1995. In 1992, Austria and Italy declared their conflict formally settled by handing over a declaration to the UN Secretary General; see, in particular, CLEMENTI and WOELK (1992), above note 13.

4.1 Equality and non-discrimination

According to Article 2 ASt: 'In the Region the equality of rights of citizens is recognised, regardless of the linguistic group to which they belong, and respective ethnic and cultural characteristics shall be safeguarded.' While the first part refers to the equality principle, understood in formal terms, and to its reverse side, i.e. anti-discrimination, the second part expressly calls for taking factual differences into account, thus allowing for special measures in order to create equality also in substantial terms.[42] Article 4 of the Framework Convention on National Minorities (FCNM) contains a similar distinction between and combination of formal and substantial equality highlighting their complementary role; it also opens to promotional measures in favour of the minority members in order to guarantee full and effective equality with those belonging to the majority.[43] Non-discrimination is further strengthened by the European Convention on Human Rights (ECHR) as a principle (Article 14 ECHR and Additional Protocol No. 12 (2000)), which can be directly invoked in case of disregard by State authorities; it is thus an important means for members of minority groups who directly file a claim to the European Court of Human Rights after exhausting domestic legal remedies.

4.2 Minority rights

Historically, the term 'minority' relates to the relationship between distinct groups of population vis-à-vis the majority of the State; it denotes power relations and different status. Consequently, in South Tyrol (and later also in Trentino),[44] the term 'language group' is used for all groups residing in the territory independently from their numerical strength in order to underline the institutional equality and equal dignity of these groups and their members. Consequently, 'minority rights' as guaranteed in international instruments, such as language and other rights laid down in Articles 7 to 18 FCNM, apply to members of the language groups on the

42 See WOELK, J. (2009) Individual and Group Rights in South Tyrol: Article 2 as '*Grundnorm*' of the Autonomy Statute. In WOELK et al., above note 1, pp. 203–218.

43 Positive or affirmative action measures, aiming at redressing discrimination, are consequently expressly mentioned as not discriminatory in Art. 4.2 FCNM.

44 In 2001, amendments to the Autonomy Statute (Art. 4 Const. Law 2/2001) introduced some principles of minority protection also for Trentino. For the three small language groups there – Ladins, Mocheni and Cimbri – a Provincial Law (No. 6, 2008) provides for a differentiated and very detailed framework of guarantees; itself a model case for the protection and promotion of small and smallest communities. See PENASA, S. (2014) From Protection to Empowerment through Participation: The Case of Trentino – a Laboratory for Small Groups. *Journal on Ethnopolitics and Minority Issues in Europe (JEMIE)*. [Online] 13(2). pp. 30–53. Available at: www.ecmi.de/fileadmin/downloads/publications/JEMIE/2014/Penasa.pdf [Accessed: 14 February 2017].

basis of the personal principle, i.e. individual choice of the group members (in conformity with Article 3 FCNM).[45]

Numerous rights are daily practice in South Tyrol, ranging from guaranteed participation in the political sphere (for example, minimum presence in executive bodies, presidents and vice-presidents from different groups and rotation of speakers in assemblies), to language rights (for example, use of language in public, in communications with public administration and authorities, as well as in courts) and cultural rights (in particular education and media), but also include socio-economic rights (quota system for proportional representation of the groups according to their demographic strength in the public administration and even in the judiciary; similar proportional distribution of resources in the area of social housing).[46]

The guarantees for linguistic groups and their members in South Tyrol correspond to the principal minority rights in international treaties and Recommendations.[47] However, they still show a strong emphasis on separate regulation and management within the groups' responsibility (for example, the three separate school systems according to Article 19 ASt),[48] even though there is a statutory duty of teaching the other language from the second year at latest. Separation in the educational sector is usually explained as a reaction to the traumatic experience of German being banned completely from school during Fascism. In other contexts, separation is increasingly criticised by international organisations as it prevents students from getting to know each other, and intercultural dialogue.[49]

4.3 Territorial governance and powers

South Tyrol's autonomous powers are quite outstanding, not only when compared to other minority situations, but even with regard to its Northern neighbour Tyrol,

45 For members of the smallest group in South Tyrol, the choice is often limited by the territorial principle to the municipalities in which most members of that group reside.

46 See the respective chapters (Part III. Minority Rights) in WOELK et al. (2008), above note 1, pp. 203–299.

47 In particular, to the Framework Convention on National Minorities (FCNM), the European Charter for Regional and Minority Languages (ECRL) and the Recommendations of the OSCE High Commissioner on National Minorities.

48 See, for a brief description of the school system in South Tyrol, BAUR, S. and MEDDA-WINDISCHER, R. (2008) The Educational System in South Tyrol. In WOELK et al., above note 1, pp. 235–258. Despite the separate organisation in schools in German and Italian (as well as Ladin) language, parents can choose which school they prefer for their children, knowledge of the language provided. Nowadays, there are numerous 'experiments' of cooperation and exchange in the school sector, including a strong increase in the number of hours taught in the 'other' language, just below the threshold of a bilingual school.

49 For instance, in Bosnia and Herzegovina, where the policy of 'two schools under one roof' in the Federation is heavily criticised as segregation based upon the ethnicity of children, see TOLOMELLI, A. (2015) 'Two Schools under One Roof'. The Role of Education in the Reconciliation Process in Bosnia and Herzegovina. *Ricerche di Pedagogia e Didattica – Journal of Theories and Research in Education.* 10(1). pp. 89–108.

a member state of federal Austria. Generally, the provincial powers relate to economic, cultural and social matters; legislative powers are exercised by the Provincial Council (assembly). Exclusive competences can be freely exercised while respecting the Constitution, international obligations and the basic principles of the Italian legal system, as well as fundamental principles of socio-economic reforms.[50] Provincial legislation in further matters (secondary legislative powers) also had to respect the ordinary laws of Italy. After the declaration of conflict settlement in 1992, the Autonomous Province in negotiations with the Italian centre-left governments obtained the devolution of a large number of additional competences (for example, roads, electricity, teachers and school staff), not foreseen and guaranteed in the Autonomy Statute.

The provisions regarding legislative and executive powers apply to both Autonomous Provinces in the same way, while further special provisions regarding the relations between the three linguistic groups apply to South Tyrol alone. Furthermore, the institutions in the Autonomous Province and their functions are identical to the general scheme of territorial government in Italy;[51] however, there are specific requirements for the representation of the groups in the composition of the institutions according to the power-sharing model. The regulatory power vis-à-vis municipalities, generally exercised by the State creating a triangular relationship between State, Region and municipalities, is vested with the Autonomous Region permitting a direct relationship and making derogations from the national framework of territorial government possible (for example, there has been a reform of the intermediate bodies).

Specific guarantees of financial resources complete the picture, making it possible to use the powers effectively. While ordinary Regions are completely dependent on State transfers, the more generous funding of the Autonomous Regions, corresponding to more competences, is guaranteed in their Autonomy Statutes reaching a share of more than 90 per cent of tax revenue raised in the Region in the case of Trentino, South Tyrol (Articles 70, 71 and 75 ASt). In addition, the Autonomy Statute contains two fundamental principles governing financial relations between State and Autonomous Region/Provinces: complete budgetary freedom in the field of expenditure, while tax collection remains the responsibility of the State; no change can be made to the financial system without agreement between Province(s) and State. Thus, the price for flexibility is, again, negotiation with protection for the weaker part (necessity of an agreement). In 2009, Italy has reformed the financial relations between State and Regions, implementing Article 119 Const. (2001, on fiscal federalism). While the autonomous Provinces of Trentino and South Tyrol are still subject to differentiated treatment

50 The 'national interest' of Italy may be a limit, too, but – as a counter-limit – it is expressly stated that this national interest 'includes the protection of local linguistic minorities' (Autonomy Statute, Art. 4).

51 Also, the judiciary is structured in the same way as in the rest of Italy, but there exists a separate order for the judicial staff.

also in the financial sphere,[52] they have concluded a bilateral agreement with the State (Milan Agreement, November 2009) taking over new powers from the State without additional resources for their exercise; as a consequence, they will not be included in a general financial equalisation mechanism among Italy's regions.[53]

In the absence of binding international provisions on regional autonomy, territorial arrangements with the purpose of minority protection are specifically addressed in a soft-law document elaborated by independent experts for the High Commissioner on National Minorities: the OSCE Lund Recommendations (19–21);[54] these guidelines for good practice highlight the need of sufficiently guaranteeing the minority's influence in the exercise of legislative and executive powers.[55] This is guaranteed in South Tyrol through the fact that German speakers are a local majority as well as through mechanisms of power sharing which also include the other two linguistic groups (see below). From a comparative perspective, the South Tyrolean autonomy arrangements can certainly be qualified as best practice. [56]

4.4 Power sharing

Due to its legal entrenchment and reliance on strong legal guarantees, the complex and highly differentiated system in South Tyrol has been characterised as 'tolerance through law'.[57] The emphasis placed upon legal guarantees is particularly evident in the relations between the groups. The South Tyrolean system shows all four structural elements of 'consociationalism' or power sharing:[58] (1) participation of all groups in government – for example, grand coalition; (2) a high degree of

52 Act 42/2009 on fiscal federalism does not apply to Autonomous Regions (Art. 27).

53 See, on financial relations in particular, BENEDIKTER, T. (2008) South Tyrol's Financial System. In WOELK et al., above note 1, pp. 105–119.

54 See text of Lund Recommendations, available at: www.osce.org/hcnm/32240?download=true [Accessed: 14 February 2017]. Also, the European Charter on Local Self-Government (1985, ETS 142) and the Reference Framework for Regional Democracy provide standards which might apply to territorial self-governance structures, insofar as these are part of territorial government, independent from the fact that they might have been established for the purpose of guaranteeing a more effective protection of minorities.

55 Paragraph 21: 'Where powers may be devolved on a territorial basis to improve the effective participation of minorities, these powers must be exercised with due account for the minorities within these jurisdictions. Administrative and executive authorities must be accountable to the whole population of the territory.'

56 See, for a comparative analysis and evaluation, the Recommendations 346(2013) of the Council of Europe's Chamber of Regions and the Explanatory Memorandum 'Regions and Territories with Special Status in Europe', CPR(25)2FINAL, 30 October 2013. Available at: https://wcd.coe.int/ViewDoc.jsp?id=2107887&Site=COE [Accessed: 14 February 2017].

57 WOELK et al. (2008), above note 1.

58 The concept as well as the four structural features go back to LIJPHART, A. (1977) *Democracy in Plural Societies*. New Haven, CT, London: Yale University Press. pp. 25–52, and have been further developed by the same author with a focus on accommodation of inter-ethnic relations, e.g. in LIJPHART, A. (2004) Constitutional Design for Divided Societies. *Journal for Democracy*. 15(2). pp. 96–109.

autonomy for the groups; (3) proportionality as the basic standard of political representation, public service, appointments and allocation of public funds; (4) minority veto for the protection of vital interests. In more detail, these elements are applied as follows:

(1) Participation of the representatives of all significant groups in the government, through jointly exercising governmental (and particularly executive) power, e.g. *grand coalition cabinet*:

According to the power-sharing model, the composition of the South Tyrolean Government must be proportional to the ethnic groups in the Council; the presidency of the Council rotates between members of the different groups.[59] This is certainly in line with the important but very generally framed provision regarding the guarantee of effective participation for minorities in public affairs, Article 15 FCNM.

(2) A high degree of *autonomy for the groups* (especially for issues which are not of common concern):

Autonomy for groups must not be confused with territorial autonomy; while the latter is granted to the Province as territorial entity (and consequently to the whole population residing in the Province) vis-à-vis the State, the former applies to the groups within the entity. The principle of cultural autonomy is established by Article 2 ASt, which states that the parity of rights of citizens of all language groups is recognised, and 'their ethnic and cultural characteristics are protected'. The provisions for the protection and promotion of cultural characteristics, including the system of separated schools, are typical means of cultural autonomy of the groups. Cultural autonomy is in line with international instruments;[60] however, separation is increasingly criticised by international organisations, in particular in the educational sphere.[61]

(3) *Proportionality* as the basic standard of *political representation, public service*, appointments and allocation of public funds:

The Autonomy Statute provides for a system of proportional representation of the language groups for public employment[62] and for the allocation of

59 The Provincial Government has to include a minimum number of Italian speakers (Art. 50); the president is a German speaker, the vice-president an Italian speaker. The same is prescribed for local authorities (Arts 61 and 62). A rotation of the chairperson of the Assembly after half of the term guarantees equality of the two major groups (Art. 48ter).

60 See, for instance, OSCE Lund Recommendations (17 and 18).

61 For instance, recently vis-à-vis Bosnia and Herzegovina, e.g. in OSCE reports criticising the 'Two schools under one roof' policy (see above), as well as in Opinions of the Venice Commission on ethnic quotas in general and in the judiciary in particular.

62 The principle of ethnic proportions, which has to be applied (in the form of earmarked posts) to all State and semi-State bodies operating in the Province (Art. 89 ASt), as well as to the provincial

funds for cultural activities of the groups, as well as for social welfare and services (i.e. housing), which has been consistently upheld by the Italian Constitutional Court. It is also generally consistent with Article 4 paragraph 3 FCNM, according to which positive actions shall not be considered as an act of discrimination; however, pursuing the aim of re-establishing equal chances and redressing historical injustice, the permanent establishment of these measures may become problematic in terms of the (constitutional) proportionality principle.[63]

(4) *Minority veto* as the ultimate weapon for the protection of vital interests, i.e. issues of fundamental importance for the group:

The principles of equality of all residents, regardless of their group affiliation (Article 2 ASt), and the quasi group personality of the language groups counterbalance the provisions on proportional representation. This is particularly true for the right to request separate voting by the language groups in the Regional or Provincial Council: whenever a draft law is judged to be in violation of the parity of rights or the cultural characteristics of one group, councillors of one linguistic group (i.e. independent from their political affiliation) can exercise a temporary veto with a two-thirds majority vote. In case of overruling by the majority in the Council, the ultimate means available to the language groups is an action before the Constitutional Court, founded on the same motivation.[64] These are emergency mechanisms in case the normal means of consultation in the organs should not work. They have very rarely been applied in practice.[65]

administration (on the basis of provincial legislation), was introduced to gradually revert the Italian dominance in the public service. The representation of language groups in their respective proportions in all these areas were to be achieved within thirty years of the implementation of the second Autonomy Statute. In practically all sectors this has been achieved.

63 Differentiation is necessary: while positive action is widely accepted as an instrument, in the political sphere, the European Court of Human Rights has considered the permanent exclusion from the right to stand for election based upon non-membership of a group as discriminatory (*Sejdic-Finci* case, 21 December 2009). In a dynamic perspective, according to the Court, certain measures might be justifiable for ending a conflict, but cannot be upheld indefinitely.

64 Compared to the Belgian 'alarm bell procedure', which relies upon a political solution in its second stage (suspension in Parliament and search for compromise in the federal government, where Flemish and Walloons have an equal number of ministers, i.e. parity), the South Tyrolean arrangement relies, again, on a legal, judicial solution.

65 By contrast with other cases, in particular Bosnia and Herzegovina, where frequent use of different veto rights has practically paralysed the institutional system and could only be overcome by direct intervention of the International Community's High Representative making use of its powers of substitution ('Bonn Powers'). In South Tyrol, the German speakers have for decades supported the South Tyrolean People's Party, which until recently had an absolute majority of seats in the assembly and therefore did not need to use the veto.

In South Tyrol, there are no special cross-community voting requirements or double majorities, which have been introduced more recently in some cases – for example, Macedonia (2001) and Northern Ireland (1998). They also guarantee the protection of smaller groups against being outvoted, while placing the emphasis on reaching an inclusive majority rather than blocking decisions.

5. Dynamic evolution of the 'model'

There is no doubt that the settlement of the conflict through implementation of the amendments to the Autonomy Statute was a first and necessary step: Italy's German and Ladin minorities were no longer threatened by assimilation. However, time has passed and the over-institutionalisation of ethnicity as well as the technique of creating stability through separation is increasingly criticised:[66] good fences may make good neighbours, but social cohesion and cooperation within a territorial community, also across ethnic or linguistic cleavages, is nowadays considered a necessary precondition for any sustainable and durable solution.

Achieving a compromise solution accepted by the majority of all those concerned – Italy, Austria and the South Tyrolean German speakers – was certainly due to tolerance and goodwill on all sides. The same should be true for the gradual development toward a society more characterised by inter-ethnic interaction and cooperation. These elements are necessary for an inclusive democratic and pluralistic society; thus, they are also increasingly emphasised in instruments at European level adopted since the 1990s (for example, Article 6 paragraph 1 FCNM).[67]

Both foundations of South Tyrol's autonomy are still present today: minority protection and territorial self-government; however, with full implementation, different balances of the two principles are perceived and developing, with more emphasis on the latter. Autonomy is a dynamic process,[68] balances established in a certain situation and within a specific context can and must adapt, if their preconditions or circumstances change. Only those processes will inspire and maintain public confidence, which are inclusive of those concerned. As territorial arrangements not only concern the minority group (at least where different groups

66 Due to the unsatisfactory results in practice elsewhere, in the European context, in particular in Bosnia and Kosovo.

67 Art. 6.1 FCNM: 'The Parties shall encourage a spirit of tolerance and intercultural dialogue and take effective measures to promote mutual respect and understanding and co-operation among all persons living on their territory, irrespective of those persons' ethnic, cultural, linguistic or religious identity, in particular in the fields of education, culture and the media.'

68 After the formal settlement of the conflict in 1992, the South Tyrolean People's Party has declared the opening of a new phase: 'dynamic autonomy'; today, in the political debate, 'integral autonomy' is used as a catchword meaning a status just short of independence. These concepts are mostly related to requests for the transfer of ever-wider powers to the Province; much less intense is the discussion regarding changes and adaptations within the autonomous Province and regarding the relationships between the language groups, as well as between the latter and individuals.

live together in the same territory), but the whole population, a shared idea of the organisation of the entity is fundamental: functional criteria (for example, merit, knowledge of language) and conditions of tolerance, but also the perception and respect of pluralism as a basic value, play an important part in the development of such a shared idea.

It is exactly this change from an area in which one group needed special protection to a situation in which it can – together with the other groups – autonomously determine many issues, which best summarises the success of the South Tyrolean autonomy system. Despite the fact that 'internal self-determination' is usually seen as a second-best choice and despite all daily difficulties and future challenges, this has made the emergence of a kind of 'autonomy-patriotism' possible, which manifests itself in the provincial institutions hosting delegations from other countries, in particular minority representatives, explaining the South Tyrolean system.[69]

After the formal recognition of full implementation in 1992, the search for new objectives began: the autonomy had to be consolidated and extended. From concentration on internal issues, such as implementation, the focus now shifted to the context in which the autonomy is placed, i.e. European integration and the Italian political and constitutional system.

Thus, after 1992, South Tyrol has become increasingly aware of the opportunities and challenges of multi-level integration within the European Union,[70] but also of potential risks for Regions. The open borders and Austria's membership are certainly huge advantages for a peripheral territory. Inter-regional networking and cross-border cooperation are additional opportunities: together with Trentino and Austrian Tyrol a joint representation office is run in Brussels and for intensifying cross-border cooperation between the three entities, in 2011 a 'Euro region' has been established as a European Group of Territorial Cooperation (EGTC).[71] However, besides capacity and resource problems for small Regions, it is hardly possible for Autonomous Regions to represent or defend their specific interests at national or European level, where the logic of the internal market and the imperative of uniform application of EU Law limit the sphere of regional differentiation and autonomous decisions.[72]

69 Visits to South Tyrol included those by delegations of the Tibetan Government in Exile; a kind of informal 'network' has emerged for cooperation and exchange on issues related to minority protection and autonomy.

70 Not by chance, the formal settlement of the conflict between Italy and Austria was declared in 1992, the year of the signature of the Maastricht Treaty on the European Union. Celebrating the fortieth anniversary of the 'Second' Autonomy Statute, the Autonomous Province organised a conference dedicated entirely to the relations between Province and the European Union.

71 See the EGTC's website for further information (www.europaregion.info).

72 There are already three ECJ judgments regarding South Tyrol: while regulations related to linguistic rights (C-274/96, *Bickel/Franz*; C-281/98, *Angonese*) have been substantially upheld although they have to be extended to EU citizens, recently, the ECJ has struck down some provisions on social housing as discriminatory for resident immigrants (C-571/10, *Kamberaj*). The number of immigrants has grown rapidly since 2000 up to c. 9 per cent today.

In the last two decades, also the Italian context has changed considerably: Italy has struggled with federalisation trying to narrow the gap between ordinary and special Regions, most notably with the constitutional reforms of 1999 and 2001.[73] However, many improvements for (ordinary) Regions have been re-dimensioned and limited by flawed and slow implementation as well as by the conservative case law of the Constitutional Court. Regionalism has come under considerable strain for various reasons. The economic and political gap between Southern and Northern Regions has, at best, not diminished. Adding to the general crisis of Italy's political system, scandals about the abuse of public money for personal matters in numerous Regions made the regional political class appear as totally unreliable, incapable and without any legitimacy. The drastic financial cuts in the wake of the economic and financial crisis and unilateral intervention by the Monti government in 2012, and its successors, in the name of general consolidation of public finances, worsened the situation for regional autonomy. The Autonomous Regions are increasingly criticised for enjoying 'financial privileges'. In this general climate, the government of Matteo Renzi, in power since March 2014, has proposed a comprehensive constitutional reform which will weaken regionalism in Italy, in particular by further reducing regional legislative powers. Although this reform will not directly apply to Autonomous Regions and Provinces, it contains a provision requiring the adaptations of their Autonomy Statute 'by agreement' (i.e. respecting the bilateral relationship between State and Autonomous Regions/Provinces). What is to happen in case such agreement cannot be reached within a reasonable time is not clear, as there are no precedents for such a procedure. However, at the time of writing, it is also not certain, due to the complex procedure of constitutional amendment,[74] that the reform will actually be adopted and enter into force.

The limits of territorial autonomy in South Tyrol deriving from its context are highlighted by the mentioned developments and have triggered a debate on the prospects for the future.[75] Proposed options oscillate between 'full autonomy', in

73 Constitutional Laws 1/1999 (ordinary Regions) and 2/2001 (special Regions). In the subsequent constitutional reform (amendments of title V of the Constitution, related to relations between State and Regions), Art. 11 of Constitutional Law 3/2001 protected the Autonomous Regions by declaring only 'more favourable provisions' (compared to the autonomy statutes) applicable to them, introducing, however, a degree of uncertainty.

74 Article 138 Italian Constitution provides for the adoption by each House, after two successive debates at intervals of not less than three months and approval in each House by at least an absolute majority with the second vote. A popular referendum may be called for, if the second vote in each House has not reached a two-thirds majority.

75 This debate has become more intense with the generational change under way: Luis Durnwalder, South Tyrol's president for the last twenty-four years, and many other politicians as well as long-serving civil servants, have retired in the last two years. In addition, the November 2013 elections have further eroded the majority of the South Tyrolean People's Party (SVP) on which the political unity in the representation of the German speakers has been based and which for decades guaranteed a power monopoly (in 2013, the SVP remained by far the strongest party with seventeen

the sense of close to complete powers for the Province, including taxation, and a 'Free State' solution, following the aspirations of Scotland and Catalonia. 'Full autonomy' is proposed by the ruling South Tyrolean People's Party (SVP) in order to protect the autonomy system from negative external interferences, in particular in the financial sphere, while remaining – a more distinct – part of the larger Italian system. The alternative demand for independence as a 'Free State', proposed by right-wing German opposition parties, surprisingly excludes return to Austria and expressly includes the Italian population, which may even be interpreted as an indicator for the beginning of the development of an inclusive identity based upon the distinct character of the territory. Both competing visions will require, however, major reform and adaptation of the current Autonomy Statute. In this regard, the inclusion (and participation) of Italian speakers together with the other two language groups will be an important as well as necessary element in forging a new compromise updating the one of 1972.[76] In May 2015, the Provincial Council adopted an Act establishing a Convention on the reform of the Autonomy Statute, as an auxiliary organ to the Council, which will guarantee broad(er) citizens' involvement and participation in the reform process.[77]

6. From compromise to compact? Conclusive remarks

The general context of a controversy to be settled after the Second World War between two democratic States, Austria and Italy, which both respect human rights and the Rule of Law principle, as well as the beginning of European integration certainly favoured a sustainable solution in the South Tyrolean case. In particular, resort to wide-scale violence could be avoided. However, it is important to stress that the solution found actually anticipated the European multilateral instruments on minority protection, which were adopted long after that compromise had been reached.[78] Thus, parties had to engage in dialogue without being able to rely on pre-established solutions or rules. Creative thinking and innovative solutions were

seats and 45.7 per cent of votes, but failed to achieve the absolute majority it held over decades). Competing visions of the Province's future, including the status issue, are therefore an obvious way to challenge the SVP's dominance.

76 Obstacles on the way to such distinct territorial identity are the strict separation in the media and the political parties; in particular, the SVP still conceives itself as the representation of the German (and Ladin) speaking minority.

77 The Convention shall elaborate proposals for reform, which will be adopted by the Council (respecting its institutional monopoly). Eight of its thirty-two members are citizens representing a 'Forum of 100' citizens, which accompanies the Convention, facilitating civil society debate; citizens could freely apply for membership in the 'Forum of 100', representative selection regarding gender, age and language groups has been guaranteed. See website: https://www.konvent.bz.it [Accessed: 14 February 2017].

78 In fact, as mentioned above, the European Charter of Regional and Minority Languages (ECRML) was adopted in 1992, the Framework Convention on National Minorities (FCNM) in 1995.

of key importance. The devolution of legislative powers from the Autonomous Region to a new institutional category, the Autonomous Provinces (not foreseen in Italy's original constitutional design of territorial government, but created in 1972), has been the decisive innovative element for a – sustainable – solution.

Above all, the South Tyrolean case shows the importance of negotiation as a principle: it was the only way to a sustainable solution, i.e. accepted by all parts. Negotiation has remained central for the implementation period, during which trust could gradually be built up (through special bilateral channels of negotiation with the State in the joint commissions). Although the compromise was mostly brokered outside the area (by the Italian and Austrian Governments), the concerned minority group was included from the beginning, through consultation by both sides. This was fundamental for successful implementation as the minority is the majority in the autonomous territory and the arrangement will guarantee above all preservation of their cultural distinctiveness.

Full implementation meant the establishment of a distinct and special subsystem within the Italian legal and political system: during the gradual establishment of such a differentiated system, the Italian group realised the risk of marginalisation, i.e. becoming a minority within a minority. The system of Complex Power Sharing based upon separation with some inclusive features has in some areas come to be seen as too rigid for a dynamic evolution of the 'model' accepted and supported across the linguistic groups. Adaptation is needed due to societal change (where a relaxation of inter-ethnic relations can be observed – certainly a success of the autonomy system), but also due to external pressures from European integration and imminent Italian constitutional reform.

The pride in the success of South Tyrol's working autonomy, a kind of 'autonomy patriotism', may even lead, in the most optimistic perspective, to a new foundation for the autonomy agreement: this time from within, in the form of an agreement between the three linguistic groups on the adaptation of the provisions on the inter-group relations. This is currently attempted with the establishment of a Convention as a consultative body which will gather the citizens' perspectives and proposals in view of a reform of the Autonomy Statute. It remains to be seen whether this ambitious objective – a 'compact' on autonomy – can be realised and what the results of the Convention will be. Of course, such a compact on autonomy would truly mean an expression of 'internal' self-determination.

Chapter 7

Asymmetric regionalism in Spain

Catalonia and the Basque Country

Rafael Bustos Gisbert

1. Introduction

Let us state some starting points. I use the term 'Spanish federalism' rather than Spanish regionalism, because I mean a broader sense for federalism. Actually, I like better its comprehension, as Friedrich[1] described it more than half a century ago, as an historical process of decentralisation. That is, a dynamic process in which centripetal and centrifugal forces reach different and changing points of equilibrium in a constitutional framework that guarantees at the same time a territorial political self-government and the existence of a minimum central government.

In this sense, all federalisms can only be understood in historical terms. For any given federal framework, the question is not what the starting point is, but rather what are its limits and, thus, how far that framework will let self-government become a reality.

In an asymmetric federalism, the historical perspective is particularly important. Asymmetry is not a common feature of federalism. On the contrary, federal systems are commonly based in the substantial identity in nature and competences of their territorial components. We should not forget Article 79.III of the German Basic Law or the senatorial equal representation clause of the US Constitution. In both rules, the substantial identity of the territorial entities that compose the Federal State has the maximum guarantee. An 'eternity clause', in the German case, safeguards the statehood nature (*Staatlichkeit*) of the *Länder* and, thus, their identical position, as true States, in the federal system. A clause, only changeable under the consent of the entity concerned, guarantees that all the States in the federation will be treated equally in the Upper Chamber of the Legislative, in the case of the United States of America.

Asymmetry, thus, breaks some of the basic logic of traditional federalism (in particular, when regulating the participation of the component entities in federal decisions). Asymmetry evokes 'difference'. And that difference, to be accepted by

1 FRIEDRICH, C.J. (1968) *Trends of Federalism in Theory and Practice.* New York: Praeger.

the Union and the rest of its territorial components, must have deep historical roots (here is another important idea for Tibetan autonomy, the differences of the Tibetan people – historically proved – justify the search for an asymmetric decentralisation). But asymmetry may also raise certain kinds of problems which are not those of typical or traditional federalism.

2. Why is there a federal asymmetric system in Spain?

At first, it is not easy to define asymmetry and its reasons, and I will not even try to do so. A good way to find the reasons for asymmetry is to follow the structure and content of the 'Memorandum on Genuine Autonomy for the Tibetan People', Dharamsala, 16 November 2008.[2]

Eleven reasons are listed in the memorandum. Let us examine which ones could also be applied to Spain.

Language is one of the main reasons for asymmetry in Spain. The existence of four official languages in Spain is well known. And what is far more important, almost 25 per cent of Spaniards speak a language that is not '*castellano*' (Castilian-Spanish). The minority languages were prohibited in the long years of Franco's dictatorship (not the Gallego, though, Franco being a Galician himself), so any federal solution for Spain could not forget about the language particularities. Even today, more than thirty years since the approval of the Constitution, the 'language question' is not completely settled and conflicts still arise when regulating subjects such as the use of these regional languages in the judiciary or in public schools.

Culture is a main reason for asymmetry too. The cultural differences among Spanish territories are important. But the true cultural difference to be considered here is that one linked to the language difference which implies most of the relevant cultural particularities in Spain. In other words, culture is different in all the territories, but they live together without any special treatment (which may demand asymmetry) until the language problem arises. Where the cultural differences result from language difference, asymmetrical treatment is unavoidable.

Again, *education* is an important factor for the asymmetry which is linked to the cultural and language differences. Self-government must include the power to rule on education if a minority language and culture have to be preserved. This is a need only felt in those territories where this language is broadly spoken. Nevertheless, it is clear that the majoritarian language has to be properly taught in schools all around the country. Again, we can conclude that the finding of a point of equilibrium is not an easy task, but it is impossible to find it from a strict symmetrical point of view.

2 The Memorandum can be consulted at www.tibetoffice.ch/web/mwa/memorandum/ [Accessed: 14 February 2017].

Last, but not least, and connected to the cultural particularity, is what the memorandum calls '*cultural, educational and religious exchanges with other countries*'. On the one hand, there is no doubt that European frontiers do not respect cultural identities and, on the other, cultural particularities imply international exchanges with other countries and communities all around the world. Again, we can assure the presence of this factor in Spanish federalism. In our case, the search for a sort of *foreign policy* in some Spanish regions has been a constant over the years. The connections existing between the Spanish Basque Country (which is considered by the Basque nationalists as 'south Euskadi') with the French Basque Country (the so-called 'north Euskadi') are difficult to exaggerate. Something similar may be said about the links between Catalonia and other countries or regions (such as, obviously, Andorra, but also the Sardegna Island in Italy where Catalan is spoken) or the links between Andalucía and Morocco; or even between regions which in the past have fed the emigration to the states in Latin America.

Two other reasons should be emphasised which do not have any relation with cultural differences.

First, *public security* has been one of the special competences, i.e. recognised only in some regions in Spain. The reasons may be found in the identification of the police forces with fascist repression. In those places where that repression was harsher or, most probably, where that repression was extended to the political aspiration to self-government, after the regime change the new democratic police had to be a *regional police*. So, in the Basque Country where the fascist police committed serious offences in the repression of the separatist terrorism (which included tortures, unlawful detentions and even assassinations), it was impossible to maintain public security in the hands of the central authorities. Something similar can be said for Catalonia, where democratic ideas, the language or the search for autonomy had been seriously repressed in the last years of Franco's dictatorship.

Second, to some extent we may accept that there are some particularities in *economic development and trade*. The economic development of the Spanish regions was, and still is, not uniform. Some regions had strong economic development, while others had evident underdevelopment, due to agriculture, tourism and public expenditure being their only source of revenue. This unequal development produced important migration movements, inside Spain and abroad, in the 1950s, 1960s and 1970s. Madrid (the Spanish capital), Catalonia and the Basque Country were, and still are, the most developed regions and the beneficiaries of the migration movements that, in the case of Catalonia and Euskadi, put at risk the traditional way of life, culture and specific language. Today, the economic differences are still important between these three regions and the rest of Spain (although some regions have had a strong development in the last decades). This raises some important questions which may be summarised in problems related to which economic policies must be implemented when the territorial economic interests are so diverse, on the one hand, and those related to solidarity among regions, on the other. In any case, we must bear in mind that, again, Catalonia and the Basque Country have a very special position among Spanish regions.

Other reasons for asymmetry in the Memorandum cannot be applied to Spain: regulation of immigrant population, religion, national resources, public health or environment protection. These are not relevant reasons for different treatments among regions in Spain.

The full picture of Spanish asymmetrical federalism[3] needs to emphasise other relevant reasons for asymmetry. In a few words, four reasons can be summarised, most with deep historical roots.

First, due to historical reasons with deep roots in the medieval era – impossible to cover in this brief chapter, there are public law particularities in the Basque Country and in Navarra. These two regions are divided into *Foral* Territories (three in the Basque Country and one in Navarra, where a distinct set of mainly pre-modern rules is in force) which have their own particular legal regulation different from the other Spanish provinces. One of the main consequences of this situation affects the public finance system. In these two regions (Euskadi and Navarra), the public finance system is different from the rest of Spain. In both regions, for centuries the 'Foral' provinces had exercised the competence to collect taxes. After collection, the provinces negotiate with the central government as to how much will be transferred to the central powers to fund its expenditure. So, in these regions the public finance system works in the opposite way to how it is implemented in the rest of Spain, where the central government is the entity in charge of collecting taxes and, afterwards, distributing the financial resources among the Autonomous Communities (CC AA). This system, known as the '*concierto*' system, implies, as anyone can imagine, a strong financial advantage for these two regions.

Second, again due to historical reasons, there are important territorial differences in Civil Law. Some regions, in particular Catalonia, had important particularities in important civil matters. The codification process implemented in Spain during the nineteenth century (as in most European countries) was not fulfilled completely so long as important specialities survived in some territories (as in Catalonia) and were applied instead of the common rules included in the civil code.

Third, some geographical circumstances have been cited as a strong reason that had justified important differences in the past. This is the case regarding the Canary Islands and the autonomous cities of Ceuta and Melilla. With regard to the former, the Canary Islands are located next to the African coast, around 1,000 miles from the Iberian Peninsula. Ceuta and Melilla, on the other hand, are two small cities situated on the north coast of Africa, a vestige of the old colony in Morocco. In the past, these territories (the Canary Islands and both cities) had numerous different legal regulations – in particular, a special regulation regarding indirect taxation.

3 For a general explanation of the most important aspects in this topic, see AJA, E. (2007) *El Estado Autonómico: Federalismo y Hechos Diferenciales*. 2nd edn. Barcelona: Alianza.

Last, but probably most important, in some regions, there have been for many years influential political forces, with strong support in their respective societies, some defending clearly the independence of these regions, some sustaining a special relationship with Spain without demanding a complete secession. This is the case with the Basque Country or Catalonia, and less important in Galicia. These political forces were strongly repressed during General Franco's dictatorship, but never disappeared. During the transition to democracy, these forces were an important element in its success. Alongside these pro-independence forces, since 1978, other political forces have appeared to defend the speciality of their own regions in different places. We may call these the 'nationalist parties' (those defending independence or a special relationship with Spain) and the 'regionalist parties' (those who do not question the region belonging to Spain). The important point is the almost continuous victory of the nationalist parties in both Catalonia and the Basque Country. Only once have the nationalist parties not been present in the governmental majority in the Basque Country and never in the case of Catalonia (although in two elections the majoritarian nationalist party lost the elections against a coalition, which included an important pro-independence party).

Summarising the reasons for asymmetry in Spain, we can conclude that most of the differences listed in the Memorandum are clearly present in Catalonia and the Basque Country. But also, further reasons not listed and peculiar to Spain are present in those two regions. Moreover, both regions have been governed almost without interruptions by nationalist parties. It is easy to understand the importance of both CC AA in the definition of Spanish federalism.

A second conclusion can already be proposed: the Spanish territorial problem is the multinational integration in a federal system. Multinational, here, means the presence of important (historical, legal, economic, linguistic and political) differences in some territories that lead the system to exist in an asymmetric pattern.

3. The constitutional (no) solution

Remembering Montesquieu's 'Persian letters', Professor Cruz,[4] in 1981, proved how the Spanish Constitution did not truly regulate the Spanish federal system. If a Persian lawyer wants to know Spanish territorial organisation, he would not find an answer in the Constitution. An innocent reader of the Spanish Constitution will have no answers for essential questions such as: What is the Spanish federal map? How many CC AA are recognised? What are the competences of the federal entities? Moreover, which are the central competences? Is Spain fully federalised? None of these questions has a clear solution in the Constitution.

4 CRUZ VILLALÓN, P. (1981), 'La estructura territorial del Estado o la curiosidad del Jurista Persa', *Revista de la Facultad de Derecho de la Universidad Complutense de Madrid*, 4 (monográfico), pp. 53–63.

Even more surprising: If we read the territorial article in the Constitutional '*Preliminar*' Title (where the constitutional principles are expressed), we find Article 2, which raises more questions than it solves:

> The Constitution is based on the indissoluble unity of the Spanish nation, the common and indivisible homeland of all Spaniards, and recognises and guarantees the right to autonomy of the nationalities and regions which make it up and the solidarity among all of them.

Is there only (indissoluble unity of) one nation (in a common and indivisible homeland of all Spaniards – the echoes of fascist terminology are quite obvious), or are there several nations ('nationalities') instead?

Is there a difference between 'nationalities' and 'regions'? It is clear that we are not talking about 'states' or '*Länder*'. But what is a nationality or a region? We are left without a further definition of either one in the Spanish territorial system in 1978 (not even in the rest of the Constitution).

What does autonomy mean? Is it the same autonomy for nationalities and regions? Can autonomy be safeguarded when at the same time the indissoluble unity of the Spanish nation is declared?

We can find answers to these questions (and to the unsatisfied curiosity of the Persian lawyer) by adopting a particular approach. The Constitution doesn't solve the territorial problem by itself. The Constitution tries to solve the problem without developing the whole federal system. What the Constitution creates is a framework where different territories (with the agreement of the central powers) can choose the form and degree of their self-government, designing different ways or trends of federalism.[5] The territories will be the fundamental actors in the definition of their powers. But the final solution will be based on the result of a dialogue between each territory and the Spanish Parliament.[6]

In that sense, the Constitution prescribes two levels of autonomy. The higher level is reserved for what Article 2 describes as 'nationalities'. The lower level is prescribed for 'regions'. But there is not a previous definition of the nationalities. A territory will become a nationality or a region depending on the autonomous level chosen by each one (with the agreement of the central powers).

Now we can rebuild the Spanish system from a historical point of view.

5 In this sense, the so-called 'autonomous process' is required for the comprehension of the Spanish way to federalism. For a complete account of the process, it is worth consulting two early, but still essential, contributions: TOMÁS Y VALIENTE, F. (1989) *El reparto competencial en la jurisprudencia del Tribunal Constitucional*. Madrid: Tecnos; and GARCÍA DE ENTERRÍA, E. (1985) *Estudios sobre Autonomías Territoriales*. Madrid: Civitas.

6 I have developed these questions in BUSTOS GISBERT, R. (2005) 'Las tensiones del Estado Autonómico ante el proceso de reforma estatutaria'. In *La reforma de los Estatutos de Autonomía*. Valladolid: Junta de Castilla y León. pp. 69–87.

There are two paths to accede to the higher level for self-government: an easy path and a difficult one.

The easy path has two possibilities:

1. Interim Disposition No. 2 of the Constitution: territories that in the past approved *Estatutos de Autonomía*, that is: Catalonia, the Basque Country and Galicia (namely, the homelands of true nations in the socio-political sense, with their own language, culture and nationalist political parties).
2. Additional Provision No. 1 of the Constitution: those territories in which access to autonomy would be an update of the medieval *foral* system (i.e. Navarra, with close links to the Basque Country).

The difficult path (Article 151 of the Constitution) requires the affirmative action of all provinces interested in autonomy, three-quarters of the municipalities and a positive referendum with absolute majority of the electoral roll in each province (only Andalucia followed this path, with serious doubts about the constitutionality in the process).

So, we can now define the legal concept the constituent had in mind for nationalities. Nationality is a region with a special will for self-government. That qualified will is presumed for some places (Catalonia, the Basque Country, Galicia and Navarra) due to historical reasons (true nations in the socio-political sense), but it has to be proved in a democratic process for the rest of Spain (Andalucía).

The regions will accede (if they wish, and it was so in the entire Spanish territory) to a lower degree of autonomy.

In both cases, the *Estatuto de Autonomia* will be the 'constitution' of each *Comunidad Autonoma*, which has to be passed both by central Parliament and by the autonomous Parliament, or directly by the people in the CA. Any change in this norm has to be a result of a consensual process between the local and central governments.

What are the differences between the two levels?

1 *Competences that can be claimed.* The nationalities can assume all of the competences not expressly reserved to central government (Article 149). The regions can only assume the competences prescribed in the Constitution (Article 148). But the central competences can, in some circumstances, be delegated to the CC AA (Articles 150.1 and 150.2).
2 *Special competences.* There are some competences that can be assumed only if there are previous differences among territorial entities. These include language (only in the CC AA with a different official language – Catalonia, the Basque Country, Galicia and Navarra, but also Valencia and the Balearic Islands), civil law (Catalonia, Navarra and, with less importance, other CC AA) and public finance (the Basque Country and Navarra). Finally, there is also a difference in public security due to the approval of *Estatutos de Autonomía* (autonomous police in Catalonia, the Basque Country and Navarra).
3 *Culture* is a *concurrent* competence which means that both the central and the autonomous governments have powers in regulating the subject.

4. The federal process in action: from success to disaster?

The apparently final design of the federal map seems to satisfy asymmetry as it was understood in the nationalities: recognition of a higher self-government and respect for their particularities in terms of culture, language, civil law or public finance law.

But new problems soon appeared in the Spanish federal process. We can classify these problems into three groups with regard to their diverse effects:

1. The '*emulation*' *effect*. All of the CC AA followed the path opened for the nationalities. Although they were free to organise and assume different competences, the regions copied (as long as it was not constitutionally forbidden) the organisation and competences of the Basque Country and Catalonia.
2. The '*territorial discrimination*' *effect*. The distinction between nationalities and regions was forgotten in less than ten years. A new terminology was adopted: 'first class' and 'second class' autonomy. The terminology illustrates the political phenomenon that took place in these years. Regions felt discriminated against with the two levels of autonomy constitutionally designed, and aspired to raise their self-government to the higher level.
3. The *birth of new reasons for asymmetry*. Insularity is the most important example with the Canary Islands and, to some extent, the Balearic Islands claiming special status. But new singularities were formulated for different reasons, and some of them were against the new CC AA rather than the federal powers.[7]

As a result of these effects, the federal process changed its course from the recognition of asymmetry to the implementation of a new equality among territories.[8] But, and this is important, this process is a *reactive* effect against a perceived discrimination. It does not have a real reflex in the political vitality of the CC AA. The self-government in most of the so-called second-class autonomies

7 In this sense, we may underline the case of Valencia, where a strong sense of rejection is felt against the way in which cultural authorities in Catalonia have tried to control every single particularity linked to a language which is broadly spoken in Valencia. Something similar may be said about the Balearic Islands, where also a version of Catalan is spoken in an insularity context. The case of Navarra is also important. A new regionalism has been born to confront not Spanish nationalism, but the growing influence of Basque nationalists in Navarra. We may find these kinds of processes in other parts of Spain where there are pressures even inside the Comunidades Autónomas.

8 A full account of the evolution of the Spanish federal system can be found in AJA, E. (2007) *El Estado Autonómico: Federalismo y Hechos Diferenciales*. 2nd edn. Barcelona: Alianza; SOLOZABAL, J.J. (1988) *Las Bases Constitucionales del Estado Autonómico*. Madrid: MacGraw-Hill; FOSSAS I ESPADALER, E. (2007) *El principio dispositivo en el Estado Autonómico*, Madrid: Marcial Pons. Also useful is the Annual Rapport on Comunidades Autónomas, which has been published by the Instituto de Derecho Público since the 1980s.

was not comparable to the self-government of the first-class ones – not only in terms of the presence of regionalist political parties (which appeared with force in the Canary Islands connected to the insularity exception and in Navarra, in contrast with the Basque nationalist political parties with an important presence in that *Comunidad Autónoma*), but in terms of the number of bills approved, electoral participation, richness of the political process, importance of the regional political class, etc. In other words, from a political point of view, the first-class CC AA (and with great difference the Basque Country and Catalonia) enjoyed a far more important self-government than the second class ones.

But, in the end, the sense of territorial discrimination was stronger (mainly due to the electoral advantages for the two national political parties when they adopted this position). So, a second federal process started with the second-class autonomies reforming their *Estatutos* to raise their self-government to the higher level (a process allowed by Article 148.2 CE five years after the approval of the *Estatutos*). The federal map, at the end of the 1990s, changed dramatically. Seventeen CC AA now had the same level of self-government. Only the competences linked to language (where an official language was recognised), civil law (where *foral* civil particularities still survived), the special regime for public finance law, autonomous police and some singularities for the Canary Islands made possible asymmetric treatment in the Spanish federal process. This situation was reached, I must repeat, with an enormously different political will for self-government: a strong will in Catalonia and in the Basque Country and a much weaker will in the rest of Spain. This situation was aggravated by the action of two new powerful trends against self-government: the European integration (which politically decreased autonomous self-government); and a Constitutional Court case law that slowly diminished the CC AA competences.

The reaction coming from the Basque Country was the adoption of the so-called Ibarretxe Plan. Formally, it was a reform of the *Estatuto de Autonomia*, but in essence it was an unconstitutional attempt to secure the Basque Country's independence (it attempted to create a sort of confederation of Spain and Euskadi as independent states). The Ibarretxe Plan was clearly defeated in the Spanish Parliament (after obtaining a slim majority in the Euskadi Parliament with the help of the political branch of the terrorist organisation ETA). Eventually, after two autonomous elections with the Ibarretxe Plan as a central issue, the nationalist government of Euskadi was defeated and for the first time in thirty years a non-nationalist leader became the president of the Basque Country.

Catalonia also reacted to the general reform of the *Estatutos* of the CC AA after a change in the political equilibrium in the *Comunidad Autonóma*. The nationalist government was defeated by a coalition of left-wing nationalist and non-nationalist political parties for nearly thirty years. The new parliamentary majority drafted a reform of the *Estatuto de Autonomía* (the '*Estatut*'). The *Estatut* was passed via a referendum after hard negotiation in the Spanish Parliament, but it lacked the consensus of the right-wing national political party (*Partido Popular* – PP), who challenged its constitutionality before the Constitutional Court. The absence of the *Partido Popular* in the drafting and passing of the *Estatut* was, as will be explained below, an 'original sin' that could not be overcome and helped to create significant problems in Spanish federalism today.

This new Statute for Catalonia tried to secure the singularity of the Catalan nationality with six major changes:

1 a Catalan Bill of Rights;
2 a stronger bilateral relationship with the central government;
3 a recognition of its international role in European affairs, but also in trans-regional cooperation and international relationships regarding culture, immigration, trans-frontier cooperation, etc.;
4 a better definition of autonomous competences to avoid the centralistic jurisprudence of the Constitutional Court;
5 an increase in the competences recognised for Catalonia – even those constitutionally reserved to the central government (using delegating and transferring statutes); and
6 better public finance for Catalonia.

The Catalan *Estatut* generated, almost at once, the reform of other *Estatutos de Autonomía*.[9] But, the emulation effect has been less significant than in the first decentralisation and so has been the intent to obtain an absolute equal level of self-government. In addition, however, not all the CC AA started reform processes.

The Constitutional Court took its time to decide the unconstitutionality application lodged by the Popular Party. Almost five years after the claim was made, the Constitutional Court, in the Decision taken on 9 May 2010 (STC 31/2010), ruled the unconstitutionality of important provisions included in that legal instrument and the reinterpretation of many others. The process inside the Court was not an easy one. The independence of one of the constitutional magistrates was challenged by the plaintiffs. His fellow magistrates, against the will of the magistrate questioned, accepted its challenge by a slim majority (six to five) due to the publication of an academic work on the matter some years before he became a member of the Court. Moreover, Decision 31/2010 was adopted after terrible negotiations inside the Court (continuously leaked to the press) where a two-block division was evident in the Dissident Opinions which defended an even stronger unconstitutionality of the text.

The decision was highly controversial from both the political and legal viewpoints. This chapter is not the place to give an account of all the questions raised by the decision, but some facts should be underlined.

9 Re. this process, it is worth consulting the Papers presented to the Annual Congress of the Spanish Association of Constitutionalists: RUIZ-RICO RUIZ, G. (ed.) (2006) *La Reforma de los Estatutos de Autonomía, Actas del IV Congreso de la Asociación de Constitucionalistas de España*. Valencia: Tirant.

From a political point of view, the decision was saluted by the Spanish nationalist forces as a great achievement. The *Estatut* had been considered by these forces to be a serious menace for the continuity of Spain as a single state. The academic literature in line with this perspective considered, from a more technical point of view, that the *Estatut* was unconstitutional because it ruled aspects reserved to the central powers and tried to fix basic constitutional concepts that should be defined by the Constitutional Court alone.[10]

In Catalonia, the decision raised strong opposition from both the political and the academic perspectives. The President of the *Comunidad Autónoma* declared he was enraged with the decision, which was considered by all political forces (except the Popular Party) an insult to Catalonia. A month after the Court's Decision, a million people took to the streets of Barcelona to demonstrate against it. From an academic point of view,[11] numerous aspects of the decision were criticised. These criticisms focused on the absence of comity to the *Estatut* by the Constitutional Court. The Court should have taken into account that the *Estatut* had strong democratic support. It was approved in the Catalan Parliament by all political parties except for the Popular Party. It was negotiated and also approved by the Spanish Parliament (again with the opposition only of the Popular Party). Last, but not least, it was approved in a popular referendum in Catalonia. A Constitutional Court should not, for these academics, be eager to declare the unconstitutionality of rules with such democratic legitimacy (based only on the Court's case law and not directly on the Constitution which, as has been stated, left a broad margin of appreciation to the territories to define their self-government).

In any case, Constitutional Court Decision 31/2010 put an end to the development of the federalising process started in the early years of the century. It declared null many of the most controversial articles, provided interpretations of others which stripped them of their original meaning and, last, but not least, conditioned the entry into force of other provisions to the approval of other bills by the central Parliament.

If we take into account the six major changes proposed in the original *Estatut*, we may summarise the judgment as follows: first, the Catalan Bill of Rights became a declaration subordinated to the national Bill of Rights without any true significance; second, the bilateral relationship with the central government was left to the goodwill of the central powers; third, the definition of competences was declared as not compelling for the Constitutional Court; fourth, the competences which could be transferred or delegated to Catalonia were left to the sole will of the central powers without any obligation coming from the *Estatut*; and, fifth, the

10 A Sample of this literature can be found in the monographic volume about the Constitutional Court Decision on the *Estatut* for Catalonia edited by *Teoría y Realidad Constitucional*, 27, 2011.

11 Again, a sample of the opinions of the Catalan academic literature can be found in a monographic volume edited by a law journal about the Constitutional Court Decision: *Revista Catalana di Dret Public*, num. extraordinario, 2011.

public finance system was not considered binding because it would depend on a general agreement among the central powers and the CC AA as whole. Only the international role in European affairs and foreign affairs remained untouched, but the Court made clear that the Catalan competence in the matter must respect the leading role of the central powers.

In other words, apart from the last point, none of the changes proposed was accepted by the Constitutional Court.

A final but symbolic blow to the *Estatut* was the Court's refusal to accept the constitutionality of the declaration contained in the Preamble of the *Estatut*, which stated that the Catalan Parliament considered Catalonia to be a nation. The Court, in an unnecessary statement, maintained that only the Spanish nation could be considered a nation under the current constitutional regime.

The political crisis provoked by the Constitutional Court Decision (in which this Court lost an important part of its well-earned prestige from the 1980s and 1990s) seemed to end abruptly due to the importance of the economic crisis and to the political changes. These political changes came from elections in Catalonia (the right-wing nationalists – CiU – came back to the executive in Catalonia in November 2010, but with a slim majority needing the support of the Popular Party) and in the rest of Spain (the Popular Party won, in November 2011, in almost all the *Comunidades Autónomas* and recovered a strong majority in the Spanish Parliament). But the problems were far more deeply rooted, as events would show a few months later.[12]

During the 2012 '*Diada*' (11 September, the National Day of Catalonia, which celebrates the resistance and destruction of Barcelona by the Borbonic troops in 1714, considered as the end of the true autonomy of Catalonia by the Nationalist parties), a great demonstration took place in the streets of Barcelona organised by a private association for independence (the Catalan National Assembly). More than 1.5 million people marched under the slogan: 'Catalonia, new state in Europe'. The demonstration gathered the discontent raised by the territorial question, but, also, the rage provoked by the hard economic measures adopted by the new Spanish Government to confront the financial crisis that razed Spain. In any case, it generated a change in the Catalan Government discourse about self-government and the adoption of a clear demand for independence. This implied the withdrawal of the Popular Party's parliamentary backing and the search for help from the left-wing Nationalist Party (ERC), which has supported for years, open and clearly, the independence of Catalonia. So, *Convergencia I Unió* (CiU), which has been the majoritarian party in Catalonia for years, and has played an essential role in the building through dialogue of Spanish federalism, gave up its

12 The literature about the *Catalan process* has multiplied in recent years and is not easy to summarise. For a general overview about its effect on the Spanish legal system, see: AJA, E. (2014) *Estado autonómico y reforma federal*. Madrid: Alianza; and MUÑOZ MACHADO, S. (2014) *Cataluña y las demás Españas*. Madrid: Critica.

traditional moderate role in the national demands of Catalonia and adopted a clear secessionist discourse. The autonomous elections in November 2012 showed strong support for parties in favour of independence: the two major parties in Parliament backed independence for Catalonia. A new minority executive was nominated. It was constituted by a weaker CiU (which lost almost 20 per cent of its seats in the House), with the backing of a stronger ERC (which increased its seats in the House by 25 per cent), and almost destroyed the political federal entity (PSC) of the Spanish Socialist Party, which had its worst results in Spain's democratic history and lost its second position in the Parliament, and was nearly defeated by the Popular Party in Catalonia.

Thus, the situation in Catalonia from the territorial point of view worsened substantially. The Parliament passed a resolution which claimed the right of the Catalan people to decide their own future (with the agreement of all parties apart from the Popular Party and a non-independentist but minoritarian party). This resolution was backed by both the nationalist parties (CiU, ERC and an extreme left-wing party, CUP) and the non-nationalist parties (PSC-PSOE and the old Communist Party, IU). Although the Spanish Socialist Party (PSOE) did not agree, the PSC approved that a referendum regarding independence in Catalonia was needed to overcome any doubt about the strength of the independence desire in that region. The resolution was annulled by the Constitutional Court in its judgment 42/2014.[13]

At the same time, in the rest of Spain, the positions also became more radical. The Popular Party, in charge of the Spanish executive, strongly fights the sole idea of a referendum about the independence of Catalonia. In this sense, it – rightly – defends the unconstitutionality of the celebration of a referendum in a *Comunidad Autónoma* without the consent of the Prime Minister (Article 99 of the Spanish Constitution). Mr Rajoy, Prime Minister, has solemnly stated that he will never authorise a referendum on this topic. The decision, he argued, about the independence of a part of Spain is a constituent decision that can only be adopted by the constituent power – that is, the Spanish people – not a part of it. The Spanish Socialist Party backs this refusal (with the exemption of the majority of its Catalan members), but underlines the necessity to change the Constitution to solve the territorial problem. This constitutional change, in the Popular Party's opinion,

13 The resolution claimed the recognition of a right of the Catalan People to decide their future by themselves. It is interesting to underline the development of a new theory about this *right to decide* apparently different from the right or secession or the right to self-determination. The Constitutional Court, surprisingly, didn't deny this right, but established that it should be exercised with full respect to the Spanish legal and constitutional order. On the 'right to decide', see RIDAO, J. (2014) *El derecho a decidir: Una salida para Catluña y España*. Barcelona: RBA. About the judgment 42/2014 and the way in which the Constitutional Court confronted the right to decide, see FERRERES COMELLA, V. (2014) 'The Spanish Constitutional Court Confronts Catalonia's Right to Decide (Comment on the Judgment 42/2014)'. *European Constitutional Law Review*. 10. p. 571.

is neither necessary nor convenient in Spain's current political and economic situation.

The President of Catalonia called for a referendum on the independence of Catalonia in September 2014. The Decree and the Statute which gave legal support to the referendum were immediately challenged in front of the Constitutional Court. Two days later, the Court agreed the admission of the challenge, and suspended the call, according to Article 161.2 of the Constitution.[14] The President of Catalonia backed by the nationalist parties called then for a 'participative process'. Their intention was to promote a sort of unofficial referendum using a different legal form, but, in the end, asking Catalans their opinion about the convenience of becoming a state (the first question in the suspended referendum) and, if so, of becoming an independent state (the second question of the referendum). This 'participative process' was called without passing any legal document or approving any public action to avoid another challenge in front of the Constitutional Court. Nevertheless, the Spanish Government challenged every 'activity' of the Catalan Government related to the 'process of citizen participation'. This 'process' was also immediately suspended by the Constitutional Court, only five days before the date planned for the 'participation process'.

On 9 November, even with the opposition of the Spanish Government and the Constitutional Court, this 'process of citizen participation' took place without any incident and in peace. Around 2,305,000 Catalans voted in the process. More than 80 per cent of the voters supported the independence of Catalonia. These numbers imply that almost 37.02 per cent of the potential voters in Catalonia (according to the rules of the referendum, which included voters over 16 years of age and foreigners) voted in the referendum and about 30 per cent did so supporting independence. After the polls, the Spanish Attorney General lodged a criminal complaint against the President of Catalonia and other members of his cabinet for disobedience to judicial orders and embezzlement.

After the informal referendum, the President of Catalonia called for elections in December 2015. This election was considered by pro-independence parties as 'plebiscitarian'. The term was used to underline that what was at stake was not (only) the composition of a regional parliament, but (politically) a decision about Catalonia's independence. In coherence with this approach, the main members of the independence movement presented a united front under a coalition (JuntspelSi–JpS) whose programme was clearly, in a very Ackermanian sense,[15] the declaration

14 This article prescribes the suspension of any autonomous act once a challenge by the President of the Spanish Government is admitted. This suspension is automatic: the Court has no option about the suspension of the act until five months have elapsed.

15 The ideas of Bruce A. Ackerman are clearly present in the Catalan 'constituent' process. In the absence of any intention to create a situation of violence or an abrupt break in historical terms, the construction of a people strictly in democratic terms which is at the core of Ackerman's understanding of the constituent power as a mobilised people who discuss and decide about their

of Catalonia's independence. The main idea was that if they could gain more than 50 per cent of the votes, they would be legitimated to declare independence. But the results did not give a clear answer. Pro-independence parties won the day, but not clearly. These parties were the governmental coalition (JpS, which won 39.54 per cent of the votes) and the CUP (an anarchist and radical left-wing party, which won 8.2 per cent of the votes). Together, both parties reached 47.74 per cent of the votes, and a clear majority in the house. Unionist parties won 41.6 per cent of the votes (C's – a new centre party born against independence in Catalonia – 17.93 per cent, the Socialist Party – 12.74 per cent, the Popular Party – 8.5 per cent and *Unió* – 2.5 per cent). Finally, a new radical left-wing party (*Catalunya si que es pot*) won 8.94 per cent of votes. This party didn't campaign in favour of or against independence; it just asked for a future referendum on independence where, apparently, it would support the union of *Cataluña* and Spain under a new constitution.

After difficult negotiations (which caused the retirement of the former President of Catalonia), a new parliamentary majority was created by an unstable coalition of JpS (in which some independent personalities of Catalan public life take part; the right-wing nationalist party and the left-wing nationalist party) with the CUP (which, as just stated above, is mainly an anarchist party sustained in a network of local assemblies). Both parties (even before the governmental coalition was agreed) passed a resolution in the Catalan Parliament, exactly one year after the celebration of the informal referendum to declare the beginning of the process to create an independent Catalan Republic.[16] The resolution was promptly challenged by the Spanish Government and annulled by the Constitutional Court.[17] It is relevant to point out that the reform of the Statute of the Constitutional Court[18] in October 2015 (just a month before and as a consequence of the attitude of Catalan authorities) gave the Court sufficient competences to assure the effectiveness of its judgments, even imposing fines or the temporal dismissal of any authority who may infringe the orders issued by the Court.

However, the annulment of the parliamentary resolution and the menace of economic and dismissal sanctions have not discouraged the Catalan Government, now under the presidency of a more radical personality, whose parliamentary

future as a polity in a context of 'constitutional politics', fits perfectly with the approach of the main theorists of the Catalan independence movement. See for his position about constitutional creation and reform the three volumes by ACKERMAN, B. (1991) *We the People*. Cambridge, MA: Harvard University Press. Ibid. (1993) *Foundations*. Vol. I; Ibid. (1998) *Transformations*. Vol. II; Ibid. (2014) *The Civil Rights Revolution*. Vol. III.

16 Resolució 1/XI del Parlament de Catalunya sobre l'inici del procés polític a Catalunya como a conseqüència dels resultats electorals del 27 de setembre de 2015.

17 STC 259/2015, 2 December 2015. It's relevant to underline the *efficiency* of the Court, which decided the case in less than a month since the challenge by the government was lodged.

18 LO 15/2015, 16 October 2015.

majority has created committees to study the passing of bills needed to create the legal conditions for the unilateral declaration of independence.

At the same time, in Spain, general elections took place in December 2015. The harsh electoral campaign highlighted that most political parties in Spain were convinced of the need to reform the Constitution, among other reasons, to propose a new status for Catalonia. Only the Popular Party was reluctant regarding these proposals (although some of its members backed the idea of the Constitutional reform). Even the new left-wing radical party (*Podemos*) assumed the proposal made by their Catalan branch (*Catalunya si que es Pot*) to celebrate a referendum about the independence of some of the Spanish nationalities (not only Catalonia, but also the Basque Country and Galicia). But again, the results were uncertain. The Popular Party won the day, but lost a substantial segment of its support in Parliament, especially the comfortable majority it had previously enjoyed. But the Socialist Party also lost many of its seats in Parliament. Its losses gave parliamentary space to the new parties such as C's and *Podemos*. In any case, the result is a hung Parliament which needs a three-party coalition (at least) to create a governmental majority. This coalition has not yet been created, and it is foreseeable that it will be impossible to form it. So, the most probable scenario in Spain (at the time of writing in March 2016) will be a new general election in the summer of 2016.

In the meantime, the situation continues to worsen. With the backing of the Parliamentarian majority, Catalan authorities seem to have started a constituent process with significant but insufficient support by the people. On the other side, Spanish authorities are frozen due to the absence of a majority that allows reform of the Constitution to satisfy, to some extent, the stronger quest for Catalonia's self-government.

While the situation in Catalonia shows increasing support in favour of independence, in the rest of Spain there is growing support of a more centralistic and homogeneous revision of the territorial autonomy without giving any space for a decision of the Catalan people on their own.

In any case, and with no regard to my personal opinion on this topic, this crisis of the federalising process in Spain was not exactly a result of the concrete regulation put in force in the new *Estatut*. Many of the provisions contained in this instrument were already declared (partially and with different formulations) in other *Estatutos de Autonomia* in force; other provisions were a codification (constitutionally impossible in the Court's opinion) of the Constitutional Court's own case law. However, that was not the real problem. The problem was that none of these provisions, included in other *Estatutos*, had been questioned before the Court. That was due to the fact that those *Estatutos de Autonomía* were a result of a successful dialogue between *all* political forces relevant in a concrete territory and *all* political forces in the Spanish Parliament. The Catalan *Estatut* lacked this essential feature. It did not have the consensus of an important political actor both in Catalonia and in Spain: the Popular Party. That is why this party questioned the *Estatut*. The *Estatut* was not a child born out of the consensus. It was a child born out of the confrontation. That is its 'original sin'.

The whole model can be criticised because it gives a strong power (even a veto power) to minorities which can block any normative change. This power was used by the Popular Party to stop the increase in Catalonia's powers. It was the party's right to do so. But that decision (the challenge of the *Estatut* before the Constitutional Court) has provoked the most important crisis of the asymmetrical federal system in Spain. The dialogue among parties and territories (among themselves and between them and the federation), which was the efficient secret of the Spanish Constitution, has disappeared. And with the disappearance of dialogue, it seems that a solution for the territorial problem in Spain is no longer possible.

But, paradoxically, both the positions of Catalan secessionists and the opinion of the rest of the Spaniards are justified from their respective perspectives.

On the one hand, the opposition of Spanish political parties (and their voters) to a referendum in Catalonia is easy to understand. A right to secession has never been recognised in any democratic state. The situation of the United Kingdom is absolutely different. Spain has been a state since the fifteenth century, not an international union by a treaty among previous states. Spain is a single state with a single constitution, a single constituent power and a single people: the Spanish people. That was solemnly declared in the Constitution not so long ago (1978). Catalonia is not a colony. Its citizens have equal rights to the rest of Spaniards, it has self-government and absolute respect for its cultural and historical peculiarities. A so-called Catalan people cannot decide on its own vital issues that touch the essence of the Spanish Constitution: its territorial and personal integrity. This cannot be accepted from the Spanish point of view.

On the other hand, it is also easy to understand the reasons of the supporters of independence in Catalonia. They thought, so they were told during the drafting of the Constitution, the *Estatutos* or even the *Estatut*, that the allocation of powers between centre and periphery was the result of negotiation among political parties and between Catalonia and the Spanish Parliament. The *Estatut*, the basic norm that performs the role of a basic law or national constitution for Catalans, was agreed by more than 80 per cent of the members of the Catalan Parliament. It was agreed with the Spanish Parliament, even if this agreement implied changes in some important provisions. And, finally, it was approved with a strong majority via referendum (almost 74 per cent of voters). But it was declared void in its most symbolic provisions at the request of a minoritarian political force in Catalonia by a non-democratic organ (the Constitutional Court) in whose composition Catalans have no participation at all. The discontent of Catalans is thus understandable. If they cannot negotiate their position in Spain, it is much better to follow their own path among European states.[19] In particular, it can be well understood, if we bear in mind that the entire process is taking place during the worst economic crisis in

19 A complete theoretical approach from a legal point of view can be consulted in BOSSACOMA I BUSQUETS, P. (2015) *Justicia i legalitat de la secessió. Una teoría de l'autodeterminació des de atalunya.* Barcelona: IEA.

the last fifty years in Spain and with no dialogue among peoples, parties and territories. This state of affairs is evidence that the seed of independence has a fertile ground in Catalonia where it may grow with deep roots.

The events in Spain over recent years prove that the dialogical pattern is essential to our federal system. We hope that this pattern will be recovered, sooner or later, in the present political and parliamentary crisis and will give us an opportunity to redesign the federal compact in such a way to satisfy both the need for unity of Spain and the singularities felt as essential by Catalans. But not even a single relevant political force should be excluded from this new compact. An inclusive agreement of all political and territorial forces is impossible without dialogue. This is essential and cannot be forgotten without paying a high price. And, as we have attempted to explain above, Spain is currently prepared to pay it.

5. Final remarks

This is the picture today. The description of the situation cannot be more depressing. But, at least, some conclusions can be drawn from the question at hand. In particular, I would like to point out, at least, eight conclusions:

1 Asymmetry can provoke a sense of territorial discrimination. The levelling of competences is not a good solution because it nullifies the special self-government a nationality feels it deserves.
2 The safeguard of the concrete special features and distinct characteristics in some regions is served better by asymmetric decentralisation, i.e. reaction to and differentiation in the individual case, rather than by establishing two (or various) levels of autonomy.
3 It is constitutionally difficult to transcribe asymmetries in competences when regulating the participation of the component entities in forming the federal will. A better way may be the establishment of bilateral organs with territorial and central representatives.
4 The specific definition of the competences in the Constitution can be a way to safeguard them against centralistic interpretations.
5 Sufficient resources are a precondition for autonomy. Any asymmetric federal arrangement will also need an asymmetric public finance framework, but it is important to avoid any sense of discrimination among territories. This will be, probably, the most difficult task: designing (or redesigning) an asymmetric federalism without generating – perceived – discrimination among territories.
6 There must be normative ways based on consensus to adapt the solutions to the changing conditions of a federal process.
7 There must be an arbiter not only to secure the competence distribution, but to supervise any change in the basic rules governing the allocation of the different powers. This arbiter should be designed in such a way that it can guarantee enormous public confidence. This public confidence has to be felt in both the central and the decentralised powers.

8 Dialogue must never be abandoned during the federal process. With dialogue continuously taking place, a solution may become possible. But without dialogue, it is evident that no solution is possible. The refusal of dialogue closes all roads for self-government and pushes minorities to secessionism as the only solution to safeguard their peculiarities. At the same time, it pushes majorities to intolerance and to a growing sense of disgust regarding any different opinion, moderate or not, that will be considered treacherous to the common and sacred interest of the state.

And, as a final remark, it appears that we Spaniards do not know where our federal process would lead us. It has been a long journey from the centralistic and fascist dictatorship in Spain until 1975. We have achieved the longest period of a peaceful (except for terrorism) solution for territorial problems. This solution, for the first time in Spanish history, has respected pluralism in law, culture and languages. This success has been possible thanks to a normative framework that demands a permanent dialogue among a new federal union (Spain) and its heterogeneous components, a dialogue that distinguishes nationalities and regions – an asymmetric arrangement and, consequently, dialogue. We did not know where that dialogue would take us, but we have checked that as long as it has continued, there has always been a solution for every problem. The most important crisis in this period is born out of the absence of dialogue and it may lead us to disaster if we do not find a way to restart the peaceful and institutional discussion regarding our territorial differences. And this is, without any doubt, the most important lesson learned during recent years in Spain.

Chapter 8

Devolution and devolution plus

Anti-foundationalist foundations for constitutionalism

John Morison

1. Introduction

The United Kingdom as one of the more established and settled countries of the world with its history as a sophisticated, first-world legal jurisdiction comprising both a strong economy and an established democratic apparatus, may appear to offer few parallels with the experience of Tibet and China. However, the real history of the United Kingdom is one of continual change and accommodation where some fundamentals relating to the very nature and extent of the polity have undergone considerable constitutional innovation. Although the United Kingdom is often presented as a paradigm example of a stable constitutional order, where constitutional verities such as democracy, the rule of law and, particularly, the sovereignty of parliament, endure, the reality is more complex. This is a continuing story and it is one which may have application beyond the very particular circumstances of the United Kingdom as developments here have required an often subtle and sometimes underestimated re-thinking of some of the basics of constitution order.

In particular, there is the story of devolution in the United Kingdom. This is an incomplete tale, but its continuing development does have wider interest beyond its constituent parts. The process by which the United Kingdom came together, and more particularly the unfolding story of how it is now potentially splitting further apart, illustrates the possibility of developing new forms of association within a changing polity where issues of sovereignty and territory, allegiance and nationality, as well as citizenship and identity, can evolve and mutate without necessarily requiring a fundamental re-establishment of the state. Indeed, the continuing experience of devolution in the United Kingdom demonstrates how a mature democracy can accommodate change, the possibility of a radical re-ordering and even dissolution of some its constituent forms, without undue trauma to the body politic. This in turn suggests possible directions for a post-sovereignty future.

This account will look at change as a motif within British constitutionalism generally before focusing particularly on the ongoing process of gradually uniting the 'home' countries into the United Kingdom of Great Britain and Northern Ireland (which took up its present configuration only in 1922). The 'big bang' devolution project of 1998 will be examined briefly. Attention will then turn to the more recent beginnings of a possible disintegration of the United Kingdom through a process of continuing devolution that has the potential to develop into something more. In particular, this account will look at the position in one of the devolved countries – Northern Ireland – where constitutional developments were required not only to deal with issues of regional autonomy, but also to resolve fundamental issues of conflict about the very nature of the polity, and how to share it. It is here, it will be argued, that the beginnings of a constitutionalism beyond sovereignty may be found in the provision of a framework for accommodating conflict without needing to resolve some of the fundamental antagonisms that remain.

2. Constitutionalism and change in the United Kingdom

The changing nature of the UK constitution is increasingly being recognised by scholars who in recent years have departed from traditional descriptions of the constitution as being stable and certain and recognised a new language of uncertainty and change. The traditional view can be illustrated by reference to the work of various luminaries such as Burke, Dicey and Bagehot, or through the view of Lindsay Keir, who, surveying the constitutional history of Britain since 1485, declared contentedly that 'continuity has been the dominant characteristic'.[1] The newer view is one which recognises uncertainty and indeed transformation as central themes, and questions the efficacy of some of the traditional ways of thinking about the constitution in the new circumstances.[2] This has caused problems with some orthodox accounts of the constitution which now struggle to accommodate newer developments. However, in part there is an issue of perception underlying this: while there have of course been significant recent developments, the UK constitution has always been subject to continual change. There has never been a 'golden age' of continuity and indeed the story of the United Kingdom has changed as a constant.

2.1 The United Kingdom in the wider world

The last century alone has involved looking back from a time of empire to a period marked by decolonisation and withdrawal. This encompasses the story of the

1 See *The Constitutional History of Modern Britain since 1485* (1964), p. 1. See also MOUNT, F. (1992) *The British Constitution Now*. London: Heinemann, who identifies a 'continuity myth' in British Constitutionalism and indicts a range of adherents from the ranks of constitutional theorists, at pp. 15–23.

2 See, e.g. NORTON, P. (2006) The Unsettled British Constitution. *Politics Review*. 16(1). pp. 6–9; BOGDANOR, V. (2009) *The New British Constitution*. Oxford: Hart; BELL, C. (2014) Constitutional Transitions: The Peculiarities of the British Constitution and the Politics of Comparison. *Public Law*. July. pp. 446–471; and WALKER, N. (2014) Our Unsettled Constitution. *Public Law*. July 2014. pp. 529–548.

Commonwealth and the history of dominion status that developed in the late nineteenth century as former colonies such as Australia, Canada and New Zealand moved toward full statehood. This involved essentially a formal handover of power into new constitutional arrangements. The Statute of Westminster 1931 broadened the powers of dominion parliaments to make law and repeal Westminster legislation.[3] While this process may have caused some difficulties to the doctrine of parliamentary sovereignty in the United Kingdom, by suggesting that one parliament can limit its successors and 'give away sovereignty', political reality soon requires legal theory to evolve. The process of fully transferring power to some major former colonies was not, however, completed in Canada until the Canada Act 1982 brought about the 'patriation' of the constitution to Canada, and it was not until 1986 that twin legislative measures in Westminster and New Zealand and Australia respectively brought about consolidation of those countries' constitutions. Such handovers of power continue. A treaty from 1898 gave the United Kingdom a ninety-nine-year lease over the three territories that now make Hong Kong and required some delicate constitutional engineering as the lease drew toward conclusion. A new Basic Law, which may be considered a mini constitution drafted with the participation of the people of Hong Kong, provided a mechanism allowing, in July 1997, a transfer of constitutional power which returned the former British colony of Hong Kong to the Peoples' Republic of China.[4]

Of course, the United Kingdom itself has not been insulated from the processes of globalisation which have impacted upon states across the world as new groupings and alliances emerge. Constitutional change of a fundamental, far-reaching and continuing nature comes from the ongoing difficulties about adopting the UK constitutional order, with its ideas of parliamentary sovereignty, to the wider European project – both in terms of the European Union and also in relation to the standards set by the European Convention on Human Rights (ECHR). The constitutional difficulties of joining Europe with its law-making and adjudication functions based outside the formal British constitution are well known and well rehearsed.[5] There are a series of important cases which together make up the reading list of constitutional law students and scholars in the United Kingdom and describe the concerns and tensions within constitutional theory over the Europeanisation project during the last four decades.[6]

3 See further, WHEARE, K.C. (1949) *The Statute of Westminster and Dominion Status*. 4th Edn. Oxford: Oxford University Press. See also GARDBAUM, S. (2013) *The New Commonwealth Model of Constitutionalism: Theory and Practice*. Cambridge: Cambridge University Press.

4 BUCKLEY, R. (1997) *Hong Kong: The Road to 1997*. Cambridge: Cambridge University Press.

5 See, e.g. CRAIG, P. (2013), The United Kingdom, the European Union and Sovereignty. In RAWLINGS, R., LEYLAND, P. and YOUNG, A. (eds) *Sovereignty and the Law: Domestic, European and International Perspectives*. Oxford: Oxford University Press.

6 In relation to the initial problems of accepting European Community law, see, e.g. *McCarthys Ltd v. Smith* [1979] 3All ER 325 and Allan (1983), at 22. Later legal difficulties about what is now termed

Also relating to the role of European standards is an even more long-standing issue relating to the status of the ECHR. As one of the original drafters of the ECHR, the United Kingdom was the first country to ratify in 1951. However the United Kingdom's dualist system, whereby treaties are not directly incorporated into law, initially made the application of the ECHR into UK law a rather roundabout process as treaties while binding in international law do not have direct effect internally. The UK courts were required to engage in a rather tortuous exercise of preserving the sovereignty of the UK Parliament, while at the same time interpreting the law, as far as possible to be consistent with European obligations.[7] However, in 1998, the Human Rights Act incorporated most of the ECHR into domestic law. The effect of this is to allow the courts to interpret primary and subordinate legislation as being compatible with Convention rights 'as far as it is possible to do so'. Where this is not possible, and in order to preserve an idea of parliamentary sovereignty, the courts can make a 'declaration of incompatibility' which does not affect the continuing validity of the provision in respect of which it is given, but may act as a signal that the legislature may wish to amend the law.

One consequence of this has been to give the European Court of Human Rights a particular significance as the interpreter of the ECHR, with the UK courts reduced to a role of reflecting the views from the ECHR in Strasbourg. The so-called *Ullah* principle arising from judicial pronouncements in a case of that name in 1994, suggests that in giving effect to the Convention rights under the Human Rights Act, the 'duty of national courts is to keep pace with the Strasbourg jurisprudence as it evolves over time: no more, but certainly no less'.[8]

While the introduction and implementation of the ECHR into UK law may, arguably, amount to a fundamental moment of change in the UK constitution, this particular instance of constitutional significance has been prolonged by the desire of the present UK Government to extract itself from European commitments generally and the ECHR in particular.[9] One significant way in which this dispute has surfaced has been in judicial pronouncements about the nature of the obligation and how it may not require as direct a process of mirroring Strasbourg

EU law can be seen in cases such as *R. v. Secretary of State for Transport, ex p. Factortame (No. 2)* [1991] 1 AC 603 and Craig (1991). See also more recently *R. (HS2 Action Alliance Ltd) v. Secretary of State for Transport* [2014] UKSC 3.

7 See, e.g. *R. v. Secretary of State for the Home Dept, ex p. Brind* [1991] 1 AC 696 and, more generally, DONALD, A., GORDON, J. and LEACH, P. (2012) *The UK and the European Court of Human Rights*. Equality and Human Rights Commission. Research Report 83.

8 *Ullah v. Special Adjudicator* [2004] UKHL 26, [2004] 2 AC 323, see: www.publications.parliament.uk/pa/ld200304/ldjudgmt/jd040617/ullah-1.htm [Accessed: 14 February 2017].

9 See Commission on a Bill of Rights, *A UK Bill of Rights? The Choice Before Us. Vol. 1* (London, Commission on a Bill of Rights 2012); and BRAVER, J. (2014) Counter-Interpretation, Constitutional Design, and the Right to Family Life: How the Conservatives Learned to Stop Worrying and Love the HRA (Briefly). *UK Const. L. Blog*. [Online] 6 January 2014. Available at: http://ukconstitutionallaw.org/blog/ [Accessed: 14 February 2016].

as was initially suggested.[10] It is interesting to note the particularly British phenomenon whereby it is in the courts that these tensions within the constitution both come to the surface and where they are smoothed over by judicial interpretation.

2.2 The constitution, re-constitution and possible dissolution of the United Kingdom

Closer to the matter of the ordering of domestic polity itself, the theme of change appears again as a constant in the very composition and nomenclature of the United Kingdom. The entity that is the United Kingdom is one which could be said to begin its story in 1282 when Prince Llywelyn was killed and his principality of Wales passed by conquest to Edward I of England. While the story of the evolving United Kingdom is far from over, it may be true to say that its present formation dates only from 1922, when the current United Kingdom of Great Britain and Northern Ireland emerged following the succession of what was to become the Republic of Ireland.[11] In between, the history of the United Kingdom has involved a series of amalgamations, formal unions and takeovers of what might be termed the 'constituent parts' of the United Kingdom.[12] Wales's history as a separate nation before the United Kingdom is somewhat ambiguous, with England dominating the legal and administrative structures of Wales since at least 1536, when an Act of the English Parliament united the two entities. Scotland, however, was unambiguously an independent nation with its own parliament, legal and educational system and established church before the Act of Union of 1707 brought together both the parliaments and crowns of Scotland and England. Ireland was the subject of conquest and colonisation by England from the twelfth century. The limited autonomy afforded for an Irish Parliament and Irish

10 For an overview of this, see MASTERMAN, R. (2013) The Mirror Crack'd. *UK Const. L. Blog.* [Online] 13 February 2013. Available at: http://ukconstitutionallaw.org [Accessed: 14 February 2016].

11 The Interpretation Act 1978, Sch. 1 gives the authoritative definition of the United Kingdom as Great Britain (England, Scotland and Wales) and Northern Ireland, excluding the Channel Islands and the Isle of Man, although s. 50 of the British Nationality Act 1981 includes these for nationality purposes.

12 Hadfield provides an interesting account of the use of terminology to describe both Scotland and Wales in official statements with, for example, a Speaker's Conference on Devolution in 1920 referring to the 'national component portions' of the United Kingdom, while a Royal Commission on Devolution in 1973 referred to Scotland and Wales as possessing 'separate national identities'. In the White Papers introducing more recent devolution legislation of the late 1990s, Scotland was referred to as a 'proud historic nation', while Wales became a European 'economic region'. See HADFIELD, B. (2003) The United Kingdom as a Territorial State. In BOGDANOR, V. (ed.) *The British Constitution in the Twentieth Century*. Oxford: Oxford University Press. The name given to Northern Ireland has varied, often in accordance with the political stance of the person deploying the description. The phrase 'region' has generally been avoided, while the term 'Province' is widely used, as is the historic label of 'Ulster' (although this is geographically inaccurate, as the traditional province of Ulster is not coterminous with the political entity that is Northern Ireland).

Government structures that was allowed was brought to an end by the Act of Union of 1800 bringing about a formal incorporation of Ireland into the United Kingdom, at least for part of its territory, for part of its history.[13]

Although the United Kingdom, in the formation dating from 1922, was initially a single, unitary state, it was not without at least some limited layers of government. In addition to a relatively complex and fast-changing local government structure,[14] there was a scheme of devolution for Northern Ireland dating from this time. This came from the Government of Ireland Act 1920, and produced fifty years of generally stable if not entirely inclusive government. Based very firmly within a sovereignty model where the Westminster Parliament retained overall authority, it provided for a bicameral Parliament in Belfast and an executive drawn from this. The Parliament possessed an unrestricted legislative competence only in transferred matters (taken to be those necessary for the 'peace, order and good government' of Northern Ireland), while there were a series of other 'excepted matters' which required the permission of the mother Parliament at Westminster, as well as a class of 'reserved matters' which were for the UK Parliament only.[15] This scheme of government remained the only operational form of devolution in the United Kingdom until its demise as a result of what is euphemistically termed 'the Troubles' in 1972.

There was, however, a serious attempt to introduce devolution for Scotland and Wales in the 1970s. Following on from the influential Royal Commission, known as the Kilbrandon Report,[16] legislation was passed in 1978 for an elected assembly in Wales and an elected assembly with executive powers in Scotland. In order for these schemes to take effect, however, they required approval by 40 per cent of the electorate in Wales and Scotland, and this was not achieved.[17] The legislation was withdrawn, but devolution did not disappear from the political agenda.

13 See further MORGAN, D.G. (1990) *The Constitutional Law of Ireland.* 2nd Edn. Dublin. Gill & Macmillan; CASEY, J.P. (2000) *Constitutional Law in Ireland.* 3rd Edn. Dublin: Round Hall, Sweet & Maxwell; FORDE, M. and LEONARD, D. (2013) *Constitutional Law of Ireland.* 3rd Edn. Haywards Heath: Bloomsbury; PALLEY, C. (1972) The Evolution, Disintegration and Possible Re-Construction of the Northern Ireland Constitution. *Anglo-Am. L. Rev.* 1. p. 368; HADFIELD, B. (1989) *The Constitution of Northern Ireland.* Belfast: SIS Legal Pub; and MORISON, J. and LIVINGSTONE, S. (1995) *Reshaping Public Power: Northern Ireland the British Constitutional Crisis.* London: Sweet & Maxwell.

14 See further LOUGHLIN, M. (1996) *Legality and Locality: The role of Law in Central-Local Relations.* Oxford: Clarendon; WILSON, D. and GAME, C. (2011) *Local Government (Government beyond the Centre).* 5th Edn. London: Palgrave MacMillan; and NEWMAN, I. (2014) *Reclaiming Local Democracy: A Progressive Future for Local Government.* London: Policy.

15 See further Calvert, H. (1968) *Northern Ireland: A Study in Regional Government.* London: Stevens.

16 Cmnd 5460 (1973).

17 See further BALSOM, D. and MCALLISTER, I. (1979) The Scottish and Welsh Devolution Referenda of 1979: Constitutional Change and Popular Choice. *Parliamentary Affairs.* 32(4). pp. 394–409.

3. The devolving United Kingdom – 1998 and beyond

The 1970s saw devolution suspended in Northern Ireland and the devolution schemes for Wales and Scotland fall at the hurdle of a referendum, but devolution remained an active element in UK politics. In Northern Ireland, there were successive attempts to restore devolved government in forms that might be more palatable across all sections of the divided society. In Wales and, particularly in Scotland, a variety of civil society organisations took up the cause of devolution and, with the election of Mrs Thatcher's Conservative Party to Westminster to follow a variety of policies that seemed to many to be inimical to the interests of traditional industries in Scotland and Wales, devolution became an increasingly popular political cause throughout the 1980s and 1990s.[18] It was one which the Labour Party in opposition was anxious to take up as official policy and make part of a manifesto promise for the 1998 general election. Following the election of a Labour Government in May 1998, the promises about devolution were followed up in Scotland with the White Paper *Scotland's Parliament*[19] and in Wales by the White Paper *A Voice for Wales*.[20] The proposals in the White Papers were submitted to referendums in both Scotland and Wales and approved by the electorate, albeit with a very small margin in Wales. Legislation in the form of the Scotland Act 1998 and the Government of Wales Act 1998 was introduced, bringing in a new era of devolution in the United Kingdom.[21]

It is noteworthy that the foundation for devolution here within a referendum, expressing the popular will of the people, can be seen as providing an alternative basis for devolution within an idea of consent, rather than as simply something that is within the gift of a sovereign Parliament at Westminster (which could of course retain the power to rescind if it chose). This is, of course, contrary to the traditional idea of sovereignty, whereby Parliament can make or unmake any law it chooses, but there are some signs that the courts may be beginning to view such statutes differently, as possessing a higher, constitutional status.[22] Although still

18 See further The Scottish Constitutional Convention, which began its work in 1989 and made its final report, *Scotland's Parliament: Scotland's Right*, in 1995. See also BURROWS, N. (2000), *Devolution*. London: Sweet & Maxwell; BOGDANOR, V. (2001) *Devolution in the United Kingdom*. Oxford: Oxford University Press; and MITCHELL, J. (2011) *Devolution in the UK*. Manchester: Manchester University Press.

19 Cm 3658/1997.

20 Cm 3718/1997.

21 See HIMSWORTH, C. and O'NEILL, C. (2009) *Scotland's Constitution: Law and Practice*. 2nd Edn. Haywards Heath: Bloomsbury.

22 See, e.g. ELLIOT, M. (2003) Embracing Constitutional Legislation: Towards Fundamental Law. *Northern Ireland Legal Quarterly*. 54. pp. 25–42, at p. 25; *Robinson v. Secretary of State for Northern Ireland* [2002] UKHL 32; and *Thoburn v. Sunderland City Council* [2003] QU 151. For some more recent highlights, see *Somerville v. Scottish Ministers* [2007] UKHL 44 at 169; and *R. (Brynmawr Foundation School Governors) v. Welsh Ministers* [2011] EWHC 519 (Admin) at 70–73. Cf. *AXA General Insurance v.*

inchoate, there is perhaps the beginning of a wider recognition that a new constitutional foundation is necessary, beyond the limits of parliamentary sovereignty, to accommodate political reality in the modern United Kingdom.

In Scotland, elections took place in May 1999 for a 129-seat Scottish Parliament with a four-year fixed life where electors had two votes: one for seventy-three constituency members and another for fifty-six additional members from a party list. The Scottish Parliament was granted the power to make acts in a range of devolved areas, but excluding 'reserved' matters (such as defence, foreign policy, customs and borders and employment and equality) and within human rights and European law limits. The Parliament was also given the power to vary income tax by 3 per cent. The Scottish Executive was headed by a nominated First Minister leading a coalition executive of eighteen ministers, with two law officers in departments of Education, Industry, Agriculture, Environment and Fisheries, Health and Culture. (The Executive has been termed the Scottish Government since 2007.) Combined with an accompanying Ministerial Code and Guide to Collective Decision-Making, all of this was suggestive of a 'new politics' beyond the traditional Westminster majoritarian system.

In Wales, the elections of May 1999 were for a sixty-member Welsh Assembly elected for a fixed four-year term with half being constituency members and half from a party list. In strict constitutional terms, the Executive was the whole Welsh Assembly, but power was delegated to a First Secretary who with eight Assistant Secretaries covering economic development, education, health and social services, education and training, agriculture and rural economy, environment and finance were to make up the Executive in a system which ran on 'cooperation' between the two main parties rather than a formal coalition. The Assembly's powers were initially modest, being restricted to debating Westminster legislative proposals and debating and drafting secondary legislation.[23]

At the same time, although through a rather different and tortuous process, devolution was being restored to Northern Ireland as part of a wider peace process.[24] Some elements were, however, common with the other devolved systems.

Lord Advocate [2011] UKSC 46 and particularly *Imperial Tobacco v. Lord Advocate* [2012] CSIH 9, where Lord Reed states clearly that the 'democratic legitimacy of the Scottish Parliament does not . . . warrant a different approach to interpretation from that applicable to Acts of Parliament . . . Nor does it impinge upon the fact that the power of the Scottish Parliament to legislate is limited by the Act of Parliament which established it' (para. 58). This view was reinforced in the Supreme Court where Lord Hope, while acknowledging that 'the purpose of the [Scotland Act 1998] has informed the statutory language', made it clear that 'the description of the Act as a constitutional statute cannot be taken, in itself, to be a guide to its interpretation. The statute must be interpreted like any other statute'. [2012] UKSC 61 at para. 15.

23 See further RAWLINGS, R. (2003) *Delineating Wales: Constitutional, Legal and Administrative Aspects of National Devolution*. Cardiff: University of Wales Press.

24 Devolution in Northern Ireland was introduced in a very different context generally to that in the rest of the United Kingdom. There it is less to do with mechanisms of governance as such and more related to a wider peace process within which devolved power appears as the least unpopular

Among a wide variety of other things, the Northern Ireland Act 1998 introduced a 108-member legislative Assembly elected by the single transferrable vote mechanism of proportional representation from which a consociational, power-sharing executive was formed via the D'Hondt mechanism to include a co-equal First and Deputy First Minister and eleven other ministers together heading up the twelve ministries. Legislative power was granted to make acts in 'transferred' matters, subject to a number of mechanisms involving cross-community voting, parallel consent and weighted majorities, as well as human rights and anti-discrimination restrictions. Legislating power was to be transferred at a later stage to 'reserved' matters (such as law and order), while Westminster retained power in the 'excepted' areas.[25]

The initial devolution settlement across the United Kingdom that appeared in 1998 was, of course, not the end of the movement toward further regional power. The often-quoted description of devolution being 'a process not an event' was realised in a number of additions and modifications to the original settlements, and is still being worked through as all the component parts of the United Kingdom consider their future in a post-crisis, austerity world.[26] Questions about the extent and desirability of further devolution to Scotland or independence, the fitness for purpose of a peace agreement as a design for government in Northern Ireland, and the nature of a more 'grown-up' version of devolution in Wales have all been, and continue to be, very live issues. At the same time, there is increasing concern about how the interests (and revenues) of the 75 per cent of the population who live in England can best be managed within the context of what might be seen as a quietly disintegrating constitutional orthodoxy.

This is not the place to review all of these in detail, but it is important to note a few general trends. First, the position of England has increasingly appeared as anachronistic.[27] Attempts made shortly after the 1998 settlement to develop some

medium-term option for government. See further McCRUDDEN, C. (2007) Northern Ireland and the British Constitution since the Belfast Agreement. In JOWELL, J. and OLIVER, D. (eds) *The Changing Constitution*. 6th Edn. Oxford: Oxford University Press, pp. 227–270.

25 See further MORGAN, A. (2000) *The Belfast Agreement: A Practical Legal Analysis*. Belfast: TSO; HARVEY, C. (ed.) (2001) *Human Rights, Equality and Democratic Renewal in Northern Ireland*. Oxford: Hart Publishing; CARMICHAEL, P., KNOX, C. and OSBOURNE, R. (eds) (2007) *Devolution and Constitutional Change in Northern Ireland*. Manchester: Manchester University Press; and CAMPBELL, B. (2008) *Agreement! The State, Conflict and Change in Northern Ireland*. London: Lawrence and Wishart; and ANTHONY, G. (2011) Northern Ireland: The Devolution of Policing in Criminal Justice. *European Public Law*. 17(2). pp. 197–211.

26 This phrase is attributed to the former Welsh Secretary who in 1997 described the devolution he had helped to design in these terms. For some discussion of general trends within this most recent phase of devolutionary activity, see, e.g. PERRYMAN, M. (ed.) (2009) *Breaking Up Britain: Four Nations after a Union*. London: Lawrence and Wishart; WYN JONES, R. and SCULLY, R. (2012) *Wales Says Yes: Devolution and the 2011 Welsh Referendum*. Cardiff: University of Wales Press.

27 See further HAZELL, R. (ed.) (2006) *The English Question*. Manchester: Manchester University Press; and WYN JONES, R., LODGE, G., HENDERSON, A. and WINCOTT, D. (2012), *The Dog that Finally Barked: England as an Emerging Political Community*. London: IPPR; and COX, E.,

units of self-government for various English regions were finally rebuffed by the electorate in 2004.[28] Only London achieved a modicum of devolved power through the Greater London Authority Act 1999 establishing an elected mayor and twenty-five-member cabinet with limited responsibility, mainly in areas of transport, policing, fire and emergency services, planning and culture.[29] However, the debate about independence in Scotland has re-ignited some enthusiasm about new structures for England.[30] In particular, the idea of an English Parliament for English issues, where members from other regions would be unable to vote on matters that were not relevant to their constituents, has emerged after the 'No' vote in Scotland as a potentially hot political topic.

In Wales, there has been a slow progression toward a devolution architecture more like that of Scotland or Northern Ireland. A de facto separation of the legislative and executive elements of the Assembly was achieved initially by re-designating a newly termed Welsh Assembly Government as distinct from the National Assembly. Following the recommendation of the Richard Commission, a formal legal separation was achieved through the Government of Wales Act 2006 so that the Welsh Government (made up of the First Minister, various Welsh ministers and deputy ministers, and legal officers) became responsible for making and implementing decisions, policies and subordinate legislation, while the National Assembly holds the government to account. The Richard Commission also recommended an enhancement of the Assembly's legislative powers. The Government of Wales Act 2006 gave some additional legislative powers on a 'conferred powers model' in some twenty areas, introducing a mechanism whereby the National Assembly could bid for further powers from Westminster in other devolved areas and on an individual basis.[31] The Act also paved the way for the Assembly to hold a referendum to gain all powers in the devolved areas by means of a referendum and without further recourse to Westminster. Following a positive

HENDERSON, G. and RAIKES, L. (2014) Decentralisation Decade: A Plan for Economic Prosperity, Public Service Transformation and Democratic Renewal in England. *Newcastle-upon-Tyne: IPPR North 2014*. [Online]. Available at: http://www.ippr.org/publications/decentralisation-decade [Accessed: 14 February 2017].

28 See Labour Party, *'A Choice for England' A Consultation Paper on Labour's Plans for English Regional Government* (London Labour Party, 1995); and HAZELL, R. (ed.) (2006) *The English Question*. Manchester: Manchester University Press.

29 It should be noted that although Liverpool elected a mayor in 2012, this trend has not been popular with nine English cities rejecting proposals for a similar system in a referendum in 2012, leaving now only Bristol to join this trend.

30 A large new survey by Cardiff and Edinburgh universities shows 54 per cent support in England for its own parliament, four times as many as those who disagreed. See further www.theguardian.com/commentisfree/2014/aug/21/guardian-view-devolution-parliament-for-england [Accessed: 14 February 2017].

31 See further Sch. 7 of the Government of Wales Act 2006. There is no comprehensive list of these areas in law. However, the main areas that are not for devolution include foreign affairs, defence, macro-economic policy, the tax and welfare system, energy policy, broadcasting and policing and justice.

vote by the Welsh electorate in March 2011, these powers were given to the National Assembly with the effect that the Assembly can now legislate in the twenty devolved areas without the permission of Westminster. A Commission on Devolution in Wales (known as the Silk Commission) was formed in October 2011 to look first at financial aspects and then at further devolution.[32] The Silk Commission's first report recommended the addition of some limited taxation and borrowing powers for the National Assembly of Wales. These were largely approved by the UK Government in late 2013 and legislation is being passed. The second Silk report recommended further devolution in a number of areas, including of policing, aspects of youth justice and planning approval, although it did not endorse the establishment of a Welsh legal jurisdiction or devolution of the courts and the legal system. It also recommended a move to the 'reserved powers' model of devolution already in use in Scotland and Northern Ireland, and an increase in the size of the National Assembly. So far, Westminster has not responded to this, and in wider Welsh society it would seem that some extended version of devolution is as far as the public would wish to go.[33]

It is, however, in Scotland that much of the devolution action has taken place. There have been two elements here operating in parallel. First, there has been a movement from the Labour Party in Scotland, some elements of the Scottish Parliament and the government in London to develop devolution. This led to the appointment of the Calman Commission, whose full report, *Serving Scotland Better: Scotland and the United Kingdom in the 21st Century*,[34] concluded that broadly devolution was working well, but could be improved by a number of changes. Some of these found their way into the Scotland Act 2012, which provided for an option for the Scottish Parliament to develop new tax-raising powers of up to one-third of its budget in areas such as landfill tax and stamp duty on house purchases (with a commensurate reduction in the block grant from Westminster), as well as some new powers in areas such as drink-driving, speeding and the regulation of airguns.

At the same time, there has been an alternative movement, from the Scottish Nationalist Party (SNP) in their position in government in Scotland gained in the 2007 elections, and its direction is firmly toward independence. Although, by a combination of section 29 and Schedule 5 of the Scotland Act 1998, constitutional issues generally (and in particular the future of the United Kingdom) are reserved matters beyond the competence of the Scottish Parliament, the SNP Scottish

32 (2009), available at: http://commissionondevolutioninwales.independent.gov.uk [Accessed: 14 February 2017].

33 See the poll taken after the Scottish Independence referendum, which has support for Welsh Independence at 3 per cent, although 49 per cent did favour some increase in devolution powers. See www.theguardian.com/uk-news/2014/sep/24/3-per-cent-back-welsh-independence [Accessed: 14 February 2017].

34 Calman Commission, 'Serving Scotland Better . . .' (full report) available at: www.scottishconstitutionalfutures.org/Resources/UsefulPublications/OfficialPublications/tabid/1778/Default.aspx [Accessed: 14 February 2017].

Government has nonetheless become engaged with the issue. It launched the 'National Conversation' in 2007 on the question of 'commencing negotiations' with the UK Government so that Scotland becomes an independent state. This was triggered by the publication of the Scottish Executive's White Paper, *Choosing Scotland's Future: A National Conversation* (2007), and involved an unusual exercise in participatory democracy whereby people and groups across Scotland took part in public meetings, written contributions and in various formats online. This was followed by the publication of the Scottish Government's White Paper, *Your Scotland, Your Voice*, in 2009 offering a comprehensive examination of the options for Scotland's future – the status quo, further devolution along the lines of the Calman proposals, full devolution (so-called 'devo max') and independence. A draft Referendum (Scotland) Bill and accompanying White Paper, *Scotland's Future*, were published in 2010. However, the SNP suspended this course of action and instead campaigned more generally on the independence issue in the May 2011 Scottish Parliament elections. The results of this election were to provide an astonishing and largely unforeseen victory for the SNP, who won 69 of the 129 seats in the Scottish Parliament.[35] This was taken to provide a mandate for independence and a three-year timetable leading to the vote in September 2014 was outlined. In January 2012, the Scottish Government issued a consultation document, *Your Scotland, Your Referendum*,[36] which received more than 26,000 responses and provided the basis to move toward a vote on the future of Scotland. There were strongly different views in Edinburgh and London on the details of who should call the referendum and the ground rules for its organisation.[37] However, agreement was reached in October 2012 in the grandly termed 'Edinburgh Agreement' signed by the Prime Minister and First Minister of Scotland.[38] The Scottish Independence Referendum Act 2013 was passed by the Scottish Parliament and the Scottish Independence Referendum (Franchise) Act 2013 extended the vote to those aged over 16 years living in Scotland. The referendum was organised to take place on 18 September 2014 on a question recommended by the Electoral Commission, 'Should Scotland be an independent country? Yes/No'.

After an initially slow start, the referendum campaign became lively, with the 'Better Together Campaign' made up of a wide coalition of opposition parties in Scotland and all the major parties in the rest of the United Kingdom, facing a

35 This compared with forty-seven SNP members, forty-six Labour MSPs, sixteen each for the Conservatives and Liberal Democrats and four others in the previous Parliament.

36 Available at: www.scotland.gov.uk/Resource/0038/00386122.pdf [Accessed: 14 February 2017].

37 For the background to this, see the House of Lords Select Committee on the Constitution Report, *Referendum on Scottish Independence*, HL Paper 263 (2012).

38 See further www.scotland.gov.uk/About/Government/concordats/Referendum-on-independence [Accessed: 14 February 2017].

yes-vote lobby led by the Scottish Government.[39] The latter group published a series of papers, including *Scotland's Future: From Referendum to Independence and a Written Constitution* (2013), indicating the possible nature of an independent Scotland where a written, right-based constitution would be developed in a consultative process, and a White Paper, *Scotland's Future – A Guide to an Independent Scotland* (2013), outlining in considerable detail the SNP's vision for the future.[40] Disputes about continuing EU membership, the currency, expenditure plans and levels of subsidy, share of national debt, limitations of North Sea reserves and nuclear facilities were all addressed.

Although the vision for independence was not to prevail in the referendum in September 2014 (with its unprecedented 85.65 per cent turnout) by a margin of 45 to 55 per cent, it does not mean that Scotland has not changed or will not continue to do so. Interestingly, the debate was not mainly about ethnic nationalism, but was built up from ideas of civic nationalism and the degree to which a government in Scotland could organise Scottish affairs better than one for the whole United Kingdom. There was also perhaps a measure of dissatisfaction with politics in general and the Westminster establishment in particular (and this is not limited to Scotland). However, the Scottish Parliament still has considerable legislative power and controls more than 60 per cent of public expenditure. Furthermore, promises from all the main UK political parties to develop devolution toward a 'devo max' suggest that the journey toward self-government has not ended.[41] A Commission chaired by Lord Smith of Kelvin was to produce suggestions for further devolution in Scotland by the end of January 2015. Its recommendations were put into effect with the 2015 General Election. There are interesting signs, too, that the Scottish experience, where just short of one-half (44.7 per cent) of its voting population expressed a desire to leave the present constitutional configuration, may be picking up on a wider unhappiness about constitutional arrangements across the United Kingdom more generally, and there are promises made by the major parties to look at further devolution for Wales and Northern Ireland, as well as measures to ensure that English representatives only will vote on English matters.

More generally, the referendum process has confirmed that devolution is undoubtedly a process rather than a one-off event. The United Kingdom has just

39 See https://noscotland.net/2012/06/26/launch-of-the-better-together-campaign/ and www.scotreferendum.com [Accessed: 14 February 2017].

40 *Scotland's Future: From the Referendum to Independence and a Written Constitution* (2013) is available at: www.scotland.gov.uk/Resource/0041/00413757.pdf [Accessed: 14 February 2017]; and Scottish Government, *Scotland's Future: Your Guide to an Independent Future* (2013) can be found at: http://scotgov.publishingthefuture.info/publication/scotlands-future [Accessed: 14 February 2017].

41 See further the various proposals contained in Scottish Liberal Democrats (2012), *Federalism: The Best Future for Scotland: Report of the Home Rule and Community Rule Commission*; Scottish Liberal Democrats (2014), *Campbell II: The Second Report of the Home Rule and Community Rule Commission*; Scottish Labour Devolution Commission (2014), *Powers for a Purpose – Strengthening Accountability and Empowering People*; and Scottish Conservatives (2014), *Report of the Commission on the Future Governance of Scotland*. The Scotland Act 2016 has delivered some aspects of some of these proposals.

undergone what Roberto Unger might describe as a 'hot moment' – that period of escalating collective mobilisation and public enthusiasm where transformative change seems possible.[42] The pace of travel toward something approaching a federal United Kingdom may or may not be slowing, but much has already changed, and it has changed irrevocably, particularly now in light of the Brexit vote. The devolution story so far has exposed tensions and conflicts in orthodox understandings of the constitution. Traditional ideas about parliaments and assemblies, about power lent and sovereign oversight, and the proper constitutional role of the judges to police the constitutional boundaries of sovereignty, are increasingly seen as ill-suited to describe the emerging constitutional reality where significant portions of the body politic are dissatisfied with the current constitutional arrangements – albeit not quite yet in numbers to seek an immediate exit from them.

But there is a part of the devolution story in the United Kingdom where some of these trends are more evolved and, most intriguingly, some of the ways forward, beyond the traditional zero-sum games of sovereignty, authority and nationality, are more fully developed in ways that might be of interest beyond the immediate context. This is, of course, the continuing story of Northern Ireland. Within this chronology, stories of national identity, historic autonomy and newly established government structures are overlaid with a chronic and deep-seated dispute over the sovereign status of the polity and widespread conflict over the legitimacy of government. The story of its combined constitutional settlement and ongoing peace process may be instructive in other contexts.

4. Devolution plus – the Northern Ireland Peace Process and transitional justice thinking

The story of the details of the Northern Ireland constitutional settlement has been extensively told elsewhere.[43] In some senses, it can be seen as part of the wider

42 MANGABEIRA UNGER, R. (1997) *Politics: The Central Texts*. London: Verso. p. 298.

43 For an account of the processes leading to the new government structures, see CAMPBELL, B. (2008) *Agreement! The State, Conflict and Change in Northern Ireland*. London: Lawrence and Wishart; and for an overview of the formal structure of government in Northern Ireland, see HARVEY, C. (ed.) (2001) *Human Rights, Equality and Democratic Renewal in Northern Ireland*. Oxford: Hart Publishing; McEVOY, K. and MORISON, J. (2003) Beyond the 'Constitutional Moment': Law, Transition, and Peacemaking in Northern Ireland. *Fordham International Law Journal*. 26. pp. 961–995; CARMICHAEL, P., KNOX, C. and OSBOURNE, R. (eds) (2007) *Devolution and Constitutional Change in Northern Ireland*. Manchester: Manchester University Press; and McCRUDDEN, C. (2007) Northern Ireland and the British Constitution since the Belfast Agreement. In JOWELL, J. and OLIVER, D. (eds). *The Changing Constitution*. 6th Edn. Oxford: Oxford University Press. For more recent updates to the original Agreement, see ANTHONY, G. (2008) Northern Ireland: The St. Andrews Agreement and the Northern Ireland Assembly. *European Public Law*. 14(2). pp. 151–164; and ANTHONY, G. (2011) Northern Ireland: The Devolution of Policing in Criminal Justice. *European Public Law*. 17(2). pp. 197–211.

narrative of devolution in the United Kingdom.[44] However, for most commentators, Northern Ireland is seen as a place apart, and its devolution scheme is about more than simply regional self-government. It is in this sense that it can provide a further and deeper illustration of how change can happen in ways that transcend formal constitutional processes and traditional understandings. The Northern Ireland peace process perhaps demonstrates not only a unique constitutional moment, but also an example of a trend in constitution-making that is gaining currency, especially in societies that are undergoing, or moving on from, conflict. In recent times, conflicted societies are not only given parliaments, power-sharing and rights mechanisms, but also more specific mechanisms of conflict resolution in the form of prisoner-release schemes, amnesties and truth commissions, as well as the establishment of a range of commissions to oversee key functions such as policing, judicial appointments systems and the like.[45] Although not always recognised as constitutional measures by some transitional justice practitioners,[46] these are clearly the stuff of constitution-making. Indeed, the 'dynamic, mediating nature of constitution-making'[47] adds weight to the contention that there is a place for constitutionalism in not just delineating the normative basis for executive governance, but in shaping the course of conflict resolution. This peace-making role in constitution-making is gathering increasing attention and ambition. Klare, for example, recognises the potentially transformative peace-making role of a constitution as inviting 'a new imagination and self-reflection about legal methods, analysis and reasoning consistent with its transformative goals . . . where judicial mindset and methodology are . . . examined and revised so as to promote equality, a culture of democracy and transparent governance'.[48] Bell recommends simply that 'peace agreements are best understood as a form of transitional constitution'.[49]

44 See, e.g. BURROWS, N. (2000), *Devolution*. London: Sweet & Maxwell, n. 19.

45 Some of the discussion in the next few paragraphs draws upon and develops earlier work published as McCONNACHIE, K. and MORISON, J. (2008) Constitution-Making, Transition and the Reconstitution of Society. In MCEVOY, K. and MCGREGOR, L. (eds) *Transitional Justice from Below: Grassroots Activism and the Struggle for Change*. Oxford. Hart Publishing, where a fuller account of the wider processes can be found.

46 Arguably, where institutional reform is identified as a tool of transitional justice, it is typically not extended to the constitutional sphere – at least in the fundamental sense of how constitutions can become frameworks to allow peoples to work out how to live together. Instead, the emphasis remains on the reform of specific state institutions such as the judiciary, security services or civil service. See, e.g. MATTAROLLO, R. (2002) The Transition to Democracy and Institution Building: The Case of Haiti. In CHERIF BASSIOUNI, M. (ed.). *Post-Conflict Justice*. Ardsley, NY: Transnational Publishers.

47 The phrase comes from TEITEL, R. (2000) *Transitional Justice*. Oxford: Oxford University Press, p. 8.

48 KLARE, K. (1998) Legal Culture and Transformative Constitutionalism. *South African Journal on Human Rights*. 14. pp. 146–188, at p. 156.

49 BELL, C. (2000) *Peace Agreements and Human Rights*. Oxford: Oxford University Press, p. 9. It must be said that this recommendation is linked to the role of peace agreements in establishing political institutions and in adopting a simultaneously backward- – and forward- – looking approach to

Such claims and objectives for constitutions and constitution-making are closely rhetorically linked to transitional justice in its formal sense.[50] A constitutional text can perform functions of securing and sustaining short-term and long-term governance, which places it within a quintessentially transitional justice rubric, for example, in the acknowledgement of past atrocities and other contributions to victim recognition and redress.[51] A constitutional text is also well placed to tackle structural causes or provocations of conflict, such as land reform,[52] or religious and ethnic cleavage (as in Northern Ireland). Through a combination of historical acknowledgement, institutional creation and protection for social and economic rights, a constitution can, as part of a wider change process, make a potent contribution to transitional justice.[53]

There may be some controversy over whether or not the Northern Ireland settlement provided by the Belfast Agreement and the subsequent legislation giving it continuing effect is in fact another instance simply of devolution or an example of transitional justice, consociationalism or something sui generis.[54] However, there is agreement that what is involved is not just a constitutional settlement which addressed issues of government and parliamentary composition – the future 'shape' of Northern Ireland's political society – but also a peace agreement which looked backwards to untangle problems of disarmament, prisoner release and the recognition of victims of the conflict.[55] As such, it is perhaps a paradigmatic

social structures (although with the caveat that, unlike a traditional constitution, peace agreements may also be intentionally partial, short-lived and overtly political in both intent and implementation).

50 Arguably, and despite this evident overlap, transitional justice has to date not been overly concerned with political structures, focusing instead on mechanisms of adversarial justice, truth-seeking, reparation and memorialisation. See further for examples of the vast literature on transitional justice: BARKAN, E. (2000) *The Guilt of Nations: Restitution and Historical Injustices*. New York: Norton; CHERIF BASSIOUNI, M. (ed.) (2002) *Post-Conflict Justice*. Ardsley, NY: Transnational Publishers; PALMER, N., CLARK P. and GRANVILLE, D. (eds) (2012) *Critical Perspectives in Transitional Justice*. Antwerp: Intersentia; and BUCKLEY-ZISTEL, S. et al. (eds) (2014) *Transitional Justice Theories*. Abingdon: Routledge. See also the International Center for Transitional Justice at www.ictj.org.

51 See TEITEL, R. (2000) *Transitional Justice*. Oxford: Oxford University Press; HART, V. (2001) Constitution-Making and the Transformation of Conflict. *Peace and Change*. 6(2). pp. 153–176; CZARNOTA, A., KRYGIER, M. and SADURSKI, W. (eds) (2005). *Rethinking the Rule of Law after Communism*. Budapest: Central European University Press.

52 E.g. Art. XIII of the 1987 Constitution of the Philippines addresses urban land reform, obligating the state to make available low-cost housing and protecting dwellings of the urban and rural poor from unlawful destruction.

53 Aeyal Gross identifies five areas in which a constitution might make a contribution to transitional justice: (1) as part of a reconciliation process; (2) in defining the nature of the state; (3) addressing the past, history and 'collective memory'; (4) addressing the distribution of property and land rights; and (5) addressing the distribution of social economic rights. See GROSS, A.M. (2004) The Constitution, Reconciliation and Transitional Justice: Lessons from South Africa and Israel. *Stanford Journal International Law*. 40. pp. 47–104, at p. 57.

54 See, e.g. TAYLOR, R. (ed.) (2009) *Consociational Theory*. Oxford: Oxford University Press.

55 See further, e.g. MORISON, J. and LYNCH, M. (2007) Litigating the Agreement: Towards a New Judicial Constitutionalism for the UK from Northern Ireland? In MORISON, J., MCEVOY, K.

example of how constitutional change can adopt the language and form of transitional justice and emerge as transitional constitutionalism looking forward to a new society.

Indeed, an analysis of Northern Ireland's ongoing transition provides an excellent illustration of how traditional constitution-making, with its grants of power, patriation clauses and formal transfers of sovereignty is in fact increasingly being displaced, as constitution-making is often better explained in terms of the creation of a whole series of governable spaces. In these constitutional spaces, the project of governance is less dependent on the formal state and the engine of sovereign law-making than on a much wider, bottom-up exercise of power.[56] There are a number of reasons why Northern Ireland demonstrates this well. There is the very nature of the conflict, whereby politics was (and indeed remains) both broader and deeper than elsewhere. There are many everyday issues – from housing to education, policing to commemorating the past, and flags to marches – which are not only highly political, but also indeed 'constitutional'.[57] This has the effect that any settlement not only had to successfully address the high politics of constitutional accommodation through a formal power-sharing agreement with institutions and recognition of the 'consent principle' as determinative of Northern Ireland's future within the United Kingdom, but also a whole range of other, continuing, smaller – but no less 'constitutional' – issues. The genius of the Belfast Agreement relates not only to how it managed to square the circle of high politics, and provide a place to park the big constitutional issue of Northern Ireland, but also to how it was able to offer ways to defuse all of these issues. The Agreement, and subsequent legislation, provides not only a variety of structures for managing the whole range of 'wicked issues' that remain 'constitutional', but also a more general paradigm for seeing how they can be worked on toward resolution.

This means that the Northern Ireland constitutional transition is not best seen – or certainly not only to be seen – as a political deal or one-off constitutional moment where a deal was brokered among elites to in some way 'solve' the Northern Ireland problem. Rather, what we have is a complex and extensive structure addressing the three strands of the big 'Political Problem', namely: the internal governance of Northern Ireland, the relationship between the Republic

and ANTHONY, G. (eds) *Judges, Transition and Human Rights*. Oxford: Oxford University Press, p. 214; CAMPBELL, C., NÍ AOLÁIN, F. and HARVEY, C. (2003) The Frontiers of Legal Analysis: Reframing the Transition in Northern Ireland. *Modern Law Review*. 66(3). pp. 317–345.

56 See also MORISON, J. (2001) Democracy, Governance and Governmentality: Civic Public Space and Constitutional Renewal in Northern Ireland. *Oxford Journal of Legal Studies*. 21(2). pp. 287–310; and McEVOY, K. and McGREGOR, L. (eds) (2008) *Transitional Justice from Below: Grassroots Activism and the Struggle for Change*. Oxford: Hart Publishing.

57 See MORISON, J. and LIVINGSTONE, S. (1995) *Reshaping Public Power: Northern Ireland the British Constitutional Crisis*. London: Sweet & Maxwell, chs 4 and 5; and MORISON, J. (2006) Constitutionalism, Civil Society and Democratic Renewal in Northern Ireland. In COX, M., GUELKE, A. and STEPHENS, F. (eds) *A Farewell to Arms? Beyond the Good Friday Agreement*. 2nd Edn. Manchester: Manchester University Press, pp. 338–353.

of Ireland and Northern Ireland, and the wider relationships among the islands in the British Isles. And it is one which enables politicians to put on hold the constitutional problem relating to the place of Northern Ireland within the United Kingdom. The other 'constitutional' issues remain, and their containment or eventual resolution is dependent on the wider range of bodies, structures and mechanisms that have been developed to accommodate them. It is perhaps a feature of the high-profile nature of the Northern Ireland settlement that these can be seen operating at multiple levels from the international to the national and local, and across the boundaries of the public, private, voluntary and community sectors. There is not space here to detail the whole range of mechanisms, bodies and modes of thinking that have been developed. I have addressed some of them elsewhere.[58] However, the Northern Ireland experience does suggest an idea of transitional constitutionalism as a mode of constitutional change that avoids foundational concepts about whose state it is, or what its eventual sovereign destiny may be. The Peace Process is just that: it is a process that remains ongoing, and it is one that offers a framework within which agonistic politics can be accommodated and conflict managed. A language of recognition is offered and a rights framework provided within which difference can be accommodated and respected.

5. The UK as an exemplar for wider change?

Although there are many aspects of the UK constitution, even beyond its largely unwritten nature, that are unique, there are elements that do have application beyond its immediate context. It is interesting that the unsettled nature of constitutionalism there, although seen by some as a new feature, is in fact a constant in the evolution of the United Kingdom. There is undoubted flexibility in a constitution that not only could lose an empire, but also facilitate a formal

58 See further MORISON, J. (2013) 'A Sort of Farewell': Sovereignty, Transition, and Devolution in the UK. In RAWLINGS, R., LEYLAND, P. and YOUNG, A. (eds) *Sovereignty and the Law: Domestic, European and International Perspectives*. Oxford: Oxford University Press. There, the outstanding issues or governable spaces are discussed under three general headings: (1) Policing, Justice and Security; (2) Identity, Culture and the Past; and (3) Rights, Equality and Good Relations. Discussion is also taken up of the history and role of important governing ideas, such as 'parity of esteem', 'mutual respect' and, of course, the idea of 'consent', which is a vital governing concept for dealing not only with the big self-determination issue, but much else besides. The role of language as a technology, an indicative conceptual apparatus and a way of seeing that allows the imagining and re-imagining of ways of living in order that conflict may be ameliorated and governed, is also mentioned as is the role and importance of funders and their particular programmes. The role of international parties and exemplars is seen as important as is the engagement of national, local and community bodies and actors. Attention is also drawn to the way in which the governing process has been widened out to include a full range of community actors to ensure that the business of government has the widest possible base of engagement. This effort to provide a bottom-up approach is intended to bring increased legitimacy to governance in a contested society, but it also has the effect of engaging and making responsible more people in what can be seen clearly in this context as an effective and ambitious technology of governance operating beyond the notion of sovereignty.

recognition of the increasingly global nature of governance through its absorption of both the European Convention on Human Rights and the European Union's jurisdiction. More recently, the latest phase of change leading to an asymmetrical scheme of devolution, allowing different parts of what remains still one polity to acquire the degree of self-government that they desire, is arguably a highly creditable feature. So, too, is a constitutional mindset that is confident enough to allow a one-off referendum on independence in relation to Scotland (as well as a standing mechanism to allow Northern Ireland to succeed if that is demonstrated to be the desire of the majority[59]). The fact that the former referendum is likely to have engendered a significant and potentially radical re-think of constitutional arrangements more generally perhaps shows simultaneously both the flexible character of British constitutionalism and the limits of its present foundations in ideas of sovereignty and a unitary state. The Scottish Referendum has occasioned a rather panicked reaction among the political classes, who are now offering a whole series of possibilities pushing at the very limits of what is possible within orthodox understandings of the constitution. The constitutional engineering required for Brexit will test this ingenuity even further.

The Northern Ireland story is one that shows even more starkly the ability of what we might term enlarged constitutional thinking to develop beyond some of the formal limits – around ideas of sovereignty, single national identity and straightforward majority rule – into an agonistic framework where difference is accommodated, and the constitutional framework itself can be used as a language and mechanism to develop ways of living together. This, after all, is the main role of a constitution, and if the example of the changing nature of constitutionalism across the United Kingdom has any lessons for any context beyond its own, it is that a whole range of interests, ambitions and political agendas can be accommodated within a wider constitutional project so long as the constitutional imagination does not fail.

59 There is a so-called 'constitutional guarantee' which asserts that Northern Ireland will remain part of the United Kingdom for as long as the majority of its population, voting in a specially commissioned border poll, wish it to remain so (with the corollary, of course, that if a majority no longer wish this, reunification of Ireland will take place). Successive Acts setting out the constitutional framework of Northern Ireland have contained this provision and it remains an essential element of the peace process architecture, with the Secretary of State having the power to call a referendum when he or she thinks fit. (See further The Northern Ireland Act 1998, s. 1.)

Chapter 9

Can Quebec's relative autonomy within Canada be a template for Tibet?

Jean-François Gaudreault-DesBiens

1. Introduction

In April 2012, the Dalai Lama used the example of the province of Quebec, which has so far held two referenda on sovereignty with the blessing of the Canadian Government, to illustrate how the People's Republic of China could be pushed to recognise Tibet's autonomy.[1] Although this reference to Quebec had a somewhat exceptional nature because it came directly from the Dalai Lama, it was not the first time that Quebec's situation was mentioned in relation to Tibet or other societies seeking to emancipate themselves within, or outside, a larger ensemble.[2] But to what extent are such analogies with Quebec appropriate?

This chapter will examine the constitutional treatment of Quebec within Canada as an illustration of the possibility of granting a national cultural minority which forms a majority on a segment of a territory with a rather significant level of autonomy. The province of Quebec is a federated unit of Canada where about 85 per cent of the population is French-speaking, most of whom descended from French settlers of Canada in the seventeenth and eighteenth centuries. Although there are French-speaking minorities in other Canadian provinces, Quebec is the only jurisdiction in Canada and North America, north of the Rio Grande, where English speakers represent a minority.

The first part of the chapter will provide a historical account of how the province of Quebec eventually managed to gain the relative autonomy it currently enjoys as a Canadian province. As will be seen, the evolution of this society was sinuous; setbacks followed periods of progress, and maintaining a predominantly French-speaking society in an overwhelmingly English-speaking continent has always been, and remains, a work in progress. The second part will then examine five different questions which, together, are indicative of the nature and actual

1 Canadian Press, 'Dalai Lama sees Canada as accepting Quebec's independence', 30 April 2012. [Online]. Available at: www.cbc.ca/news/canada/ottawa/story/2012/04/30/dali-lama-quebec-independence.html. [Accessed: 14 February 2017].

2 See, e.g. SAUTMAN, B. (2002) Resolving the Tibet Question: Problems and Prospects. *Journal of Contemporary China*. 11(30). p. 88.

degree of autonomy enjoyed by Quebec within Canada. They are, in turn, the autonomous powers it is constitutionally allowed to exercise, the means by which it can affirm its cultural autonomy, the relations between groups within the province, the institutional guarantees that protect its status within the federation and, last, its peculiar position regarding external relations. After these first two parts, which will be primarily descriptive, the third and concluding part of the chapter will be devoted to a broader reflection on the conditions that led to the recognition of Quebec's relative autonomy within Canada and on the thorny question as to whether this path is of any relevance to Tibet within the People's Republic of China.

As my readers will realise, the analysis of Quebec's current politico-constitutional situation cannot be divorced from an examination of the particular history of that society. This examination crucially reveals that the position that Quebec enjoys within the Canadian federation, relatively enviable when compared to other stateless nations at least in terms of autonomy, as well as the peaceful coexistence (or indifference) that nowadays characterise its relationship with the other parts of Canada, simply cannot be projected in the past. Indeed, the history that I am about to examine is one of struggle and tension between oppression and emancipation. In this respect, rosy narratives where 'unpleasant facts'[3] have been carefully obscured must be avoided at all costs.

Two final caveats are warranted before going further: such a short chapter can only provide a glimpse into the issues addressed. Thus, its breadth somewhat entails a loss in depth, and several questions that could legitimately arise in the minds of my readers will remain unanswered. Furthermore, since this chapter is about Quebec as a potentially relevant springboard for a comparison with Tibet, a certain form of Quebecocentrism becomes inevitable. This chapter should therefore not be read as willingly wishing to obscure the perspective of other regions or communities in Canada. Its Quebecocentrism is just a collateral damage of its primary focus.

2. A sinuous path to relative autonomy

As mentioned, understanding Quebec's path to autonomy requires examining its history. Putting the province's current political and constitutional status in a historical perspective is indeed critically important, as it reveals that such status is both relatively old and the result of a long and rather sinuous struggle.

The history of the *territory* currently known as Quebec is very ancient. Like the rest of North America, this territory was occupied by Aboriginal peoples long before Europeans landed on the east coast of the continent. However, the main constitutive elements that influenced the constitution of the particular *society* that

3 WEBER, M. (2003) *Le savant et le politique*. Paris: Éditions La découverte (translation by COLLIOT-THÉLÈNE, C.). p. 96.

is now called Quebec must be traced back to the settling of the territory by French explorers. It is on these constitutive elements that I will focus in this chapter.

Although it is in 1534 that France took possession of Canada, it is only at the beginning of the seventeenth century that real attempts were made to create a colony that was to be called New France. This French colony lasted a little longer than 150 years, i.e. until 1763. Many factors explain this relatively short life, as compared to English or Spanish colonies on the continent. One lies in the fact that France primarily sought to exploit the natural resources of its colonies rather than to populate them. Moreover, being the dominant, albeit declining, empire of that age, the country was constantly embroiled in wars that were extremely expensive and left only scarce resources to devote to the colonies. These wars were inevitably exported abroad and, in North America, New France had to defend itself against numerous attacks from Britain. As a result of the 1713 Treaty of Utrecht, it lost a significant part of its North American territory when it ceded to Britain most of its Eastern Canadian colonies in Acadia. It initially became the colony of Nova Scotia, from which were later carved out New Brunswick and Prince Edward Island. After a truce, war resumed between the two empires and it reached a peak with the Seven Years' War, or, as it is called in the United States of America, the French and Indian War.

An episode that certainly impacted on the psyche of French-speaking North Americans at this time, and ever since, was the deportation of the Acadians in 1755. The French inhabitants of Acadia had remained neutral after the cession of this territory to Britain in 1713. However, given the increasing tension between France and England, the colonial administration of Nova Scotia asked them to pledge their unconditional allegiance to the British Crown, a demand that was accepted but not without hesitation, which prompted the administration to expel the French inhabitants from the colony. Since the deportation continued until 1762, the overall number of Acadians uprooted from their land is estimated at between 12,000 and 18,000. They were forcibly boarded on vessels and many of them died at sea. Survivors were disseminated in the British colonies to the south. Some managed to resettle in France, the land of their ancestors, or in New France. A significant number of them found a haven in Louisiana, where they became known as 'Cajuns'. Some went into hiding, eventually returning to the northern part of the colony when allowed to do so by the British in 1762. In the meantime, the British had seized all of their lands and property, and destroyed most of the remnants of Acadian presence in Nova Scotia, so as to discourage the original owners from returning. The legislative assembly of Nova Scotia even enacted a statute to ensure that returning Acadians could never claim their lands back, positing that the province of Nova Scotia, and the property thereof, had 'always of right to belong to the Crown of England, both by priority of discovery and ancient possession'.[4] It is well accepted that this administrative action was at least

4 Act for the Quieting of Possessions of the Protestant Grantees of the Lands formerly occupied by the French Inhabitants, and for preventing vexatious Actions relating to the same, SNS 1758–1759, 30 Geo. III, c. 3.

as much one of economic appropriation of the most fertile lands in the colony as one of military retaliation.[5] Irrespective of one's preferred interpretation, however, this episode reveals that the Seven Years' War was a dirty war. Both the French and the British committed exactions, but, from the standpoint of New France's inhabitants, who had to fight with scarce resources because of France's decision to invest in European battlefields rather than North American ones,[6] it was indeed a war of conquest, which reached its apex when, after many unsuccessful attempts, Britain finally captured Quebec City in 1759, the capital and then metropolis of New France. Montreal fell the next year. Three years after having begun exercising de facto control over New France, Britain's *de jure* control over the colony was confirmed in the Treaty of Paris of 1763. Protestant and English-speaking Britain was now formally reigning over a Catholic and French-speaking colony.

The first significant constitutional instrument that followed the Treaty of Paris was the Royal Proclamation of 1763,[7] which provided for the executive government of the newly created 'province of Quebec' in the St Lawrence valley. The Royal Proclamation pledged that a legislative assembly would eventually be created for the province. Of particular interest for this chapter is the fact that the Royal Proclamation imposed English law on the colony, even though the new British subjects were not acquainted with that body of law, the laws of former New France essentially consisting of the customs of Paris ('*Coutume de Paris*') and of various administrative ordinances, local and regal.[8] The imposition to the colony of the British 'Test Oath', which excluded Roman Catholics from public office unless they abjured central tenets of their faith, also created a bone of contention between the British administration and its new subjects: almost all of them being Roman Catholics, they were thus *de jure* and de facto excluded from public office since they were not ready to renounce their faith.

Such provisions obviously provoked reactions in the colony and, on the ground, the imposition of English private law proved unworkable. In practice, it is French law that continued to govern private relationships between individuals; even judges continued to apply it in spite of its abrogation.[9] A lobbying campaign to restore

5 On Acadia, see, inter alia: GRIFFITH, N.E.S. (1992) *The Contexts of Acadian History, 1686–1784*. Montreal/Kingston: McGill-Queen's University Press; and JOBB, D. (2005) *The Acadians. A People's Story of Exile and Triumph*. Toronto: Wiley.

6 Contrary to British Prime Minister William Pitt, King Louis XV of France believed that the war would be won on European battlefields rather than on North American ones, which explains his decision to concentrate his military forces in Europe. This decision predictably left New France in a very difficult position against British armies.

7 Royal Proclamation (1763), RSC (1985), app. II, no. 1.

8 As will become evident, we will only mention the features of various constitutional documents that have directly impacted on the evolution of the relationship between what was to become Quebec as a predominantly French-speaking society and Canada as a predominantly English-speaking federation. Other significant features will thus be ignored.

9 See DECROIX, A., GILLES, D. and MORIN, M. (2013) *Les tribunaux et l'arbitrage en Nouvelle-France et au Québec de 1740 à 1784*. Montréal: Éditions Thémis.

French law in private matters (essentially those governed by the Coutume de Paris under the former colonial regime and nowadays governed by the Civil Code of Quebec) was thus launched and eventually prevailed in spite of the opposition of British merchants.[10]

Indeed, the Quebec Act of 1774[11] restored the pre-conquest French civil law, called in the Act the 'laws of Canada in all matters relative to property and civil rights', while maintaining English public law and criminal law in the colony. It is at this juncture that the province of Quebec became a 'mixed' legal system, which it still is today. In addition to guaranteeing the free exercise of Roman Catholicism, it further replaced the Test Oath by another more generic one, which allowed Roman Catholics to occupy administrative positions in the government. Moreover, it restored the system of land tenure – the *seigneuries* – that had existed under the French administration. Last, but not least, the Quebec Act also expanded the territory of the province of Quebec in the Ohio Valley, much to the displeasure of British colonists residing in neighbouring American colonies. However, it did not create the legislative assembly promised in the Royal Proclamation of 1763.

The context surrounding the adoption of the Quebec Act is crucially important to understand why it was enacted. There was indeed agitation in the thirteen American colonies, notably as a result of the imposition upon them of taxes perceived as arbitrary because of their lack of representation within British institutions. To wit, the famous Boston Tea Party had taken place a year earlier. In such a context, the British Crown wanted to ensure the loyalty of its papist subjects in Quebec. It did so by enacting provisions that sought to induce the collaboration of both the clergy and the local nobility, in the hope that they would discourage the gentry from embracing the increasingly critical stance adopted by American colonists toward British colonial policy. Although this strategy proved only to be a moderate success in Quebec, it fuelled the resentment of American colonists who could not accept what they viewed as the preferential treatment granted by Britain to its newly acquired papist colony. The Quebec Act thus became one of the springboards of their discontent, which eventually built up into a fully fledged revolution against the British Crown.

This revolution culminated with the Declaration of Independence of the United States of America in 1776. Ironically, exactly as developments in Quebec impacted on the future of the American colonies, the 1776 Declaration of Independence had a significant effect on what Quebec would later become. Indeed, the revolution triggered a wave of immigration of loyalists to the Northern British colonies of Canada, including the province of Quebec. In that province, most loyalists settled west of the Ottawa River, a territory that later became the province of Ontario. This influx of English-speaking Protestants – the bulk of English-speaking, Roman

10 See MORIN, M. (2013) The Discovery and Assimilation of British Constitutional Law Principles in Quebec, *Dalhousie Law Journal*. 36(2). pp. 581–616.

11 Quebec Act of 1774, SRC (1985), app. II, no. 2.

Catholic Irish came later in the nineteenth century – had a significant impact on Quebec's politics. First, religious and linguistic tensions arose between these immigrants and the French-Catholic population who still constituted a majority, albeit a dominated one. Moreover, the private law applicable in the province, i.e. French civil law, was unknown to the Loyalists. Last, these Loyalists, who had experienced an embryonic form of parliamentary democracy with the legislative assemblies that existed in the former American colonies, resented the absence of such an assembly in the province of Quebec. All of these factors led to an uneasy coexistence between the various segments of the province's population and shed light on the institutional inefficiencies plaguing the regime established in 1774.

The table was set for an important constitutional overhaul, which took place with the enactment of the Constitutional Act of 1791.[12] This Act divided the province of Quebec into two distinct political entities, Lower Canada (now Quebec) and Upper Canada (now Ontario), each with its own legislative assembly. These political entities were by and large carved along religious and linguistic lines. Thus, the majority of Lower Canada's population was Roman Catholic and French-speaking, while Protestant Anglophones constituted the majority in Upper Canada. This religious-linguistic divide soon overlapped with a legal one, as the first statute adopted by the legislative assembly of Upper Canada sought to replace by British common law the French civil law applicable in private matters in the former province of Quebec.

Although the creation of Lower Canada and Upper Canada aimed in part at appeasing inter-group tensions, it only moderately succeeded in this respect and triggered other problems. The main one concerned the institutional relations between the elected legislative assemblies and the executive power. Indeed, in both provinces, chronic conflicts arose between elected assemblies, on the one hand, and British governors and their appointed executive councils, on the other, the latter disregarding many decisions taken by the former. The problem lay in the fact that the governor received advice from an executive council whose members he appointed and who were part of a local financial elite often ferociously opposed to the policies adopted by the assemblies. As a result, laws enacted by the assemblies were not enforced, policies opposed by the assemblies were implemented and tax revenues were spent for purposes disapproved by the assemblies. This legitimacy deficit was more acutely felt in Lower Canada, as those controlling the executive were all members of the province's English-speaking, Protestant minority. Therefore, an unelected group of people belonging to the minority could promote their interests against the wishes of the elected representatives of the majority in the legislative assembly.

All this took place before the recognition in the British constitutional tradition of the principle of responsible government. It should come as no surprise that once this principle was recognised in the United Kingdom, elected officials from

12 Constitutional Act of 1791, SRC (1985), app. II, no. 3.

both Lower and Upper Canada petitioned the British Government to implement it in Canada, a demand that was rejected. This refusal added fuel to an already tense situation, and, in both provinces, armed rebellions erupted in 1837 to 1838. While rebels in the two provinces asked for a more democratic, and thus responsible, form of government, the claims of Lower Canadians also aimed at obtaining tangible political powers for the French-speaking and Roman Catholic majority. In both provinces, the rebellion proved unsuccessful, but the repression was particularly violent in Lower Canada. Several leaders were hanged, many deported to Australia and others fled to other countries.

These rebellions prompted the British Government to send a civil servant, Lord Durham, to inquire about the situation in those British North American provinces. In 1840, he submitted a report in which he recommended the institution of responsible government for a unified province, United Canada. Durham's project was to assimilate the French of Lower Canada, whom he deemed were without culture or history, believing that they would benefit from integrating into the British mainstream. Although his recommendation about the implementation of responsible government was not accepted, that concerning the merger of the two provinces was. In the Union Act of 1840,[13] a single legislature was thus created, with an equal number of members from Canada East (the former Lower Canada) and Canada West (the former Upper Canada), despite the fact that Canada East's population was much higher at the time. Quite simply, the goal was to ensure the presence of an English-speaking majority in the legislature, that is, one that would be more inclined to promote the interests of the Crown in the newly united province. However, private law matters continued to be governed by civil law in Canada East and common law in Canada West, with statutes often being applicable in one part of the province and not in the other.

But not only did this new regime prove to be non-functional from an institutional perspective; it also failed to achieve its objective of assimilating the French population and, in Canada East, to assuage tensions between Anglo-Protestants and Franco-Catholics. Taking stock of these deficiencies, representatives from various parts of Britain's North American empire eventually met in the mid-1860s to discuss the parameters of a constitutional reform that could address the fears and expectations of both ethno-linguistic groups and of all of Britain's remaining colonies in North America. For English-speaking Canada West, whose population had by that time outnumbered that of Canada East, a guarantee of representation by population in a new national Parliament represented a critically important gain, as it could enshrine the Canada-wide dominance of the English-speaking majority. For predominantly French-speaking and Roman Catholic Canada East, a separate provincial legislature de facto controlled by a French majority, with authority over education, culture and most private law matters, was also a significant gain, as it provided it with institutional guarantees capable of ensuring its cultural survival.

13 Union Act, 1840, RSC (1985), app. II, no. 4.

This process culminated with the enactment in 1867 of the British North America Act, now called the Constitution Act 1867,[14] which gave birth to contemporary Canada.

Other factors accelerated the process. On the military front, the fear of American expansionism played an important role in convincing colonial representatives to consider the union of their colonies. Economically, they wanted to expand their networks beyond that of the mother-country and the creation of a common market made sense in this regard. Moreover, the pooling of the financial resources of the colonies involved in the discussions was perceived as a way to facilitate the undertaking of large public projects, such as railways. The implementation of these ideas in the Constitution Act 1867 took the form of a federal union of three of the remaining British North American colonies in Canada (United Canada, Nova Scotia and New Brunswick), United Canada being re-divided into two distinct provinces, Ontario and Quebec.

The Constitution Act 1867 allocates distinct and exclusive powers to the federal Parliament and to provincial legislatures. It establishes a bicameral national Parliament with representation by population in the elected lower house – the House of Commons – and representation by region in the appointed upper house – the Senate. It also creates equivalent provincial institutions, but provinces have since abolished their upper houses.

It is now time to examine to what extent this federal regime, and the constitutional developments that took place after 1867, affected Quebec's status of relative autonomy within Canada.

3. Some concrete aspects of Quebec's autonomy

3.1 Autonomous powers

It is important to clarify at the outset the main parameters governing the interpretation of the division of powers found in the Constitution Act 1867, which applies to legislation and administrative action.[15]

First, federal and provincial levels of government are co-equal and autonomous in their areas of constitutional jurisdiction within the Canadian federation,[16] subject to the primacy of federal legislation in case of operational conflict with provincial laws.[17]

14 Constitution Act 1867, RSC (1985), app. II, no. 5.

15 *Liquidators of the Maritime Bank of Canada v. Receiver General of New Brunswick* [1892] AC 437 (Judicial Committee of the Privy Council).

16 *Hodge v. The Queen* [1883] 9 AC 117 (Judicial Committee of the Privy Council).

17 For a first iteration of federal paramountcy, see: *A.G. Ontario v. A.G. Canada* [1896] AC 348 (Judicial Committee of the Privy Council). For a more recent iteration, see, inter alia: *Rothmans, Benson & Hedges Inc. v. Saskatchewan* [2005]1 SCR 188.

Second, the federal division of powers is symmetrical, which means that all provinces are vested with the same powers, at least as far as formal law is concerned. The extent to which and the ways in which they actually exercise them may vary, however. In this respect, Quebec has historically tended to exercise them to the fullest extent possible and to constantly push their boundaries so as to increase its margin of autonomy.

Third, Canada's division of powers dates back to 1867, an era where the state was much less active than today. This conception of a minimalist state is reflected in the types of powers explicitly allocated to one or the other level of government. For instance, many areas of jurisdiction which currently entail high spending, such as education and health care, are devolved to provinces, whose fiscal powers are not as broad as the federal government's. Yet, such an imbalance is not intentional, as governments in 1867 were investing very little in those areas. Moreover, the Constitution Act 1867 contains provisions that give rather extraordinary powers to the federal government, such as that of disallowing provincial legislation, to such an extent that some commentators have argued that Canada was not a true federation, structurally speaking. However, to get the real picture, one must go beyond black-letter law to make sense of the Canadian constitutional *dynamic*. Indeed, judicial interpretations since 1867 have made sure that if Canada does not have a perfect federal structure, its government, to quote Kenneth Wheare, is unmistakably federal.[18] For example, partly because of the judicial enshrinement of the provinces' co-equal status, the extraordinary powers granted to the federal government have fallen into disuse and can no longer be exercised as a matter of constitutional conventions, even if they are still part of the country's constitutional law.

Fourth, conflicts about the division of powers are ultimately settled by the Supreme Court, whose judges are appointed by the federal government, with a legal minimum of three Quebeckers out of nine judges,[19] this in view of ensuring a minimal presence of judges trained in the civil law of Quebec.

Fifth, courts always try to allocate 'new' subjects by referring to already explicit or recognised heads of power, which are deemed 'exclusive'. They have thus given a narrow scope to the federal residuary power. However, the actual impact of the doctrine of 'exclusiveness' is attenuated by the 'double aspect' doctrine, which essentially seeks to give as much constitutional space as possible to the regulatory endeavours of each level of government. Under this doctrine, many topics may be regulated by both levels of government, if each one's regulation is, in essence, related to one or many of its areas of jurisdiction.

Sixth, while it is true that the federal Parliament is vested with some potentially expansive areas of jurisdictions, which could threaten provincial ones if too broadly construed (for example, the powers to legislate for the peace, order and

18 WHEARE, K.C. (1963) *Federal Government.* 4th Edn. London: Oxford University Press. pp. 19–20.
19 Supreme Court Act, RSC (1985), c. C-S-26, s. 6.

good government of Canada,[20] to regulate trade and commerce,[21] and to legislate with respect to criminal law[22]), provinces are not deprived either of important areas of jurisdiction. These include 'property and civil rights', which encompasses most of private law, including family law, as well as local matters in general, and health care.[23] They also possess jurisdiction over some core identity markers to which we will return hereafter. It is worth noting here that one of the reasons that justified the allocation of property and civil rights to provinces was the need to respond to Quebec's desire to maintain its civil law identity.

Provinces also own the natural resources on their respective territory, which can obviously be an important source of autonomous revenues.[24] They further enjoy significant taxation powers.[25]

Topics such as the environment and economic development are shared jurisdictions, as none is explicitly allocated to one or the other level of government. The same is true for culture, each level of government being able to legislate over it from its specific heads of powers. It remains that particular fields of interesting culture have been allocated either explicitly or by interpretation to one level of government or another. For example, telecommunications fall under federal jurisdiction,[26] but education is a provincial jurisdiction,[27] which encompasses the language of instruction.

Unsurprisingly, the question of language bears a special importance given Quebec's interest in preserving French, a minority language in Canada. In this respect, provinces possess jurisdiction over language, except (1) in respect of the federal administration, and (2) subject to their respect of the rights of official language minorities, as enshrined in the Canadian Charter of Rights and Freedoms.[28]

In Quebec, several language laws have been adopted over the years, but the most famous is the Charter of French Language,[29] which inter alia restricts access to non-French schools and imposes conditions for advertising in a language other than French. This controversial piece of legislation sought to challenge a negative social and cultural dynamic that long affected the preservation of the French language in Quebec, this, in spite of the presence of a majority of French speakers in the province. Indeed, until 1977, one of the most important challenges facing

20 Constitution Act 1867, above note 14, s. 91.
21 Ibid., para. 91(2).
22 Ibid., para. 91(27).
23 Ibid., para. 92(13), (16) and (7).
24 Ibid., s. 109.
25 Ibid., para. 92(2).
26 Ibid., para. 92(10); *Téléphone Guèvremont Inc. v. Québec (Régie des télécommunications)* [1994] 1 SCR 878.
27 Ibid., s. 93.
28 Canadian Charter of Rights and Freedoms, Part I of the Constitution Act 1982, which constitutes Sch. B of the Canada Act, 1982 (UK), 1982, c. 11 (hereinafter referred to by its full title, or as 'the Charter' or 'the Canadian Charter').
29 Charter of French Language, RSQ, c. C-11.

Quebec was the assimilation of most immigrants to the province into its English-speaking minority, and the risk that its distinct French culture would be lost. Moreover, relatively few English speakers could then speak French, even among those born in the province. Vested with a strong symbolic capital as the privileged vehicle of wealth and prestige in Canada and North America, English remained a magnet which was perceived by many French speakers as enjoying an unfair competitive advantage over French. Seeking to redress that imbalance, the Charter of French Language launched a major exercise of social (re-)engineering, notably by coercing immigrants, French speakers and English speakers whose parents had not received education in English in Canada to attend French schools in Quebec. This constraint initially applied to all English speakers coming from Canadian provinces other than Quebec, but it was deemed to contravene the minority language educational rights entrenched in the 1982 Canadian Charter of Rights and Freedoms, partly to counter some of the effects of the Charter of French Language. The enactment of this historical statute basically asked the following questions. To what extent can a community, which forms a culturally fragile majority in a federated unit but a minority in the larger federation, legislate in view of ensuring its perpetuation and cultural blossoming? To what extent can it limit the individual rights of parents to choose the language of education of their children? To what extent can it legislate to preserve the 'linguistic visage' of its society? Originally raised in the context of the adoption and implementation of the Charter of French Language, these questions have now spread to other 'small nations' which have adopted language policies inspired by the Quebec model.

Sociologically, the Charter of French Language has proved a success. It has indeed facilitated the integration into the French mainstream of immigrants who, prior to its enactment, would probably have attended English schools. Its downside was to provoke an exodus of English Quebeckers shortly after its enactment. But its main outcome is undeniable: it has significantly altered the linguistic dynamic and the ethno-linguistic make-up of Quebec society. Perhaps paradoxically as it was denounced outside of Quebec as a blow to a bilingual – and largely idealistic – representation of Canada given the abysmally low rate of French–English bilingualism outside of Quebec, the Charter of French Language may have helped sustain Canadian unity by providing French Quebeckers with a stronger sense of cultural security. Since linguistic insecurities propelled to a large extent the secessionist movement in Quebec, one can argue that while being a clear affirmation of cultural nationalism,[30] the Charter of French Language contributed to defuse separatism to a certain extent. This is true even if some provisions of the Canadian Charter of Rights and Freedoms, adopted after the Charter of French Language, served as springboards for successful challenges to various aspects of that Charter. Such was the case of provisions guaranteeing access to minority

30 See generally: HANDLER, R. (1988) *Nationalism and the Politics of Culture in Quebec*. Madison: University of Wisconsin Press.

language instruction to the children of all Canadians who have received instruction in either French or English in Canada,[31] or of provisions protecting freedom of commercial expression.[32] Such provisions have had the effect of limiting Quebec's autonomy when it comes to legislating over language.

The adoption of the Charter of French Language somehow constituted the apex of a process, which had begun in the early 1960s, with the launch of the so-called 'Quiet Revolution'. At stake in this process was a quest for the recognition of Quebec as a distinct nation within Canada. One hurdle to this quest, at least according to nationalist Quebeckers, was the adoption of the federal policy of multiculturalism and its eventual inclusion in the Constitution Act 1982 as a principle of interpretation of the Canadian Charter of Rights and Freedoms. This policy is still seen in some circles as a challenge to Quebec's affirmation of its distinct national identity and as a guise through which that identity could be diluted.[33] The *political* recognition of the Quebec nation in 2006 by the House of Commons, with no tangible legal consequences, has hardly changed that prevailing view.

3.2 Cultural autonomy and its impact on inter-group relations within Quebec

The genesis of Canada shows that it was structured as a federation in large part in view of responding to the collective concerns of the French-speaking Catholics who, for the most part, *lived* in Quebec under a legal regime different from the ones existing elsewhere in North America and, most importantly, whose cultural traits distinguished them from other Canadians of European origins.[34] Indeed, absent this particular vector of deep diversity, it is by no means clear that Canada would have been constituted as a federation, and this, in spite of the strong regional diversity that existed beyond the linguistic-religious divide brought about by the presence of Quebec and that still persists today.

Concerns for the diversity brought about by the presence of Quebec within Canada are reflected in some of the most important provisions of the Constitution Act 1867.

In a nutshell, this constitutional instrument vested in the federal Parliament jurisdiction over matters of 'national' interest, while provinces were given the power to deal with 'local' issues. For example, provinces were allocated jurisdiction over education, which did allow them, to some extent, to exercise control over a critically important field for the purpose of maintaining distinct regional or

31 Canadian Charter of Rights and Freedoms, above note 28, s. 23.

32 Ibid., para. 2(b).

33 See LAFOREST, G. (1995) *Trudeau and the End of a Canadian Dream*. Montreal/Kingston: McGill-Queen's University Press.

34 *Reference re. Secession of Quebec* [1998]2 SCR 217, at para. 59.

cultural identities. This proved especially significant for Quebec, the only jurisdiction in North America where a government, albeit a provincial one, was controlled by a Franco-Catholic community. However, this provincial jurisdiction over education was constrained by the religious rights entrenched in the same constitution. For instance, Protestants in Quebec and Catholics in Ontario, who respectively formed the religious minority in these provinces, were granted rights to state-sponsored religious schools.[35] This was seen as an acceptable compromise by two communities whose relations were quite tense at the time. What is important to understand here is that under this regime, the protection of linguistic rights was merely derivative of that afforded to religion. To the extent that they respected the constitutional guarantees given to Catholic or Protestant minorities, provinces could implement whatever educational policy they wanted. It is on the basis of that logic that it was held that Ontario could validly impose English as the only language of instruction in the province, in spite of the vigorous opposition of its French-speaking minority.[36] The province of Quebec made no attempt at retaliating through the adoption of an equivalent policy, largely because of the political and economic clout of its Anglo-Protestant minority.

On another front, the 1867 Constitution only bound the federal Parliament and the Quebec legislature to enact their laws in English and French, and their courts to hear cases in both languages.[37] Afterwards, a similar provision was imposed on the newly created province of Manitoba, but the province deliberately decided to ignore its constitutional obligations in this respect. In spite of the protest triggered by this decision, especially in Quebec, the federal government, which had the constitutional power to disallow the province's action, refused to intervene. Almost a century later, the Supreme Court declared unconstitutional all the laws of Manitoba enacted solely in English, but suspended the effects of this declaration in order to avoid legal chaos.[38] In the meantime, a province that was largely bilingual at its inception had become, thanks to that particular policy and to immigration and educational policies favouring the assimilation of non-English speakers into the English-speaking community, a largely unilingual, English-speaking one, with only a small minority of French speakers remaining.

Institutional bilingualism was thus initially conceived of as asymmetrical in nature, by imposing *de jure* institutional bilingualism only on the province of Quebec.[39] As to the educational rights provided in the Constitution Act 1867, they

35 Constitution Act 1867, above note 14, s. 93.

36 *Ottawa Roman Catholic Separate School Trustees v. Mackell* [1917] AC 62 (Judicial Committee of the Privy Council).

37 Constitution Act 1867, above note 14, s. 133.

38 *Re. reference Manitoba Language Rights* [1985] 1 SCR 721.

39 Since then, the province of New Brunswick, where the French-speaking Acadians roughly form a third of the population, has become officially bilingual. See: Canadian Charter of Rights and Freedoms, above note 28, s. 16.1. For its part, Quebec has tried, to the extent allowed by the Canadian Constitution, to increase through regulatory means the presence of French at both

largely failed to protect linguistic minorities because, as alluded to, these rights were primarily concerned with religion, not language. This is how the protection of minority language rights soon became, in practice, a political question rather than a legal one. At this game, the immediate losers were clearly the French-speaking minorities outside Quebec. This marked the first step toward the rejection of a 'dualist', or bicultural, conception of the country that would be applicable at a pan-Canadian level. This conception, popular in Quebec but much less so elsewhere, somehow mirrored the 'two nations' conception of Canada that would long inform, and still informs, Quebec's attitudes toward Canada. That both were eventually rejected by the majority somehow reveals the self-deluding nature of the beliefs minority groups may entertain about their ability to impose their views in a political context where they precisely constitute a minority and where there is hardly any formal legal foundation to justify these beliefs. These observations concerning the early political dynamic of the relations between the two main linguistic groups in Canada are of the utmost importance, as religion eventually yielded to language as the main fault line in Canadian constitutional politics.

It bears remembering at this stage that very early on in the development of the Canadian federation, a legally enshrined asymmetry was supplemented by an asymmetry in political leverage. But although some level of asymmetry was formally enshrined in the Constitution Act 1867, most notably through the above-mentioned religious and linguistic rights and through the particular conditions provided for the admission of provinces in the federation, the approach informing the management of cultural diversity in 1867 by and large relied on a logic of symmetry: all the provinces were given the same powers, with some of these, like education, directly relevant to the preservation and management of cultural diversity. In this way, the constitutional *imprimatur* to any provincial expression of some form of cultural distinctiveness through its legislation was real, but nevertheless indirect. For instance, no formal constitutional acknowledgement of the bi- or multinational nature of the federation, and of the existence, *qua* nations, of the national communities composing it, was ever made. And given this prejudice in favour of symmetry, a direct, explicit and exclusive recognition of Quebec's distinctiveness was simply not on the cards. It still remains a bone of contention, especially when discussions revolve around the potential *constitutional* recognition of that distinctiveness.

All this had an impact on what Canada later became. Indeed, as French-speaking minorities outside Quebec were shrinking, this particular province increasingly saw itself, rightly or wrongly, not only as the stronghold of French

institutional and societal levels. A series of statutes designed to enhance the status of French have thus been adopted since the early 1970s, the most recent of which is the 1977 Charter of French Language, above note 29. Although this law has drawn international attention for restricting the use of languages other than French on public signs and for imposing upon non-Francophones who were not schooled in English in Canada the duty to send their children to French school, Quebec remains in practice the most bilingual jurisdiction in Canada.

culture in Canada, but also as its only sustainable bastion, and, over the years, the identity of a significant number of its inhabitants shifted. From French-Canadians with a pan-Canadian ethno-cultural identity, they became Quebeckers with a narrower territorial identity.[40] They later drew consequences from this territorial refocusing, and began redefining their identity on a civic rather than merely ethnic basis. Yet, recent episodes, such as the 2008 crisis over the 'reasonable accommodation' of religion[41] and the 2013 crisis provoked by a planned 'Charter of Quebec values',[42] show that this process is not only far from completed, but also possibly recessing, as ethno-nationalism seems to enjoy a resurgence. As is the case in other Western societies, it is religion that stirs passion, and most particularly Islam.

The discussion above unsurprisingly reveals that power imbalances always risk constraining or limiting the effectiveness of legal norms, even constitutional ones. But further evolutions also demonstrate that, to some extent, legal norms may help alleviate, and even reverse, the effects of the most deleterious power imbalances. We have already mentioned the electroshock brought about by the Charter of French Language on the language dynamic in Quebec. Immigrants started integrating into the French-speaking majority and the English-speaking community was substantially transformed: after the exodus of a good number of its members, those who stayed learned to speak French, to such an extent that English-speaking Quebeckers are now the most bilingual group in Canada. One of the virtues of the Charter of French Language is that it provides a decently stable and clear framework. While it symbolically purports to make French the only official language of Quebec, subject to constitutional guarantees pertaining to the institutional bilingualism and applicable to the legislature and the court system, it allows for the coexistence of separate, English-speaking, educational and health care institutions. To be sure, language will always remain a divisive issue, but intergroup relations are in a significantly better shape now than they were in the past.

Yet, grey areas remain. Quebec's nationalist policies constantly risk clashing with the interests of various communities living on its territory. I have so far

40 On this, see notably: DUMONT, F. (1993) *Genèse de la société québécoise.* Montreal: Boréal; and LÉTOURNEAU, J. (2000) *Passer à l'avenir. Histoire, mémoire, identité dans le Québec d'aujourd'hui.* Montréal: Boréal.

41 See: GAUDREAULT-DESBIENS, J.-F. (2009) Religious Challenges to the Secularized Identity of an Insecure Polity. A Tentative Sociology of Québec's Reasonable Accommodation Debate. In R. GRILLO et al. (eds) *Legal Practice and Cultural Diversity.* London: Ashgate. p. 151. See also, generally: GAUDREAULT-DESBIENS, J.-F. (ed.) (2009) *Le droit, la religion et le 'raisonnable'. Le fait religieux entre monisme étatique et pluralisme juridique.* Montréal: Éditions Thémis.

42 The 'Charter of Quebec Values', later renamed the 'Charter of Secularism' in a bill tabled before Quebec's National Assembly, never became law, as the Parti Québécois Government which promoted it suffered a crushing electoral defeat in 2014. Since then, various episodes have shown that religion remains a thorny issue in the province. Recurrent debates, mostly about Islam, have fuelled the re-emergence of a form of 'identity' nationalism akin to that experienced in many European countries.

mentioned the province's English-speaking communities, but one cannot ignore the competing nationalist agendas of the thirteen Aboriginal peoples of Quebec, who hold significant rights under the Canadian Constitution.[43] There have been episodes where such clashes arose, most recently during the 1990 Oka crisis, where a stand-off between an Aboriginal group and the Quebec provincial police and eventually the Canadian Armed Forces paralysed an entire region for a whole summer.

3.3 Guarantees and integration into the federation

I have so far examined the extent to which the Canadian constitutional regime enables Quebec to promote a political agenda seeking to reflect and protect its unique culture. A further question is whether Quebec enjoys, within the federation, any specific guarantee that preserves its political and constitutional status. This question must be distinguished from that concerning the rights that individual French-speaking Quebeckers enjoy, as citizens of Canada, if they want to perpetuate their culture outside of Quebec. I have by and large answered the latter; I shall now turn to the former.

As mentioned, the Canadian Constitution mostly treats provinces in a symmetrical way. Thus, the fact that Quebec is, culturally speaking, quite different from the other provinces does not entail a significantly different constitutional status. Some guarantees nevertheless ensure that the province's status within the federation is institutionally protected, at least in some respects.

First, a set of rather complex constitutional rules provides the province with a guarantee as to the minimum number of members to which it is entitled in the House of Commons and in the Senate.[44] However, as Quebec's population tends to grow less rapidly than elsewhere, fears of being dwarfed in spite of the presence of such a threshold remain. Moreover, contrary to the structure that exists in other federations such as Germany, the Canadian Senate is not composed of representatives appointed by the federated units, which means that provinces do not have a direct institutional say in federal politics.

Second, the Supreme Court Act expressly provides that out of nine judges, a minimum of three must come from Quebec.[45] Again, we need to relativise the protection that this guarantee affords the province of Quebec. On the one hand, the reason why this minimum number of judges from Quebec is legally enshrined in the Supreme Court Act lies not in the need to provide an institutional protection to the province as such, but rather in the need to ensure that there is a critical mass of civil-law-trained judges on the Supreme Court of Canada. On the other hand, given the principle of judicial independence, judges in a state where the rule of

43 Constitution Act 1982, above note 28, s. 35.

44 Constitution Act 1867, above note 14, ss. 37 and 22, as amended.

45 See above note 19.

law prevails simply cannot be depicted as 'representatives' of one level of government or another, as this would go against the very mission underlying their function.

A further significant issue concerning the Supreme Court and not dealt with by its enabling statute is the thorny question of the judges' command of Canada's two official languages, English and French.[46] Although the English and French versions of federal statutes are equally authoritative – which is also the case with statutes enacted by the legislatures of Quebec, Manitoba and New Brunswick – and although legal interpreters should, as a matter of principle, look at both versions to decipher the legislative intent, there is currently no formal obligation of bilingualism imposed upon Supreme Court judges. Some are already actively bilingual when they are appointed, which means that they understand and speak both official languages. Some are passively bilingual, i.e. they can understand, but not speak, one of the official languages. Finally, some are unilingual, and even though they are encouraged to develop some proficiency in the other official language, they can always rely on the court's translation services if they so wish. In the past decades, some unilingual judges have managed to learn the other official language, but others have not. The debate on Supreme Court judges' bilingualism is regularly reignited by bills seeking to formally enshrine this obligation in the Supreme Court Act, with little success so far. This debate shows that Canada's main historical fracture line, i.e. language, continues to sharply divide the country. It also sheds light, if need be, on the power imbalances that still exist between the two formally equal official languages of Canada, and, concretely, between the two communities congregated around one or the other of these official languages. Be it within or outside the legal community, most English-speaking commentators reject the idea of demanding bilingualism from Supreme Court appointees, while most French-speaking ones have lent their support to it.

Opponents of the idea essentially argue that merit should be the only criterion applicable to Supreme Court appointees, and that imposing a bilingualism requirement would automatically exclude a number of superbly qualified candidates, especially in Western provinces where the level of bilingualism in the population is even lower than in other parts of the country. They further expound the view that judges can incrementally begin to learn the other official language once they are appointed to the court. They also note that there is no evidence that the lack of bilingualism of some judges has negatively affected the work of the Supreme Court of Canada, whose international reputation is stellar. Some have gone as far as characterising a formal bilingualism requirement as some kind of a French-speaking conspiracy to take control of the Supreme Court, an argument which, ironically, is not flattering to English speakers as it seems to (wrongly) assume their inability to learn French. Others have finally referred to European

46 The following paragraphs draw heavily on the following report: GAUDREAULT-DESBIENS, J.-F. (2011) International Survey: Canada. *Public Law*. pp. 827–833.

judicial practice to question the need and realism of a formal bilingualism requirement. Are European judges asked to understand all the official languages of the Union? But unlike Canada, the European Union does not pretend to be a single, unified, sovereign country, albeit a federal one, with *two* official languages. This comparison thus has limits.

While agreeing that merit is the most important criterion determining Supreme Court appointments, supporters of the idea argue that merit includes, or should include, minimal competencies in both official languages, given the official bilingualism of federal institutions and legislation. They also point out that a judge who has to rely entirely on the court's translation services inevitably loses part of the legal argument that is made in the official language he or she does not master, and this, even if the translation is reasonably competent, may ultimately cause prejudice to litigants. This is especially the case in the field of criminal law, with the recognition of a limited, but recently expanded, right to have one's trial in one's official language, given the stakes involved.[47] Supporters of the idea further note that, in practice, unilingual judges are inevitably English speakers, as no unilingual French speaker could ever dream of being appointed to the Supreme Court of Canada. They then observe that this asymmetry has the effect of imposing an extra burden upon bilingual and generally French-speaking or Quebec-based judges, who, in addition to being forced to interact with their colleagues in English whenever insufficiently bilingual judges attend a meeting, often have to write their judgments in English so as to ensure that their unilingual colleagues are able to read their prose and that the work of the court will not be unduly delayed by the translation of mere draft opinions. In other words, they have to bear with the negative externalities created by their colleagues' unilingualism or insufficient bilingualism.

Both views can be defended, but it is hard not to be struck by the formal conception of equality that transpires from the arguments made by the opponents of the idea. Indeed, while it is correct to state that a formal bilingualism obligation imposed upon Supreme Court candidates would exclude otherwise qualified candidates, it is equally true that opponents to the bilingualism project obscure the fact that this argument only applies, in practice, to unilingual English-speaking judges, as no unilingual French-speaking judge has ever been appointed to the court, or could be seriously considered as a candidate to such an appointment, irrespective of his or her qualifications as a jurist. There is a clear double standard applied here, even if it is never formally expressed. A second assumption that informs the arguments of many opponents of the idea seems to be that French is relevant only for interpreting Quebec civil law, which is blatantly incorrect. Quebec civil law expresses itself in both French and English, and so does the Canadian common law tradition. Most importantly, federal legislation in Canada is bilingual, and the principles of bilingual interpretation command that both

47 *R. v. Beaulac* [1999] 1 SCR 768.

versions of a statute should be examined to identify the legislative intent. It may even happen that it is the French version which better reflects that interpretation. Very often, however, this polyphonic reading is not performed, sometimes at the expense of litigants themselves. But this apparent reluctance is more than often an outright impossibility given the low level of bilingualism of the population outside Quebec and, to a lesser extent, outside Ontario and the Maritime provinces.

In all likelihood, the status quo will probably prevail for a long time, which means that bilingual judges will be appointed when possible, but that it will never become a formal requirement. In any event, this debate has the virtue of exposing the limited reach of bilingualism in Canada. By and large, the official bilingualism of federal institutions was adopted in view of allowing one to use one's mother tongue, provided it is either French or English, when dealing with the federal administration.[48] In a certain way, it implies a right to remain unilingual. Contrary to the idealised image of Canada often projected abroad, Canadian bilingualism thus remains essentially institutional rather than cultural.[49] The generally very low level of bilingualism, except in French-speaking communities (within and outside Quebec) and in Quebec's English-speaking community, is partly explainable by the fact that apart from some demographically marginal, but successful, experiments such as French-immersion curricula, public instruction is a provincial jurisdiction under the current federal division of powers and that provinces have historically been less than eager to board the bilingualism train. Misunderstandings due to confusions between the minimalist institutional iteration of bilingualism that is currently in force and a broader cultural conception one might eventually wish to take hold are thus bound to continue.

Third, the Canadian Constitution provides another layer of protection for provinces, namely, through provisions that require various levels of provincial consent for constitutional amendments. Some of these provisions practically give provinces a veto over amendments that would bring about substantial structural change by requiring the unanimity of all provinces and the federal Parliament to proceed to such amendments. The types of changes contemplated are changes to the office of the Head of State and its representatives, to the minimum number of members in the House of Commons that each province has, to the use of English and French, to the composition of the Supreme Court of Canada, and to the amending procedures of the Constitution Act 1982.[50] Moreover, many potentially significant amendments require the support of seven provinces representing at least 50 per cent of the population of all the provinces and of the

48 See FRASER, G. (2006) *Sorry, I Don't Speak French. Confronting the Canadian Crisis that Won't Go Away.* Toronto: McClelland & Stewart.

49 On this distinction and on the interplay between legal bilingualism and bijuralism, see: GAUDREAULT-DESBIENS, J.-F. (2007) *Les solitudes du bijuridisme canadien. Essai sur les rapports de pouvoir entre les traditions juridiques et la résilience des atavismes identitaires.* Montréal: Les Éditions Thémis.

50 Constitution Act 1982, above note 28, s. 41.

federal Parliament – the so-called '7-50 formula'.[51] Amendments to the federal division of powers would be covered by this formula. It is, however, expressly provided that an amendment transferring to the federal Parliament provincial powers relating to education or cultural matters can be subject to a provincial opting-out with a reasonable compensation from the federal government.[52] Thus, should such an amendment take place, with Quebec dissenting and not wanting to lose its jurisdiction over a topic deemed core to its distinct identity, it could opt out of this amendment and receive a reasonable compensation from the federal government. Other notable changes contemplated by the 7-50 formula also include the principle of proportionate representation of the provinces in the House of Commons, the powers of the Senate and the method of selecting Senators.[53] Importantly, amendments affecting one or more, but not all, provinces require the assent of all the provinces concerned. This notably applies to amendments changing provincial borders.[54]

As can be seen, the processes that must be followed to amend the Canadian Constitution are rather complex and onerous.[55] As such, they protect provinces relatively well against undesired amendments that would affect either their competencies or their interests. On the other hand, the difficulty of getting multilateral constitutional amendments adopted tends to lead to a sclerosis of the formal constitutional structure of the federation. In 1990, the province of Quebec somehow fell victim of that complexity when the Meech Lake Accord, which would have formally recognised the province as a 'distinct society' within Canada, could not gather the unanimous support of all other provinces and could thus not enter into force. Arguably, Canada also lost, with the demise of this Accord, the opportunity to inflict a lethal blow to Quebec secessionism, because, if adopted, the Accord would possibly have met the constitutional expectations of a vast majority of Quebeckers.

3.4 External relations

For small, stateless nations who fear disappearing or being swamped by a larger whole, the international arena is often seen, rightly or wrongly, as providing a kind

51 Ibid., s. 38.
52 Ibid., s. 40.
53 Ibid., s. 42.
54 Ibid., s. 43.
55 A federal statute adopted in 1996 further increases the complexity of constitutional amendments by preventing the federal Parliament from tabling a constitutional amendment to which the 7–50 formula applies unless specific targets are met in terms of provincial support. Under that legislation, Parliament must therefore obtain the consent of Quebec, Ontario, British Columbia, two of the Atlantic provinces comprising at least 50 per cent of that region's population, and two of the Prairie provinces comprising at least 50 per cent of that region's population. See Act respecting constitutional amendments, SC 1996, c. 1.

of protective shield against such a fate. It may indeed offer a stage where they can publicise and politicise their existence, sometimes at the risk of irritating the state of which they are part.

The province of Quebec, which was undeniably a pioneer in affirming the legal personhood of federated states on the international scene, has inspired many other 'culturally distinct' sub-state nations in that regard, from Catalonia to the Belgian Flanders. However, on what legal basis could Quebec blossom to such an extent on the international scene? The answer is somewhat surprising.

It should first be stated that Canada, aligning itself with the British legal tradition, is a dualist state, which means that conventional international law needs to be incorporated through domestic legislation to take effect. However, the country's federal structure also has a bearing on how international law can be implemented. This is the result of the 1932 *Labour Conventions* case, where it was decided that international obligations agreed to by the federal government representing Canada as a whole – the *jus tractatus* is a plenary federal prerogative – but dealing with provincial areas of jurisdiction can only take effect in a province if its legislature agrees to it.[56] In other words, although the federal government may theoretically conclude a treaty regulating a matter that entirely falls under the provinces' domestic constitutional jurisdiction, it possesses no legislative means to implement it, nor can it compel provinces to do so. Provinces thus enjoy some autonomy regarding the integration into their domestic realm of international obligations internally falling in their areas of jurisdiction. Even though the *Labour Conventions'* approach was vigorously criticised outside Quebec as potentially impeding Canada's role in the international arena, no such thing ever really happened, as pragmatism led to the emergence of cooperative practices between the federal and provincial governments which sought to resolve potential conflicts before the signing of any international instrument by the federal government.

As the *Labour Conventions* regime equally applies to all provinces, Quebec's position is neither better nor worse than that of other provinces. However, what really distinguishes Quebec's position from that of other provinces at the international level is how the province conducts, and conceptualises, its international relations. The Canadian Constitution does not expressly refer to external relations, except in a now obsolete provision that deals with Canada's limited powers in this area when it was a dominion of the British Empire.[57] While the Constitution does not formally prohibit provinces from establishing external relations with other countries or federated states, it is well-settled law that it is the federal Crown that, under the auspices of its prerogative powers, is competent to

56 *A.G. Ontario v. A.G. Canada* [1937] AC 326 (Judicial Committee of the Privy Council).
57 Constitution Act 1867, above note 14, s. 132.

conduct Canada's foreign policy.[58] Following the same logic, it is the federal Crown that may bind Canada through international treaties and conventions. However, amplifying the ratio of the *Labour Conventions* case, the province of Quebec has challenged that vision since the 1960s by officially adopting the doctrine that its domestic jurisdictions extend on the international plane and that the province is competent to sign treaties recognised as such under the Vienna Convention on the Law of Treaties.[59] Although this 'doctrine' – named 'Gérin-Lajoie' after the minister who first iterated it – has no legal foundation in either Canadian law or international law, the Quebec Government keeps pushing it and it has become over the past fifty years a kind of pseudo-legal fetish that even federalist governments promote, practically turning it into a 'belief', albeit an erroneous one, about what the law allows the province to do.[60]

That being said, nothing, as a matter of principle, precludes provinces from acting as *private* actors on the international scene – for example, when they open a commercial office or delegation abroad. It is when they pretend to act as *public* powers, namely, when they seek to act as sovereign or quasi-sovereign powers (such as states under public international law), that the situation gets more complicated. The only Canadian province that has shown any willingness to challenge this private/public dichotomy is, predictably, Quebec, given its distinct identity, particular cultural network and, of course, nationalist policies. It should come as no surprise, then, that as of the 1960s, Quebec's international activities have been a cause of frictions with Ottawa, especially with the creation of international francophone organisations such as the Francophonie. France played an instrumental role in supporting Quebec's aspirations in that regard, often at the risk of undermining its relations with Canada. For example, it gave the Quebec delegation in Paris full diplomatic recognition, in spite of the fact that it is not a sovereign state. It postponed its support of the creation of the Francophonie until Ottawa agreed that Quebec could be a participating government, which it did in the 1980s. Since then, successive federal governments have come to accept Quebec's wishes to act on the international scene and have administratively agreed to give Quebec, or other wishing provinces, the possibility to speak in some international forums on issues pertaining to their constitutional jurisdictions. Recently, an administrative agreement was signed respecting Quebec's participation within the Canadian delegation at UNESCO.

58 On this, see generally: BEAULAC, S. (2012) The Myth of *Jus Tractatus* in *La Belle Province*: Quebec's Gérin-Lajoie Statement. *Dalhousie Law Journal*. 35(2). pp. 237–266.

59 Vienna Convention on the Law Treaties, 1155 UNTS 331 (1969).

60 For a recent, and ultimately unconvincing, justification of that doctrine, see: CYR, H. (2009) *Canadian Federalism and Treaty Powers – Organic Constitutionalism at Work*. Brussels: PIE Peter Lang. For a rational demolition of the belief in the legal foundation and nature of that doctrine, see: BEAULAC (2012), above note 58.

4. Can Quebec's experience provide any guidance for Tibet?

The Memorandum on Genuine Autonomy for the Tibetan People (hereinafter 'the Memorandum') is currently regarded as the blueprint for any discussion on Tibet's political future within China, at least from Tibet's perspective. While affirming Tibet's distinct identity and positing the requirement that the integrity of the Tibetan nationality be respected, it clearly rejects separatism, preferring instead to situate Tibet's claim for autonomy within the realm of the People's Republic of China. To do so, the Memorandum refers to several provisions of that country's Law on National Regional Autonomy or to other constitutional provisions pertaining to minority autonomy.

Practically, the Memorandum emphasises, not unlike Quebec did with its Charter of French Language, the need to ensure that the Tibetan language be recognised as Tibet's 'main spoken and written language'.[61] It remains vague, however, as to the means preferred for the protection of Tibetan culture, merely referring to 'protection through appropriate constitutional provisions'.[62] Yet, it iterates Tibet's desire to administer its own educational system and stresses the importance of guaranteeing religious freedoms, Tibetan-style Buddhism being presented as central to Tibet's identity. Other cultural specificities of Tibetan culture are addressed under various headings, such as traditional medical practices that are posited as worth promoting. Crucially, the Memorandum seeks to ensure that a majority of the region's security personnel be composed of members of the local nationality by virtue of their familiarity with local customs and traditions. Most importantly, it aims at limiting Han migration, which is deemed to threaten not only Tibet's distinct culture, but also its ability to claim an autonomous status under Chinese law, by potentially altering the demographic conditions necessary for claiming it. Following that logic, the Memorandum calls for a broader control of the residence, settlement and economic activities of non-Tibetans in Tibet. Clearly, the Tibetan people's fear of marginalisation and absorption into the Chinese mainstream inspires the Memorandum.

The Memorandum also directly addresses Tibet's economic and political claims. For instance, control over the region's natural resources, and ownership of some of these resources, are presented as important objectives, especially in light of the overarching goal of promoting Tibet's economical self-reliance. Furthermore, like many other sub-state nations (including Quebec), Tibetans are seeking the recognition of their power to conduct external relations in areas that would fall under their jurisdiction should they ever obtain a political and legal status akin to that contemplated in the Memorandum. Predictably, the Memorandum understands autonomy as implying the creation of institutions responsible for

61 Memorandum on Genuine Autonomy for the Tibetan People, para. IV Basic needs of Tibetans.
62 Ibid.

exercising Tibet's autonomous powers-to-be, as well as the enshrinement of guarantees of representation within national decision-making processes in the People's Republic of China. In this respect, it seeks to prevent such institutions and powers from being unilaterally abrogated or modified, while deploring its current status of autonomy which is regarded as either ineffective or unduly open to arbitrary decisions by China's central authorities. In so doing, it reveals an acute awareness of the fact that any ambiguity in the region's legal entitlements is likely to benefit the central government in an institutional context characterised by a weak rule of law and a non-independent judiciary.

At the time of writing, it is far from clear whether Tibet can realistically entertain the hope that its claims, as laid down in the Memorandum, can be met in whole or in part. Indeed, the reception of such claims seems to face significant politico-legal and psycho-cultural challenges.

The politico-legal challenges are numerous. As Ghai, Woodman and Loper argue, they lie primarily in the central government's priority on unity, stability and sovereignty, in the weak rule of law, in the lack of democratic development, in Communist Party supremacy (where minorities are not formally represented) and in a constitutional ideology that, being informed by both Chinese-Confucian philosophy and Marxist theory, is inclined to reduce or dissolve difference in view of promoting minority integration.[63] In such a context, the formal recognition of regional autonomous statuses has a cosmetic dimension, the Law on National Regional Autonomy being 'an attempt to lend legitimacy and predictability to government policies rather than to make significant changes in relations between minority areas and the central government'.[64] Thus, autonomy is not a right or entitlement strictly speaking, but a mere 'administrative device'[65] where subordination to the central government remains the rule.[66] This situation is comforted by the fact that there is no independent judiciary to arbitrate conflicts[67] and no system of constitutionalism which would facilitate the tangible enforcement of relevant constitutional provisions[68] – it is not the constitution that is supreme, but the Communist Party. This sheds light on a crucial epistemological problem when trying to tackle questions pertaining to 'autonomy' in China: the baggage that is traditionally associated with this concept in Western legal systems, notably

63 GHAI, Y., WOODMAN, S. and LOPER, K. (2010) Is There Space for 'Genuine Autonomy' for Tibetan Areas in the PRC's System of Nationalities Regional Autonomy? *International Journal on Minority and Group Rights*. 17(1). p. 184.

64 Ibid., p. 39.

65 Ibid.

66 Ibid., p. 154. See also: GHAI, Y. and WOODMAN, S. (2009) Unused Powers: Contestation over Autonomy Legislation in the PRC. *Pacific Affairs*. 82(1). pp. 29–46.

67 GHAI et al. (2010), above note 63, p. 154.

68 Ibid., p. 157.

in reference to federalism,[69] may not be relevant or applicable in China.[70] Therefore, when Tibetans refer to 'autonomy' in the Western sense of the word, representatives of the Chinese Government may easily refer to something else.

These significant hurdles could alone prevent the reception of Tibet's project of 'genuine autonomy'. However, there might be deeper, psycho-cultural problems to overcome. According to the literature, the most important one seems to be the ethnocentrism of the Han-dominated central leadership, which presumes the inferiority of the Tibetan culture.[71] There is thus clearly a need to offset the effects of such ethnocentrism by elaborating policies that would neutralise this anti-minority bias and reduce the economic disparities that still plague minority areas as opposed to Han areas, especially considering the fact that the autonomy policies were designed under a system of planned economy which has since then been radically transformed.[72]

The paths identified for a solution of the Sino-Tibetan conflict are equally numerous. A first step would be, according to some, the recognition of the ethnic nature of the conflict – which is highlighted in the Memorandum – and the latter's irreducibility to a mere question of economic development, as the central government sometimes has it.[73] Arguably, this could only come about if China showed more self-confidence in assessing the risks linked to granting Tibet a tangible level of autonomy. For now, however, fear of separatism still dominates the agenda.[74] However, this confuses nationalism and separatism. While one may obviously lead to the other, this relation is only contingent. For example, although most Quebeckers are nationalist and privilege their Quebec identity over their Canadian one, only a minority of them wants separation from Canada.

That being said, most legal solutions envisaged to resolve the Sino-Tibetan conflict remain largely formalistic and idealistic. Some call for the clarification of ambiguous legal constraints, 'such as specifying which national laws do or do not apply to Tibet and the extent of local legislative power and central or Party supervision over Tibetan autonomy'.[75] Such a proposal is reminiscent of the relatively narrow interpretation that was given to the doctrine of 'repugnancy', as enshrined in the now-repealed Colonial Laws Validity Act,[76] when Canada was still a dominion of the British Empire.

69 See BASTA-FLEINER, L. and GAUDREAULT-DESBIENS, J.-F. (2013) Federalism and Autonomy. In FLEINER, T., SAUNDERS, C. and TUSHNET, M. (eds) *Handbook of Constitutional Law*. Oxford: Routledge. p. 143.

70 GHAI et al. (2010), above note 63, p. 157.

71 See KARMEL, S.M. (1995–1996) Ethnic Tension and the Struggle for Order: China's Policies in Tibet. *Pacific Affairs*. 68(4). pp. 485–580.

72 SAUTMAN, B. (1999) Ethnic Law and Minority Rights in China: Progress and Constraints. *Law & Policy* 21(3). pp. 283–314, at p. 301.

73 GHAI et al. (2010), above note 63, p. 184.

74 Ibid., p. 185.

75 Ibid., p. 186.

76 Colonial Laws Validity Act, 1865, 28-28 Vict., c. 63.

Others promote the actual enforcement of existing constitutional provisions regarding national minority laws or the expansion to Tibet of the 'one country, two systems' formula that is applied to Hong Kong.[77] Moreover, some favour a fully fledged recognition of an asymmetrical status for Tibet, taking into account this region's deep diversity when compared to other autonomy-seeking regions.[78] The problem of this latter solution is that the fear of the consequences of asymmetry may be as high as the fear of separatism. In this respect, fear is as much a problem of social psychology as it is one of political trust, as Quebec's vain claims for a formally asymmetrical constitutional status have demonstrated. One way in which to assuage such fears could be to work on the process of intercultural encounters itself. Baogang He has argued in this respect that leaving more space and creating more opportunities for citizen-initiated meetings where deliberative approaches to conflict resolution are used could eventually reduce the level of mutual distrust between Hans and Tibetans. Indeed, experiencing intercultural encounters without official, institutional filters could lead to moderate changes of opinion, with participants to the dialogue 'locked into a polarized position on independence and sovereignty issues, but the level of polarization over social and cultural policies can be reduced'.[79] In other words, deeper disagreements on existential issues would persist, but some consensus could be built on questions standing at the core of the (Western) concept of autonomy. Finally, some count on the impact of migrants to China and of returning Chinese nationals who have been exposed to other value systems to change the culture of distrust that remains prevalent in China vis-à-vis Tibet.[80]

That being said, can Quebec's path to relative autonomy be of any guidance for Tibet, assuming that Tibet would in all likelihood be happy to enjoy the level of autonomy Quebec currently enjoys within Canada? It is on purpose that I have emphasised in this chapter the historical aspects of Quebec's evolution, as it has allowed me to expose political dynamics that unfolded over many decades. It is true that there are superficial connections to be made between the experiences of both societies: a certain form of cultural isolation, a military conquest, the resilience of a distinct culture almost against all odds, including assimilation strategies. However, differences abound. Among the most important ones, the first is that when New France suffered the trauma of conquest at the hands of Great Britain – the upcoming dominant empire of the time – this empire was nevertheless in a rather uncomfortable geopolitical situation in North America, with its American colonies on the verge of revolution. The second significant difference is that even then, the overall political dynamic was pointing toward more, and not

77 DAVIS, M.C. (2012) Tibet and China's 'National Minority' Policies. 56. *Orbis*. [Online]. Available at: http://ssrn.com/abstract=2127403 [Accessed: 14 February 2017].

78 GHAI et al., above note 63, pp. 140, 185.

79 HE, B. (2010) A Deliberative Approach to the Tibet Autonomy Issue. Promoting Mutual Trust through Dialogue. *Asian Survey*. 50(4). p. 733.

80 PIEKE, F.N. (2012) Immigrant China. *Modern China*. 38(1). pp. 40–77.

less, democracy. In the decades that followed, responsible government came to life in Great Britain, later spreading to the colonies. Moreover, democratic ideals were increasingly becoming a beacon that Western states could hardly ignore. While China has recently witnessed a significant rise of economic liberties, it is far from clear that the same is happening, or will happen any time soon, with respect to political liberties. And, of course, the reception of a demand for more autonomy on the part of Tibet is conditioned upon the status and meaning given to political liberties in China.

Returning to the question as to whether or not Quebec's experience can inspire Tibet, it is worth recalling, first, that the historical evolution of this province's status since 1763 reveals struggle and progress, as well as a 'convergence of interests'.[81] It is indeed especially important to observe that Quebec progressed on the path of autonomy not only because it wished so or because its new British master or, later, the federal government and the other provinces were particularly 'generous', but primarily because it was in the interest of the coloniser or the pan-Canadian majority to support, often reluctantly, Quebec's wish for more autonomy. However, it is probably fair to say that the logic that has inspired the management of Quebec's deep diversity has been one of *silent enablement*. 'Silent', because of a refusal, or rather a fear, to symbolically enshrine the sociological fact of the multinational (or, to understate it, the 'multi-societal') nature of Canada; 'enablement' because of the array of implicit or explicit norms that, in practice, allow the distinct identity of Quebec to blossom in spite of a lack of fully fledged formal recognition of its nationhood or of its distinct political consciousness.[82] In other words, this silent enablement, notably through federalism, has concretely allowed Quebeckers to build a power relationship with their Canadian counterparts that is significantly more favourable than that of, say, Aboriginal peoples, which are still trying to extirpate themselves from a colonial relationship with their non-Aboriginal neighbours. Yet, many Quebeckers still resent the lack of formal constitutional recognition of their nationhood or lament the symmetrical status of their province.

That being said, in a context where the rule of law prevails and where there is an old democratic political culture, such a lack of formal recognition is less problematic if specific autonomous powers are otherwise conferred and protected, than in a system with a less robust conception of the rule of law and with a weak democratic culture. Autonomy is conceptually and technically distinct

81 Critical Race scholar Derrick Bell coined this expression as an overarching idea explaining why the famous *Brown* case, dismantling legally grounded racial segregation in the United States, was decided the way it was. See BELL, D. (1980) *Brown v. Board of Education* and the Interest-Convergence Dilemma. *Harvard Law Review.* 93(3). pp. 518–533.

82 I have elaborated on this in GAUDREAULT-DESBIENS, J.-F. (2010) The State Management of Legal and Cultural Diversity in Canada. In FOBLETS, M.-C., GAUDREAULT-DESBIENS, J.-F. and DUNDES RENTELN, A. (eds) *Cultural Diversity and Law. State Responses from Around the World.* Brussels: Bruylant. p. 195.

from any formal constitutional recognition of a society's alleged nationhood. However, it is directly connected with the ability to exercise tangible powers, without external subordination, in a context where there is a reasonably neutral arbitrator taking the form of an independent judiciary. Tibet and China are clearly not at this stage.

Arguably, the problems raised outside Quebec by this province's claim for a formal constitutional recognition of its nationhood evince English-speaking Canada's lack of trust in Quebeckers' loyalty to Canada, this in spite of successive rejections of the secessionist option, and insecurity about its own collective identity, which no legal cosmetic reference to bilingualism or multiculturalism can obliterate. Furthermore, one cannot ignore the impact of majority nationalism, which is often all but visible and which may have problematic effects on minority aspirations. However, the externalities that such majority nationalism produces on their aspirations are necessarily tempered in a democratic state where legality and legitimacy are in constant dialogue. Such is the case of Canada. As the Supreme Court of the country points out in the Quebec Secession Reference:

> In our constitutional tradition, legality and legitimacy are linked. The precise nature of this link will be discussed below. However, at this stage, we wish to emphasize only that our constitutional history demonstrates that our governing institutions have adapted and changed to reflect changing social and political values. This has generally been accomplished by methods that have ensured continuity, stability and legal order.'[83]

Again, according to the literature, it does not seem to be the case in China.

On the other hand, the refusal by many Quebeckers to acknowledge that their society has made tremendous progress, politically and culturally, and that its distinctiveness is probably on firmer grounds today than it was a century ago in spite of not being constitutionally recognised as a 'people' or 'nation' may reflect the action of the common nationalist pathology of insatiable thirst. At the very least, it compels reflection on the limits, or lack thereof, of politics of recognition, and on the deleterious effects of methodological nationalism. More than anything, this old debate reveals fundamental disagreements about what Canada is, or what it should be in the abstract, and about the meaning of equality and nationality in a federal setting. But, still, these disagreements are peacefully voiced. To wit, there were two referenda on independence (or a version of it) in Quebec since 1980, and decisions on such a divisive issue were taken without any violence, which is not a negligible achievement in today's troubled world.

The question of Quebec secession remains unresolved and increasingly seems unresolvable, as a certain segment of the province's population staunchly supports it. Yet, at the time of writing, there is no indication that a clear majority of

83 *Reference re. Secession of Quebec*, above note 34, para. 33.

Quebeckers would say 'yes' to the province's independence if they were asked a clear question about it. But this issue of clarity remains litigious. In its 1998 advisory opinion on the legality of a potential unilateral declaration of independence by Quebec, the Supreme Court of Canada confirmed that Quebec had no right, either under domestic constitutional law or international law, to unilaterally secede from Canada. However, bridging legitimacy with legality, it also held that should a clear majority of the Quebec electorate vote, on a clear question, in favour of secession, the federal government and Quebec would be bound by a duty to negotiate in good faith. However, no obligation of result would be attached to this process, and the Supreme Court even alluded to the hypothesis that should the negotiations fail and Quebec decide to declare independence nonetheless, it is very likely that the international community would be the final arbitrator, with all the political uncertainty that it presupposes.[84] Thus, the bottom line of this opinion is that while Quebec cannot secede unilaterally, Canada could not ignore a clear repudiation of its constitutional order by the province's population.[85]

Following this opinion, the federal government enacted the Clarity Act,[86] which establishes parameters governing a potential federal involvement in a referendum campaign on a province's secession. Particularly, it sets the conditions under which the Canadian Government could consider a question and a majority 'clear' under the Secession Reference regime, and thus be bound to negotiate with the seceding province. It precludes the federal government from negotiating anything if these conditions are not met. This statute, which enshrines a plausible interpretation of the Supreme Court's observations in the Secession Reference, predictably provoked the ire of Quebec's nationalist political class, which denounced it as a denial of Quebec's alleged absolute right to external self-determination. That such an absolute right does not legally exist and that some form of negotiation would have to take place – be it only to divide assets and liabilities – is somehow irrelevant in Quebec's political debate because it essentially takes place in the realm of symbolic politics. Thus, in response to the Clarity Act, the Quebec National Assembly, led at the time by the separatist *Parti québécois*, enacted the Act respecting the Exercise of the Fundamental Rights and Prerogatives of the Québec People and the Québec State,[87] which reiterates Quebec's position that it alone can decide the terms under which a referendum on secession can be held and which otherwise legally affirms some traditional nationalist policies, including the 'Gérin-Lajoie' formula on the province's international powers. The constitutionality of some of its provisions, which are mostly declaratory, is dubious

84 *Reference re. Secession of Quebec*, above note 34.

85 For a contextual analysis of this advisory opinion, see: GAUDREAULT-DESBIENS, J.-F. (1999), The Quebec Secession Reference and the Judicial Arbitration of Conflicting Narratives About Law, Democracy and Identity. *Vermont Law Review*. 23. pp. 792–843.

86 Clarity Act, SC 2000, c. 26.

87 Act respecting the Exercise of the Fundamental Rights and Prerogatives of the Québec People and the Québec State, RSQ, c. E-20.2.

at best.[88] That being said, irrespective of these federal and provincial responses to the Secession Reference, it remains clear that any tangible attempt at seceding would be evaluated in light of legal *and* political standards – not solely in light of one *or* the other. The 2014 referendum process in Scotland, which was held under a framework mutually agreed by London and Edinburgh and which emphasised clarity, has arguably raised the stakes in that regard.

5. Conclusion

It is by definition difficult to conclude about a story that is still unfolding. We cannot precisely know where Quebec and Canada are going. But from their ongoing experience, it is relatively easy to identify some hurdles that should be avoided in order to facilitate dialogue.

The first one is symbolic violence. Events that are perceived, or risk being perceived, as frontal attacks on a nation's identity and status will inevitably lead to a negative reaction and to some form of retrenchment. For example, the repatriation of Canada's Constitution in 1982, without Quebec's approval and with the adjunction of a charter of rights that effectively restricted federal and provincial legislative powers, was received in Quebec as a repudiation of the compact underlying the federation,[89] and further estranged the French-speaking majority of the province from Canada. Of course, this 'reception' was also a 'construction', in the sense that Quebec's nationalist political class, from both federalist and secessionist allegiances, almost unanimously interpreted the events as a repudiation of that compact. Hence, the second hurdle that needs to be avoided in order to ease dialogue, i.e. methodological nationalism, which has been plaguing the Canada-Quebec debate for decades.

Methodological nationalism induces one to construe every single event in a polity through the monist and exclusive prism of one's preferred locus of belonging, this locus – be it the nation, the state or another type of community – being elevated as the pre-eminent 'natural' political form available.[90] In other words, methodological nationalism incites us to more or less consciously reduce our complex identities to monolithic ones. The offsprings of methodological nationalism are, in a system of multi-level governance entrenching the relative autonomy of each level of government, competence-narcissism and jurisdictional

88 BEAULAC (2012), above note 58.

89 For the two advisory opinions rendered by the Supreme Court of Canada in the course of that repatriation process, see: *Reference re. Amendment of Constitution of Canada* [1981] 1 SCR 753; and *Reference re. Amendment of Canadian Constitution* [1982] 2 SCR 793.

90 For an interesting study on that, see: WIMMER, A. and GLICK SCHILLER, N. (2002) Methodological Nationalism and Beyond: Nation-State Building, Migration and the Social Sciences. *Global Networks*. 4(2). pp. 301–334. For a Canadian application of the concept, see: LECLAIR, J. (2013) Socrates, Odysseus, and Federalism. *Review of Constitutional Studies*. 18(1). pp. 1–18.

fetishism, 'where the mere sake of protecting [competences] prevails over any other concern'.[91] Under that view, a Quebecker can hardly be both Quebecker and Canadian, or both Canadian and Quebecker, as if a definitive choice between the two identities had to be made irrespective of the contexts in which such a choice may take place. From that perspective, establishing a fruitful dialogue between the People's Republic of China and Tibet would require reducing the deleterious effects of methodological nationalism, be it Han or Tibetan.

Finally, the third hurdle that needs to be avoided, which is directly related to the preceding one, is to evaluate loyalty from a monist perspective. The loyalty of a member of a national minority simply cannot be asserted using the standards applicable to the majority nation. For instance, many Quebeckers declare themselves to be Quebeckers before being Canadians. Their first loyalty is thus to Quebec, which is perceived as their primary homeland, that is, where they feel the more secure culturally speaking. This sentiment is captured by the motto '*Le Québec ma patrie, le Canada mon pays*'. In a way, their loyalty to Canada is conditional upon the respect by this broader polity of their distinct culture and identity; this typifies political minorities as opposed to mere social ones.[92] But this does not mean that they are, or will be, disloyal to Canada, even though their claims may indeed end up questioning the political legitimacy and even authority of the broader polity. Many factors other than culture or identity are at play when making practical decisions about the fate of a nation. Neither Canada nor the People's Republic of China can afford the luxury to ignore that when dealing with their internal political minorities.

91 GAUDREAULT-DESBIENS, J.-F. (2009) The Fetishism of Formal Law and the Fate of Constitutional Patriotism in Communities of Comfort: A Canadian Perspective. In FOSSUM, J.E., MAGNETTE, P. and POIRIER, J. (eds) *Ties That Bind. Accommodating Diversity in Canada and the European Union*. Brussels, Bern and Berlin: P.I.E. Peter Lang. p. 319.

92 Canadian legal theorist Andrée Lajoie states that *political* minorities are those whose primary locus of identification is a sub-state entity (which in and of itself forms a political community) rather than the global polity constituted by the state, and for whom belonging to the latter is conditional upon the respect by that polity of their primary identification with the sub-state entity. In contrast, *social* minorities are those who are in a legitimate position to advance an equality claim, but whose sense of belonging to the political community formed by the state is not conditioned by any prior, and primordial, identification with another sub-state political community. As a result, claims made by political minorities potentially threaten the integrity of the state, while those made by social minorities do not. See LAJOIE, A. (2002) *Quand les minorités font la loi*. Paris: Presses Universitaires de France.

Chapter 10

The autonomy of Aceh

Hans-Joachim Heintze

1. Introduction

Indonesia is one of the most diverse states in the world and became independent in 1945. It is the fourth most populous state and inhabited by more than fifty ethnic groups who speak more than 450 languages. There is no clearly dominating group; however, it has the world's largest Muslim population.

Prior to Dutch colonialism, there had been no state. The Dutch educated some people to serve in its colonial administration. During the time of Dutch colonialism, the country was governed according to federal structures. After the withdrawal of the Dutch, the independent United States of Indonesia – a federation – were inaugurated. This federation lasted only nine months.[1] As a reaction against the colonial rule, the new Constitution of 1945 – which was drafted in haste during the last days of the Japanese occupation – established the independent Indonesia as a unitary state. Ultimate power was vested in the People's Consultative Assembly. Ethno-nationalism and resistance to the unitary state came later, when the government became increasingly repressive and tried to enforce the assimilation.[2] The response of the Suharto regime to the regional challenges was the acceptance of a certain degree of decentralisation within that huge state and therefore some powers were delegated by the Constitution to the provinces and other sub-state entities. But the important political power had been strongly concentrated with the central government and the most important obligation of all local administrations was the loyal support of the national government.

This system had become quite unpopular because the results of the exploitation of natural resources were channelled to the parasitic and brutal central government.[3] The Constitution was only a piece of paper: according to Article

1 SCHILLER, A.A. (1955) *The Formation of Federal Indonesia 1945–1945*, The Hague/Bandung: W. van Hoeve. p. 18.

2 FEITH, H. (1962) *The Decline of Constitutional Democracy in Indonesia*. Ithaca, NY: Cornell University Press. p. 541.

3 BUTT, S. (2010) Regional Autonomy and Legal Disorder: The Proliferation of Local Laws in Indonesia. *Sydney Law Review*. 32(2). p. 21.

18(2), the provinces, regencies and municipalities enjoyed self-government and regional autonomy. In principle, they were entitled to administer their own affairs. Moreover, the understanding of the term 'autonomy' in the Constitution was quite vague. Article 18(5) ruled that only matters which are defined by law belong to the affairs of the central government.[4]

2. The 1999 decentralisation caused confusion

After the collapse of the Suharto Government in 1998, the claim for real self-administration could no longer be suppressed and the country faced strong separatist movements. There was only one way for the central government to keep the state together and this was to devolve a significant power to local entities.[5] According to the concept of decentralisation, the authority was granted to two kinds of regional entities: the provinces and the districts. The idea behind this kind of decentralisation is subsidiarity, i.e. to bring the government closer to the people. Foreign donors in particular were very much in favour of that principle and Indonesia has transformed to be one of the most decentralised states in the world. In 1999, the government started an ambitious programme of decentralisation which led to significant law-making powers of more than a thousand legislatures and executive bodies. The number of such bodies has continued to increase. One of the consequences has been a great complexity of the law, which has led to uncertainty in the legal system and even to violations of Indonesia's international obligations. The system can be described as a 'vast and extensive jungle of law',[6] because the local lawmakers lack legal drafting skills. The consequences are unclear or unworkable laws which sometimes contradict other laws.

Indonesia after Suharto remained a unitary state, albeit with far-reaching centralisation. After regional autonomy was introduced, the central government was confronted by a strong tendency of the newly established regions to regulate as much as possible and to enlarge their jurisdiction step by step. Consequently, many scholars criticised the content of various local laws and demanded an effective review mechanism. The number of these laws is small; the consequences, however, may be considerable, because they concern many autonomous local entities. Butt argues, therefore, that the system of regional autonomy creates 'nothing short of legal chaos'.[7] Bell also concludes that the 1999 autonomy statute had caused significant confusion because the relationship between the powers of the provinces and local governments in the districts and cities within the provinces

4 SETYOWATI, H. and TOENGKAGIE, M.S. (2006–2007) Introduction to the Indonesian Legal System: Major Developments in the Past Decade. *YB Islamic & Middle East Law*. 13. p. 66.

5 FERRAZZI, G. (2000) Using the 'F' Word: Federalism in Indonesia's Decentralization Discourse. *Publius – The Journal of Federalism*. 30(2). p. 64.

6 BUTT (2010), above note 3, p. 3.

7 BUTT (2010), above note 3, p. 4.

was quite unregulated.[8] Provinces were in legal terms not superior to the local authorities and cities.

Against this background, the central government wanted to regain power and to overcome the legal chaos. This was achieved by the enactment of the Autonomy Law 2004. It gives local governments the 'broadest' autonomy concerning matters not reserved for the central government. The Autonomy Law 2004 specifies the obligations of the provincial, district and city governments in the fields of development planning, public order, public infrastructure, health, education, labour, small and medium-sized enterprises, environment, land affairs, public administration and investment. Matters like foreign affairs, defence, security, finance and religion are reserved for the central government, in addition to the justice sector and immigration. However, there are, according to Article 10 of the Autonomy Law, limitations on regional law-making because the central government retains the power to regulate any matter. Ultimately, one cannot speak about an 'exclusive' law-making jurisdiction of local entities. Moreover, the Autonomy Law 2004 empowers the governors to guide and supervise the districts and cities and to coordinate the implementation of central government affairs in the provinces, districts and cities. Thus, the implementation of the laws made by the central authorities (House of Representatives) is with the self-administrated entities. The central authorities are obliged to respect these powers of the regional entities.

Among them are also special and distinct entities which are regulated by law. Aceh and Papua belong to these units. For the understanding of the autonomy issue in Aceh, it is important to know the conflict parameters. This is, on the one hand, the history of its Islamic social society and, on the other, the structure of the Indonesian state with its military. The military plays a role both in domestic affairs (it is involved in generating business for profit) and in defence.

3. Aceh within the Indonesian legal order and its political background

Aceh emerged as a sovereign state in the sixteenth century and preserved its independence against the Portuguese until Dutch colonisation. The Acehnese joined Indonesia and rejected attempts by the Dutch to create a separate state of Aceh. In the 1940s, the Acehnese supported the independence of Indonesia and were incorporated into the new state. They enjoyed a de facto autonomy, but were ruled via the central government. There were 'classic centre-periphery dynamics here (decisions were made in Jakarta, taxation going to Jakarta, political

8 BELL, G.F. (2001) The New Indonesian Laws Relating to Regional Autonomy: Good Intentions, Confusing Laws. *Asian-Pacific Law and Policy Journal*. 2(1). p. 21.

appointments coming from Jakarta)'.[9] Acehnese resistance arose in reaction to the integrationist, assimilationist and repressive policies of the Indonesian Government. The Acehnese feared that the role of Islam would be undermined and thus Islamic scholars supported armed resistance from 1953 until the 1960s. The Islamic rebellion was met with repression.

The reaction of the Indonesian Government under President Sukarno was the granting of autonomous rights in religious and cultural matters. The autonomous character of Aceh had already been recognised by Indonesian Law 24 (1956) in 1956.[10] However, after Suharto came to power, Aceh lost in this period autonomy and control of local resources which they had enjoyed after 1946.[11] Due to the plunder of natural resources, corrupt governance, underdevelopment and revenue drain to the central government, the struggle for secession began. It was organised by the Free Aceh Movement (GAM). The people experienced military repression and human rights violations and the GAM enjoyed ever-increasing public support. In response, the government imposed the status of a Military Operation Zone on Aceh. During so-called anti-insurgency campaigns, the inhabitants experienced military repression and serious human rights violations, resulting in thousands of peoples losing their lives.

After the fall of Suharto in the 1990s, the regulations were lifted and this enabled a new approach of the Indonesian Government to implement general decentralisation legislation. The first entity they dealt with was Aceh. The government recognised the special characteristics of the governance in Aceh as an autonomous entity with competencies in the fields of religion, education and customary law in 1999. Nevertheless, the people of Aceh were not satisfied with the implementation of these autonomy rights and were still fighting for an independent state. They felt supported by the 1999 NATO intervention in Serbia in defence of Kosovo and the separation of Eritrea from Ethiopia. The GAM set up a government in exile in Stockholm and claimed the right of self-determination for the people of Aceh. They argued that the territory was illegally annexed to the Dutch West Indies in 1873. Thus, the Aceh people were entitled to fight for decolonisation and independence by all means, including armed struggle. They were also influenced by similar claims in Irian Jaya (now West Papua). In both Aceh and Irian Jaya, ethno-nationalist movements claimed independence. The Indonesian Government perceived these attempts as foreign subversion and insisted on the principle of non-interference. They were especially suspicious of foreign NGOs. Other states, however, denied recognition of secession claims.

9 AGUSWANDI and LARGE, J. (2008) *Reconfiguring Politics: The Indonesia-Aceh Peace Process*. London: Conciliation Resources. p. 8.

10 MILLER, M.A. (2009) *Rebellion and Reform in Indonesia – Jakarta's Security and Autonomy Policies in Aceh*. London: Routledge. pp. 41 ff.

11 REID, A. (2007) Indonesia's Post-Revolutionary Aversion to Federalism. In BAOGANG, H., GALLIGAN, B. and INOGUCHI, T. (eds) *Federalism in Asia*. Cheltenham: Edward Elgar. p. 153.

At the same time, a strong civilian movement claimed greater autonomy within Indonesia.[12] In 1999, a Swiss NGO was allowed to begin a humanitarian dialogue for an end to the hostilities and access to the victims. This led to the enactment of Law No. 18 concerning the Special Autonomy of Nanggroe Aceh Darussalam in 2001. The special characteristic of this law is the implementation of Syariat Islam and the customary ways of life within the unitary Indonesian State.[13] Another outcome was a ceasefire and in 2002 the Cessation of Hostilities Agreement. This initiative ended again in violence and the agreement broke down. Fighting resumed on an unprecedented scale. New talks took place and collapsed again. Martial law was imposed once again, but there was a complete lack of public order and security. Poverty, displacement, rape, threat of attack, intimidation and a shadow economy characterised life in Aceh. Then an underwater earthquake caused a tremendous tsunami in 2004, resulting in the death of over 128,000 people.

Faced with such destruction, the GAM declared a unilateral ceasefire. The impact of the tsunami enabled opportunities for peace negotiations. The government was ready to enter into negotiation with the exile government. A Finnish businessman took the initiative to enable a high-level mediation with the support of the European Union and the Association of Southeast Asian Nations (ASEAN). The talks dealt with many fundamental issues such as self-governance, poverty reduction, lack of access to resources, education, revenue sharing and electoral participation and representation. The outcome of the mediation was a Memorandum of Understanding (MoU) signed in Finland in 2005.

According to the preamble, the parties commit themselves 'to creating conditions within which the government of Acehnese people can be manifested through a fair and democratic process within the unitary state and constitution of the Republic of Indonesia'. Thereby, the MoU underlines the unitary state structure and rules out 'federalism in its paradigmatic sense'.[14] However, the term autonomy does not appear in the MoU. This can be considered both cause and consequence of the bad reputation of autonomy after the former experiences. The document also avoids the concept of self-governance and self-determination.

Instead, the MoU refers five times to the 'people of Aceh' and notes their historical traditions and customs, their aspirations for local political parties, their right to nominate candidates for the positions of all elected officials and the guarantee of full participation in local and national elections. This approach means a kind of recognition that there is a distinct people of Aceh within Indonesia.

12 BERTRAND, J. (2007) Indonesia's Quasi-Federalist Approach: Accommodation amid Strong Integrationist Tendencies. *International Journal of Constitutional Law*. 5(4). p. 578.

13 Unpublished manuscript of the presentation given at the Symposium on Legitimacy and Western & Non-Western Views of Human Rights, University of South Carolina Law School, 3–4 February 2006, p. 1.

14 MARASIGHE, L. (2007) Federalism: Lessons from Aceh and Sudan. *Sri Lanka Journal of International Law*. 19(1). p. 321.

Suksi is rightly arguing that the concept of 'people' is used in a 'collective sense with more than allusions in the direction of the existence of an entity of self-determination'.[15] Without using the terminology of autonomy, the new Law No. 11 of 2006 on Governing Aceh deals with the distribution of powers between the government and the executing branches of Aceh.[16]

4. The self-government regulation

The Aceh situation meets all the criteria of a secessionist conflict since a relatively homogenous people within a multi-ethnic state fights against oppression and for self-determination. The confrontation between the reassertion of rights by the population of Aceh and the resistance of the unitary state to accept meaningful pluralism has resulted in the demand for broader political and economic power.[17] Therefore, the state institutions have been transformed in response to ethnic tensions. The economic conflict follows from the exploitation of natural gas in northeastern Aceh which intensified the appropriation of revenues by the central government. The military protects the gas fields and uses the gas as an extra budgetary source for the financing of the military leadership. This kind of exploitation of the natural resources led to local impoverishment.[18] However, in January 2005, the GAM accepted self-government instead of independence because they realised that the negotiations could otherwise collapse.

Self-government or autonomy regulations have in principle the capability to satisfy the aspirations of minorities and peoples to a degree of political and economic power, while preserving the territorial integrity and sovereignty of the state. Therefore, it is often seen as an instrument of conflict resolution.[19] The main advantage of autonomy follows from the fact that the suppression of a group calls for their resistance, thus disturbing peace and public order. This general lesson is also true for Aceh and the need for a new approach by the central government was obvious. In 2006, the government declared in accordance with Article 272 of the Law No. 11 of 2006 on Governing Aceh, that the old 2001 Law No. 18 concerning the Special Autonomy of Nanggroe Aceh Darussalam was no longer in force.

The new law touches upon the distribution of powers, the foreign affairs and the relationship between the central government and the administration of Aceh. It is a kind of further elaboration of the governance rules which had been

15 SUKSI, M. (2011) Sub-State Governance through Territorial Autonomy, Berlin: Springer. p. 252.

16 Republic of Indonesia, Law No. 11/2006 on the Governing of Aceh. Available at: www.ucdp.uu.se/gpdatabase/peace/Ind%20050815.pdf [Accessed: 28 March 2016].

17 HEINTZE, H.-J. (2005) Legal Appraisal of Autonomy. In SKURBATY, Z.A. (ed.) *Beyond a One-Dimensional State: An Emerging Right to Autonomy?* Leiden: Brill. p. 53.

18 WENNMANN, A. and KRAUSE, J. (2009) Resource Wealth, Autonomy, and Peace in Aceh. The Centre on Conflict, Development and Peacebuilding Working Paper 3. Geneva. p. 5.

19 MUSGRAVE, T.D. (1997) *Self-Determination and National Minorities*. Oxford: Oxford University Press. p. 208.

developed in Indonesia since the 1990s.[20] Thus, the confirmed norms concerning the Islamic law in Aceh and the financial regulations concerning the revenue allocation between the central government and the local administration can be seen against this background. The national legislation of Indonesia is powerless concerning matters that affect Aceh as long as there is no consultation and prior consent of the Aceh bodies. That leads to the consequence that the Aceh administration has a veto right in the unitary state and is the supreme legislator. This regulation enables Aceh to be an integral part of the national constitution of Indonesia on the one hand and strengthens the unitary state structure with devolved powers on the other. The blanket power of veto means also that Aceh is not bound by international treaties which may adversely affect the interests of that province.

4.1 Politics

Within a period of a few years, Indonesia has shifted from an integrationist approach to a system which permits more flexibility. The advanced kind of provincial self-administration includes the devolution of several competencies to the provincial level. The fields of governance, economy and human rights belong to the local authorities, while the central government takes care of defence, fiscal and monetary policy, foreign relations, justice and freedom of religion. All decisions on national, regional and international levels relating to Aceh need to have the consent of the Aceh Administration.[21] The Aceh authorities are entitled to use regional symbols and specific names and titles, as well as customary law according to the Aceh traditions. The political participation is guaranteed by the right to establish provincial parties and to take part in elections on the district, provincial and national levels. An independent candidate can stand for the direct election of the head of Aceh's administration. The administrative and fiscal decentralisation contains elements of a quasi-federal system. However, the unitary state forms the core and the autonomous entities do not coincide with ethnic groups. Since 2004, the legal system has dramatically shifted the balance of power between the central government and the regions.

The Acehnese are Muslims with a strong antipathy to radical Islam. Former rebels of the Free Aceh Movement were not involved in any significant way in the actions of the jihad. Therefore, the discovery of a jihadi training camp in Aceh in 2010 was a surprise.[22] The Indonesian Government is no doubt taking terrorism seriously, but the training camp proves that jihadism has taken root in Aceh. To tackle this challenge in Aceh means fighting corruption and strengthening the police activities in the region because corrupt police officers became the lubricant

20 SETYOWATI and TOENGKAGIE (2006–2007), above note 4, pp. 65–66.
21 AGUSWANDI and ZUNZER, W. (2008) *From Politics to Arms to Politics Again: The Transition of the Gerakan Acheh Merdeka*. Berlin: Berghof Conflict Research. p. 18.
22 International Crisis Group, Asia Report No. 189/2010, p. 1.

for terrorist activities. Therefore, the struggle against terrorism belongs to the most important tasks of the Aceh self-government.

4.2 Economy

The thirty years of armed conflict devastated the economy and resulted in 15,000 deaths and the displacement of 100,000 human beings. Poverty rates increased from 14.8 per cent in 1998 to 36.2 per cent in 2005. Aceh became one of the poorest parts of Indonesia despite its natural resources. In 1990 Aceh represented 3.6 per cent of the gross domestic income, by 2001 only 2.1 per cent.

After the conflict, Aceh received significant support from Indonesia and it has the right to raise funds with external loans and the setting and raising of taxes. Seventy per cent of the revenue from all hydrocarbon deposits and other natural resources in the territory of Aceh and in its surrounding sea can be retained by the local authorities. Aceh's budget revenue can be collected from different sources such as regional taxes and regional charges. Sea and air traffic takes place under the control of the Aceh administration, as well as the exploitation of living natural resources in the territorial waters. The collecting and allocation of revenues between Aceh and the Indonesian Government is to be transparent. The administration can also seek foreign direct investment.[23]

Despite the improvements, problems still exist with regard to the post-conflict reconstruction efforts. The inequalities between the tsunami- and conflict-affected areas have resulted in disparities which have created some unrest. Restrictions on the use of international support have meant that the conflict-affected areas have not received assistance. In 2005, conflict-affected areas were 44 per cent more likely to be poor than average regions.[24] Against this background, it cannot be surprising that tensions are rising at the local level. The same is true concerning the uneven support for different groups of conflict-affected persons. Yet, certain groups enjoyed more benefits, especially the GAM-linked people. Another major problem is the lack of capacity and transition strategy.

The problems with the reconstruction efforts undermined the fragile peace. The inequalities between areas and people benefitting from support as well as corruption and weak capacities can be seen as the main reasons for the difficulties.

4.3 Law

The acceptance of the creation of local-level political parties was a significant improvement for the establishment of a real local government in Aceh. It allowed the transformation of a rebel group into a non-violent political party. A precondition

23 SUKSI (2011), above note 15, p. 263.

24 BARRON, P. (2008) Managing the Resources for Peace. In AGUSWANDI and LARGE, J. (eds) *Reconfiguring Politics: The Indonesia-Aceh Peace Process*. London: Conciliation Resources. p. 60.

for this new approach was the amnesty for the members of the Free Aceh Movement which allowed the release of prisoners and detainees. Those who lived abroad could return home unconditionally.[25] This has enabled the reintegration of the former fighters into society and the elaboration of a new legal order. The practical issues of reintegration were regulated by the Aceh Reintegration Agency, which dealt with ex-combatants, victims of the conflict and the settlements of compensation claims.[26] The Agency was confronted with the overlap between its tasks and the competencies of the Truth and Reconciliation Commission in the field of reparation payments, which is not primarily an issue of reintegration, but one of justice and fact-finding.

The Law on Aceh Government of 2006 has 210 articles and contains detailed regulation of the rights and duties of the governor and the Aceh legislature, the local electoral process, determinants of fiscal revenues and control over the exploitation of natural resources. It is an 'extremely complex piece of legislation and is not limited to the core issues of "autonomous" regional governance'.[27] It also covers areas which are in most cases ruled by sectorial laws. It includes human rights issues, armed forces, police and judiciary, education, and the social and health sectors, as well as natural resources, economic development and investment.

This broad approach and the direct involvement of a large number of stakeholders with varying interests in all stages of the elaboration led to greater public support than for the 2001 Special Autonomy Law. The 2006 Law reflects the involvement of the Free Aceh Movement in the peace negotiations and contains their major demands. However, there are weaknesses concerning the clarity and consistency of the law. Some stakeholders in Aceh have also had the expectation that Aceh would be entitled to exercise all authorities concerning all fields of public affairs. This was unrealistic because those functions which belong to the constitutional obligations of the central government are excluded. These obligations include, for instance, the transformation of international treaties into the law of Indonesia, because such treaties have to be implemented all over the country. However, this norm contradicts the second MoU principle that international agreements, which relate to Aceh, will be discussed between the central government and the autonomous government and they will enter into force only with the consent of the legislature of Aceh.

Another issue of concern is that, according to Article 11 no. 1, the central government sets norms, standards and procedures and conducts the supervision over the implementation of government functions by the Government of Aceh

25 AWALUDDIN, H. (2008) Why Is Peace in Aceh Successful? In AGUSWANDI and LARGE, J. (eds) *Reconfiguring Politics: The Indonesia-Aceh Peace Process*. London: Conciliation Resources. p. 25.

26 FRÖDIN, L. (2008) The Challenges of Reintegration in Aceh. In AGUSWANDI and LARGE, J. (eds) *Reconfiguring Politics: The Indonesia-Aceh Peace Process*. London: Conciliation Resources. p. 54.

27 MAY, B. (2008) The Law on the Governing of Aceh. In AGUSWANDI and LARGE, J. (eds) *Reconfiguring Politics: The Indonesia-Aceh Peace Process*. London: Conciliation Resources. p. 42.

and district/city governments. Such a rule allows a broad range of interference by the central government in the affairs of the autonomous entity.

In the past, there was no direct reference to Islamic law in the agreements between Aceh and Indonesia. However, many references to the historical traditions and customs of Aceh were understood in relation with the religious background of the people. Therefore, most of the rules of Islamic law were already applicable in Aceh before its self-government. The Law on Aceh of 2006 recognises the application of Islamic law and entitles the provincial government to implement and enforce it. Aceh is therefore the only part of Indonesia with the legal rights to apply certain parts of Sharia law outside matters of family and inheritance.

Law No. 44/1999 on the implementation of Aceh's special status already allowed the application of Sharia for Muslims and entitled the local government authority to enact norms on religious life, customs and education. Regulation No. 5/2000 on the implementation of Islamic law ruled the application of all aspects of Islamic law. The Special Autonomy Law for Aceh 2001 allowed the establishment of Sharia courts with jurisdiction over family law, property rights and criminal cases. Sharia was applied in the narrowly conservative interpretation. In 2003, the Sharia court dealt with cases of gambling, sale and consumption of alcohol and illicit relations between men and women. The application of the conservative interpretation of Sharia has caused much consternation among moderate and secular Muslims.[28] It was argued that this approach violated the Indonesian legal order. The first laws on Sharia in Aceh were enacted by the unrepresentative and corrupt Parliament 'elected' in 1999 (the election was boycotted by most Acehnese). There was hope that the Law on Aceh 2006 would be an opportunity to overcome the debatable interpretation of Sharia. However, the promise to redraft the legal order of Aceh in the light of the UN Human Rights Covenants and general human rights principles have had little effect. Most of the provisions of Islamic law enacted prior to the Law on Aceh 2006 are still in force.[29]

The appointment of judges to the Islamic court remains the remit of the central government. Parallel to the Islamic court, secular courts were established which deal with specific fields of Islamic law. Executive and legislative powers are specified in the Law on Aceh of 2006 and the tasks of the governor are laid down. He is responsible for enforcing Islamic law and improving the standard of life of the Acehnese people, as well as the enhancing of democratic life. Corruption and nepotism are prohibited. Bertrand argues rightly that such explicitness gives greater impetus to possible future actions in a country where the judiciary is sometimes subjected to political interference.[30] The same is true for the right to

28 WILMOT, F. (2008) Shariah in Aceh. In AGUSWANDI and LARGE, J. (eds) *Reconfiguring Politics: The Indonesia-Aceh Peace Process*. London: Conciliation Resources. p. 78.

29 SUKSI (2011), above note 15, p. 262.

30 BERTRAND, J. (2007) Indonesia's Quasi-Federalist Approach: Accommodation amid Strong Integrationist Tendencies. *International Journal of Constitutional Law*. 5(4). p. 602.

form local political parties. This right creates an exception because in Indonesia, in general, only countrywide organised parties are allowed. Ultimately, this allowed the Free Aceh Movement to reconfigure itself as a political party.

In general, one can evaluate that the Law on Aceh Government is a vast improvement because it has to be considered as a far-reaching institutionalisation of its autonomy.

4.4 Implementation

The codified regulation on emergency powers of the Indonesian President entitles the central government to override decisions of the Aceh Government. This is doubtless a matter of concern in addition to the imposition of Sharia law. This creates a challenge which might have a long-term impact on the region.[31] Against this background, Aceh is obliged to respect the universal human rights norms as laid down in the UN Covenant on Political and Civil Rights, as well as economic, social and cultural rights. An independent and impartial court system has to be established. This also includes the establishment of a court of appeals.

The Aceh administration has to approve the appointment of a police chief and the prosecutor, as well as recruit police officers. All the civilian crimes committed by military personal in Aceh are to be tried by civilian courts. Besides a human rights court, a commission for truth and reconciliation has been established. All the people who had been detained for activities in the freedom movement have now been released under an amnesty law. The rehabilitation of the ex-combatants was enabled under the reintegration fund administrated by the Aceh Government. The fund provides them with farming land and adequate social security.

The Indonesian Government committed itself to withdrawing its troops and special force police with the exception of 14,700 soldiers for external defence and 9,100 policemen for upholding internal security in Aceh. The monitoring of the implementation of the Agreement lies in the hands of the Aceh Monitoring Missions, composed of 230 observers from ASEAN and EU countries. Therefore, a private conflict resolution institution takes care of the implementation.

As elections approached in 2009, it became obvious that the core of the Aceh problem was the mutual fear between the Free Aceh Movement and the Indonesian military. The deep distrust proves that perceptions from the time of the armed conflict still exist. Many in the Indonesian army were still convinced that the Acehnese were committed to independence.[32] However, these fears were misplaced. There is little danger in the short term of violence escalating out of control.

The real challenge is better law enforcement and the development of a civil society. Therefore, the International Crisis Group argued in 2009 that employment

31 AGUSWANDI and ZUNZER (2008), above note 21, p. 21.

32 International Crisis Group, Update Briefing No. 90/2009, p. 1.

and good policing is needed – not the deployment of more soldiers.[33] Better policing is the key and, therefore, the international community needs to support training in human rights and community relations. The solving of crimes committed by and against ex-combatants is essential. Moreover, some of the Aceh leaders are using democratic means not to claim independence, but to acquire access to the spoils. They are interested in getting their fair share of post-conflict benefits. Decentralisation has turned into a fractured association that is composed of small units only interested in themselves. The former guerrillas 'still use a modified version of their old hierarchical structures, but the power is locally concentrated'.[34] Against this background, there was a need for better law enforcement, in addition to an increase in employment and targeted civil society efforts.

In February 2012, the Acehnese went to the polls again to elect a governor and vice governor, as well as seventeen district heads. Mechanisms were again needed to avert election violence because the potential for unrest was high. The local political party, Partai Aceh, tried to influence the voters by arguing that there was a threat of a renewed conflict: 'To this end, it engaged in a number of legal manoeuvres, on the pretext of safeguarding Acehnese autonomy and the integrity of the 2006 Law on the Governing of Aceh.'[35] This may be rhetoric about the commitment to the MoU; however, there is no doubt that the legal basis of the status of Aceh has been recognised by all parties. This is the starting point for further improvements of living conditions in Aceh.

5. Conclusion

Aceh is still in the post-conflict rebuilding phase. Despite its resources, the entity is confronted with hidden economies and predation for profit. The system of self-governance offers opportunities, but autonomy is not as such a guarantee for improvement in the lives of the people.

33 Ibid., p. 14.
34 Ibid., p. 3.
35 International Crisis Group, Update Briefing No. 135/2012, p. 1.

Chapter 11

Sometimes guns are the answer

The path to autonomy in Tibet, Burma and South Sudan

David C. Williams

1. Introduction

In Tibet, autonomy is still only a distant dream, as the Chinese Government consistently maintains that no 'Tibetan issue' even exists.[1] In its intransigence, China is bucking what might be a global trend: in recent years, other countries have proved more willing to adopt autonomy schemes for their national minorities. The contrast raises the question of why autonomy has become a realistic goal elsewhere, but not in Tibet. At least part of the answer, this chapter will suggest, is that resistance movements elsewhere have adopted a different strategy: they have taken up arms. Though such resistance seldom achieves clear military victory, national governments are often prepared to concede autonomy to buy peace because the many years of conflict have brought the two sides to a mutually hurting stalemate, a situation that is often conducive to peace settlements.

In other words, sometimes guns are the answer – or at least a piece of it. To some, that conclusion may seem obvious, but in fact, the international community exhibits a distinct aversion to armed resistance. Some have gone so far as to argue that violence can never lead to good results. But, in fact, military capacity is sometimes the key to success. In denigrating armed resistance, the international community has rejected a strategy that is sometimes the only way for people to protect themselves.

The international community presumably developed this aversion from a concern that some armed resistance movements are themselves oppressive and that civil war causes lost lives and property destruction. As a result, it might seem better always to champion non-violence. But by rejecting armed resistance across the board, the international community has chosen to prioritise the unimpeachability of its own moral purity over the welfare of suffering people. And in so doing, it has lost the very thing it was trying to retain: the moral high ground.

1 SMITH Jr., W.W. (2009) *China's Tibet?: Autonomy or Assimilation*. Plymouth: Rowman & Littlefield. p. 13.

I advance this thesis by comparing Tibet to South Sudan and Burma. I choose these two both because they effectively illustrate the point and also because as Executive Director of the Center for Constitutional Democracy, I have personally advised resistance leaders in those countries on constitutional reform. I disclose this personal knowledge for two reasons: on the one hand, the reader should know that I am friends with a number of resistance leaders and am therefore not a detached, 'outside' observer; on the other hand, precisely because I am not an outsider, I have access to information that I would not otherwise have.

In Burma and South Sudan, minorities conducted long and bloody armed resistance that, for all its costs, gained them substantial autonomy, in the case of Burma, and actual independence, in the case of South Sudan. By contrast, although Tibetans did resort to arms in the early years after the Chinese invasion, that resistance was short-lived.[2] More recently, the Dalai Lama has strenuously insisted that Tibetans should employ only non-violent resistance.[3] Non-violence has, however, proved quite unsuccessful in practice: the Chinese Government insists that it will not allow any genuine autonomy for Tibet.[4]

On the other hand, the Dalai Lama's non-violence has earned him enormous credibility with the international community, which has pressured China to negotiate with him.[5] Indeed, although the Dalai Lama's pacifism grows from his religious conviction, it is also a clever strategy: because the Tibetans pose no military challenge to the Chinese army, their only hope is to appeal to the international community by principled adherence to non-violence. By contrast, the international community's support for the Burmese resistance armies has been virtually non-existent; they are lucky if they can stay off terrorist watch lists. And the support for the southern Sudanese fighters was late in coming.

In other words, sometimes violent resistance can secure autonomy on the ground, but it can also lose international enthusiasm. And sometimes non-violence can create international enthusiasm, but it is often ineffective on the ground.

The second section of this chapter outlines the history of armed resistance in Burma from independence to the present ceasefire negotiations. The third section outlines the history of armed resistance in Southern Sudan from shortly after the independence of Sudan to the independence of South Sudan. These movements were long, grinding affairs that eventually wore down both parties sufficiently to bring them to the bargaining table. By contrast, as the fourth section shows, although Tibet possesses a proud warrior tradition amply manifested after the Chinese invasion, its leaders turned to non-violence when violence proved hopeless.

2 SMITH (2009), above note 1, pp. 45–49.

3 LLOYD-ROBERTS, S. (2012) Self-Immolations Shake Tibetan Resolve. *BBC*. [Online] 18 April. Available from: www.bbc.co.uk/news/world-asia-17745634 [Accessed: 14 February 2017].

4 SMITH (2009), above note 1, pp. 292–293.

5 Ibid., pp. 268–269.

2. Burma's armed path to negotiated autonomy

Armed struggle between Burma's majority ethnic group, the Burmans, and its ethnic minorities goes back centuries.[6] The Burmans occupied what is now central Burma, and the minorities inhabited a horseshoe of mountains along the borders of the country.[7] The Burman kings sought to extend their jurisdiction over the neighbouring kingdoms and tribal groups in the hills, but they never wholly succeeded.[8]

The British then occupied the country.[9] Burman armed resistance to the British subsided once the king was forced to leave the country.[10] Resistance by the minorities went on longer, but eventually it too stopped.[11] The British then enlisted soldiers from the minorities in disproportionate numbers because they thought that the hill peoples were 'warrior races' like the Gurkhas or Sikhs.[12] The British governed central Burma separately from the ethnic areas: they governed the former directly, but the latter only indirectly, through local leaders.[13]

During the Second World War, the Japanese quickly drove the British out of Burma.[14] The Burmese army joined the Japanese, but the ethnic minorities mostly joined the Allies.[15] As a result, the hostilities between the minorities and the Burmans continued through the war. Even after the Burmese army switched sides to join the Allies late in the war, it continued to attack minority populations, especially Karen villagers.[16]

After the war, as Britain prepared to grant the country independence, many minority groups wished to take their homelands out of the Burmese union, and others were prepared to stay only if granted substantial autonomy.[17] The new constitution satisfied neither group, and eventually, every large minority group would field a resistance army.[18] Very early, the Karen mustered a force that once

6 SMITH, R. (1999) *Burma: Insurgency and the Politics of Ethnicity*. New York: St Martin's Press. pp. 31–33.
7 Ibid., pp. 29–38.
8 Ibid., p. 39.
9 Ibid., pp. 40–59.
10 Ibid., p. 41.
11 Ibid., pp. 41–42.
12 Ibid., pp. 44–45.
13 Ibid., p. 42.
14 CHRISTIE, C.J. (1998) *Southeast Asia in the Twentieth Century: A Reader*. London: I.B. Tauris. p. 98.
15 For Burman collaboration with the Japanese, see SMITH (1999) above note 6, pp. 58–59. Regarding minority Kachin resistance to the Japanese, see BAYLY, C. and HARPER, T. (2004) *Forgotten Armies: The Fall of British Asia, 1941–1945*. London: Allen Lane. pp. 204–206, 279, 352–353.
16 SMITH (1999), above note 6, pp. 60–64.
17 MYINT-U, T. (2006) *The River of Lost Footsteps: Histories of Burma*. New York: Ferrar, Straus, & Giroux. p. 253; LINTNER, B. (1999) *Burma in Revolt: Opium and Insurgency Since 1948*. Bangkok: Silkworm Press. p. xiv.
18 SMITH (1999), above note 6, pp. 79–87.

had prospects of capturing Rangoon itself.[19] In addition, the Communist Party of Burma left the government and formed its own force, and later Kuomintang remnants retreated into north Burma.[20]

The parliamentary government tried unsuccessfully to cope with these threats, and eventually the army – called the Tatmadaw – seized control and kept it until very recently.[21] Thereafter, more ethnic groups went into resistance. Although the military was largely able to convince the people of central Burma that it stood between them and death at the hands of the rebels, it was unable to destroy any of these armies.[22]

At first, the Tatmadaw ruled central Burma by coercing key players to unite in support of the army.[23] As time went on, however, that unity started to disintegrate. On the one hand, the threat from the ethnic armies decreased because with military equipment from China, the regime won a series of victories, culminating in the destruction of the KNU stronghold at Manerplaw.[24] But as the threat level went down, so did the junta's unity: absent the unifying threat from without, the government broke down into rival factions, each seeking to capture income and resource streams for its people. Gradually, the regional commanders asserted greater independence from the centre, becoming almost fiefdoms.[25]

As the regime governed ever more harshly, it rapidly lost whatever support it once had among the central Burmans. In 1988, protests racked the country, and to stem the discontent, the junta agreed to hold elections in 1990.[26] Aung San Suu Kyi's National League for Democracy handily won these elections, but the regime refused to allow the party to govern.[27] Many of those in opposition then joined hands with the ethnic minorities.[28] This whole process further eroded the military's ability to govern the country. They were, for the first time, faced with an opposition that included both Burmans and minorities and that reached into central Burma.

19 Ibid., pp. 110–112, 118.
20 Ibid., pp. 106, 120.
21 LINTNER (1999), above note 17, pp. 143–145, 169.
22 Although the allegiances of the ethnic armies and organisations are ever-shifting, many of those that remain opposed to the Burmese Government have joined a defensive alliance. WENG, L. (2010) Ethnic Groups Enter Alliance. *The Irrawaddy*. [Online] 27 March. Available at: www.burmanet.org/news/2010/05/27/irrawaddy-ethnic-groups-enter-alliance-%E2%80%93-lawi-weng/ [Accessed: 14 February 2017].
23 SMITH (1999), above note 6, pp. 179–183.
24 YAN NAING, S. (2010) KNU Eye Manerplaw. *The Irrawaddy*. [Online] 17 December. Available at: www2.irrawaddy.org/article.php?art_id=20339 [Accessed: 14 February 2017].
25 CALLAHAN, M.P. (2003) *Making Enemies: War and State Building in Burma*. Ithaca, NY: Cornell University Press. pp. 212, 217–218.
26 CHARNEY, M.W. (2009) *A History of Modern Burma*. Cambridge: Cambridge University Press. pp. 155–163.
27 Ibid., pp. 173–176.
28 SMITH (1999), above note 6, p. 430.

Even though the minorities had been weakened, so too had the Tatmadaw. In the 1990s, the junta entered into ceasefire agreements with some of the powerful armies, granting them territory, resources and income streams in exchange for peace.[29] In other words, violence proved to be a successful strategy for these groups. Because they were viable fighting forces, the regime gave them what they had always demanded: meaningful home rule.

In non-ceasefire areas, especially Karen and Shan States, the war raged on.[30] Although the minorities were never able to vanquish the regime, the regime was never able to crush the resistance. In many areas, the Tatmadaw almost entirely stopped fighting the resistance armies; instead, they confined their attacks to the civilian population.[31] These human rights abuses are early signs of the army's increasing desperation. Gradually, the fighting was grinding down the mighty Tatmadaw.

For many years, the situation seemed to have reached stasis: neither side could win. Recently, however, events have taken a new turn. In 2008, the junta held a sham referendum on their new constitution, and then in 2010, it held elections.[32] The Tatmadaw announced that its own parties had won the lion's share of seats, although it did permit some token oppositionists to be elected.[33] Before the election, the military government revoked all its ceasefires, giving the resistance armies three options: disband, become part of the Burmese army, or face renewed fighting.[34] Almost all chose the last option, and at the time of writing, the civil war is raging.

But the Tatmadaw is not the mighty force that once it was. For years, the central government has given it only meagre supplies and pay. By report, some soldiers are starving, and some soldiers' wives have turned to prostitution.[35] Morale is very low, as is the general quality of the conscripts. Again by report, the junta ordered the Northern Regional Commander to attack the Kachin Independence Army, but he refused. As a result, the junta kept extending the deadline for the ethnic armies to disband, and many thought that the government seemed uncertain and afraid.

29 CHARNEY (2009), above note 26, pp. 188–190; CALLAHAN (2003), above note 25, p. 220.

30 ZOM HSENG, S. (2011) Human Rights Abuses Reported in Shan State Clashes. *The Irrawaddy*. [Online] 22 April. Available at: http://burmamonitor.blogspot.it/2011/04/human-rights-abuses-reported-in-shan.html [Accessed: 14 February 2017].

31 Human Rights Watch, *Burma: Army Attacks Displace Thousands of Civilians*. [Online] 14 August 2009. Available at: www.hrw.org/news/2009/08/14/burma-army-attacks-displace-thousands-civilians [Accessed: 14 February 2017].

32 Burmese Junta Sets Voting Dates. *BBC*. [Online] 9 February 2008. Available at: http://news.bbc.co.uk/2/hi/asia-pacific/7236648.stm [Accessed: 14 February 2017].

33 GYI, T. (2010) USDP Wins 76.5 Percent of Vote. *The Irrawaddy*. [Online] 8 November. Available at: http://election.irrawaddy.org/news/612-usdp-wins-765-percent-of-vote.html [Accessed 14 February 2017].

34 WENG, L. (2010) KIO Calls for Free and Fair Election. *The Irrawaddy*. [Online] 1 September.

35 (2011) A Soldier's Escape: Maung Lwin Soe's Story. *Burma Issues*. 21(7/8). Available at: www.burmalibrary.org/docs13/BI-2011-08.pdf [Accessed: 14 February 2017].

The fighting resumed only when the government sent elements of the better-equipped Central Command to Kachin State.

Meanwhile, the political situation had changed. Although no grass-roots democrat, the new President Thein Sein proved to be a pragmatist. Desiring closer relations with the West and the end of sanctions, he took tentative steps toward reform – not free and fair elections, but relaxation of censorship, release of political prisoners and the like.[36] He is also seeking renewed ceasefires and political talks to address the minorities' demands for constitutional reform.[37]

His childhood friend, Aung Min, is the chief negotiator.[38] At the time of writing, the KNU has agreed ceasefire terms with the government, ending the longest running civil war in the world.[39] The government has agreed to schedule political talks to address the Karen's underlying concerns, and the list of issues includes constitutional devolution, power-sharing and minority rights. For full disclosure, I should reveal that I am advising the Karen on those negotiations. Other groups will follow the Karen's lead. At the time of writing, the Shan State Army-South has concluded a preliminary ceasefire. The New Mon State Party,[40] the Chin National Front,[41] the Karenni National People's Party[42] and the Arakan League for Democracy[43] are in negotiations. The Burmese Government has largely left the very strong United Wa State Party in peace, but signs are good that it will join the others at the negotiation table. At the time of writing, the most intense combat is occurring in Kachin State; negotiations for a ceasefire are ongoing, but have made only limited progress. Nevertheless, the writing seems to be on the wall: eventually, the war in Kachin State will wind down.

The point is that armed resistance has worked for these groups. They wanted a constitution that would allow them meaningful home rule; the government refused for decades even to talk about the question; they took up arms to press their demands. At times, it seemed that the fight would be endless and futile. But, in the

36 ZAW, A. (2012) Thein Sein: Reformist or Caretaker? *The Irrawaddy*. [Online]. Available at: www2.irrawaddy.org/article.php?art_id=23034 [Accessed: 14 February 2017].

37 Ibid.

38 YAN NAING, S. (2012) KNU, Govt Reach Historic Agreement. *The Irrawaddy*. [Online] 12 January. Available at: www2.irrawaddy.org/article.php?art_id=22826 [Accessed: 14 February 2017].

39 Ibid.

40 WENG, L. (2012) NMSP, Govt Sign Peace Agreement. *The Irrawaddy*. [Online] 27 February. Available at: www2.irrawaddy.org/article.php?art_id=23102 [Accessed: 14 February 2017].

41 MOE, W. (2011) Govt Agrees Ceasefire Talks With Karen Rebels. *The Irrawaddy*. [Online] 21 December. Available at: www2.irrawaddy.org/article.php?art_id=22695 [Accessed: 14 February 2017].

42 Ibid.

43 See MOE, W. (2011) The Ethnic Issue: Following in the Footsteps of Kings. *The Irrawaddy*. [Online] 10 November. Available at: www.burmanet.org/news/2011/11/10/irrawaddy-the-ethnic-issue-following-in-the-footsteps-of-kings-%E2%80%93-wai-moe/ [Accessed: 14 February 2017], discussing the need for tripartite negotiations between the Arakan League for Democracy, the Burman democracy movement and the government.

1990s, some secured ceasefires that gave them most of what they wanted. Shortly, all will be in political talks. At the date of writing, it is impossible to know how many concessions the government will make. But the fact that talks are occurring at all is startlingly different from the past. If the government makes any concessions, then the battle will have borne fruit.

Equally importantly, waging the war has required the minorities to create and sustain resistance organisations. These organisations often sub-divided and re-combined in various ways, but nonetheless the hills of Burma are home to intact resistance armies that command the loyalty and even affection of much of the local population. As a result, there are organisations to represent these populations at the negotiating table and to organise the people under the revised constitution. If the ethnic groups had given up fighting, they would likely have become subject populations, an undifferentiated mass of individuals as politically inert as most people under authoritarian rule. The horizon is brightening for these minorities; if they had lain down their arms, it would likely be still as dark as midnight – as it is for Tibetan patriots.

3. South Sudan's armed path to negotiated independence

The parallels between the histories of South Sudan and that of Burma are many and striking. Like Burma, the country is ethnically and religiously divided, between the largely Muslim and Arab north and the largely African, Christian and animist south.[44] As in Burma, one part, the north, sought to extend its control over the other part, the south, but never succeeded until the British conquered the whole area.[45] As in Burma, the British ruled the north directly and the south only indirectly.[46] The imperial authorities viewed the two regions as culturally distinct, isolated the south to prevent the spread of Islam, and underdeveloped the south.[47] After the Second World War, as independence approached, southerners demanded a federal system to protect them against the alien but more sophisticated northerners,[48] but instead the elected colonial government in Khartoum Sudanised the army and administration, replacing British officials with northern Sudanese, even in the south.[49] The south took up arms in protest, and as in Burma, the army seized control of the country – although only episodically rather than continuously.

44 JOHNSON, D.H. (2011) *The Root Causes of Sudan's Civil War: Peace or Truce*. Rochester: James Curry. pp. 1–2.
45 Ibid., pp. 2–11.
46 Ibid., p. 11.
47 COLLINS, R.O. (2010) *A History of Modern Sudan*. Cambridge: Cambridge University Press. pp. 54–55.
48 Ibid., p. 66.
49 JOHNSON (2011), above note 44, p. 27.

By independence in 1956, Sudan was already plunged into civil war and would remain so with only one respite until 2005. The two sides contended over demands very similar to those at stake in Burma. On the one hand, some southerners sought outright independence, and others desired a secular, federal Sudan with strong autonomy for the south.[50] On the other side, although its policy varied somewhat, the government wanted to impose Sharia on the whole of the country, including the largely non-Muslim south.[51]

As in Burma, although the government forces outnumbered and out-spent the south, it could never extinguish the resistance. Similarly, although the south always managed to field a fighting force and control territory, it could never overthrow the government in Khartoum. The fighting in the south did, on the other hand, contribute to political instability in the north. Waging the war put great stress on the northern economy and social harmony, and the government's conduct of the war bred resentment, especially when it introduced conscription. As a result, control of the government often passed from one coalition to another, and the north had difficulty waging a focused, sustained war effort.[52]

The resistance began when southern soldiers in the Torit garrison mutinied, but at first the struggle was limited and fitful.[53] When they realised that the north would not keep its promise of federalism for the south, southern parliamentarians broke the governing coalition, and in response General Abbud seized control.[54] It was Abbud's Arabisation policy – seeking to impose Arab identity and language, even in the south – that ignited widespread resistance.[55] Cells of fighters across the south gradually coalesced into the Anya-Nya movement.[56]

In Khartoum, the government returned to civilian control until 1969, when Colonel Ja'afar Numayri seized control.[57] A hard-liner toward the south, Numayri was unable to crush the resistance, in part because Israel supplied arms to the southerners and in part because Joseph Lagu managed to unify the movement under his rule.[58] With no military solution in sight, Numayri adopted a unilateral ceasefire and was virtually forced into political negotiations with the south.[59] During the talks, secession was never discussed as a serious possibility, but from the beginning, all assumed that the south would be given a measure of autonomy.[60]

50 Ibid., p. 30.
51 Ibid., pp. 30–32.
52 COLLINS (2010), above note 47, pp. 72–92.
53 JOHNSON (2011), above note 44, p. 28.
54 COLLINS (2010), above note 47, p. 72.
55 Ibid., pp. 77–78.
56 Ibid., p. 79.
57 Ibid., p. 92.
58 Ibid., pp. 103–106.
59 JOHNSON (2011), above note 44, pp. 36–37.
60 Ibid., pp. 38–41.

And so it transpired: the 1972 Addis accords created an autonomous government with meaningful powers of self-rule.[61]

Once the southern fighters laid down their arms, however, Numayri reverted to his hard-line approach. The southerners had anticipated this prospect, and in the Addis negotiations they had demanded that the southern government be allowed to maintain its own army.[62] They ended up accepting a compromise: elements of the Anya-Nya movement would be integrated into the Sudan army.[63] With no effective resistance to oppose him, Numayri became increasingly autocratic and intent on Islamising the south.[64] When the southern government refused to accept his proposal that the south be divided into several states, he dissolved it and abrogated the Addis accords.[65] Critically, he repudiated the provision that southern fighters would be absorbed into the army in proportional numbers, and he transferred the southern units to the north and west.[66]

Numayri was plainly gambling that he could militarily control the south, but he lost the bet. A new insurrection swiftly grew up; southern units of the military mutinied, especially at Bor; and the southern command defected to the guerrilla movement.[67] John Garang eventually welded many of these resistance elements into the SPLM/A.[68] Yet again, southern unrest undid a northern leader: with the economy in shambles and rampant corruption, Numayri alienated his political allies one by one, until the military again seized control in 1985.[69]

As the southern victories piled up, some in the north began to contemplate that it might be better for the south to secede.[70] In 1986, Sadiq al-Madhi became the leader of a coalition government,[71] and in 1989 he ordered a ceasefire with the SPLM.[72] In response, Brigadier Omar Hasan Ahmed al-Bashir perpetrated yet another coup in conjunction with the National Islamic Front.[73] At this point, both the government in Khartoum and the SPLM believed that military victory was possible, as control over southern towns passed back and forth.[74]

As Garang became more autocratic, internal unrest boiled over: Riek Nachar and Lam Akol formed their own armed force, the Nasir Faction, pledged to

61 COLLINS (2010), above note 47, pp. 108–110.
62 JOHNSON (2011), above note 44, p. 40.
63 COLLINS (2010), above note 47, pp. 110–113.
64 Ibid., p. 133.
65 Ibid., pp. 123–138.
66 Ibid., p. 138.
67 JOHNSON (2011), above note 44, pp. 61–62.
68 COLLINS (2010), above note 47, p. 139.
69 Ibid., pp. 143–156.
70 Ibid., p. 167.
71 Ibid., p. 162.
72 Ibid., p. 170.
73 Ibid., pp. 170, 185.
74 Ibid., p. 200.

independence, rather than the federal 'New Sudan' preferred by Garang.[75] The Nasir Faction, composed primarily of Nuer people, commenced attacks on Dinka civilians, and for a time, the south was consumed by ethnic civil war.[76] During the fighting, the northern army took advantage of the split by retaking lost territory and supporting the Nasir Faction, which took the name SPLM-United.[77] The breakaway was, however, short-lived. Within a few years, Garang held unquestioned authority, and with the new unity, the SPLM again racked up startling successes. The NIF was forced to institute conscription in the north, and the army at times refused to fight.[78] The SPLM seemed unstoppable.

International involvement helped to hasten the end of the war. From 1994 forward, the governments of Kenya, Ethiopia, Eritrea and Uganda, working through the Intergovernmental Authority on Drought and Development (IGAD), sought to mediate the conflict.[79] After 9/11, the US Government pressured the Khartoum Government and gave support to the SPLM.[80] In 2003, as part of the IGAD process, the Sudanese Government and the SPLM signed the historic Machakos Protocol, under which the south would be allowed to vote on independence in six years' time.[81] In the event, it took the parties another thirty months to codify the Machakos Protocol in the Comprehensive Peace Accord, signed in 2005.[82] During the ensuing six years, Khartoum did little to convince the south to stay, and in January 2011, southerners voted overwhelmingly to become a new country.[83] Independence came six months later amid great jubilation.[84] It remains to be seen what the new government of South Sudan will do with its independence.

Although international intervention may have helped the southern cause, independence was really won on the battlefield. The Khartoum Government finally realised that it would never be able to vanquish the SPLM. In the months leading up to the Machakos Protocol, Sudan saw heavy fighting in which the advantage lay with the southerners, who were strongly motivated and fighting on their home ground.[85] Although the north had more men, equipment and money, its army had become a largely ineffective fighting force, just as the Burmese army has. Officers gained advancement through orthodoxy or nepotism rather than

75 JOHNSON (2011), above note 44, pp. 93–97.
76 Ibid., pp. 67–69.
77 COLLINS (2010), above note 47, pp. 206–207.
78 Ibid., p. 211.
79 Ibid., p. 207.
80 Ibid., pp. 239–244.
81 JOHNSON (2011), above note 44, pp. 167–169.
82 Ibid., pp. 167–169.
83 Ibid., p. 177.
84 FLICK, M. (2011) South Sudan Formally Declares Independence. *The Independent*. [Online] 9 July. Available at: www.independent.co.uk/news/world/africa/south-sudan-formally-declares-independence-2309751.html [Accessed: 14 February 2017].
85 COLLINS (2010), above note 47, p. 259.

ability, and foreign training was largely unavailable.[86] Increasingly, the military was filled with conscripts whose morale and discipline were both very low, and who came from people without martial traditions.[87] The army's heavy equipment such as tanks and aeroplanes was often useless in South Sudan's terrain and inoperational because of poor maintenance.[88] Because the northern army received no guerrilla training and fought on alien ground, it generally remained in garrison.[89] One historian explains: 'In the seclusion of their forts fear of the dark and dense bush beyond spread like a cancer that sapped their effectiveness.'[90]

As the war entered this 'mutually hurting stalemate', it at last became clear that the struggle would be interminable and its costs limitless. As a result, the war became unpopular, and al-Bashir suffered the political fallout. The same historian details some of these costs:

> [T]heir conduct of the war had produced an increasing volume of international condemnation [. . .]. Instead of victories, the number of body bags from southern Sudan had escalated, and at the same time the number of eager recruits had drastically declined. Finally, the diversion of oil revenues into military expenditure simply exacerbated the perennial economic problems that had bedeviled Sudan since the Numayri years. [. . .] [P]rices were high, and discontent was running deep. Unemployment among university graduates who had completed their military service was nearly 70 percent, small business firms were unable to secure loans, medical services were expensive and only for the rich, civil servants were still not regularly paid [. . .] and schools closed when unpaid teachers took other jobs. Budgets were never balanced, and so the debt relentlessly expanded [. . .]. Many members of the NCP [the governing party] now began to accept peace as the best possible solution to resolve or at least ameliorate Sudan's socio-economic problems.[91]

In other words, for the southern Sudanese, as for Burma's ethnic rebels, guns really were the answer, or at least a necessary part of it. The SPLM could never vanquish the Sudanese army, but it could impose sufficient costs that Khartoum felt it had to come to the bargaining table. Like so many countries before it, South Sudan may have been conceived in a dream of self-determination, but it was born in blood.

86 Ibid., p. 253.
87 Ibid., pp. 253–254.
88 Ibid., pp. 254–255.
89 Ibid., pp. 253–259.
90 Ibid., p. 253.
91 Ibid., p. 262.

4. Tibet's unarmed path to helplessness

In the late 1950s, Tibet bore many resemblances to both Burma and South Sudan: an ethnic resistance movement was fighting for either independence or autonomy against a government intent on assimilating them to the dominant culture.[92] But in the early twenty-first century, the dissimilarities are more striking: South Sudan has achieved independence; Burma's ethnic minorities will likely achieve some degree of autonomy; but China continues to suppress Tibetan culture and to send ever larger numbers of Han people to colonise the region. These differing outcomes cannot be explained by different levels of international support: the CIA funded the Tibetan resistance in the 1950s,[93] and Tibet has received at least as much international attention as the other two. The real difference lies in the nature of armed resistance. In Tibet, the resistance forces were massively outnumbered. They still might have been able to mount a long-lasting guerrilla campaign, leading to a mutually hurting stalemate, but they faced another obstacle: their spiritual leader the Dalai Lama was morally opposed to violence.

Because the Dalai Lama is so strongly associated with non-violence, it surprises many that Tibetans have traditionally been no strangers to bellicosity. The men in many regions of Tibet, especially the eastern areas of Kham and Amdo, valued themselves for their warrior prowess and loved weapons.[94] Even the monasteries housed ferocious warrior-monks charged with defending their domains. To outsiders who equate Tibetan Buddhism with pacifism, the concept of a *warrior* monk may seem a contradiction in terms, but after all, someone had to defend the community.[95]

Although many of his admirers view the Dalai Lama as purely non-violent, his thinking also reflects the warrior culture of his youth. Thus, he wrote in the foreword to a recent book:

> Although I believe that the Tibetan struggle can only be won by a long-term approach and peaceful means, I have always admired these freedom fighters for their unflinching courage and determination.[96]

Similarly, when he was fleeing to exile in India, he had kind words for his Khampa guards:

> I thanked them for their strength and bravery, and also, more personally, for the protection they had given me [. . .]. By then, I could not in honesty advise

92 See generally DUNHAM, M. (2004) *Buddha's Warriors*. New York: Jeremy P. Tarcher/Penguin. pp. 153–394.

93 Ibid., pp. 191–210.

94 Ibid., p. 7.

95 Ibid., pp. 145–150.

96 Ibid., frontispiece.

them to avoid violence. In order to fight, they had sacrificed their homes and all the comforts and benefits of a peaceful life. Now they could see no alternative but to go on fighting, and I had none to offer.[97]

When the Chinese People's Liberation Army (PLA) invaded Tibet in 1950, it met little resistance, in part because its soldiers were told to be well behaved[98] and in part because, in the 17-Point Agreement, the Chinese Government promised the Tibetan Government that it would not change political or social institutions in the Tibetan Autonomous Region.[99] The agreement did not, however, cover Kham or Amdo, and even in the TAR, the Chinese Government quickly made clear that it would not allow the Tibetan Government to run the country and that it intended to assimilate the Tibetans to Chinese socialist culture.[100]

Although non-elite Tibetans were not very nationalistic before the invasion, Chinese repression created a new consciousness.[101] When the PLA began to search monasteries, the warrior-monks protested because they feared that the army would find their treasured stores of weapons.[102] When the PLA began to confiscate arms in Kham, the warriors took to the hills, and the whole eastern region ignited in 1956.[103] The main resistance army adopted a flag bearing two crossed swords of traditional Tibetan type, much loved because they were the only sort of weapon that Tibetans could fabricate themselves.[104] The eastern resistance was effective enough to cause China to postpone further assimilationist moves in the TAR, for fear of resistance there as well.[105]

Like the Burmese ethnic minorities and the SPLM, the resistance fighters were effective because they knew the terrain, came from a martial tradition and were highly motivated.[106] At first, the PLA remained confined to forts, just as the Sudanese army in South Sudan, but the Chinese Government had a trump card not available to the Sudanese Government: overwhelming military power.[107] China sent in very large numbers of soldiers, heavy artillery and aircraft, for which the Tibetans had no answer.[108]

Throughout the struggle, the Dalai Lama urged non-violence. Traditionally stand-offish toward Lhasa, the men of eastern Tibet ignored these imprecations.[109]

97 Ibid., p. 289.
98 SMITH (2009), above note 1, p. 19.
99 Ibid., p. 22.
100 Ibid., pp. 23–26.
101 Ibid., pp. 37–38, 46–47.
102 DUNHAM (2004), above note 92, p. 146.
103 Ibid., pp. 154–165; SMITH (2009), above note 1, pp. 37–40.
104 DUNHAM (2004), above note 92, pp. 196–197.
105 SMITH (2009), above note 1, p. 40.
106 Ibid., p. 38; DUNHAM (2004), above note 92, p. 261.
107 SMITH (2009), above note 1, p. 38.
108 Ibid., pp. 39, 45.
109 DUNHAM (2004), above note 92, pp. 174–175.

Even when the fighting moved into central Tibet, the Dalai Lama had only limited control, as best illustrated in the events surrounding his flight into exile. In order to prevent the Dalai Lama from accepting an invitation to visit the Chinese commander in his camp, a crowd encircled the palace. When the Dalai Lama asked the crowd to disperse, they instead set up a permanent guard and then declared Tibetan independence. In the days following, Tibetan officials and monasteries signalled their support for independence. Finally, the Dalai Lama escaped. Not knowing that he was gone, the PLA bombarded the palace, killing thousands. The Dalai Lama then declared a government in exile and entered India.[110]

The demise of Tibetan resistance may have been inevitable, given China's military superiority. The only hope was to sustain a guerrilla movement, not to win battles, so as to bring the PLA to a mutually hurting stalemate leading to autonomy for Tibet. Today, of course, China's control is absolute, and the military option seems forever foreclosed. Under such circumstances, the Dalai Lama's strategy – working non-violently to publicise the conditions in the country and to negotiate with the Chinese Government – may be the only option. But although his non-violence may have earned the admiration of the rest of the world, it has proved entirely ineffective in his dealings with China.

China has been negotiating with the Dalai Lama's government in exile at Dharamsala since 1979, but no progress of any kind has been made.[111] China maintains that Tibet has been part of China for a very long time, so autonomy would be inappropriate.[112] It insists that the Tibetan negotiators are appearing in their private capacity and that the only issue is whether the Dalai Lama will be allowed to return home once he has renounced his splittist claims.[113] The Chinese negotiators have never hinted that autonomy was on the table, and the most recent round of talks was so negative that Dharamsala did not even attempt to give its usual hopeful spin.[114]

But if the Dalai Lama's strategy of non-violence has not helped his own people, it has made him a star with the international community, an icon of spirituality, one of the world's most popular figures.[115] It is clear that his commitment to non-violence is a large part of his appeal.[116] For example, in his presentation speech awarding the Nobel Peace Prize to the Dalai Lama, the chair of the Norwegian Nobel Committee praised his non-violence, implicitly criticising those resistance movements which use arms:

110 SMITH (2009), above note 1, pp. 45–56.

111 FRENCH, P. (2003) *Tibet, Tibet: A Personal History of a Lost Land.* New York: Vintage Departures. p. 110.

112 SMITH (2009), above note 1, p. xi.

113 Ibid., pp. 213, 226.

114 Ibid., pp. 262–263.

115 Ibid., p. 254; French (2003), above note 111, pp. 27–30, 107–117.

116 SMITH (2009), above note 1, pp. 268–269.

> This is by no means the first community of exiles in the world, but it is assuredly the first and only one that has not set up any militant liberation movement. This policy of nonviolence is all the more remarkable when it is considered in relation to the sufferings inflicted on the Tibetan people during the occupation of their country.[117]

Clearly, the Dalai Lama appeals to such people because it allows them to support resistance to oppression while remaining unsullied by association with violence. But such people have chosen to prioritise their own purity over helping oppressed people for whom violent resistance is a sensible strategy. And although the international community may have embraced the Dalai Lama for his pacifism, it has been entirely unable to help him win autonomy for Tibet. The United States and other countries have pressured China to negotiate with the Dalai Lama in good faith, but as already noted, China has shown no openness to Tibetan autonomy.[118]

The Dalai Lama has explained that, in his view, non-violence is the only effective and acceptable strategy for resisting oppression anywhere in the world, not merely in Tibet, where armed opposition would be futile. He writes:

> I believe that ultimately it is only through kindness and nonviolence that we human beings can create a more tranquil and happy atmosphere that will allow us to live in harmony and peace [. . .]. Responding to violence with more violence is rarely appropriate [. . .]. It is precisely when things become really difficult, urgent, and critical that we should think and act with nonviolence.[119]

The irony is that non-violence has been wholly ineffective in Tibet, and armed opposition ultimately successful in Burma and South Sudan.

5. Conclusion

In both Sudan and Burma, those struggling for autonomy relied on both international intervention and armed struggle. Ultimately, the most effective strategy may be a combination of these two approaches. That strategy will work only if the two are not inconsistent, that is, only if the international community will lend support to armed movements fighting against genuine oppression. The experience of South Sudan and Burma indicates that, sometimes, the international

117 Aarvik, E. (1989) Chairman of the Norwegian Nobel Committee. Award Ceremony Speech. Nobel Peace Prize, Oslo, Norway. Available at: www.nobelprize.org/nobel_prizes/peace/laureates/1989/presentation-speech.html [Accessed: 14 February 2016].

118 SMITH (2009), above note 1, pp. 216, 227–228, 231–232, 268–269.

119 KURLANSKY, M. (2008) *Nonviolence: The History of a Dangerous Idea*. New York: Random House. pp. xii–xiv.

community eventually overcomes its squeamishness toward armed resistance movements. Through a series of military successes, the SPLM finally convinced the international community to support its desire for a vote on independence; and in the newly reforming Burma, the international community is finally pressuring the government to negotiate settlements with the resistance armies, who still exist only because they kept fighting.

The irony in this comparison between Burma and South Sudan, on the one hand, and Tibet, on the other, is that the Dalai Lama's insistence on pacifism as the only enlightened form of resistance may actually be undercutting those movements for whom violence is an effective course. It is one thing to argue that armed insurrection is an unfeasible strategy for Tibet – which it is. It is wholly different to argue that armed insurrection is in principle wrong for all oppressed people. To the extent that the international community buys into that argument, it puts fighting groups to an impossible choice: give up your guns and whatever security they may give you; or give up the support of the international community.

Whether foreign governments should support violent resistance movements against unjust governments is, of course, a difficult and complicated question, but despite what many claim, Tibet does not demonstrate that there is an effective alternative to armed struggle. What Tibet actually demonstrates is that pacifism is sometimes completely ineffective. It shows that guns are sometimes the answer.

Chapter 12

Territorial autonomy in India

Thomas Benedikter

1. Introduction

Before giving an overview on territorial autonomy in the Indian Union, it is useful to recall a suitable definition of territorial (in Europe also 'regional') autonomy as used in the present chapter:

> Autonomy can be defined as a means of internal power-sharing aimed to preserve the cultural and ethnic variety, while respecting the unity of a state. It consists in permanently transferring a certain amount of powers suitable for those purposes to a certain territory, giving its population the possibility of self-government, and leaving only residual responsibilities to the central state.[1]

As a general rule, autonomous territories possess no international character, and are not treated as states for the purposes of international law. Thus, autonomy can be defined as a means of internal power-sharing aimed at preserving cultural and ethnic variety, while respecting the unity of a state. According to another scholar, who has been a consultant for autonomy issues around the world including Nepal, autonomy is '. . . a device to allow ethnic or other groups that claim a distinct identity to exercise direct control over affairs of special concern to them while allowing the larger entity to exercise those powers that cover common interest'.[2]

Autonomy is a special device designed to accommodate a particular part of a state if its population differs from the majority population of that state. It should

1 See BENEDIKTER, T. (2010) *The World's Modern Autonomy Systems*. Bozen: EURAC Research. p. 19. Available at: www.eurac.edu/en/research/autonomies/minrig/Documents/benedikter/Autonomies%20Benedikter%2009%20FINAL-FINAL.pdf [Accessed: 14 February 2017].

2 See GHAI, Y. (ed.) (2000) *Autonomy and Ethnicity: Negotiating Competing Claims in Multi-Ethnic States*. Cambridge: Cambridge University Press. p. 484. Joachim Heintze defines territorial autonomy as follows: 'In international law autonomy means that a part or territorial unit of a state is authorised to govern itself in certain matters by enacting laws and statutes, but without constituting a State of their own'; furthermore: HEINTZE, H.J. (1998) On the Legal Understanding of Autonomy. In SUKSI, M. (ed.) *Autonomy: Implications and Applications*. The Hague: Kluwer Law International. p. 7.

be remarked that territorial autonomy, as today operating in about sixty regions in twenty states in all continents, has been established also in federal states in two forms: on sub-state level (as a unit of a federated subject of that state, as in India and Belgium) or as a special category of territorial power sharing along the ordinary federated units of that federation (as in Canada). Ethnic-linguistic or national minorities are the classic population to demand autonomy, especially when settling homogeneously in their original homeland, but autonomy has been accorded also due to geographical ('islandness') and historical reasons.[3]

This above definition focuses on the fundamental purposes of autonomy of a legally defined scheme of territorial power sharing, mostly established to protect minority groups, in which legislative and executive – and sometimes jurisdictional – powers are attributed to a territorial community (region, province, district) endowed with a freely elected regional assembly. A clear distinction has to be drawn with regard to other concepts and forms of power-sharing and self-rule such as reservations for indigenous peoples, asymmetrical federalism and associated statehood. Moreover, the criteria by which a regional autonomy can be considered to be a 'genuine autonomy' must be clarified from the very outset, as they clearly distinguish this particular democratic and ethnically non-exclusive form of self-government under the full sovereignty of a central state, from some hybrid or non-perfect arrangements that can also be found under the label of 'autonomy' in some states. Under this approach, both non-democratic autonomous areas or autonomies operating in a non-democratic state cannot be regarded as 'genuine working autonomies' (for example, Pakistan's FATA and Northern Areas (Gilgit-Baltistan), Uzbekistan's, Tajikistan's or China's autonomous entities). Furthermore, a minimum standard of legislative and executive powers is required in order to be qualified as a genuine autonomy. Sub-state entities not vested with legislative and executive powers cannot be branded as autonomies (for example, the Union Territories in India and the Chittagong Hill Tracts in Bangladesh, Corsica in France, Rodriguez in Mauritius). To put it bluntly, there is a minimum standard of powers and democratic procedures of self-government of a regional polity, without which talking about 'autonomy' becomes meaningless.

2. Territorial (sub-state) autonomy in India

India is the only South Asian state that has enshrined some forms of regional territorial autonomy in its Constitution (Fifth and Sixth Schedules) for some few districts and regions at the sub-state level.[4] Some of these provisions of speciality

3 For the complete list of working territorial autonomies and further definitions, see: BENEDIKTER (2010), above note 1, pp. 16–20.

4 The Fifth and Sixth Schedules of India's Constitution can be found at www.constitution.org/cons/india/shed05.html and www.constitution.org/cons/india/shed06.html Respectively [Accessed: 14 February 2017].

are no longer applied, as is the case with Article 370 with respect to Jammu and Kashmir.[5] Others are an expression of India's 'asymmetrical federalism'. This concept, beyond the Union and the centre, provides for some additional rights to single states, based on their special character and interests. In India, apart from the federated states with special features, there are also Union territories and autonomous districts on a sub-state level, known as 'entities with a limited autonomy'. Moreover, the 73rd and 74th Amendments to the Constitution ensured the devolution of some limited powers at the village and town levels defined *Panchayati Raj*.

Under the special protection clause in Article 371 of the Constitution, tribal customary laws, procedures and land rights are protected. Part XVI of the Constitution also ensures special provisions for scheduled castes, scheduled tribes and other underdeveloped classes, which are usually not linked to territories, but to specific social groups.[6] Some of them can be compared to concepts of 'cultural autonomy' applied in Europe, while some are established on a territorial basis.[7] Under the Fifth Schedule, some provisions for 'local autonomy' are provided in order to protect the interests of smaller tribal groups who are placed within larger units of a state.[8] This annex to the Constitution provides a limited platform by way of formation of 'Tribes Advisory Councils', which can articulate the aspirations of the indigenous communities. Yet, neither the Council has any executive power nor does it enjoy any legislative or judicial powers in administering the justice within the scheduled areas. The legislative power is vested with the Governor, and the Council has the duty to advise him on his desire. The Governor is empowered to apply his discretion regarding the applicability of any law passed by the parliament or the state legislature in the scheduled areas. In consultation with the 'Advisory Council', he can make laws for the scheduled areas:

- prohibiting or restricting transfer of land;
- regulating the allotment of land; and
- regulating money-lending business.

5 Among various analysis of the Kashmir-conflict there is one essential for a basic understanding: BOSE, S. (2003) *Kashmir – Roots of Conflict, Paths to Peace*. Massachusetts, UK: Harvard University Press. The author also published his analysis in Italian language after months of ground research: BENEDIKTER, T. (2005) *Il groviglio del Kashmir*. Genoa: Fratelli Frilli.

6 See the full text at: www.constitution.org/cons/india/p16.html. [Accessed: 14th February 2017].

7 Two basic works on this issue are: ADENEY, K. (2002) *Federalism and Ethnic Conflict Regulation in India and Pakistan*. New York: Palgrave McMillan, and ASHRAF, A. (ed.) (1994) *Ethnic Identity and National Integration*. New Delhi: Concept Publishing.

8 See Article 244A on the scheduled and tribal areas at: www.constitution.org/cons/india/p10244a.html as well as the Fifth Schedule of India's Constitution at: www.constitution.org/cons/india/shed05.html [Accessed: 14 February 2017].

The Union President should assent to all these regulations. Thus, the Fifth Schedule, although envisaging to protect tribal interests, does not assign any concrete right of territorial autonomy to the tribal peoples.[9]

In contrast to Article 371, 'genuine' territorial autonomy, as defined in the introduction, has been established in India since 1951 under the Sixth Schedule of her Constitution.[10] The Sixth Schedule contains detailed provisions for 'Autonomous District Councils' (ADC) in districts dominated by so-called 'tribal peoples'.[11]

The main purposes of the provisions of that part of the Indian Constitution are again to preserve the distinct cultures of tribal peoples, to prevent economic exploitation of such peoples by non-tribal peoples, and to allow them to develop and administer themselves. This scheme, although termed 'Provisions as to the Administration of Tribal Areas in the States of Assam, Meghalaya, Tripura and Mizoram', departed from a mere concept of 'ethnic reservations' as provided by the Fifth Schedule, establishing autonomous territories with mixed populations and fully democratic institutions based on general suffrage.

Although limited in their scope, the legislative councils of the autonomous districts established by the Sixth Schedule are based on a very elaborate legislation and are safeguarded by the Union government. They were tasked with granting sufficient autonomy to prevent radical secessionist claims and movements and thus the further splitting up of the states, especially in the northwest and northeast of the country.[12]

Ten out of thirteen ADCs have been established in the four northeastern states of Meghalaya, Assam, Mizoram and Tripura, one in West Bengal and two in Jammu and Kashmir (Leh and Kargil). The latter three have been established under state law, not under the Sixth Schedule, but are very similar to the Sixth-Schedule arrangements. In the rest of the country, however, no such district autonomies have been created, although India has no less than 330 districts, many of which host ethno-linguistic or tribal minorities. About fifty of these districts have an ethno-linguistic majority different from the majority population of their respective federated state and thus would be eligible for a certain degree of cultural

9 The denial of substantial autonomy to India's Adivasi peoples is described by BOSE, S. (2003) *Kashmir – Roots of Conflict, Paths to Peace.* Massachusetts, UK: Harvard University Press.

10 For the full text of the Sixth Schedule of India's constitution see: www.constitution.org/cons/india/shed06.html [Accessed: 14 February 2017].

11 On the issue of India's indigenous peoples see: ERNI, C. (ed.) (2008) *The Concept of Indigenous Peoples in Asia – A Resource Book.* Copenhagen/Chiang Mai: International Work Group for Indigenous Affairs (IWGIA) document no. 123; and MANCHANDA, R. (ed.) (2006) *The No Nonsense Guide to Minority Rights in South Asia.* New Delhi: South Asian Forum for Human Rights (SAFHR).

12 There are three basic researches which helped the author to understand the complex situation of India's Northeast: BARBORA, S. (2002) Ethnic Politics and Land Use: Genesis of Conflicts in India's Northeast. *Economic and Political Weekly.* 37 (13), pp. 1285–1292; BARUAH, S. (2005) *Durable Disorder: Understanding the Politics of Northeast India.* New Delhi: Oxford Press; BARUAH, S. (1999) *India against itself: Assam and the Politics of Nationality.* New Delhi: Oxford Press; BHANMIK, S. (1996) *Insurgent Crossfire: Northeast India.* Delhi: Lancers.

or territorial autonomy in order to preserve the particular cultural character of the concerned area.[13]

As far as genuine territorial autonomy is concerned, the Sixth Schedule of the Constitution is India's present standard. On the other hand, the regional councils constituted by the northeastern states by State Act do not enjoy all the powers available under the Sixth Schedule. Even within this schedule, certain autonomous councils, like Bodoland, Karbi Anglong and North Cachar, managed to obtain greater powers granted by specific constitutional amendments made to this schedule. Hence, there is a certain flexibility in the application of the Constitution's provisions concerning district autonomy. At present, India counts thirteen autonomous territories on the sub-state level,[14] as follows:

The legislative powers of these autonomous districts include:[15]

- land transfer;
- forest (other than reserved forest);
- water bodies (for the purpose of agriculture);
- regulation of shifting cultivation;
- village or town committees and administration;
- appointment or succession of chiefs or headmen;
- inheritance or property;
- marriage and divorce;
- social customs;
- money lending and trading activities of non-residents or non-tribal people living in the area;
- primary education;
- dispensaries, markets, cattle pounds and fisheries; and
- roads, road transport, ferries and waterways.

13 The author has elaborated these issues in his recent research: BENEDIKTER, T. (2013) *Minority Languages in India - An appraisal of linguistic rights of minorities in India*. Bozen. [Online] Available from: www.gfbv.it/3dossier/asia/india2013.pdf [Accessed: 14th February 2017].

14 Autonomy provisions in India available online: Tripura Tribal Areas: http://tripura.nic.in/ttaadc; Jaintia Hills Autonomous District Council: http://jaintia.nic.in; Khasi Hills Autonomous District Council: http://khadc.nic.in; West Garo Hills Autonomous District Council: http://westgarohills.nic.in; Ladakh (Leh) Autonomous Hill Development Council: http://leh.nic.in; Ladakh (Kargil) Autonomous Hill Development Council: http://kargil.nic.in; North Cachar Autonomous District Council: http://nchills.nic.in; Karbi Anglong Autonomous District Council: http://karbianglong.nic.in; Mara Autonomous District Council (Mizoram): www.maraland.net; Maraland (Mizoram): http://samaw.com/maraland; Bodoland Territorial Council: www.bodolandcouncil.org; Bodoland general: www.bodoland.org; Darjeeling Gorkha Hill Council: http://darjeeling.gov.in; Darjeeling's most important weekly magazine: http://darjeelingtimes.com; Gorkha major political party: www.gorkhajanmuktimorcha.org; Kokborok of Tripura: www.boroksite.co; Northeastern Council: http://necouncil.nic.in [Accessed: 14 February 2016].

15 See Art. 3 of Sixth Schedule of the Constitution at: www.constitution.org/cons/india/shed06.html [Accessed: 14 February 2017].

Table 12.1 India's autonomous districts and autonomous hill districts[1]

Autonomous District	*Area (in km²)*	*Population (2001)*	*Capital*	*Ethnic composition*[2]	*Year of Constitution*
1. Bodoland	8,970	2,631,289	Kokrajhar	ST: 1,354,627 SC: 137,594	07.12.2003
2. Karbi Anglong	10,434	813,311	Diphu	ST: 452,963 SC: 29,200	17.11.1951 14.10.1976
3. North Cachar	4,890	186,189	Haflong	Dimasa, Kuki, Hmar, Zemei, Hrangkhawls	17.11.1951 02.02.1970
4. Garo Hills	8,167	865,045	Tura	Garo, smaller groups	22.02.1972 (1979 division)
5. Jaintia Hills	3,819	295,692	Jowai	Pnar, Jaintia, Khasi	22.02.1972
6. Khasi Hills	7,995	1,060,923	Shillong	Khasi, smaller groups	22.02.1972
7. Tripura Tribal Area	7,132	679,720[3]	Khumwng	ST: 679,720	n.d.a.[4]
8. Chakma ADC	n.d.a.	n.d.a.	Chawngte	Chakma	1987
9. Lai ADC	n.d.a.	n.d.a.	Lawngtlai	Lai	1987
10. Mara ADC	n.d.a.	55,000	Siaha	Mara	1987
11. Darjeeling Gorkha Hill Council Since Sept. 2011: Gorkhaland Territorial Administration GTA	3,144	1,609,172	Darjeeling	ST: 179,153 SC: 209,856	22.08.1988 02.09.2011
12. Auton. Hill Development Council Leh	45,110	117,232	Leh	ST: 92,200 (Ladakhi)	28.08.1995
13. Auton. Hill Development Council Kargil	14,086	119,307	Kargil	ST: 105,377 (Purigba, Balti, Brokpa)	01.07.2003

Source: *official websites of the Autonomous District Councils. Elaboration by the author.*

Notes:

1. The Darjeeling Gorkha Hill Council and the Autonomous Hill Councils of Leh and Kargil have been established by state laws of West Bengal and Jammu and Kashmir respectively, and are not enshrined in the Sixth Schedule of the Constitution.
2. SC = scheduled caste; ST = scheduled tribe.
3. This figure accounts for the tribal population of the district only, which accounts for at least 90 per cent of the total population, which is more than 700,000. Ethnic groups in the Tripura Tribal District: Bhil, Bhutia, Chainel, Chakma, Garo, Holan, Kuki, Lepcha, Lushai, Mog, Munda, Moatia, Orang, Riang, Santal, Tripura and Uchai.
4. n.d.a. = no data available.

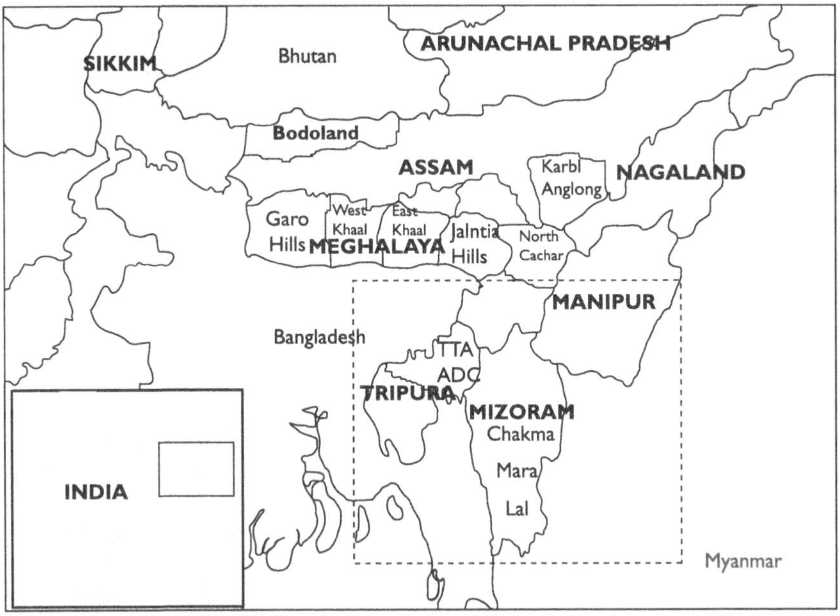

Figure 12.1 Autonomous areas in India's northeast

Source: Archbishop's House, Guwahati (Thomas Menamparambilsdb), Anthropological Map of North-East India (integrated by the author).

The District Council of these entities is allowed to levy and collect taxes on land and buildings, as well as tolls on persons. Moreover, it can collect taxes on professions, trades, callings and employment, animals, vehicles, boats, entry of goods into the local markets, goods carried on ferries, the maintenance of schools, dispensaries and roads. The ADCs are also entitled to receive a share of royalties accruing to the state annually on account of extraction of minerals. The management of these revenues is guided by rules and regulations set by the Governor.

All the matters on which district council is empowered to legislate are also enumerated in the so-called 'State List'. In order to ensure the legislative autonomy of the district council, the Sixth Schedule provides that no act of the state legislature shall apply to any autonomous district unless the respective district council adopts and approves the same.

Regarding the judiciary, the Sixth Schedule provides for a two-tier system at the district and village levels.[16] At the village level, the village council is empowered to

16 The administration of justice in the autonomous districts and autonomous regions is regulated by p. 4 of the Sixth Schedule. See www.constitution.org/cons/india/shed06.html [Accessed: 14 February 2017].

trial suits and cases between the parties belonging to scheduled tribes. At the district level, the district courts are empowered to act as a court of appeal in respect of all suits and cases triable by a village court. This differentiation in the judiciary mirrors the original 'tribal character' of the Sixth Schedule autonomy. Originally, it has created a legal framework specifically for tribal communities, allowing self-administration on social and economic fields deemed most relevant for tribal communities, such as agriculture, forests, fishery and local markets. But it is highly questionable whether this form of autonomy really covers all relevant powers required by such peoples for the preservation of their ethnic and cultural identity and for acting as a comprehensive agency for the economic and social development of their homeland.

For their financial funding, the ADCs are mostly dependent on grants-in-aid, coming from the central government in New Delhi, but mainly routed through the state government. This mechanism provides a leverage, which is often being used to bring the ADC in line with state policies. The resulting financial dependence and the instrumental use of dependency of state decision-makers remain a major bone of contention in relations between the district council and the state governments.

Under the autonomous councils, constituted under the Sixth Schedule, there is no adequate devolution of powers to the village level and most power is concentrated at the district level itself. Instead, if there are different scheduled tribes in an autonomous district, the Governor may, by public notification, divide the area or areas inhabited by them into autonomous regions.[17] Whereas in other states of India a certain amount of administrative power has been attributed to the institution of *Panchayati Raj* under the new Eleventh Schedule of the Constitution, the areas covered by the Sixth Schedule are not encompassed in this form of decentralisation.[18] In these mostly tribal areas, there are traditional systems of governance at the village level, ranging from autocracy or semi-autocracy to full participative democratic procedures and institutions. Thus, there is a certain discrepancy between autonomy at district level and the denial of municipal or local administrative autonomy of the village bodies. The village development boards in Nagaland offer one example of the models that can be adopted. Even in Arunachal Pradesh and in the plain areas of Assam, Manipur and Tripura, where *Panchayati Raj* have been established, just a few powers are devolved to these institutions.

The role of the Governor, appointed by the Union's president for each federated state of India, is considerable also vis-á-vis the Sixth Schedule autonomies. Apart

17 Art. 1(2) of the Sixth Schedule. Art. 2(2) reads: 'There shall be a separate Regional Council for each area constituted an autonomous region under subparagraph (2) of para (1).' See www.constitution.org/cons/india/shed06.html [Accessed: 14 February 2017].

18 See www.constitution.org/cons/india/shed11.html [Accessed: 14 February 2016]. The Bodoland Memorandum in point 4.8 abolishes the Panchayati regime on the autonomous territory. See www.bodolandcouncil.org [Accessed: 14 February 2017].

from the matters on which the district council has legislative powers, the Governor has the discretionary power in deciding whether the laws, made by the state legislature on matters not covered by autonomous legislation of the district, will be directly applicable to the autonomous district or not.[19] The applicability of the laws made by the parliament in these areas is also put under the discretion of the Governor, in the case of Assam, and the President, in the case of other northeastern states. The Governor is also entitled to nominate a certain number of the members of the Autonomous Councils and to suspend the legislation if he deems them to be no longer effective. Thus, the district councils have been provided with a certain legal shield against encroachment by the respective state, but they are fully exposed to the discretionary power of the Governor.

The limited form of autonomy provided by the Sixth Schedule of the Constitution could not quell the quest for self-determination of the Naga peoples, who in 1963 achieved 'statehood' in India without giving up military resistance for full independence. Nor could such a form of autonomy, granted in the form of ADC, meet the widespread demand of some smaller peoples of India to have their own federated state, especially in the northeast. Fully federated 'statehood' was eventually accorded to Meghalaya, Mizoram, Arunachal Pradesh and Tripura. Later, and with the creation of the Bodoland Territorial Council in 2003,[20] a range of further clauses were added to the Sixth Schedule, extending the scope of their autonomy. Nevertheless, some of the Autonomous Districts went on claiming for full statehood in India, but have not been accommodated.

Hence, in India, the pattern of combining ethnicity – regarding small peoples or national minorities – with exceptional autonomies remains quite contradictory. The Indian Constitution emphasises republican values and fundamental human and civil rights standards throughout the whole territory, and in principle does not allow 'ethnic autonomy'. In practice, in order to solve local and regional conflicts, forms of limited territorial autonomy had to be created, admitting implicitly that on a state level the majority rule of a liberal democracy generates a permanent threat to every minority representation and participation in politics and power. On the other hand, new indigenous elites dominating autonomous districts have been tempted to transform such autonomous regions into 'ethnic spaces', as some Indian scholars assert.[21]

19 The Governor's powers to annul, suspend acts and resolutions of District and Regional Councils is provided by Art. 15 of the Sixth Schedule, his power to dissolution of ADCs in Art. 16 of the Sixth Schedule. See www.constitution.org/cons/india/shed06.html [Accessed: 14 February 2017].

20 See the Bodoland Accord at: http://peacemaker.un.org/sites/peacemaker.un.org/files/IN_030210_MemorandumSettlementBodolandTerritorialCouncil.pdf [Accessed: 14 February 2017].

21 See BARBORA, S. (2003) *Experiences of Autonomy in the East and North East – A report on Third Civil Society Dialogue on Human Rights and Peace.* Kolkata: Calcutta Research Group (CRG) and BASU RAY CHAUDHURY, S., KUMAR DAS, S., SAMADDAR, R. (eds.) (2005) *Indian Autonomies – Keywords and Keytextes.* Kolkata: Sampark.

3. India's sub-state autonomies: new 'ethnic spaces'?

Some Indian scholars warn about the risk that territorial autonomy might lead to new ethnically biased states and sub-state entities by vesting their indigenous peoples with special privileges, leaving out other 'denizens', in other words, recent immigrants not members of the titular ethnic groups or not members of 'scheduled tribes'.[22] They warn against the creation of autonomous entities with two or three classes of citizens:

- citizen members of the titular ethnic group;
- Indian general citizens; and
- foreign immigrants.

As a matter of fact, in India's northeast a large share of the population is registered under Scheduled Tribes (STs) status, and some groups and individuals not belonging to such STs appear to be excluded from some benefits of the territorial autonomy provided by either the states listed under Article 371 of the constitution or by the Sixth Schedule – to autonomous districts. Non-members of STs, for example, may be excluded from exercising some trades and business,[23] and they are partly excluded from political representation. In the states of Assam, Meghalaya, Tripura and Mizoram seats are reserved for SC and SC in the legislative assemblies of the states and of the ADCs.[24] As such scholars assert, new social injustices are brought about that carry the potential for social and ethnic conflict. At this point, the very rationale of territorial autonomy has to be recalled: autonomy in a modern democratic sense cannot allow for new discrimination (reversed, for example, against the members of the national majority population living in the area), privileging just one group at the expense of smaller groups. Modern autonomies are incompatible with the idea of indigenous reservations as existing in the Americas.[25]

Autonomy exists to give ethno-linguistic communities the chance to preserve their identity in their traditional homeland, but within a democratic setting inclusive of all legally resident people, with and without citizenship. In a region

22 See BARUAH (2005), above note 12, Section V on 'Citizens and Denizens', pp. 183–210; and BARBORA (2003), above note 20.

23 According to Art. 10 of the Sixth Schedule, the ADCs have the power to make regulations on money-lending and trading by non-tribals. See www.constitution.org/cons/india/shed06.html [Accessed: 14 February 2017].

24 See Part XVI, Art. 332 of the Constitution, on 'Reservation of Seats for SC and ST in the Legislative Assemblies of the States'. See www.constitution.org/cons/india/p16.html [Accessed: 14 February 2017]. Such reservation of seats, however, will cease after sixty years from the commencement of the constitution (Art. 334).

25 For the distinction between ethnic reservation and territorial autonomies see BENEDIKTER (2010), above note 1.

where these communities are compactly settled, it exists to redress the structural disadvantages of ethnic minorities in states with a different titular majority. In India, this also refers to federated states' linguistic majorities. The national majority's implicit power in all domains of life, from culture to media, from economy to politics, from public jobs to military careers, remains largely unquestioned. Territorial autonomy's rationale is not to create a similar 'ethnic space' that allows reverse discrimination, but to establish a legal space wherein substantial equality of opportunity is ensured for all groups sharing the same region.[26] If conceived as a common democratic space with consociational power sharing, territorial autonomy is not exclusive, but inclusive by nature, as long as the necessary institutional safeguards are provided.

This is a normative statement against which working autonomies must be measured. Neither in Europe nor on other continents do territorial autonomy systems always coherently act in accordance with such principles. The challenge lies in making arrangements to ensure that full civil rights are granted to all legally resident citizens irrespective of ethnic affiliation, as well as arrangements for protecting internal minorities. Thus, the concept and the scope of powers of the Sixth Schedule autonomy is obviously too narrow for both enhancing and stabilising the position of the 'titular' tribal or indigenous or minority peoples of a given area and ensuring the consociational participation of all ethnic groups sharing the same territory. The titular majority itself is called upon to strike a balance between the interests of indigenous peoples and non-tribal resident citizens who contribute to regional welfare. Or in other terms: within an autonomous region or district, internal minority protection has to be reconciled with democracy.[27]

4. Conclusion: Transcending the 'Sixth Schedule autonomy'

India's federal system in its sixty-two years of history was repeatedly reshaped: it was first reorganised along linguistic lines, and later further states were carved out from existing ones. In addition, India adopted forms of sub-state autonomy or special autonomy, in which smaller ethnic groups were to be accommodated

26 Substantial equality means not only the absence of individual discrimination, but equal opportunities: a regime of full public bilingualism, official recognition of minority languages and religions, provision of equal means for cultural services and for all groups, an education system in mother tongue, no discrimination on ethnic grounds in recruitment for public jobs, same opportunities in achieving political charges, affirmative action for historically discriminated groups.

27 This issue is further developed by the author in: BENEDIKTER, T. (2009) Regional Autonomous Democracies: New 'Ethnic spaces'? In BENEDIKTER, T. (ed.) *Solving Conflict through Self-Government – A Short Guide to Autonomy in South Asia and Europe*. Bozen: EURAC Bozen. pp. 86–87. Available at: www.eurac.edu/en/research/autonomies/minrig/Documents/Eurasia/Deliverable_No_9_Update_Set_educational_material.pdf [Accessed: 14 February 2017].

or 'minor conflicts' to be settled, but without a coherent scheme. Whereas all major linguistic groups during the linguistic reorganisation of the Indian Union in the 1950s and 1960s were granted their own state, the smaller peoples in the northeast were not, or at least, only much later (Manipur, Meghalaya, Arunachal Pradesh) or only after protracted military violence (Mizoram, Nagaland). While the Sixth Schedule autonomy was applied to some areas in the northeast, in order to avoid the further division of Assam, other states in central India including West Bengal refrained from granting such autonomy even to numerically very sizeable regional or tribal communities (Gorkhaland, Santals, Bhili, Gondi, Ho, Kurukh/Oraon and others).

Thus, both the basic constitutional principles of territorial power sharing in India appear far from being coherently applied: on the one hand, there is federalism for equal or symmetric power sharing between the centre and all federated units, and on the other, territorial autonomy to meet requirements for territorial power sharing at the sub-state level has been established only exceptionally. This is a serious problem, as India's federalism is marked by strong centralism: the federal government is vested with a range of powers unusually large for a federation, while at state level most powers are concentrated in the hands of the federated state administration. Local democracy is provided only by the institution of the *panchayats* – the democratic councils in villages and municipalities. We have to bear in mind that European federations and regional states are not bigger than West Bengal (Germany, the most populous European state after Russia, has 82 million citizens), but are articulated in federal units or autonomous communities with the size of Indian districts. Therefore, there is still a great need and potential for further decentralisation to the lower units that make up the single federated states. This can occur in a symmetric form, including all sub-state entities, or in an asymmetric form, reserved for some districts with special needs and interests, such as those inhabited by ethnic minorities and tribal peoples. Territorial autonomies can be established even outside the federal units, as claimed by concerned political organisations from Ladakh and Gorkhaland. But if regional autonomy on a sub-state level does not match the people's expectations, demands for a fully fledged federated state will reappear on India's political agenda.

The institution of India's 'Autonomous District Councils', under the Sixth Schedule of the Constitution, was originally conceived as a solution for tribal peoples and ethnic conflicts in the northeast during the initial period of nation building. Established by the fathers of the Constitution to avoid splitting up the multi-ethnic northeast, which was faced with a variety of self-determination claims by tribal peoples, the ADCs in their current form cannot meet the political requirements on the ground. It worked as a temporary painkiller, but the pain was to remain.[28] Assam was split up, and four resulting states (Assam, Meghalaya,

28 See SAMADDAR, R. (2005) Minority Rights and Forms of Autonomy in South Asia. In SKURBATY, Z.A. (ed.) *Beyond a One-Dimensional State: An Emerging Right to Autonomy?* Leiden: Martinus Nijhoff. p. 551.

Manipur and Tripura) adopted the Sixth Schedule autonomy to accommodate sub-state self-government demands by smaller ethnic communities and peoples. The very ethnically homogeneous northeast remained conflict ridden. After many uprisings, violent rebellions, and years of low intensity warfare and military resistance by guerrilla groups and 'national liberation fronts', some ethnic groups and peoples managed to obtain their own federated states, including Mizoram, Nagaland and Meghalaya. Other states, such as West Bengal, Jammu and Kashmir, and Assam, had to accord territorial district autonomy to their own minorities (Leh and Kargil, Karbi Anglong and North Cachar Bodoland). The smaller northeastern states, such as Tripura and Mizoram, had to come to terms with their internal ethnic heterogeneity. Nevertheless, the existing legal setting and scope as given by the Sixth Schedule does not offer sufficient political space for a fully autonomous cultural and language policy or for the comprehensive range of powers needed to allow the ADC to be the most important agent for social and economic development in the area. The state government and the Union governor of the respective state exert major hierarchical control, while the ADC neither has a sufficient nor an autonomously controlled financial base.[29]

In addition to the limited scope of the Sixth Schedule autonomy, there is a need to focus on the quality of democracy and governance allowed by these territorial autonomies. The population of some ADCs in the northeast sees autonomy as just an institutional process, and does not feel sufficiently involved. The participation of the people and civil society of some ADCs remained very low. This is due to both the weak institutional design and the particular form of the elite-determined political setting at the sub-state level in India. The mere decentralisation of power to local elites is not enough. There must be provisions to ensure good governance, accountability of the politicians, minority protection and consociational mechanisms of power sharing.

Some other features of the Sixth Schedule autonomy, however, no longer appear appropriate for genuine autonomous legislation and decision-making: relying on the Governor's strong role in surveillance rather than giving the judiciary the main responsibility for resolving disputes, financial dependency on the respective state, the ADCs' lack of power to create their own revenues, gaps in the application of official language policies, the need for fair regulations for recruitment on territorial basis, and the need for forms of immigration control to the autonomous area that are compatible with fundamental rights of all citizens.

The Sixth Schedule has implicit limitations, as unrest in several autonomies such as Karbi Anglong, North Cachar and Mizoram's ADCs demonstrates. Some features of this autonomy were extended in 2003, when the Sixth Schedule was amended to accord greater autonomy to Bodoland. But the Gorkhaland issue can no longer be met with the means of limited self-governance offered by the Sixth

29 For a meticulous critique of the ADC regime in India's northeastern region, see: BARUAH (2005), above note 12.

Schedule.[30] The political evolution of India's northeast clearly shows that continuous pressure from the ground, political organisation and popular pressure led first to serious negotiations between the regional communities and the centre, then to the establishment of autonomies, and eventually to an increase in territorial autonomy. The complex power-sharing settlement in the northeastern states has not yet come to an end, nor has the Kashmir issue been resolved. The majority of tribal peoples still live in states like Madhya Pradesh, Orissa and Jharkhand, while several peoples, such as the Santhali, Gonda, Munda and Ho, are mostly scattered across several states, but often form a majority on the district level. Lacking political organisation and influence, they could generate movements for territorial or cultural autonomy, and it is high time they do so if they want more attention and a real commitment for the protection of their minority rights. The Sixth Schedule autonomy might not be enough to meet this demand of autonomy, let alone reservations and tribal councils under the Fifth Schedule.

30 The region of *Gorkhaland,* so called by its mostly Nepali speaking inhabitants, in northern West Bengal after years of violent clashing, uprising and repression, in 1988 was accorded a rather weak form of territorial autonomy under West Bengal legislation, termed 'Darjeeling Gorkha Hill Council'. After the failure of this first experiment with very limited autonomy in 2007 a new political force, the Gorkha Janmukti Morcha GJM, turned back to mass protest with the basic demand of a separate state of Gorkhaland as a member of the Indian Union. After four years of tug-of-war, but with non-violent means, on 18 July 2011 the GJM signed an agreement with the Government of West Bengal for the Constitution of the 'Gorkhaland Territorial Administration' (GTA), an autonomous body which replaced the Darjeeling Gorkha Hill Council. On 2 September 2011, the GTA was confirmed with a bill by the West Bengal Parliament in Kolkata. While the first Minister, Mamata Banerjee, reiterated that this Act should be a durable solution for the conflict in Gorkhaland, the leader of the GJM, Bimal Gurung defined the GTA just a further step toward statehood separate from West Bengal. The GJM won the GTA elections in July 2012, but its leader Bimal Gurung resigned in order to renew the agitation for full statehood of Gorkhaland. In 2013 the popular agitation on this issue flared up with strong forms of protests of *bandhs* (civil strikes). After a marathon all-party meeting convened by the GJM in August 2013 at Darjeeling, the pro Gorkhaland parties informally formed the 'Gorkhaland Joint Action Committee' in order to continue the movement. For the first time in 106 years, all the major political parties of Gorkhaland agreed to jointly press for statehood within the Union. See http://darjeelingtimes.com [Accessed: 14 February 2017]; for a concise history of Gorkhaland and an interview with Roshan Giri (GJM), see BENEDIKTER (2009), above note 26, pp. 104–111.

Chapter 13

Is Malaysian federalism a good example or a warning for solving the China/Tibet issue?

A brief inquiry into a half-century experiment in asymmetric federalism

Andrew Harding

On 22 July 2013, the residents of Kuching, the capital of the Malaysian state of Sarawak, on the island of Borneo, were treated to a strange spectacle. They saw actors performing a re-enactment of the actual ceremony in 1963 when the last British Governor of Sarawak, Governor Sir Alexander Waddell, sailed from the Astana, the ancient seat of government, directly across the Sarawak River to greet and officially hand over his duties to his Sarawakian successor, signalling the end of colonial rule.[1] For this staged re-enactment, the State Government even arranged for Caucasian actors to play the role of Waddell and his entourage as they walked toward the Square Tower at the Kuching Waterfront, where the Union Jack was lowered as the newly independent state's flag was raised.[2] The event was billed as a celebration of '*liberation day*' (22 July 1963), and the end of the colonial period in Sarawak.

The symbolism of all this would not have been lost on Kuching residents. Between 22 July and 16 September 1963, Sarawak had been an independent territory, its brief independence terminated when it agreed to join the new Federation of Malaysia on the latter date. It was an existential statement of underlying independence and, ultimately, sovereignty. It was a reminder that adherence to the Malaysian federation, created in 1963, was a matter of *choice, not compulsion*, reminiscent of Canada's declaration of war on Germany in 1939 – *a day after* the United Kingdom declared war.

A few days after this staged re-enactment, on 16 September 2013, Malaysia celebrated the 50th anniversary of its creation as a result of the federation of four

1 For a century before Sarawak became formally a British colony in 1945, it had been ruled by the 'white rajahs', the Brooke family, who derived the legitimacy of their rule from a grant of sovereignty over Sarawak by the Sultan of Brunei in 1842. This story of the white rajahs is one of strangest stories of the entire colonial period; here we are concerned only with its aftermath.

2 Sarawak Observes Big Day. *New Straits Times*. Kuala Lumpur, 23 July 2013.

entities: the existing Federation of Malaya (created in 1948 and becoming independent on 31 August 1957); and the British Crown colonies of Singapore, Sabah (known then as North Borneo) and Sarawak. Six years earlier, on 31 August 2007, the 50th anniversary of Malayan 'independence' (*Merdeka*) had been celebrated with gusto in what was from 1963 called 'West Malaysia' (i.e. the Federation of Malaya), but those anniversary celebrations seemed quite foreign to Sabah and Sarawak, which were under British rule for another six years after 1957; for them, 1957 had no significance at all. For these East Malaysian states on the island of Borneo, separated from West Malaysia by a stretch of the South China Sea, it was not, they appeared to think, their party.

A further oddity in this arrangement is that, while the Federation of Malaysia was formed on 16 September 1963, the anniversary of *Malaysia*'s National Day (now usually referred to as *Merdeka Day*) is regularly celebrated on 31 August, commemorating the day in 1957 when the *Federation of Malaya* gained independence. It was not in fact until 2003 that the Government of Malaysia proclaimed *Malaysia Day* to be 16 September, the actual date of the creation of the country we know as 'Malaysia'. Forty years is a long time for the correction of such a basic historical and diplomatic error.[3]

The confusion deepens further when one looks at the Federal Constitution of 1957, which is now known as the Federal Constitution of (please note) *Malaysia*. The creation of Malaysia did not apparently merit a new Constitution, but only amendment (and of course a renaming) of the existing Constitution, called the 'Constitution of the Federation of Malaya'. Article 1(1) clarifies that 'the Federation' shall be known, in Malay and in English, by the name 'Malaysia'. Yet Article 160 of the Constitution provides that '*Merdeka* Day' (celebrating independence) refers to 31 August 1957, and defines 'the Federation' as the Federation established under the *Federation of Malaya Agreement 1957, not the Malaysia Agreement 1963*. The legal position can probably be best expressed by saying that 'the Federation' referred to repeatedly in the Constitution is the Federation established by the 1957 Agreement *as modified by* the 1963 Agreement, and whose powers and structure are defined extensively in the Federal Constitution. So, it seems that after fifty years, or fifty-seven according to one's calculation, Malaysia still has an existential problem that is seen quite differently from Kuching and from Putrajaya, which is now the seat of the federal government near Kuala Lumpur. Even the black letter of the Constitution seems to skate over the momentous events of 1963 and the creation, on 16 September of that year, of a new federation. Interestingly enough, the validity of the 1963 federation was challenged, unsuccessfully, by one of the existing states of the Federation of Malaya – Kelantan – in legal proceedings the day before the new federation took effect. They argued,

3 See, further, HARDING, A. and CHIN, J. (2014) 'Fifty Years of Malaysia: Reflections and Unanswered Questions'. In HARDING, A. and CHIN, J. (eds) *50 Years of Malaysia: Federalism Revisited*. Singapore: Marshall Cavendish. p. 8.

very plausibly, that this change was a fundamental one on which they should have been consulted. Indeed, it was, and they should have been.

This might all seem to be purely technical confusion for draftsmen to sort out, but it is not so. There was a palpable sense in September 2013 that federation itself was an issue only for Sabah and Sarawak. And even in Sabah and Sarawak it seemed as if the prevailing view was that federation was not something to be celebrated with great (or for some people, actually any) enthusiasm. Casual treatment of the 'details' discussed above is seen in those states as symbolic of dismissive attitudes, and a form of neo-colonialism in which the Malaysian Prime Minister stands in for Sir Arthur Waddell. In federalism protocol matters deeply; appearances can reinforce or damage the federal structure.

The fact is, however, that, despite the lack of enthusiasm for the federal arrangement in Sabah and Sarawak, not only has Malaysia succeeded as a federation, but it is plausibly the only Asian example of a successful federation east, that is, of Kolkata. So, from the point of view of China and Tibet, here is something worth investigating in a comparative perspective.

Now, it may be objected that mere survival is not the test of success, but rather the test should be whether the federal bargain of 1963 has been observed and has led to stability and development. Many Sarawakians, and even more Sabahans, would likely dispute that stability, or even development, has actually occurred. They might point to their states being swamped with illegal migrants who are given citizenship with alacrity to subvert the electoral politics of their states; to a brief insurgency in favour of the claim of the Sulu Sultanate (now part of the Philippines) to Sabah; and to West Malaysian colonialism – in politics, economics and religion/culture.[4] It is objected that the federal power interferes in and manipulates state politics in a manner not in the spirit of federalism.[5] It is maintained that these two states, having the most abundant natural resources, remain the poor relations among Malaysia's thirteen states.[6] Still, the general trend of discussion around and after the anniversary in 2013 is not toward advocating independence for those states, but rather toward the decentralisation of more powers to the state level. Significantly, however, advocacy of secession is defined as sedition and is punishable under Malaysia's increasingly draconian sedition law.[7]

4 For contemporary discussion of these grievances, see CHIN, J. (2014) 'Federal-East Malaysia Relations: Primus-Inter-Pares?' In HARDING, A. and CHIN, J. (eds) *50 Years of Malaysia: Federalism Revisited*. Singapore: Marshall Cavendish. p. 152.

5 HARDING, A. (2014) 'Protection of the Indigenous Peoples of Sabah and Sarawak'. In HARDING, A. and CHIN, J. (eds) *50 Years of Malaysia: Federalism Revisited*. Singapore: Marshall Cavendish. p. 186; MOHKTAR, K.A. (2014) 'Confusion, Coercion and Compromise in Malaysian Federalism'. In HARDING, A. and CHIN, J. (eds) *50 Years of Malaysia: Federalism Revisited*. Singapore: Marshall Cavendish. p. 220.

6 WELSH, B. (2014) 'Interview with Tan Sri Simon Sipaun'. In HARDING, A. and CHIN, J. (eds) *50 Years of Malaysia: Federalism Revisited*. Singapore: Marshall Cavendish. p. 50.

7 (2015) '4 Charged with Sedition over Sabah, Sarawak Secession, Reports Says'. *The Malaysian Insider*. [Online] 16 March. Available at: http://m.themalaymailonline.com/malaysia/article/court-drops-sedition-charges-against-four-sabah-secessionists [Accessed: 14 February 2017].

Clearly, therefore, there is deep disagreement about the nature of federalism in Malaysia and in looking at a possible future for Tibet we could learn valuable lessons, both positive and negative, from the experience of the East Malaysian states of Sabah and Sarawak. The example is salient in the sense that although these two states are two of thirteen, their position under the Constitution evinces more autonomy than the states of West Malaysia, where the federalism we see is characterised by Watts as quasi-federalism. It will be argued here that if Tibet is to become politically part of the People's Republic, then whatever special guarantees are put in place will have to be carefully negotiated, drafted and implemented. If Sabah and Sarawak can remain part of the Malaysian federation, albeit with many grievances, historic and current, despite some lack of care in negotiating, drafting and implementing their guarantees, then perhaps – just perhaps – there is a possibility of reaching a successful conclusion for Tibet. But the example here also shows that Tibetans had better be wary of such processes. Federalism can also be a spider's web of deceit.

Let us begin the inquiry by discussing federalism itself as a concept, and how it is applied in Malaysia.

1. Federalism

The term 'federalism' itself originates from the Latin *foedus* which means 'treaty'. States have always tried to find structures for peace, cooperation and mutual benefit, and federalism is one such structure. 'Federalism' is used these days to denote a state with more than one level of government operating each within its own constitutionally protected sovereign sphere. It does not have to be based on a treaty; in fact, a treaty system would these days more likely fall within the notion of a '*con*federation', a looser arrangement in which states come together for certain limited purposes.

The Federation of Malaysia on the other hand *is* based on a treaty – the Malaysia Agreement of 1963; and the original Federation of 1957 was also based on a treaty, the Federation of Malaya Agreement. The Malaysia Agreement was an international agreement involving the Federation of Malaya, the United Kingdom and the then colonies of Singapore, North Borneo (now Sabah) and Sarawak. It needed to be effected and enforced by constitutional law. Accordingly, amendments were made to the Constitution of the Federation of Malaya of 1957, giving the country a new name and a modified constitutional structure taking account of the three new states and their enhanced status, compared with the existing states, within the Federation.

Federalism has been looked at as a blueprint for decentralisation; as a way of resolving ethnic or central-local tensions; as a way of maximising economic benefits; and as a way of resolving long-standing geopolitical cleavages. It has also had its disasters such as Yugoslavia in the 1990s and the West Indies in the 1960s.

It is also true, however, that we no longer regard federalism as the only way of solving these problems. Europe in particular has experimented with various kinds of 'devolution', which involve a form of delegation of executive and legislative powers to a sub-national unit, but without implications for national sovereignty. These arrangements are typically one-off or asymmetrical, rather than a system adopted for all sub-national units, and respond to particular demands for autonomy. Asymmetry here means that the powers being exercised are not the same as in the other sub-national units. In Asia, Aceh within Indonesia provides a good example of an asymmetrical devolution of power, based on agreements between the separatist movement and the central government in Jakarta. This too might be of interest in Tibet. The people of West Papua are also seeking the same arrangement. And another clear example is the recently established Moro autonomous government in the Southern Philippines. As we can see from the symbolic enactment with which this chapter began, where sovereignty is an issue, federalism rather than devolution is a better fit: devolution assumes continuation of the sovereignty of the larger unit, whereas federalism merely suspends or limits the sovereignty of the smaller. That was essentially the message of the Kuching re-enactment. In this sense, the one-country-two-systems approach relating to Hong Kong and Macau may not be suitable for the case of Tibet, where sovereignty is a hugely important issue.

In federal systems, many tensions can arise, and federal systems tend to evolve over time, as has clearly been the case with Malaysia. To take an obvious example, the current phenomenon, since 2008, of opposition parties controlling a number of states brings an important new factor into the practice of federalism in Malaysia.[8] Office-holders at both levels have been exploring the political, legal, administrative and fiscal consequences of this novel situation. At the same time, politicians on both sides have not been above exploiting some of these issues for political gain. The Constitution brings opposing coalitions into a direct relationship within a structure that each has to render effective, albeit in different ways. The test is whether the Federal Government can live with state governments of a different political stripe; and whether state governments can in practice operate within the constraints imposed by the Constitution. These practical issues are often obscured or complicated by political rhetoric. Most distinctly and positively in the case of Penang one can see the results of federalism at its best; this state thrives under opposition rule and has carved out its niche within the system, in terms of economic progress and internal governance.[9]

Federalism, despite the complexity it entails, is often considered to bring the benefit of requiring compromise and cohabitation between opposed parties, lessening tension and creating a positive competitive environment that is conducive to democracy. Of course, in China, democracy is not an ambition, but a federal arrangement could nonetheless facilitate the kind of cohabitation in which the

8 HARDING, A. (2012) *The Constitution of Malaysia: A Contextual Analysis*. Oxford: Hart Publishing. ch. 5.

9 YEOH, T. (2012) *States of Reform: Governing Selangor and Penang*. Penang: Penang Institute.

issue of sovereignty is fudged and both sides benefit. It is built around the idea of dividing powers and accepting that winners do not necessarily take all. In this sense, federalism can reinforce constitutional government, as well as provide a measure of autonomy for ethnic and religious groups. Whether China really wants this is a large question. In Malaysia's case, while across most of the states pluralism is fairly evenly spread rather than geographically concentrated (except in urban areas where the Chinese minority is predominant), this is far less true in East Malaysia, the subject of our concern here, where indigenous people are in the majority.

Federalism is nonetheless a concept that varies psychologically according to one's perspective and according to the dynamics of a given context. It offers the prospect of building a new entity out of states or territories that may not have much in common except geostrategic interests or markets for their products; here, it offers harmonisation and maximisation of value instead of fragmentation. It can on the other hand offer decentralisation in the place of an authoritarian centre. Then again, for some people, such as Kuching residents in 2013, it represents the surrender of *already existing autonomy*, and is therefore to be regarded with deep suspicion.

Because of the inherent tensions in a federal system, it is also difficult to maintain a federation in a state of stability. This we will see from the Malaysian example. It can easily succumb to the assertion of central, federal power, dissolving in practice the elements of autonomy that are guaranteed legally, but are subsumed in a political imperative that draws power towards the centre. This is the 'centripetal' (centre-seeking) tendency with a federal system, and it is very apparent in Malaysia. But a federation can also tend toward fragmentation and the breaking up of the federation, which is known as the 'centrifugal' (centre-fleeing) tendency, the ultimate end of which would lead to the breaking up of the federation, as was seen with Yugoslavia in the 1990s.

For this reason, we need to pay close attention to the institutions that create and enforce federalism, especially those that protect states' rights; and these institutions need to work in a way that understands and supports the distribution of power that federalism entails. Federalism needs to be constantly maintained through politics, administration, economics and law, and is therefore a real responsibility of all branches of government, legislative, executive and judicial. This is true not just at the federal level, but at the state level too. It is all very hard work.

One obvious and essential element of a federation, therefore, is a process of dispute resolution, which polices the boundaries of state and federal powers, ensuring that the original bargain is not contravened by either or any side of that bargain. In Malaysia, the Federal Court performs this task, just as the Supreme Courts of India, Canada and the United States, and the High Court of Australia do within their respective federal systems. Given the precedents in Malaysia, it is difficult to say that the Federal Court has maintained a balance between federal and states' rights over the last fifty years. Most decisions have gone against the latter.

The courts are not, however, the only forum for settling such disputes. One should add the legislature as a forum for raising federal-state issues, and in those jurisdictions which have a bicameral legislature, like Malaysia, one would expect state representatives in the upper house at least, if not all representatives in both houses who represent non-federal areas, to be prominent in advocating the interests of the states. In addition, there is usually a consultative body that pays attention to state and federal financing (in Malaysia, it is the National Finance Council) and this body affords a non-confrontational method of settling all-important fiscal issues.[10] With this background, let us see how Malaysian federalism has been arranged and implemented with regard to Sabah and Sarawak.

2. The basic structure of Malaysian federalism

Federalism, as we have seen, is a complex system of government and it is especially so in Malaysia given its complex, multi-layered nature. Malaysia is a federation of two states (originally in 1963 three, including Singapore) with an already existing federation of eleven states, the Federation of Malaya, which came into being in 1948 and became independent, as we have seen, in 1957. The Federation of Malaya had brought within the federal structure the nine Malay states (which were already either federated or unfederated, and had their own traditional Rulers) and the two former Crown colonies of Penang and Melaka (Malacca). Additionally, the Federation of 1963 is an asymmetrical federal system in which Sabah and Sarawak have more powers, and more constitutional protection for their powers, at least in theory, than the other eleven states. The word 'complex' actually hardly does justice to the intricate, cultural and history-ridden nature of these constitutional arrangements.

In Malaysia's case, federalism was essentially, as we have seen, an outcome of decolonisation, and the need to create some kind of viable unification across the former British territories, of various kinds, in Southeast Asia. The object was to create a new entity powerful enough to compete economically and politically with rising nationalisms in the region such as those of Indonesia and Vietnam, in the context of the Cold War. Indeed, the Malaysian Federation was opposed by Indonesia during 1963 to 1965, but faced down the larger bully.[11] The Federation thus survived its first test. It survived its second test, too, when in 1965 Singapore left the Federation. Arguably, however, this departure, in which the views of Sabah and Sarawak were not sought, did alter fundamentally the nature of the bargain, which formed the basis of the Malaysia Agreement.

10 HARDING, A. (2012) *The Constitution of Malaysia: A Contextual Analysis*. Oxford: Hart Publishing. p. 144.

11 POH-LING TAN (2007), 'From Malaya to Malaysia'. In HARDING, A. and LEE, H.P. (eds) *Constitutional Landmarks in Malaysia: The First 50 Years, 1957–2007*. Petaling Jaya: LexisNexis. pp. 30 ff.

The Reid Commission, which drafted the Federal Constitution in 1957, was constrained by its terms of reference to bestowing on the states only a 'measure of autonomy'. This implies that most legislative and executive powers are vested in the Federation rather than the states. This is confirmed by an examination of Schedule 9 of the Constitution. Schedule 9 contains three lists, pertaining to federal, state and concurrent powers. Concurrent powers can be exercised by either state or federal authorities, and any residual powers not mentioned belong to the states. The lists designate both legislative *and* executive powers. If there is any inconsistency between federal and state law, federal law prevails.

As one would expect, the Federation deals with all of the larger issues affecting the country as a whole, such as external affairs, defence, energy, the legal system and citizenship. Trade, industry and transport are also federal powers, as well as social issues such as health care and education. Most importantly, finance and general taxation are federal matters. State powers, on the other hand, are largely limited to Islamic law and custom, land, agriculture, forests and natural resources; however, local government and therefore all of its functions are also under state control. The concurrent powers, such as social welfare, planning and public health, are in general exercised by the states. We should note here that Sabah and Sarawak have additional powers over immigration, as well as over native customary and personal law, and some other functions such as harbours and posts. They also have the power to impose a sales tax, but have not exercised it (the Federation has imposed a general sales tax from 1 April 2015).

It is immediately apparent that the Federation has much more power than the states, and that Sabah and Sarawak have much more power than the other states. Sabah and Sarawak's control over immigration, not only from outside Malaysia but also from the rest of the country, is very unusual in a federal system.

The exclusive arbiter over the constitutional division of powers is, as discussed above, the Federal Court. It is also the exclusive arbiter of disputes of any kind between states or between the Federation and a state. Although the Federal Court has on occasion decided disputes of this kind, it has only rarely struck down a statute as being a trespass on state powers. In one case, *Mamat Daud*, it laid down the applicable criteria in such cases.

In *Mamat bin Daud v. Government of Malaysia*, all five judges in the apex court, which struck down a federal law, were agreed on the test to be applied:

> it is the substance and not the form or outward appearance of the impugned legislation which must be considered . . . no amount of cosmetics used in the legislative make-up can save legislation from being struck down for pretending to be what it is not. The object, purpose and design of the impugned section must therefore be investigated for the purpose of ascertaining the true character and substance of the legislation and the class of subject-matter of legislation to which it really belongs.[12]

12 *Mamat bin Daud v. Government of Malaysia* [1986] 2 *Malayan Law Journal* 192.

The dissenting judgments, however, applied the test differently from the majority. Therefore, this 'pith and substance' test is not necessarily easy to apply, and much depends on the court's willingness to protect states' rights, as the majority did in this case. The point here is that even in a common-law system with a stable constitutional order and a measure of judicial independence, judicial protection of states' rights cannot be taken for granted. China does not even have an independent judiciary; therefore, some other method of dispute settlement would have to be found. Constitutional law is not replete with examples of such mechanisms.

The division of federal and state powers also has to be read against provisions that give the Federation even greater powers than appear in Schedule 9. Under Article 76, the Federal Parliament is empowered to legislate in respect of matters on the State list in three situations.

First, it may legislate for the purpose of implementing international agreements. Here, however, it cannot legislate with respect to Islamic law or Malay custom, and not in any case without consulting the State Government.

Second, it may legislate to promote legal uniformity between two or more states; in this case as well as for the first situation, the law only takes effect when passed by the state legislature, when it becomes state law. Additionally, Parliament is given a specific power to legislate for ensuring uniformity of law and policy in relation to land and local government; but in this instance the law does not have to be passed by the state legislature and remains federal law. The Constitution also recognises the importance of creating uniformity in relation to these issues by creating a National Land Council and a National Local Government Council. These provisions concerning land and local government do not, however, apply to Sabah or Sarawak.

Third, Parliament can legislate where simply requested to do so by a state legislature. The National Land Code 1965 is a good example of the use of this power. Like the Local Government Act 1976, it is a federal law dealing with a state matter; it was passed at the request of all the states rather than under the special powers mentioned above for land and local government. The two statutes mentioned here were passed following agreement between the Federation and the states in their respective national councils. But again, they do not apply to Sabah or Sarawak, which, as on many other issues, have their own laws. It is, of course, axiomatic that it is perfectly possible for a subject of a federation to maintain its own legal system as quite distinct from the federal system and that of other subjects.

Although executive powers follow legislative powers, Article 80 provides similar flexibility to Article 76 by allowing federal law to confer executive authority on a state. A good example is the Immigration Act 1959, as amended in 1963, which gives the Governments of Sabah and Sarawak control over immigration in their respective states. It is also permissible for state and federal authorities to exercise executive powers on behalf of each other. State powers must also be exercised so as to ensure compliance with federal laws, and not so as to impede the exercise of federal powers.

The structure created in 1957 clearly bestows a preponderance of power on the federation without reducing states to the position of mere agents of the federal power. It is also a flexible arrangement and therefore much depends on observing the spirit of federalism in practice. The division of powers outlined above has not, however, required any significant adjustment since 1957, or since 1963 for Sabah and Sarawak, which indicates that on this issue the Reid Commission at least successfully reconciled the aspiration for State Government with the needs of national development and nation-building. Whether this applies also to Sabah and Sarawak under the Malaysia Agreement of 1963 remains disputed. The consensus among scholars discussing this issue at a seminar in Singapore in 2013 was that the balance of powers as it exists needs to be adjusted in favour of more state powers for Sabah and Sarawak, despite the already asymmetrical nature of the federal structure.

3. Fiscal federalism

Desiring to create strong central government with limited powers for the states, the Reid Commission placed financial matters firmly in federal hands. The idea was to enable the states to draw on federal resources while exploiting the possibilities for maximising their own revenue. An important example is taxation of income, where they refused on grounds of efficiency to give powers to the states, as a result of which there is an imbalance between federal and state finances. The total revenue of all of the states combined in 2006 was less than RM9 billion, compared to federal revenue of more than RM120 billion in the same year. Expenditure showed a similar imbalance. In practice, state governments have found it difficult to avoid an operating deficit, and development funding normally has to come from federal sources. For states, fiscal issues are therefore fundamental to the exercise of their powers.

States are entitled under the Constitution to certain grants, which are calculated according to formulae. These grants are constitutionally guaranteed and set out in detail in Schedule 10 of the Constitution, so that there is no element of discretion involved.

First, there is a Capitation Grant, which is based on the annual population projection for the state, as assessed by the Federal Government; being graduated, it favours states with a small population. The amounts payable are amended from time to time by Parliament according to inflation and population increase, but Parliament may not reduce the grant to less than 90 per cent of the previous year's grant.

Second, there is a State Road Grant. Maintenance of state roads is an important function and a large expenditure. This grant is calculated by multiplying an average maintenance cost per mile by the number of miles of road the state has, and so favours those states with extensive highways and therefore high maintenance costs. Arguably, this leaves states that need infrastructural *development* at some disadvantage; however, since this argument applies principally to Sabah and Sarawak, whose development needs are dealt with by other means, a problem of entrenched underdevelopment seems not to arise from this system.

In theory, therefore, state finance does not depend on federal approval; but in practice the situation tends to be otherwise. Mandatory grants are in general terms barely sufficient for state governments to perform their basic functions, and they have usually been run on deficit funding, which is then made up by the Federation. In order to take development initiatives, however, states need finance over and above the mandatory grants, and unless they can find the resources otherwise, they will be dependent on discretionary federal grants.

Nonetheless, states also have some sources of revenue based on their own powers, which are similarly guaranteed by the Constitution. They can, for example, charge rents on state property, impose licence fees and charge water rates. In practice, the most important elements are the royalties and other revenue derived from land and natural resources, such as tin, petroleum, oil, minerals and timber; however, Parliament may restrict the levying of royalties or similar charges made in respect of mineral concessions. Conflicts have occurred constantly between the Federation and states over natural resources.[13]

It can be seen that a successful federal fiscal arrangement, which Malaysia by and large can claim to have, requires a good deal of negotiation and compromise. This is achieved through the mechanism of the National Finance Council (NFC), whose main task is to iron out difficulties of a fiscal nature arising in the federal context. It consists of the Prime Minister, such Ministers as the Prime Minister shall appoint and one representative from each state. It must meet at least once every twelve months, and is summoned, as often as he or she considers necessary, by the Prime Minister (or else by three or more state representatives), who presides. The Federal Government is under a constitutional duty to consult the NFC in respect of matters such as the making of federal grants to the states; the assignment to the states of federal taxes or fees; and the making of loans to the states. Parliament is required annually to pay into a State Reserve Fund such sums as are deemed by it, after consultation with the NFC, to be necessary; and the Federation may from time to time make payments out of the Fund to the states for the purposes of development or to supplement revenues. All matters of potential controversy are dealt with by the NFC, and it is interesting to note that open fiscal controversy between a state and the Federation, or between states (with the exception of the issue of natural-resource revenues, as mentioned above), is rare.

Sabah and Sarawak have some fiscal advantages over the other states.

First, unlike the other states, they may borrow money with the consent of Bank Negara (the Central Bank of Malaysia).

13 See, e.g., KHALID, R.M., JALIL, F. and MOKHTAR, M.B. (2014) 'Fifty Years of Water Resource Management in Malaysian Federalism: A Way Forward'. In HARDING, A. and CHIN, J. (eds) *50 Years of Malaysia: Federalism Revisited*. Singapore: Marshall Cavendish. p. 266; HARDING, A. (2012) *The Constitution of Malaysia: A Contextual Analysis*. Oxford: Hart Publishing. p. 143.

Second, Schedule 10 also provides for special grants for Sabah and Sarawak, over and above the Capitation Grant and the Road Grant, the bases of which were negotiated at the time of their accession. The object of these is to ensure that state revenue is adequate to meet the cost of existing state services, with reasonable provision for their expansion.

Third, they are allowed eight further sources of revenue not accorded to the other states.

Fourth, the restrictions on the proportion of export duty on minerals do not apply to Sabah and Sarawak.

4. The politics of federalism

While the preceding sections dealt with the legal and financial aspects of the Federation, this section will deal with the politics. The first thing to recognise is that for the past fifty years, in fact since independence, the Federation has been ruled by a single coalition, called the Alliance until 1973, and thereafter the Barisan Nasional (National Front, or BN). The core of the coalition consists of three political parties, each representing the three major ethnic groups in Malaysia. They are: United Malays National Organisation (UMNO), the Malaysian Chinese Association (MCA) and the Malaysian Indian Congress (MIC). As the name suggests, UMNO represents Malays, MCA the Chinese and MIC the Indians. The BN is arguably one of the most successful political alliances in the world, and for the majority of the past fifty years, the coalition commanded more than a two-thirds majority in Parliament. This allowed BN to alter the Malaysian Constitution at will.

At the state level too the BN has been politically successful, although it has problems with three states: Kelantan, Terengganu and Sabah. Kelantan has been ruled by Parti Islam Malaysia (PAS) for most of the past fifty years, while Terengganu was under PAS rule for several terms. Sabah presents an interesting case study. While the Parti Bersatu (PBS) state government was officially part of the BN from 1986 to 1990, it behaved like an opposition party within the BN. It took a strong 'state-rights' stand against the federal power, so much so that on the eve of the 1990 elections, it left the BN and joined an opposition alliance. Since 2008, Penang and Selangor have joined Kelantan as opposition-ruled states, suggesting that the dominance of the BN may be coming to an end. In fact, in the 2013 general elections, BN lost the popular vote to the opposition, although it won a majority of parliamentary seats.[14]

Nevertheless, when Tun Dr Mahathir Mohamad was Prime Minister (1981–2003), he centralised power at Putrajaya,[15] and within the BN power was decisively

14 IN-WON HWANG (2003) *Personalized Politics: The Malaysian State under Mahathir.* Singapore: ISEAS.

15 HARDING, A. (2012) *The Constitution of Malaysia: A Contextual Analysis.* Oxford: Hart Publishing. ch. 2.

shifted towards UMNO. Mahathir himself did not really believe in federalism, being more comfortable with a strong central power that was in his view needed to transform Malaysia into a fully developed country.[16] He maintained a tight control over the states. In every state where UMNO operates (the only exception was Sarawak), the Chief Minister's post was not only given to UMNO, but personally approved or nominated by the Prime Minister.

Thus, federal–state relations were smooth as long as both the federal and state governments were ruled by the BN. When the state was ruled by the opposition, the Federal Government tended to do its utmost to make life difficult for the state, even punishing it by use of its fiscal control and withholding development funding in order to weaken the State Government with a view to replacing it with a BN State Government in the next election.[17] The same pattern is repeating now – Kelantan, Selangor and Penang are experiencing little or no cooperation from Putrajaya when it comes to issues such as trade and investment regulation, which are under the purview of the Federal Government.

The lesson to be drawn from the politics of Malaysian federalism is that if a single party holds power at the federal level, it can assert overwhelming power and effectively demolish all but the appearance of federalism.

5. Position of Sabah and Sarawak

Let us turn now to the salient question of Sabah and Sarawak's membership of the Federation, and how and on what terms it came about.

These states had few viable options in 1963 other than joining Malaysia. At the same time, there was unease about the possibly deleterious effects of joining the Federation. A Memorandum of the Malaysia Consultative Committee, a Committee of the Commonwealth Parliamentary Association, consisting of representatives of the Governments of Britain, Malaya, Sabah and Sarawak, supported the federation of Sabah and Sarawak with Malaya and Singapore in its Memorandum of February 1962. The Cobbold Commission, consisting of representatives of the British and Malayan Governments, visited Sabah and Sarawak in 1962 and reported that the majority supported federation with Malaya, provided due regard was had to the special position of Sabah and Sarawak, the ethnic implications, the physical distances involved and these territories' political immaturity compared to the Federation of Malaya and the then colony of Singapore.

The Legislative Assemblies of both territories voted in favour of federation subject to appropriate safeguards. An Inter-Governmental Committee was then

16 YATIM, R. (1995) *Freedom under Executive Power in Malaysia: A Study of Executive Supremacy*. Kuala Lumpur: Endowment Books.

17 CHIN, J. (1997) Politics of Federal Intervention in Malaysia, with Reference to Kelantan, Sarawak and Sabah. *Journal of Commonwealth and Comparative Politics*. 35(2). pp. 96–120.

set up, comprising representatives from the same four governments, to thrash out constitutional safeguards for Sabah and Sarawak, reporting in February 1963. Negotiations with Singapore proceeded separately, and a referendum in Singapore also supported federation. The Malaysia Agreement was eventually signed on 9 July 1963 by all the governments concerned, and Malaysia came into being, as we saw earlier, on 16 September 1963. This was effected not by a new Federal Constitution, but simply by the admission of new states to the existing but renamed Federation under Article 1 of the Constitution, and by numerous amendments to the Constitution giving effect to the negotiated settlement that was embodied in the Malaysia Agreement.

The principal point of concern was the possible effect of migration on land, commerce, and the employment and professional opportunities of East Malaysians faced with competition from more qualified people from Malaya and Singapore. In this connection, a draft Bill on immigration was appended to the Malaysia Agreement and promptly passed into law as the Immigration Act 1963 a few days before Malaysia came into being. However, there was also concern about other issues: financial arrangements and development; the special position of natives of Sabah and Sarawak; the national language; religion; the legal system; representation in the Federal Parliament; and, of course, how these states would be protected from future constitutional changes affecting any of these issues. Between them, Sabah and Sarawak have about 60 per cent of Malaysia's land, but only about a fifth of its population. The Cobbold Commission had stressed the need for a sense of equality and partnership in the new federal scheme. According to Lord Cobbold, it was to be a 'partnership', not a 'takeover'. In retrospect, those words carry some irony.

Sabah and Sarawak were thus placed in a position that was not available to the other states that formed the Federation in being able to negotiate their participation. Sabah and Sarawak were both resource-rich and underdeveloped.

Quite apart from the central issue of immigration, Sabah and Sarawak have, as we have seen, substantially more powers than the other states. Parliament's powers to legislate for land and local government, for example, do not apply to Sabah and Sarawak; this allows these states exclusive legislative control over these two matters. Crucially, the Governments of Sabah and Sarawak also have special powers to veto constitutional amendments affecting their states. Under Article 161E(2), no amendment shall be made to the Federal Constitution without the concurrence of the Government of Sabah or Sarawak, as the case may be (oddly, *not* the State Legislative Assembly), if the amendment is such as to affect the operation of the Constitution with regard to: Malaysian citizenship and the equal treatment of persons born or resident in the state; the constitution and jurisdiction of the High Court of Sabah and Sarawak, and the appointment, removal and suspension of its judges; the state's legislative and executive powers and financial arrangements between the Federation and the state; religion and language in the state, and the special treatment of natives of the state; and the quota of MPs allocated to the state in proportion to the total number of MPs.

The demarcation of powers as between the Federation and Sabah and Sarawak has remained unaltered since 1963. But although the Federation has not sought to alter the balance of legislative powers in its favour, the underlying reality of federal politics means there are limits to states' political autonomy, even where they receive special constitutional protection.

6. Secession and other remedies

For Sabah and Sarawak, Malaysian federalism has proved to be centripetal in a way that deprives these states of real autonomy and this has been deleterious to their interests. The question then arises, what is the remedy? Three remedies are raised: namely, political process at the federal level; secession; and a 'Second Malaysian Federation',[18] or renegotiation of the federal bargain.

Federal constitutions rarely mention secession, and therefore when it is raised it is necessarily a grey area. We cannot deny that, legally, where there is a federal agreement, this could be repudiated by an aggrieved party. This is simply part of international law. But it does not get us very far. In the case of Singapore in 1965, secession (by expulsion in this case) is possible, and can even be effected with great rapidity; and there are, of course, many other examples across the world such as the collapse of the Soviet Union and Yugoslavia.

Nonetheless, many questions arise with regard to secession. How could secession be effected in a situation where even raising the issue might be seen as treasonable and a reason for armed intervention? Who would have the right to declare secession and how would the exercise of such a right be rendered legitimate? Could a State Government make such a declaration? Would the people have to be consulted in a referendum (the recent example of Crimea springs to mind)? Would such consultation even be possible in a fast-moving environment? Is the reality that, in these days of political, administrative, legal and economic complexity, secession could only be effected cleanly by mutual consent and careful negotiation? And would such negotiation not also involve renegotiation of the federal bargain itself, given the effects of secession on the other units?

In the case of Sabah and Sarawak, secession is probably impossible in practice, and perhaps not even desirable given (in Sabah's case) the prospect of an independent state being taken over by the large numbers of illegal migrants from the Philippines.

It is also worth mentioning here Article 159 clause 4 (bb), which states that Parliament can admit new states by amending the Constitution, based on a Bill which receives a simple majority (ordinary majority) in both Houses of Parliament. So, the nature of the Federation can be altered by the federal power acting unilaterally, it seems.

18 CHIN-HUAT WONG (2013) 'Time for a Second Federation in Malaysia?' *Penang Monthly*, 13 September 2013.

In Tibet's case, thought would have to be devoted to the issue of how it might be protected in terms of severance of any agreement that might be made with China. My conclusion here is that it would have to be specifically provided for.

Given the economic imbalance between Malaysia's states that are rich in natural resources and those with the best economic position, it can be seriously questioned how federalism as implemented for the past fifty years could be justified. One answer is that these states have special funding and it is up to their leaders, not the Federal Government, to distribute it for the benefit of their states and to defend states' interests through the political process. Unhappily, attempts to do this have not been looked upon with favour by federal leaders. In an early instance, in 1966, a Sarawak Chief Minister seen as recalcitrant was turned out of office by constitutional manipulation, including an emergency proclamation, which ought to have been impossible in a federal system. Similar episodes have continued to occur over the last half century.

This leaves the question of how a Second Malaysian Federation might differ from the first, the 1963 model. In the view of many observers, states have too few powers, so that possibly education, health care, transportation and police could be assigned to the states. In this way, the states would have enough power to devolve, in turn, to local government, making a genuinely three-tier government system possible. Decentralisation would have to be asymmetric in favour of the larger and more inherently autonomous states of Sabah and Sarawak. In order to prevent the decline and extinction of native languages and cultures in Sabah and Sarawak, which has become a real fear (and very salient with regard to Tibet), devolved powers should allow these states to preserve native languages.

7. Conclusion

Federalism is not, as we can see, a self-executing concept, and it needs to be enacted very carefully, but also judiciously enforced and carefully maintained by a process of continual dialogue. So, the fact that Malaysia has survived as a federation is notable. But why has it survived?

The fundamental issue is that independence is not a realistic option fifty years down the track of federal government. It does not seem as though there is an 'East Timor' solution to the problems of Sabah and Sarawak; indeed, there is no international interest in or support for such an outcome. If decentralisation is the remedy to the issues raised in this chapter, rather than complete independence, then the present Federation must make *some* sense (political, geostrategic, economic?), even in the eyes of its fiercest critics. Even if the Federation of Malaya with Sabah and Sarawak was just a way of dealing with what Charles de Gaulle once called 'the dust of empire', it is apparently a Federation that is even now worth having, albeit perhaps on different terms from those of 1963, or perhaps on 1963 terms if actually adhered to in practice.

In Malaysia, one does not hear federalism per se criticised as a bad method of territorial organisation. What one does hear is that federalism or the spirit of federalism has not truly been practised or experienced in Malaysia.

Perhaps dissatisfaction or even depression is an occupational hazard for federalists. Federalism is always a least-worst solution to territorial organisation. It seems to leave all parties feeling they have less than they should have had. But . . . do they not also have more than they could have had? This counterfactual scenario is worth considering. For Tibetans, it should be clear that federal solutions carry many intractable problems. The issue is whether there is a solution that offers more hope than the present impasse.

Concluding observations

One country, *three* systems: The Tibetan quest for genuine autonomy between European experiences and Asian perspectives

Roberto Toniatti

1. Introductory observations

There is a Tibetan question. It is a domestic question – both for the People's Republic of China (PRC) and for Tibetan identity[1] – as well as a domestic question of international concern, because of humankind's interest in the preservation of the uniqueness of Tibetan culture, as it is also the case with other endangered cultures. The ground for asserting a legitimate international concern in the Tibetan question is thus rooted in a humanist attitude of respect for the essence of the human condition and for its collective capacity to produce history and culture, as it appears to be the case with Tibet – by virtue of its spiritual dimension as well of its (more than simply) physical attachment to the land of traditional settlement. Such ground, therefore, is not connected with any a priori anti-Chinese attitude, or with an a-critical partisan political support for Tibet, or in an exclusive interest for the dignity of this people alone.

That there is a Tibetan question is in fact acknowledged, in particular, by the willingness of the PRC authorities to entertain direct or indirect forms of official dialogue with representatives of Tibet (other than officials of the Tibet National Autonomous Region: Tibet NAR),[2] as historically indicated by and since the 1951

1 In this chapter, reference to Tibet, unless otherwise specified, is not meant to include the present Tibet National Autonomous Region (Tibet NAR).

2 And yet, even within the framework of Tibet NAR, the Chinese authorities have been producing a good number of White Papers concerning various aspects of life and development and stressing and even exhibiting the progressive achievements in the region: Tibet's Path of Development Is Driven by an Irresistible Historical Tide (2015), Successful Practice of Regional Ethnic Autonomy in Tibet (2015), Development And Progress in Tibet (2013), Sixty Years Since Peaceful Liberation of Tibet (2011), Fifty Years of Democratic Reform in Tibet (2009), Protection and Development of Tibetan Culture (2008), Regional Ethnic Autonomy in Tibet (2004), Ecological Improvement and Environmental Protection in Tibet (2003), Tibet's March Toward Modernisation (2001), The Development of Tibetan Culture (2000), New Progress in Human Rights in the Tibet Autonomous Region (1998), Tibet – Its Ownership and Human Rights Situation (1992), all to be found in

17-Point Agreement and, more recently, by the rounds of talks between 2000 and 2010.[3] And that international concern for the preservation of Tibetans' own identity and culture through autonomy and self-government may be thought of as thoroughly compatible with a legal obligation to respect PRC's sovereignty is confirmed worldwide by similar arrangements to be found in sources of constitutional and international law.[4]

The legitimate international concern for the Tibetan question, therefore, is not now to raise the whole body of controversial issues related to the principle of sovereign self-determination of peoples as a political precondition for the valuable preservation of Tibetan culture and identity.

The perspectives disclosed by the Memorandum on Genuine Autonomy for the Tibetan People (hereinafter, 'the Memorandum'), inspired by a balanced policy approach indicated as the 'Middle Way', appear to suggest a distinctively different setting, one of effective recognition of Tibetans' status as a cultural minority and of related powers of regional self-government in their ancestral territory: in other words, the Memorandum – supported by reference to Asian as well as to European experiences and not yet properly and analytically addressed by the Chinese authorities within their own constitutional scenario – provides for a new institutional solution whereby the right to self-determination is expressed in the framework of Chinese domestic constitutional law instead of one of international law.

The present commitment to achieving a Tibetan 'genuine' autonomy within Chinese sovereignty thus fully replaces the former ideal of reaching a Tibetan sovereign independent statehood;[5] and it is to be acknowledged as being functional

Information Office of the State Council of the PRC (available at: http://english.gov.cn/archive/ [Accessed: 14 February 2017]). This circumstance – especially when compared to only three (and recent) White Papers on Xinjiang (2015), Historical Witness to Ethnic Equality, Unity and Development in Xinjiang (2015), Development and Progress in Xinjiang, (2009) – makes of such reports a sort of indirect answer to specific concerns raised by the Tibetan Government in Exile.

3 For an overview of the Sino-Tibetan Renewed Contacts (2002–10) elaborated by the Central Tibetan Administration, see http://tibet.net/important-issues/sino-tibetan-dialogue/an-overview-of-sino-tibetan-dialogue/sino-tibetan-dialogue-renewed-contacts-2002/ [Accessed: 14 February 2017].

4 A recent relevant example of the latter is offered by the 2007 UN Declaration on the Rights of Indigenous Peoples (supported and eventually voted for by the PRC) whose Art. 46 provides for a guarantee of the consistency of self-government by those populations with not only the territorial integrity, but also with the political unity of sovereign States. Art. 46 clearly states that: '1. Nothing in this Declaration may be interpreted as implying for any State, people, group or person any right to engage in any activity or to perform any act contrary to the Charter of the United Nations or construed as authorizing or encouraging any action which would dismember or impair, totally or in part, the territorial integrity or political unity of sovereign and independent States.'

5 The solution is, in fact, presented as a commitment by Tibetans, as stated in the Introduction of the Memorandum: 'The essence of the Middle Way Approach is to secure genuine autonomy for the Tibetan people within the scope of the Constitution of the PRC. This is of mutual benefit and based on the long-term interest of both the Tibetan and Chinese peoples. We remain *firmly committed* not to seek separation or independence. We are seeking a solution to the Tibetan problem through

to overcoming the inherent limits of the present solution – the Tibet NAR – (that the Memorandum claims to be non-genuine), while attempting at the same time to be consistent with the view of a 'harmonious society' celebrated so much by the official rhetoric of PRC's leadership.

The view of a harmonious society is critically tested mainly with regard to the 'one country two systems' constitutional philosophy, originally thought of as applicable to Taiwan and already applied in Hong Kong and Macao. The Memorandum may be read as an attempt to further develop that specific approach, in the assumption that it may accommodate also the specific needs of Tibet. Thus, it elaborates a challenging vision inspired by a 'one country *three* systems' constitutional philosophy, whereby the relationship of compatibility – between the one country, on the one side and, on the other, each one of the polities that, although parts of the PRC's sovereignty, constitute a different system – is expanded beyond the economic capitalist diversity of the political systems of Taiwan, Hong Kong and Macao as to include a different cultural world view and lifestyle reflective of the Tibetan soul.

The adoption of a 'one country *three* systems' approach is not suggested by or contained in the Memorandum and yet it appears to be the only reasonable constructive alternative to the inherent – or, at least, alleged – inappropriateness of the Tibet National Autonomous Region model currently applied, as well as of the Special Administrative Region according to the Hong Kong and Macao experiences.

The 'one country three systems' perspective is a formula suggested by this chapter as an innovative conceptual framework: it is the outcome of an analysis of the present setting of socialist constitutionalism with Chinese characteristics and of an assessment, on the one hand, of the inadequacies of other current solutions for the Tibetan world view, but also, on the other hand, of the potential for further evolution of China's own original constitutionalism in the light of developments that have already taken place in the area of adoption of a (socialist) market economy.

The formula has a weakness, but also an element of strength: in the first place, it appears to be strong because of its consistency with the wording (although certainly not with the original intent of the historical constitution-maker) of the 1982 PRC Constitution, the specific provision of which is written in such a loose way as to acknowledge a limitless discretionary power of its implementing enactments;[6] in other words, the Constitution not only does not rule out the

genuine autonomy, which is compatible with the principles on autonomy in the Constitution of the People's Republic of China (PRC)' (emphasis added).

6 Art. 31: 'The State may establish special administrative regions *when necessary*. The systems to be instituted in special administrative regions shall be prescribed by law enacted by the National People's Congress *in the light of specific conditions*' (emphasis added). The provision, read with a Western background, contains a very broad, general and generic attribution of power with regard to the 'when necessary' and the 'in the light of specific conditions' clauses. It would have one element of

solution, but could even provide a favourable ground for it. The Hong Kong and Macao Basic Laws, adopted by the National People's Congress (NPC), have introduced a suspension of relevant parts of the PRC Constitution in those territories – as we shall see later – and such circumstance is self-eloquent in highlighting the systemic wide margins of political appreciation available.

Nevertheless, the weak element of the 'one country *three* systems' approach is that the Constitution does not bind in any affirmative way the political process that might lead to the decision of establishment of a 'Third (Cultural-Spiritual) System' – along with the 'Second (Economic-Capitalist) System' – within the 'one country'; in other words, there is no constitutional justiciable collective right of self-determination for the Tibetan people under Article 31 and until the PRC's authorities see the advantages (if any) of such solution – as they have seen and see the advantages of incorporating, effectively or potentially (in the case of Taiwan) the capitalist economies – it is doubtful that any pressure – whether Tibetan, international or foreign – may be able to achieve the purpose.

The legitimacy of the unlimited political discretion enjoyed by the PRC's leadership – the weak and at the same time the strong element of a 'one country *three* systems' approach – is therefore likely to be *the* crucial factor in any deliberative process. And yet, the current emphasis on the rule of law and on the primacy of the Constitution in the framework of governance of the PRC encourages having a constitutional ground for the exercise of political discretion. In other words, what matters is the political decision, but a political decision appearing to be constitutional is preferable.

Considering that the Memorandum relies very much on the apparent constitutional consistency of its proposal, it is necessary, at this stage, to turn the attention to a short critical assessment of constitutionalism and constitutional law in the PRC in order to elaborate a closer and realistic evaluation of the perspectives of its implementation as the result of an agreement by the authorities of the PRC.

It is convenient to anticipate, in short, the result of such an assessment, confirming – and it could not be otherwise – the previous remarks: relying on the present constitutional ground for any implementation of the Memorandum is legally unrealistic and unfounded, as the issue remains entirely within the political process, in conformity with the specific character of the Chinese Constitution. Any positive political response in the (near or far) future, nevertheless, would be likely to be framed within the constitutional setting, as such dynamics seems presently to be a political priority of Chinese authorities, in view of achieving a somehow more effective rule of law foundation of the regime's legitimacy.

guarantee in the requirement of a law, as long as such a law should be a normative enactment produced by a representative parliament resulting from a free and competitive election among a plurality of political parties enjoying equal freedom of communication, the law being likely to be judicially reviewed by an independent judiciary. It's obvious that in the Chinese situation, none of the foregoing elements exists and the provision may be interpreted only as the source of unlimited discretionary decision-making power.

The next paragraph will analyse the nature of constitutional law in the PRC and will emphasise its constant and consistent conformity with the socialist legal tradition founded on Marxism-Leninism, the official qualification referring to 'Chinese characteristics' as an effort of asserting the national 'ownership' of the legal system.[7] In fact, the formula 'socialist system of laws with Chinese characteristics' doesn't serve any purpose other than allowing the government to root in the rule of law whatever political priority they may have irrespective of its ideological 'orthodoxy' – including the legitimacy of the (socialist) market economy – as long as it reflects the immediate interests of the country in its movement toward modernisation.

2. Chinese constitutionalism and its distinctiveness

More and more, historical developments and the world practice of constitutionalism – resulting from the bare circumstance of most countries showing to have a set of rules, which more often than not bear some fundamental substantive relevance for the polity concerned and are formally recognised as such – require to add to the word and concept of constitutionalism a further qualification, be it historical (for example, nineteenth-century constitutionalism as distinct from twentieth-century one), ideological (for example, liberal constitutionalism as distinct from a socialist one), geopolitical (for example, Western constitutionalism as distinct from an illiberal one), geographical (for example, Asian constitutionalism as distinct from a Latin American one), religious (for example, secular constitutionalism as distinct from an Islamic one) or otherwise. The alternative of not employing any such additional qualifications would entail either not seeing the differences among constitutions or reserving the word/concept to Western constitutionalism and denying that there is any constitutionalism other than the Western one (although even in this more limited circuit many distinctions ought to be drawn).

Reference to such further qualifications is the outcome of the comparative analysis of a plurality of constitutional documents (and, possibly but not necessarily, of their relative implementation) sharing some identical features that distinguish them from other groupings of constitutional documents having their own distinct commonalities. And yet, each national constitution obviously also has some distinguishing features of its own that may be either an adaptation of those of the pertinent classification or a solution with a thoroughly original character. What is said about the Constitution can of course be said with regard to the main features

7 The adoption of the general Principles of Civil Law in 1986 has been an important milestone in the process of shaping, although not without selectively choosing foreign references, the legal system of the PRC: see ZHENG, H. R. (1986), 'China's New Civil Law'. *American Journal of Comparative Law*. 34(4). 669.

of the form of government (State) that 'must be' in conformity with the normative effects expected from that specific constitution.

Furthermore, each country presents constitutional features that allow its inclusion in one or another of the comparative synchronic classifications and nevertheless have a constitutional history of its own, not only for a number of constitutional documents, but also for the experience of a plurality of constitutional regimes, being therefore entitled to registration in distinct comparative classifications in different historical periods. So, for instance, Chinese constitutionalism refers to the various constitutions that have been enacted in the country[8] and such unitary historical focus serves the purpose of contributing to the identification of the different constitutional regimes that have been established there since the beginning of the twentieth century.[9] At the same time, the assumption is that each type of constitution that China has had in the past and at present does offer features that are directly and invariably reflective of Chinese culture.[10]

The potential of this method for the interpretation and comparative classification of any constitution is to be considered in approaching the analysis of the present 1982 Constitution – as amended in 1988, 1993, 1999 and 2004 – making it clear

8 A number of twelve constitutions is reported as having been adopted in China, 'eight of which were enacted between 1908 and 1954', in KILLION, M. U. (2005), 'China's Amended Constitution: Quest for Liberty and Independent Judicial Review'. *Washington University Global Studies Law Review*. 4(1). 43.

9 An interesting historical reconstruction of the early steps of China on the track of introducing modern constitutionalism (leaving aside that '*li* was not only one type of social norm but the ultimate source from which imperial laws and edicts derived. It was, virtually, a "constitution" for pre-modern China', at 9), since the Qing dynasty's promulgation of an Outline of the Imperial Constitution in 1908 and the imperial concession of a Doctrine of Nineteen Articles in 1911 that 'envisioned a constitutional monarchy borrowed from the British model' (at 13), through the 1923 one that 'was the closest that China has ever achieved to a federal constitution' (at 24), to the 1947 Nationalist Constitution that is still in force in Taiwan today, can be found in ZHANG, Q. (2012), *The Constitution of China. A Contextual Analysis*. Oxford and Portland: Hart. On the pre-modern constitutional setting in China and its strong current influence, see HAHM, Ch. (2009), 'Ritual and Constitutionalism: Disputing the Ruler's Legitimacy in a Confucian Polity'. *American Journal of Comparative Law*. 57(1). 135.

10 It has been written that 'Confucianism, tradition, and Asian values in general constitute China's "history of the present". It is through China's distinctive ontological base in tradition that it will potentially make progress in the area of political and economic development, and in the area of constitutionalism, rule of law, and judicial review. Confucianism and Asian values serve as harbingers of foundational or societal values, encompassing the forces, if not the values, of China's political, socio-economic, and legal institutions. These foundational values will likewise translate into a genuine indigenous ethos for Chinese constitutionalism', in KILLION (2005), above note 8, p. 67. From a more limited point of view of political culture, but within the axiological scenario indicated above, it is interesting to recall, for instance, how also the Nationalists' approach was founded on the 'logic of tutelage' and that they 'initiated China's first experiment with "rule of the party" (*dangzhi*), as opposed to both the modern rule of law and the ancient rule of virtue', ZHANG (2012), above note 9, p. 27. As a matter of fact, the inclusion of Taiwan in the number of Asian democracies dates back only to the 1980s.

that: (i) modern Chinese constitutionalism is a long period in history, covering more than the present socialist period and amendments to the Constitution between 1982 and 2004; (ii) another constitutional document – the 1947 Constitution now in force in Taiwan (although virtually the constitutional source for the whole of China) – is part of it; (iii) the most significant historical segment of Chinese constitutionalism is to be attributed to the category of 'socialist constitutionalism' as originally elaborated within the philosophical framework of Marxism-Leninism in the Soviet Union and other socialist countries; (iv) the PRC has adopted four socialist constitutions (1954, 1975, 1978 and 1982, amended in 2004);[11] and (v) the category of socialist constitutionalism includes now only a few other countries (Cuba, North Korea and Vietnam) that are not easily comparable with China for complexity (and size).

In other words, in reading the Chinese 1982 to 2004 Constitution, we must be aware of those features that are typical of the socialist model and are to be interpreted accordingly, on the one hand, and, on the other, of those characters that are reflective either of Chinese cultural identity more in general and of Chinese socialist option more in particular, both requiring a deeper understanding of the country that goes well beyond the legal system. Therefore, it would be wrong to try to read the constitutional provisions and interpret them through the lens of the Western lawyer, leaving aside fundamental structural principles of the socialist legal tradition that are radically distinct, such as the unity of power (as opposed to separation of powers), democratic centralism and one-party rule (inherently incompatible with any pluralism of political parties and diversity of social and territorial interests), the principle of socialist legality (not amenable to any system of checks and balances and entailing the non-justiciability of the Constitution) and the prevalence of unchecked political discretion (as a consequence of the absence of a political opposition and resulting in the judiciary's formalised lack of independence).[12] Even harder might be, for the Western lawyer, trying to further detect the Chinese characteristics of the legal system.

Nevertheless, it's also important to stress that current Chinese constitutionalism is all but static. Quite to the contrary, although the purpose of 'modernisation' has

11 The Common Program of the Chinese People's Political Consultative Conference adopted in 1949 before the convening of the First National People's Congress may be regarded as an early quasi-constitutional source, although provisional and formally atypical and yet substantively effective.

12 It has been written – in a first stage of modernisation – that 'ideology remains a potential and self-contradictory inspiration, both for further and far-reaching reform and for the continued maintenance of Communist authoritarianism', in LUBMAN, S. (1999–2000), 'Bird in a Cage: Chinese Law Reform after Twenty Years'. *Northwestern Journal of International Law & Business*. 20(3). 399; and yet, although 'the genesis of the legal system lies, without much doubt, in the Soviet model', 'however, after some 80 years of trial and error, legal developments in the present China depend more on breaking off the shackles of ideological domination than on being guided by it. Indeed, the major breakthrough in legal developments in post-Mao China can largely be attributed to the abandonment of ideology', in CHEN, J. (2008), *Chinese Law: Context and Transformation*. London and Boston: Brill-Nijhoff. p. 75.

been a permanent source of institutional dynamism, there is a good deal of tension between two ways of interpreting the term:[13] modernisation as Westernisation *tout court*, or modernisation through pragmatic cherry-picking – originally, from the Soviet model and, more recently, from Western law – only what appears to be really unavoidable, strictly instrumental to solving present difficulties and standstills and in particular to increasing the rhythm and size of economic development and indulging in 'GDP worship'. In the public sphere, such an attitude appears to suggest investing more in administrative law than relying on the beneficial effects of constitutional freedoms and pluralism.

Within this general framework – which underlies the overall importance of the interface between the substance of any research and the required appropriateness of its own methodology – it is easier to explain the choice of those formal and substantive features of the PRC Constitution that affect the conformity of the Memorandum.

In fact, reference to Asian and European experiences of minorities' autonomy is not as easily done as it is easily said, though, not only because such experiences do not always rule out all political claims for independent statehood – thus appearing to confirm one of the main criticisms to the Memorandum by Chinese authorities – but also and especially when such comparative reference concerns a proper appreciation and interpretation of the very meaning of constitutional law

13 It's interesting to compare the two attitudes as largely reflected in a divided scholarship. On the one hand, Chinese constitutionalism, insofar as it hasn't developed into sharing what is regarded to be the essence of constitutionalism – 'a system of government committed to the enforcement of rules spelled out in the constitution', referring mainly to judicial review of constitutionality, at 951 – has been defined as resulting from a 'façade constitution', or a 'dormant' or 'unenforced constitution'; nevertheless, a series of episodes (including the first and only case in which the constitution has been cited by the Supreme People's Court (SPC) as the independent ground for the decision, the *Qi Yuling v. Chen Xiaoqi* case (2001), the ruling having later been withdrawn by the same SPC) suggest that 'the Constitution, particularly its subsequent amendments, plays a vitally important role in China today', 960 as argued by ZHANG, Q. (2010), 'A Constitution without Constitutionalism? The Paths of Constitutional Developments in China'. ICON. 8. On the other, after stating that 'notably, at this time, judicial constitutionalism is even becoming attractive in socialist East Asian nations such as China and Vietnam', in the case of China, the "judicialization of the constitution" (*xianfa sifahua*) has been a remarkable movement in which judges, activist lawyers, and Chinese citizens have attempted to use the courts as a mechanism for constitutional litigation'; this circumstance makes the author argue against 'the trend towards judicial constitutionalism among the Chinese and Vietnamese constitutionalists. It holds that judicial review is not the sine qua non of a true constitutionalist State. Neither is judicial review the best alternative for constitutional enforcement. It submits that a mechanism of constitutional enforcement should be developed under the grounds familiar with the local people. For the cases of China and Vietnam, Confucianism should be taken into account for this purpose. This article proposes the constitutional academy as a Confucian institution of constitutional enforcement. It is a mixed model of constitutional enforcement in which some Confucian constitutionalist ideas and institutions are integrated with some ideas and institutions of the Marshallian and Kelsenian models of constitutional review', BUI, N. S. (2014), 'Beyond Judicial Review: The Proposal of the Constitutional Academy'. *Chinese Journal of Comparative Law*. 2(1). p. 43.

in the distinct regional contexts: the status of the Constitution in the system of sources of law – even when proclaimed to be the fundamental rule of the country – is not necessarily the same when construed in Europe or in Asia and in the PRC especially, and the interpretation of its normative force and reach also may be quite diversified.

2.1 The evolving concept of the Constitution in the PRC

It should be acknowledged that there has been a crescendo in the explicit recognition of the Constitution as the foundation of the socialist legal system in the PRC.

In the 1954 and 1978 constitutional texts, respecting and observing the Constitution did not mean much more than being one of the duties of the personnel of the State's institutions and one component of their ideological training for performing their respective public functions.[14] The 1975 Constitution mentions the Constitution in the framework of the fundamental rights and duties of citizens, although rather as the duty to abide by it than as a source of their rights.[15]

Eventually, in 1982 in the Preamble[16] as well as in the text (Article 5),[17] the Constitution is attributed a reinforced and even emphatic formal acknowledgement

14 See Art. 18 of the 1954 Constitution ('All personnel of organs of state must be loyal to the system of people's democracy, *observe the Constitution and the law* and strive to serve the people') and Art. 16 of the 1978 Constitution ('The personnel of organs of state must earnestly study Marxism-Leninism-Mao Tsetung Thought, wholeheartedly serve the people, endeavour to perfect their professional competence, take an active part in collective productive labour, accept supervision by the masses, *be models in observing the Constitution and the law*, correctly implement the policies of the state, seek the truth from facts, and must not have recourse to deception or exploit their position and power to seek personal gain' (emphasis added in both extracts)).

15 See Art. 26 of the 1975 Constitution: 'The fundamental rights and duties of citizens are to support the leadership of the Communist Party of China, support the socialist system and *abide by the Constitution and the laws* of the People's Republic of China' (emphasis added).

16 'This Constitution, in legal form, affirms the achievements of the struggles of the Chinese people of all nationalities and defines the basic system and basic tasks of the State; it is the fundamental law of the State and has supreme legal authority. The people of all nationalities, all State organs, the armed forces, all political parties and public organizations and all enterprises and institutions in the country must take the Constitution as the basic standard of conduct, and they have the duty to uphold the dignity of the Constitution and ensure its implementation.'

17 The Constitution contains provisions that are more or less thoroughly in line with mainstream (Western) constitutionalism in the area of sources of law, such as Art. 5, paras 3–5: 'No laws or administrative or local regulations may contravene the Constitution'; 'All State organs, the armed forces, all political parties and public organizations and all enterprises and institutions must abide by the Constitution and other laws. All acts in violation of the Constitution or other laws must be investigated' (although including the armed forces and enterprises as directly bound by the Constitution is formally unusual in a comparative perspective; furthermore, the inconsistency between higher and lower sources of law ought to deserve something more than mere 'investigation'); 'No organization or individual is privileged to be beyond the Constitution or other laws'.

as *the* fundamental law, with regard to the context of the (socialist) rule of law and to its hierarchical supremacy over other legal sources, to its binding effects over the State's institutions, and to its providing the normative framework for rights and duties of citizens.[18] Nevertheless, the Constitution itself makes it clear that the normative force and meaning of the constitutional source is to be understood within the framework of the legal theory of socialism.[19] In fact, Article 5 clearly states that 'the People's Republic of China governs the country according to law and makes it a socialist country under rule of law' and that 'the State upholds the uniformity and dignity of the socialist legal system'.[20]

The text of the 1982 Constitution of the People's Republic of China, as amended, offers an interesting blend of statements concerning pluralism and plurality, as well as of rules establishing unity and uniformity. Statements are descriptive and rules, of course, are (expected to be) prescriptive and yet, in a context of socialist legality, it is not always clear what is a statement describing the current advancement of the country on the way of building a stateless socialist society and what is properly a binding legal rule – considering also the lack of judicial enforcement – so that eventually the bias in the combination of the two is quite self-evident. Furthermore, socialism with Chinese characteristics – as constitutional and legislative sources repeatedly insist on qualifying the PRC's socialist way – does make constitutional interpretation even more complex for a lawyer not specifically trained in Chinese law.

An important recent development affecting the role of the Constitution concerns not the institutions and political officials, but citizens at large: the need is felt to reinforce the awareness of the central relevance of the Constitution and to foster a widespread constitutional culture.[21]

18 See Art. 33, para. 4: 'Every citizen is entitled to the rights and at the same time must perform the duties prescribed by the Constitution and other laws.'

19 It shouldn't be forgotten that 'strictly interpreted, the Communist conception of a constitution is inseparable from the Marxist doctrine of class struggle. A constitution is not just the fundamental law of a regime, but is also necessarily a reflection of the power relationships between classes. It is, therefore, an instrument of struggle and a justification for dictatorship over the class enemies as well. From this perspective, the relationship between Party and state (government) represents a legal dilemma which defies any neat, logical solution' in WENG, B. (1982), 'Some Key Aspects of the 1982 Draft Constitution of the People's Republic of China'. *China Quarterly*. 91. p. 492.

20 The Preamble is just as explicit: 'the Chinese people of all nationalities will continue to adhere to the people's democratic dictatorship and the socialist road, persevere in reform and opening to the outside world, steadily improve socialist institutions, develop the socialist market economy, develop socialist democracy, improve the socialist legal system and work hard and self-reliantly to modernize the country's industry, agriculture, national defence and science and technology step by step and promote the coordinated development of the material, political and spiritual civilizations, to turn China into a socialist country that is prosperous, powerful, democratic and culturally advanced'.

21 See LAIFAN, L. (2015), 'Constitutional Culture to be Cultivated in China'. *China Law*. 112. p. 133, commenting favourably on the decision to set up the 'National Constitution Day' (4 December). An important case, often referred to, of citizens' mobilisation in support of the Constitution is examined in HAND, K.J. (2009), 'Citizens Engage the Constitution: The Sun Zhigang Incident

2.2 China as a socialist State and legal system

According to Article 1 of the 1982 Constitution, 'the People's Republic of China is a socialist State' and, according to Article 2, 'the socialist system is the basic system of the People's Republic of China'.

Both statements may be read as to provide a twofold meaning: a first interpretation – more in line with a notion of a normative constitution, indicates that the PRC *must* be a socialist State,[22] while, alternatively, it may be read more as a descriptive indication, certifying that the PRC is a socialist State and it also specifies – again normatively and descriptively at the same time – what being a socialist State means. It entails operating 'under the people's democratic dictatorship led by the working class and based on the alliance of workers and peasants' (Article 1).[23]

The second descriptive reading is closer to socialist legal theory and is to be interpreted as stating a reality, the achievement of a stage in a progressive movement ultimately establishing Communism:[24] in fact, in conformity with constitutional theory and practice as experienced in the former Soviet Union,[25]

and Constitutional Review: Proposals in the People's Republic of China'. In BALME, S. and DOWDLE, M.W. (eds), *Building Constitutionalism in China*. New York: Palgrave Macmillan. p. 221.

22 The 1982 Constitution contains a provision introducing a rule of protection of the socialist regime (Art. 2: 'Disruption of the socialist system by any organization or individual is prohibited') structured with the rationale of a militant and self-defending political regime. In this context, Art. 36, al. 3 is also worthy of being mentioned ('The State protects normal religious activities. No one may make use of religion to engage in activities that disrupt public order, impair the health of citizens or interfere with the educational system of the State').

23 Interesting elaborations on the meaning of the innovative formula 'people's democratic dictatorship' founded on a subtle compromise can be found in WENG (1982), above note 19, p. 494.

24 Although in the 1982 text (as in Art. 1 of the 1954 Constitution: 'The People's Republic of China is a people's democratic state led by the working class and based on the alliance of workers and peasants'), the Communist Party is not expressly mentioned (in both the constitutional texts, repeated references to the Party are in the Preamble), there is a clear ideological continuity with the 1978 constitutional text (Art. 1: 'The People's Republic of China is a socialist state of the dictatorship of the proletariat led by the working class and based on the alliance of workers and peasants'; Art. 2: 'The Communist Party of China is the core of leadership of the whole Chinese people. The working class exercises leadership over the state through its vanguard, the Communist Party of China. The guiding ideology of the People's Republic of China is Marxism-Leninism-Mao Tsetung Thought'); and with the 1975 text (Art. 1: 'The People's Republic of China is a socialist state of the dictatorship of the proletariat led by the working class and based on the alliance of workers and peasants'; and Art. 2 'The Communist Party of China is the core of leadership of the whole Chinese people. The working class exercises leadership over the state through its vanguard, the Communist Party of China. Marxism-Leninism-Mao Tsetung Thought is the theoretical basis guiding the thinking of our nation').

25 Nevertheless, explicit reference to the Soviet Union is found only in the 1954 Preamble: 'Our country has already built an indestructible friendship with the great Union of Soviet Socialist Republics and the People's Democracies; and the friendship between our people and other peace-loving peoples all over the world is growing day by day. These friendships will continue to be developed and consolidated.'

building socialism is framed as the outcome of the leadership of the Communist Party[26] and as a gradual and progressive accomplishment,[27] each subsequent constitutional document having the task of registering how much of the process has been achieved, as stated also in the 1982 Preamble:[28]

> After the founding of the People's Republic, China gradually achieved its transition from a New-Democratic to a socialist society. The socialist

26 See the 1954 Preamble: 'In the year 1949, after more than a century of heroic struggle, the Chinese people, led by the Communist Party of China, finally won their great victory in the people's revolution against imperialism, feudalism and bureaucrat-capitalism, and thereby brought to an end the history of the oppression and enslavement they had undergone for so long and founded the People's Republic of China – a people's democratic dictatorship. The system of people's democracy – the system of new democracy – of the People's Republic of China guarantees that our country can in a peaceful way eliminate exploitation and poverty and build a prosperous and happy socialist society [. . .] In the course of the great struggle to establish the People's Republic of China, the people of our country forged a broad people's democratic united front led by the Communist Party of China and composed of all democratic classes, democratic parties and groups, and people's organizations.' The role of the Communist Party has been further codified in the text of the 1975 Constitution, as indicated above.

27 As clearly stated in the 1954 Preamble: 'From the founding of the People's Republic of China to the attainment of a socialist society is a period of transition. The general tasks of the state during the transition period are, step by step, to bring about the socialist industrialization of the country and, step by step, to accomplish the socialist transformation of agriculture, handicrafts and capitalist industry and commerce [. . .] This Constitution consolidates the gains of the Chinese people's revolution and the new victories won in the political and economic fields since the founding of the People's Republic of China; and, moreover, it reflects the basic needs of the state in the period of transition, as well as the common desire of the broad masses of the people to build a socialist society.'

28 The original 1982 text of the Preamble stated: 'China will be in the primary stage of socialism for a long time to come. The basic task of the nation is to concentrate its effort on socialist modernization along the road of Chinese-style socialism. Under the leadership of the Communist Party of China and the guidance of Marxism-Leninism, Mao Zedong Thought, Deng Xiaoping Theory and the important thought of Three Represents [as taught by former President Jiang Zemin], the Chinese people of all nationalities will continue to adhere to the people's democratic dictatorship and the socialist road, persevere in reform and opening to the outside world, steadily improve socialist institutions, develop the socialist market economy, develop socialist democracy, improve the socialist legal system and work hard and self-reliantly to modernize the country's industry, agriculture, national defence and science and technology step by step and promote the coordinated development of the material, political and spiritual civilizations, to turn China into a socialist country that is prosperous, powerful, democratic and culturally advanced.' The 2004 amendment replaced that part of the Preamble with a new text: 'China is at the primary stage of socialism. The basic task of the nation is, according to the theory of building socialism with Chinese characteristics, to concentrate its effort on socialist modernization. Under the leadership of the Communist Party of China and the guidance of Marxism-Leninism and Mao Zedong Thought, the Chinese people of all nationalities will continue to adhere to the people's democratic dictatorship and follow the socialist road, persevere in reform and opening to the outside, steadily improve socialist institutions, develop socialist democracy, improve the socialist legal system and work hard and self-reliantly to modernize industry, agriculture, national defense and science and technology step by step to turn China into a socialist country with prosperity and power, democracy and culture.'

> transformation of the private ownership of the means of production has been completed, the system of exploitation of man by man abolished and the socialist system established. The people's democratic dictatorship led by the working class and based on the alliance of workers and peasants, which is in essence the dictatorship of the proletariat, has been consolidated and developed.

In other words, the advent of socialism is not an event or a punctual starting point, but rather an ongoing process based on steady leadership and constant support by the people: inevitably, what the Constitution reflects at one stage along the way is not necessarily what the Constitution will reflect at a later stage and what and how this later stage will be like is part of policies to be discretionally developed rather than of constitutional obligations to be fulfilled. The overall governmental architecture is therefore instrumental to such progressive achievements and the unitary political control is necessary. The consequences on the institutional structure of the state in the 1982 Constitution is essentially coherent with the ideological foundation of socialist constitutionalism in the Soviet Union and in China since the 1954 Constitution: the acknowledgement of the principle of democratic centralism and that 'all administrative, judicial and procuratorial organs of the State are created by the people's congresses to which they are responsible and by which they are supervised' (Article 3).[29]

The structure of public power is thus inherently consistent with the ideological foundation of the PRC since its very establishment, as essentially confirmed by the sequence of constitutions, all reflecting the culture and practice of Marxism-Leninism and as still unaffected by the 2004 radical economic reforms that have introduced the socialist market economy.

2.3 China as a socialist State with Chinese characteristics

The above short survey of constitutional texts indicates to what extent the theoretical foundations of Chinese socialist constitutionalism appear to rest entirely on European culture, both with regard to the philosophy and the typical features of legal theory of Marxism-Leninism and to the normative setting and political practice in the Soviet Union and, although not without differences, in Central and Eastern European countries.

The further and repeatedly emphasised official qualification of the Chinese reception of the European socialist model with reference to the notion of *Chinese*

29 With regard to the judiciary, although Art. 126 establishes that 'people's courts exercise judicial power independently, in accordance with the provisions of law, and not subject to interference by any administrative organ, public organization or individual', Art. 128 states that 'the Supreme People's Court is responsible to the National People's Congress and its Standing Committee. Local people's courts at various levels are responsible to the organs of state power which created them'.

characteristics clearly appears to be an attempt to connect the importation of the leading revolutionary movement with domestic sources – which could not be even remotely connected to traditional Confucian thought, although the functional authoritarian similarities were fairly evident – and consequently to confer some national features to socialism in the PRC as distinct from other national socialisms.

Such national qualification is achieved, in the first place, through recalling the struggle of the Chinese people from feudalism and capitalism and with even more evident commitment through the integration of Marxism-Leninism by the contribution, both theoretical and of historical statesmanship, of the great national leaders of the PRC.

It is significant that it is up to the 1975 Constitution – that is, the normative document that was meant to reflect the impact of the Cultural Revolution[30] – to introduce such reference to the thought of Chairman Mao, together with Marxism and Leninism, into the Preamble as well as into the text.[31] The same approach, updated to the succeeding leaders, has been adopted by the 1978[32] and 1982[33] Constitutions.

Another relevant component of the Chinese characters of socialism may be seen in the historical circumstance of socialism that affirmed and established itself not in an industrially developed capitalistic social context, as sustained by Marx, but in a sort of semi-feudal and mainly rural system.

But what is really distinguishing Chinese socialism and adding Chinese characteristics is, since the Constitution of 1982, the establishment of a socialist

30 It has been written that 'the 1975 Constitution was merely a political declaration, at most an outline for a politicised constitution; a constitution was in any case meaningless in an era when rights and laws were trampled on with disdain as "bourgeois influences"', in ZHANG (2012), above note 9, p. 46.

31 See, respectively, 'We must adhere to the basic line and policies of the Communist Party of China for the entire historical period of socialism and persist in continued revolution under the dictatorship of the proletariat, so that our great motherland will always advance along the road indicated by Marxism-Leninism-Mao Tsetung Thought'; 'Marxism-Leninism-Mao Tsetung Thought is the theoretical basis guiding the thinking of our nation' (Art. 2); and 'State organizations and state personnel must earnestly study Marxism-Leninism-Maoism Tsetung Thought, firmly put proletarian politics in command, combat bureaucracy, maintain close ties with the masses and wholeheartedly serve the people' (Art. 11).

32 Reference in the 1978 Preamble is to 'our great leader and teacher Chairman Mao Tsetung', to Chairman Mao's 'proletarian revolutionary line in the political, economic, cultural and military fields and in foreign affairs' and to 'the Great Proletarian Cultural Revolution' of Marxism-Leninism-Mao Tsetung Thought. See also Art. 2: 'The guiding ideology of the People's Republic of China is Marxism-Leninism-Mao Tsetung Thought.'

33 The 1982 Preamble declares: 'the basic task of the nation is to concentrate its effort on socialist modernization along the road of Chinese-style socialism [. . .]under the leadership of the Communist Party of China and the guidance of Marxism-Leninism, Mao Zedong Thought, Deng Xiaoping Theory and the important thought of Three Represents'. It is meaningful also that the Preamble draws back in time the reference to Chinese leaders whose commitment reinforces the Chinese characteristics of the national endeavour, by recalling that 'the Revolution of 1911, led by Dr. Sun Yat-sen, abolished the feudal monarchy and gave birth to the Republic of China'.

market economy, through a process of constant and increasing revision of the Constitution by way of a sequence of amendments between 1988 and 2004.[34]

The development of the PRC Constitution as well as of its legal system as a whole through the qualification provided by the formula 'with Chinese characteristics' has therefore achieved an important twofold result: on the one hand, not only the original ideological origins of the struggle of the Chinese people for modernisation have been at least symbolically preserved and, along with the symbols, the reality of an authoritarian structure of public power consistent with the foundational values remains unaltered and perhaps results may even be strengthened; on the other hand, a process of emancipation from a foreign source of inspiration has been put in motion, providing for the establishment of a new constitutional and legal autochthonous socialist orthodoxy expressed by the Chinese characteristics.

It would be hard to try to describe analytically what exactly such Chinese characteristics are, except for an inherent connection to the national interest as interpreted and safeguarded by the political leadership: an intrinsically pragmatist approach, which has the power of engrafting contingent substantive policy options on the ground of constitutional and legal legitimacy and axiological dignity.[35]

34 The first amendment in 1988 has added a new paragraph to Art. 11: 'The State permits the private sector of the economy to exist and develop within the limits prescribed by law. The private sector of the economy is a complement to the socialist public economy. The State protects the lawful rights and interests of the private sector of the economy, and exercises guidance, supervision and control over the private sector of the economy.' In 1993, among many others, a new text of Art. 15 declares that 'the State has put into practice a socialist market economy. The State strengthens formulating economic laws, improves macro adjustment and control and forbids according to law any units or individuals from interfering with the social economic order', while an amended Art. 16 establishes that: 'State-owned enterprises have decision-making power in operation and management within the limits prescribed by law. State-owned enterprises practice democratic management through congresses of workers and staff and in other ways in accordance with the law.' In 1999, the revised text of Art. 6 proclaims that 'the basis of the socialist economic system of the People's Republic of China is socialist public ownership of the means of production, namely, ownership by the whole people and collective ownership by the working people. The system of socialist public ownership supersedes the system of exploitation of man by man; it applies the principle of "from each according to his ability, to each according to his work". During the primary stage of socialism, the State adheres to the basic economic system with the public ownership remaining dominant and diverse sectors of the economy developing side by side, and to the distribution system with the distribution according to work remaining dominant and the coexistence of a variety of modes of distribution'; finally, in 2004, among several others, an amendment to Art. 13 introduces the following provision: 'Citizens' lawful private property is inviolable', 'The State, in accordance with law, protects the rights of citizens to private property and to its inheritance' and 'The State may, in the public interest and in accordance with law, expropriate or requisition private property for its use and shall make compensation for the private property expropriated or requisitioned.'

35 See JIANWEI, Z. (2014), 'The Three Perspectives of the Rule of Law'. *China Law*. 6. p. 68.

Even an authoritative governmental source such as the 2011 White Paper on the Establishment of the Socialist System of Laws with Chinese Characteristics[36] does not go much beyond a very detailed survey of legislative enactments by the PRC, a presentation of the 'tiers of the socialist system of laws with Chinese characteristics' – starting with the Constitution and ending with local regulations – followed by a commented-upon list of legislation covering a plurality of material areas of public action.[37] Indeed, some comments are quite interesting, as the remark concerning the strong connection between the strategic decision of establishing a socialist market economy – since 1992 – and the related requirement that it 'must be regulated and guaranteed by a complete legal regime'. And yet, all explanations prove to be little more than tautological statements.

Economic modernisation then proves to be central in the configuration of the socialist system of law and of the socialist market economy, both qualified as 'with Chinese characteristics'. The economic achievements of the reforms are well known and don't need to be celebrated again here. Nothing equivalent, though, has taken place or even appears to be in the process of taking place in some future time to come in the field of a different conception of human rights and of the rights of minorities.[38] It may then be that with regard to both issues the present constitutional and legal condition is already consistent either with Chinese characteristics or with traditional socialism (of Soviet origin). From the point of view of both perspectives, the insistence of the Constitution (text and preamble)

36 Issued on 27 October 2011 and available on the website of the Information Office of the State Council of the PRC.

37 In the Foreword, one is to read that 'the socialist system of laws with Chinese characteristics is a legal foundation for socialism with Chinese characteristics to retain its nature, a legal reflection of the innovative practice of socialism with Chinese characteristics, and a legal guarantee for the prosperity of socialism with Chinese characteristics. Its establishment is an important milestone in China's development of socialist democracy and the legal system, and showcases the great achievements of reform, opening up and the socialist modernization drive. It is of great realistic and far-reaching historic significance.' Indeed, the White Paper does offer further explanations of the specific features, such as: 'the socialist system of laws with Chinese characteristics embodies the essential requirements of socialism with Chinese characteristics' (III.1); 'Socialist system of laws with Chinese characteristics meets the demand of the reform, opening up and socialist modernization of the current times' (III.2); 'The socialist system of laws with Chinese characteristics reflects the requirements of an inherently unified and structurally multilevel legal system' (III.3); 'The socialist system of laws with Chinese characteristics meets the cultural demand of carrying forward the fine traditions of Chinese legal culture and drawing on the achievements of human legal civilizations' (III.4); or 'The socialist system of laws with Chinese characteristics reflects the development demand of being dynamic and open, and of advancing with the times' (III.5). Furthermore, in the Concluding Remarks, it is stated that: 'Social practice is the foundation of laws, and laws encapsulate practical experience. Social practice is endless, and legislative work should also constantly move forward with the times. Building socialism with Chinese characteristics is a long-term historic task. Improving the socialist system of laws with Chinese characteristics is also a long-term and arduous historic task, and it must advance in tandem with the practice of socialism with Chinese characteristics.'

38 See SUN, Y. (2014), 'The Roots of China's Ethnic Conflicts'. *Current History*. 113. p. 231.

and implementing legislation with national or ethnic pluralism appears to be consistent with the descriptive reading of the Constitution rather than with a normative force: nationalities are to be protected just as they are presently protected and do not have a justiciable right to be protected more or differently; regional special ethnic and national self-government is established and does not require further guarantees. Wider protection and expansion of the quality of self-government is not a proper constitutional matter, but a policy issue in the hands of the governmental leadership, whose political discretion is constitutionally unlimited, not amenable to any political control or judicial scrutiny.

The multinational clauses of the Constitution, therefore, as dealt with in the following paragraph, are highly descriptive of their Chinese characteristics and are to be read in conformity with traditional socialist constitutional theory and practice.

2.4 China as a unitary multinational state and national regional self-administration under central political control

Both the multinational character of the social and cultural fabric of the Chinese people as well as its political unity and unitary governmental control (in spite of a pattern of socialist decentralisation and a sort of functional asymmetry, to be shortly dealt with below) have been formally and expressly acknowledged as inherent features in the structure of the PRC since the 1954 Constitution:[39] in fact, union and solidarity of the working class is the authentic bond on which the coexistence of state unity and national plurality is achieved, such aggregating bond depending on a strong common ideological vision and on a shared political commitment to radical reforms.

In this perspective, since its early approach to socialist State-building in the context of modernisation in 1949, China has had to cope with the complexities of nation-building as well.[40] The path undertaken has entailed a firm reliance on ideological uniformity, centralised political control and also a realistic

39 The Preamble declares that 'all the nationalities in our country have been united in one great family of free and equal nationalities. The unity of our country's nationalities will continue to gain in strength on the basis of the further development of the fraternal bonds and mutual aid among them, and on the basis of opposition to imperialism, opposition to public enemies within their own ranks, and opposition to both big-nation chauvinism and local nationalism. In the course of economic construction and cultural development, the State will concern itself with the needs of the different nationalities, and, in the matter of socialist transformation, pay full attention to the special characteristics in the development of each nationality'.

40 For an interesting essay on the Chinese understanding of concepts such as nationalism, nation-state, patriotism and others, in comparison with their Western equivalents and on the historical scenario of China having rather been for centuries a 'civilisation state', see BISLEY, A. and LI, X. (2014), 'Conceptualizing the Cultural and Political Facets of "Chinese Nationalism" in an Era of China's Global Rise'. In *International Communication of Chinese Culture.* Berlin and Heidelberg: Springer-Verlag. p. 21.

acknowledgement of existing national or ethnic diversities, in spite of the overwhelming majority of the Han population and the fragmentation into fifty-five minorities of the remaining 10 per cent. Once again, also from this point of view, the PRC has been able to profit from theoretical speculation and historical practice of the Soviet Union and its approach to handling its own nationalities problem:[41] giving nationalities their due would eventually prove to be of support for the revolutionary process as long as the political unitary leadership were not questioned.

The first constitutional source of the PRC has also established the structural elements of the system: explicit recognition of the plurality of nationalities within the established and protected unity of the State, proclamation of their equality and prohibition of discrimination, territorial autonomy and local use of their national languages.[42]

The same elements are also to be found in the 1975 Constitution,[43] which reinforces the principle of equality among the nationalities by introducing a

41 It is well known that the Soviet Union adopted a federal solution – obviously made compatible with the theory and practice of democratic centralism – to the extent of creating a bicameral parliament in which one of the Chambers was the Soviet of Nationalities. However, the socialist federal model (adopted as well by Yugoslavia and Czechoslovakia) has been rejected by China. Nevertheless, the Preamble of the White Paper on Regional Autonomy for Ethnic Minorities in China (2005) states that: 'Regional ethnic autonomy is the basic policy adopted by the Communist Party of China for resolving the ethnic issue in China through its application of Marxism-Leninism. It is an important political system of the State.'

42 See Art. 3 (1954 Const.): 'The People's Republic of China is a unitary multinational state. All the nationalities are equal. Discrimination against or oppression of any nationality, and acts which undermine the unity of the nationalities, are prohibited. All the nationalities have the freedom to use and develop their own spoken and written languages, and to preserve or reform their own customs and ways. Regional autonomy applies in areas where a minority nationality lives in a compact community. All the national autonomous areas are inseparable parts of the People's Republic of China.'

43 The Preamble states that 'for the last twenty years and more, the people of all nationalities in our country, continuing their triumphant advance under the leadership of the Communist Party of China, have achieved great victories both in socialist revolution and socialist construction and in the Great Proletarian Cultural Revolution, and have consolidated and strengthened the dictatorship of the proletariat'; that 'We should consolidate the great unity of the people of all nationalities led by the working class and based on the alliance of workers and peasants, and develop the revolutionary united front'; and finally exhorts, 'People of all nationalities in our country, unite to win still greater victories!'; while Arts 4 and 24 confirm the structural components: 'The People's Republic of China is a unitary multi-national state. The areas where regional national autonomy is exercised are all inalienable parts of the People's Republic of China. All the nationalities are equal. Big-nationality chauvinism and local-nationality chauvinism must be opposed. All the nationalities have the freedom to use their own spoken and written languages' and, respectively: 'The autonomous regions, autonomous prefectures and autonomous counties are all national autonomous areas; their organs of self-government are people's congresses and revolutionary committees. The organs of self-government of national autonomous areas, apart from exercising the functions and powers of local organs of state as specified in Chapter Two, Section III of the Constitution, may exercise autonomy within the limits of their authority as prescribed by law.

negative value judgement for both 'big-nationality chauvinism' and 'local-nationality chauvinism', the latter being likely to be the authentic target and the former being presumably mentioned for an exhibition of fairness.

In the 1978 Constitution, along with the repeated formalisation of the same basic rules,[44] the focus on the duo 'unity-pluralism' is somehow changed: plurality is expanded as to include Chinese populations and territories not presently within Chinese sovereignty and is no longer limited to the nationalities within it. Explicit reference is made, in fact, to Hong Kong, Macao and, with specific emphasis, to Taiwan.[45]

The 1982 Constitution presents a fundamental continuity with the previous documents: in the Preamble, a 'culture of grandeur' and a 'glorious revolutionary tradition' are attributed to the achievement by 'the people of all China's nationalities', or by the 'Chinese people of all nationalities'; furthermore, it is stated that:

> the People's Republic of China is a unitary multi-national State created jointly by the people of all its nationalities. Socialist relations of equality, unity and mutual assistance have been established among the nationalities and will continue to be strengthened. In the struggle to safeguard the unity of the nationalities, it is necessary to combat big-nation chauvinism, mainly Han chauvinism, and to combat local national chauvinism. The State will do its utmost to promote the common prosperity of all the nationalities.

The higher organs of state shall fully safeguard the exercise of autonomy by the organs of self government of national autonomous areas and actively support the minority nationalities in carrying out the socialist revolution and socialist construction.'

44 The Preamble proclaims the continuity between the past (since the founding of PRC 'the people of all our nationalities have carried out Chairman Mao's proletarian revolutionary line [. . .]') and the future ('the fundamental guarantee that the people of all our nationalities will struggle in unity and carry the proletarian revolution through to the end is always to hold high and staunchly to defend the great banner of Chairman Mao'); according to Art. 4: 'All the nationalities are equal. There should be unity and fraternal love among the nationalities and they should help and learn from each other. Discrimination against, or oppression of, any nationality, and acts which undermine the unity of the nationalities are prohibited. Big-nationality chauvinism and local-nationality chauvinism must be opposed. All the nationalities have the freedom to use and develop their own spoken and written languages, and to preserve or reform their own customs and ways. Regional autonomy applies in an area where a minority nationality lives in a compact community. All the national autonomous areas are inalienable parts of the People's Republic of China.'

45 Again in the Preamble, the following statements: 'We should consolidate and expand the revolutionary united front which is led by the working class and based on the worker-peasant alliance, and which unites the large numbers of intellectuals and other working people, patriotic democratic parties, patriotic personages, our compatriots in Taiwan, Hong Kong and Macao, and our country-men residing abroad. We should enhance the great unity of all the nationalities in our country'; and 'Taiwan is China's sacred territory. We are determined to liberate Taiwan and accomplish the great cause of unifying our motherland'.

Reference to Taiwan is repeated in the Preamble: 'Taiwan is part of the sacred territory of the People's Republic of China. It is the inviolable duty of all Chinese people, including our compatriots in Taiwan, to accomplish the great task of reunifying the motherland.' Honk Kong and Macao are not directly mentioned again, although – as indicated above – the provision for the establishment of Special Administrative Regions (Article 31) is specifically introduced for them.

The pattern of recognition and regulation of nationalities is confirmed in Article 4 through a variety of provisions.[46]

In the first place, equality is the object of various provisions: that 'all nationalities in the People's Republic of China are equal' and that 'discrimination against and oppression of any nationality are prohibited' are confirmed. The prohibition of 'any act, which undermines the unity of the nationalities or instigates division' is added. Moreover, 'the State protects the lawful rights and interests of the minority nationalities and upholds and develops a relationship of equality, unity and mutual assistance among all of China's nationalities'; a specific assistance by the State is to be made available for accelerating the 'economic and cultural development according to the characteristics and needs of the various minority nationalities'. No criteria are indicated that will allow to distinguish between lawful and unlawful rights and interests of the minority nationalities, so that granting or non-granting of State protection may be based on the rule of law.

It's quite evident that the status of minority nationalities is not given any justiciable right to access a special condition differentiating one group from the others outside of central determination that remains thoroughly political and discretionary – even more so when considering that the crucial issue of decision-making on 'economic and cultural development according to the characteristics and needs of the various minority nationalities' is indicated as part of the protective role of the State and not of regional self-government.

The only factor to be taken into account for the purpose of implementing the Constitution is the physical concentration of national groups on the same territory, although that same factor does not prevent the distribution of the national group into different regional borders.[47] Regional autonomy is consequently not normatively regulated on any fundamental principle, but is rather framed as a practice, thus mirroring whatever existing practice is in place.[48]

46 It is also confirmed by Art. 4 that 'all national autonomous areas are integral parts of the People's Republic of China' and that 'all nationalities have the freedom to use and develop their own spoken and written languages and to preserve or reform their own folkways and customs'. In 2009, the Government issued a White Paper on China's Ethnic Policy and Common Prosperity and Development of All Ethnic Groups (hereinafter, 'White Paper on Ethnic Policy') that, among other interesting data and general narratives, consolidates the switch in the official language from 'nationalities' to 'ethnic groups'.

47 This is indeed the case with Tibetans today.

48 See Art. 4 Const.: 'Regional autonomy is practiced in areas where people of minority nationalities live in concentrated communities; in these areas organs of self-government are established to

The constitutional regulation of regional autonomy qualified by the national or ethnic factor is established in Section 6 ('The Organs of Self-Government of National Autonomous Areas') of Chapter III ('The Structure of the State') as a form of exception to the general pattern of sub-central government (regulated in Section 5, 'The Local People's Congresses and Local People's Government at Local Levels'); in fact, the national factor applies to 'self-government' at various territorial levels (autonomous regions, prefectures and counties, as indicated by Article 112 of the 1982 Const.). The rules of the Constitution have been implemented by the Regional Ethnic Autonomy Law (REAL, 1984, as amended) and are to be read in the framework of the White Paper on Regional Autonomy for Ethic Minorities in China (2005) and the White Paper on China's policy and Common Prosperity and Development of All Ethnic Groups (2009).

Indeed, this form of Regional Autonomy may easily be qualified as corresponding at the most to a regime of self-administration in a twofold sense: first, such Regions are bound to give execution to legislation and policies decided and deliberated centrally;[49] and, second, 'the regulations on the exercise of autonomy and other separate regulations of autonomous regions shall be submitted to the Standing Committee of the National People's Congress for approval before they go into effect', although their autonomy is nominally allowed to be entitled to 'the power to enact regulations on the exercise of autonomy and other separate regulations in the light of the political, economic and cultural characteristics of the nationality or nationalities in the areas concerned' (Article 116 Const.).[50]

exercise the power of autonomy'. Art. 2, al. 3 specifies that: 'Ethnic autonomous areas are classified into autonomous regions, autonomous prefectures and autonomous counties.'

49 See Art. 3, al. 1 of REAL, which defines them as 'autonomous agencies that function as local agencies of state power at their respective levels'; the same provision clarifies that 'Autonomous agencies in ethnic autonomous areas shall apply the principle of democratic centralism'. Furthermore, Art. 5 states that 'Autonomous agencies in ethnic autonomous areas must uphold the unity of the country and guarantee that the Constitution and other laws are observed and implemented in these areas', Art. 6 that 'Autonomous agencies in ethnic autonomous areas lead the people of the various nationalities in a concentrated effort to promote socialist modernization. Under the principle of not contravening the Constitution and the laws, autonomous agencies in ethnic autonomous areas have the power to adopt special policies and flexible measures in the light of local conditions to speed up the economic and cultural development of these areas. Under the guidance of State plans and on the basis of actual conditions, autonomous agencies in ethnic autonomous areas steadily increase labour productivity and economic results, develop social productive forces and gradually raise the material living standards of the people of the various nationalities'; and, as stated by Art. 7, 'institutions of self-government in ethnic autonomous areas shall place the interests of the state as a whole above all else and actively fulfil all tasks assigned by state institutions at higher levels'. According to Art. 118 Const.: 'The organs of self-government of the national autonomous areas independently arrange for and administer local economic development under the guidance of State plans. In exploiting natural resources and building enterprises in the national autonomous areas, the State shall give due consideration to the interests of those areas.'

50 In Chapter IV of the White Paper on Ethnic Policy (Fundamental Political System for This Country), it is clearly stated that 'regional ethnic autonomy is a self-government system under the

In other words, the regional autonomy attributed to minorities is constrained by both positive and negative limits and the scope and quality of their autonomy does not appear to be substantially different from the one enjoyed by other territorial units – such as 'provinces, municipalities directly under the Central Government, counties, cities, municipal districts, townships, nationality townships, and towns' – where people's congresses and people's governments are established (Article 95 Const.).[51]

Constitutionalism with Chinese characteristics does, therefore, prove to be compatible with an asymmetric regime of territorial self-administration with regard to the ethnic (or, formerly, national) factor, but only as far as the organisational configuration of regional institutions is concerned. However, such distinguishing features do not have the functional legal consequence of affecting authentic self-government, of providing for exemption from strict central control and policy-making, of connecting the minority status to a differentiated setting that would accommodate diversity properly. Such consequences, on the contrary, are indeed present within constitutionalism with Chinese characteristics, but only where the diversity to be accommodated is the economy.

2.5 Regional self-government and the economy factor: Special Economic Zones and Special Administrative Regions

Constitutionalism with Chinese characteristics has developed two more institutional patterns for sub-state regional government: both of them are referred to as 'special', indicating that they enjoy a status of exception to general rules and both of them have their origins and *raison d'être* in economic development

unified leadership of the State. Every ethnic autonomous area is an inseparable part of the country. Organs of self-government in ethnic autonomous areas must follow the leadership of the central government'.

51 According to Art. 99 Const.: 'Local people's congresses at various levels ensure the observance and implementation of the Constitution and other laws and the administrative regulations in their respective administrative areas. Within the limits of their authority as prescribed by law, they adopt and issue resolutions and examine and decide on plans for local economic and cultural development and for the development of public services. Local people's congresses at or above the county level shall examine and approve the plans for economic and social development and the budgets of their respective administrative areas and examine and approve the reports on their implementation. They have the power to alter or annul inappropriate decisions of their own standing committees. The people's congresses of nationality townships may, within the limits of their authority as prescribed by law, take specific measures suited to the characteristics of the nationalities concerned'; while Art. 100 establishes that: 'The people's congresses of provinces, and municipalities directly under the Central Government, and their standing committees may adopt local regulations, which must not contravene the Constitution and other laws and administrative regulations, and they shall report such local regulations to the Standing Committee of the National People's Congress for the record.'

policies (Special Economic Zones, SEZ) and in sheer economic and financial capitalism (Special Administrative Regions, SAR).

The SEZs – started and framed after the end of the cultural revolution – are in fact the best evidence of the pragmatism of Chinese authorities in dealing with the problems of economic development of a massive population with their basic needs unsatisfied within an ideological scenario as compelling as Marxism-Leninism: 'the emphasis on unified policy and unified coordination make it difficult for local authorities to realize even the degree of independence and autonomy provided by the constitution. The situation can be changed only under the condition of a market economy'; granting legislative power to Shenzen 'is an example of how a market economy will require the enlargement of local autonomy'.[52]

Since 1980, when the new experiment started, SEZs have the autonomy to elaborate and implement their own market-oriented policies, and to attract foreign investments through tax incentives that shape territorial competitiveness as related to increasing production, export and further investments. The economically aggressive policies by SEZs have initially greatly increased the income of coastal areas; the establishment of free trade zones, technological development zones and high-tech industrial districts has later expanded the geographical areas interested by the profit-making attitude of the socialist market economy and made the asymmetric setting of regional autonomy more complex.[53] SEZs have a thoroughly functional rationale, therefore, to be identified in their potential of contributing to the increase of economic production according to capitalist modes.[54]

Such an important innovative feature of the PRC speaks of, some have suggested, a 'de facto federalism' in China, possessing 'the advantage of flexibility. What the center needs is the creative ambiguity implicit in *de facto* federalism. In other words, the centre needs, for the time being, not a clear-cut division between the center and the provinces, but ambiguity between them'.[55]

SARs are the second innovative functional solution that allows a somehow substantial regional autonomy under Chinese state sovereignty and gives strong evidence of the pragmatic approach of socialist constitutionalism with Chinese characteristics: as a matter of fact, the flexibility of such a peculiar arrangement, constitutionally formalised in Article 31 – although very vaguely, as indicated above – goes as far as introducing a sort of provisional suspension of the

52 Quotations from BUYUN, L. (2006), *Constitutionalism and China*. Beijing: Law Press. p. 9.

53 It has been written that 'they were established in 1982 as "windows" for the reform and open-door experiment. Although the SEZs are no longer so "special" today, given the widespread delegation of legislative power to the local governments as the reform proceeds, they nevertheless illustrate how certain yokes of the unitary framework may be shaken off to allow trials of far-reaching institutional breakthroughs', in ZHANG (2012), above note 9, p. 109.

54 On recent developments, see BIN, L. (2015), 'Institutional Innovation and Breakthrough in the Free Trade Zones'. *China Law*. 113. p. 62.

55 See YONGNIAN, Z. (2007), *De facto Federalism in China: Reforms and Dynamics of Central-Local Relations*. Singapore: World Scientific. p. 382.

effectiveness of the PRC Constitution, such suspension presently being a promise only in the case of Taiwan, but actual with regard to SAR Hong Kong and SAR Macao.[56]

In all three cases, the 'one country two systems' formula – originally devised for Taiwan,[57] although first applied to Hong Kong and Macao – is mainly instrumental to achieving peaceful reunification of all those parts of China that for different reasons are not within the motherland's full unified and unitary sovereignty.

The White Paper on Taiwan (1993) emphasises that:

> this position is an important component of the theory and practice of building socialism with Chinese characteristics and a fundamental State policy of the Chinese Government which will not change for a long time to come. Its basic contents are as follows: 1. Only one China [. . .]'Self- determination' for Taiwan is out of the question. 2. Coexistence of two systems. On the premise of one China, socialism on the mainland and capitalism on Taiwan can coexist and develop side by side for a long time without one swallowing up the other [. . .]It will be a unique feature and important innovation in the state system of a reunified China. After reunification, Taiwan's current socio-economic system, its way of life as well as economic and cultural ties with foreign countries can remain unchanged. Private property, including houses and land, as well as business ownership, legal inheritance and overseas Chinese and foreign investments on the island will all be protected by law. 3. A high degree of autonomy. After reunification, Taiwan will become a special administrative region. It will be distinguished from the other provinces or regions of China by its high degree of autonomy. It will have its own administrative and legislative powers, an independent judiciary and the right of adjudication on the island.[58]

56 The suspension, as said in the text, is meant to be provisional, though, as a deadline for its validity has already been indicated in the year 2047 for Hong Kong and 2049 for Macao. Neither the Constitution nor the Basic Laws indicate what the status of the two SARs is going to be after that deadline and from this point of view the future of all three systems (Hong Kong, Macao and Taiwan) appears quite uncertain.

57 See the White Paper on the Taiwan Question and Reunification of China, 1993: 'To settle the Taiwan question and achieve national reunification – this is a sacrosanct mission of the entire Chinese people. The Chinese Government has persistently worked towards this end since the founding of the People's Republic. Its basic position on this question is: peaceful reunification; one country, two systems'; and 'Chinese leader Deng Xiaoping pointed out on 11 January 1982 that this in effect meant "one country, two systems", i.e., on the premise of national reunification, the main body of the nation would continue with its socialist system while Taiwan could maintain capitalism. On 26 June 1983 Deng Xiaoping further enunciated the concept of peaceful reunification, stressing that the crucial point was national reunification. He went on to expound the Government's policy on reunification and on the creation of a Taiwan special administrative region'.

58 The White Paper continues: '[Taiwan] will run its own party, political, military, economic and financial affairs. It may conclude commercial and cultural agreements with foreign countries

With regard to the previous British and Portuguese colonies, the first domestic acts of implementation of this constitutional regional policy have been the enactment of HK Basic Law (1997) and Macao Basic Law (1999) which, although approved by the National People's Congress, are meant to serve as the two SARs' respective own constitutions, marking the boundaries of SARs' self-government: according to Article 5 of HK Basic Law, 'the socialist system and policies shall not be practiced in the Hong Kong Special Administrative Region, and the previous capitalist system and way of life remain unchanged for 50 years'.

In short, with the exception of general foreign and defence policies, the two SARs enjoy a 'high degree of autonomy under the law'[59] unparalleled by any other existing regional arrangement in the PRC:[60] the common law tradition in Hong Kong and the civil law of Portuguese origin in Macao continue to be in force as well as their distinct judicial systems – up to the respective court of last instance; most of the main policies – monetary and financial affairs (including their own currency), taxation, domestic and international trade (and separate membership in the WTO), education, culture and science, public health and social welfare – are part of HKSAR's and Macao SAR's 'high degree of autonomy in accordance with the law', thus establishing 'two systems' within 'one country'.

Nevertheless, how high the degree of autonomy is and may be is to be tested over time, as the framework designed by the Basic Laws does ensure a relevant role of oversight to the PRC authorities.[61] The Chinese Government's White Paper on 'One Country, Two Systems' Policy in the Hong Kong Special Administrative Region, for instance, is quite generous both in acknowledging the high degree of autonomy of HKSAR, but also in framing its actual exercise within and under unitary control by national authorities. In fact, the qualification of the Special

and enjoy certain rights in foreign affairs. It may keep its military forces and the mainland will not dispatch troops or administrative personnel to the island. On the other hand, representatives of the government of the special administrative region and those from different circles of Taiwan may be appointed to senior posts in the central government and participate in the running of national affairs.' In 2005, the PRC has adopted an Anti-Secession Law, expressly concerning Taiwan (apparently as a response to the growth of the Independentists there), which confirms the features of the promise of a high degree of autonomy (Art. 5, al. 3, 'After the country is reunified peacefully, Taiwan may practice systems different from those on the mainland and enjoy a high degree of autonomy'), but warns also (Art. 8) that 'the State shall employ non-peaceful means and other necessary measures to protect China's sovereignty and territorial integrity'.

59 The formula is to be repeatedly read in the White Paper on The Practice of the 'One Country Two Systems' Policy in the Hong Kong Special Administrative Region, 2014.

60 Art. 11 of the Basic Law states that 'in accordance with Article 31 of the Constitution of the People's Republic of China, the systems and policies practised in the Hong Kong Special Administrative Region, including the social and economic systems, the system for safeguarding the fundamental rights and freedoms of its residents, the executive, legislative and judicial systems, and the relevant policies, shall be based on the provisions of this Law'.

61 The White Paper specifies that 'the organs of power by which the central leadership directly exercises jurisdiction over the HKSAR are the NPC and its Standing Committee, the president of the state, the Central People's Government, and the Central Military Commission'.

Region as merely 'administrative' and not as 'political' may prove to be, on the one hand, an understatement – as the differentiation of policies is real – but, on the other, a symptom indicating that the political dimension is inherently unitary, that it belongs exclusively to the national authorities and that the special autonomy of the second (capitalist) system depends on the assessment by the one (socialist) country only. The image of an attitude established on the carrot and the stick is quite appropriate, although the stick appears to have rather a deterrent function only and the priority of economic welfare does not really need the incentive of the carrot.[62]

For instance, as established by Article 17, al. 3 of the Basic Law, the Standing Committee of the NPC may declare 'a law enacted by the legislature of the Region [. . .] not in conformity with the provisions of this Law regarding affairs within the responsibility of the Central Authorities or regarding the relationship between the Central Authorities and the Region and, although without the power of amending it, the SC has the authority of having such law "immediately [. . .] invalidated", with no retroactive effect, unless otherwise provided for in the laws of the Region'.

Other important examples concern the power of amendment of the Basic Law, which belongs exclusively to the NPC – which originally enacted it – and, mostly, the power of interpretation, which is attributed to the Standing Committee of the NPC.

More in detail, with regard to the consequences for the independence of the judiciary, Article 158 of the Basic Law provides that 'the Standing Committee of the NPC shall authorize the courts of the HKSAR to interpret on their own, in adjudicating cases, the provisions of this Law which are within the limits of the autonomy of the Region': in fact, interpretation of the law does not belong inherently and structurally to the judicial function per se, as 'this power of interpretation comes from the authorization of the NPC Standing Committee'.

The Basic Law has also introduced a sort of *referé legislatif* 'with Chinese characteristics', insofar as 'if the courts of the HKSAR, in the process of adjudicating cases, need to interpret the provisions of the Basic Law concerning affairs which are the responsibility of the central government, or concerning the relationship between the central authorities and the HKSAR, and if such interpretation will affect the judgments on the cases, the courts of the HKSAR shall, before making their final judgments which are not appealable, seek an interpretation of the relevant provisions from the NPC Standing Committee through the Court of Final Appeal of the HKSAR'. The NPC Standing Committee's interpretation is binding on the courts of the HKSAR as such interpretation 'enjoys the same status with HKSAR laws'. The Basic Law also explains that the Standing Committee's 'power of interpretation of the Basic Law

62 And yet see comments and documents in CHOU, Bill K.P. (2012), 'Implementation Measures of China's Macao Policies'. *Chinese Law and Government*. 45(5). p. 3.

in accordance with the law is aimed at maintaining the rule of law in Hong Kong, as it oversees HKSAR's implementation of the Basic Law and protects the high degree of autonomy of the region'.

Under the heading 'Fully and Accurately Understanding the Meaning of "One Country, Two Systems"', the philosophy of the approach is clearly described by the White Paper as being founded on a 'holistic concept': first, 'as a unitary State, China's central government has comprehensive jurisdiction over all local administrative regions, including the HKSAR. *The high degree of autonomy of HKSAR is not an inherent power, but one that comes solely from the authorization by the central leadership. The high degree of autonomy of the HKSAR is not full autonomy, nor a decentralized power. It is the power to run local affairs as authorized by the central leadership*'.[63] Second, 'the "two systems" means that, within the "one country", the main body of the country practices socialism, while Hong Kong and some other regions practice capitalism. *The "one country" is the premise and basis of the "two systems," and the "two systems" is subordinate to and derived from "one country." But the "two systems" under the "one country" are not on a par with each other*'.[64]

3. One country *three* systems: establishing a 'Special Cultural Region' for genuine autonomy in Tibet

The critical examination of the systemic framework of socialist constitutionalism with Chinese characteristics may have aggregated sufficient evidence so far to the purpose of highlighting the strategic lucidity of the Chinese Communist Party (CCP), as well as the normative transparency of governmental authorities of the

63 Emphasis added. The White Paper further specifies that 'the high degree of autonomy of HKSAR is subject to the level of the central leadership's authorization. There is no such thing called "residual power." With China's Constitution stipulating in clear-cut terms that the country follows a fundamental system of socialism, the basic system, core leadership and guiding thought of the "one country" have been explicitly provided for. The most important thing to do in upholding the "one country" principle is to maintain China's sovereignty, security and development interests, and respect the country's fundamental system and other systems and principles'.

64 Emphasis added. The White Paper explains that 'the fact that the mainland, the main body of the country, embraces socialism will not change. With that as the premise, and taking into account the history of Hong Kong and some other regions, capitalism is allowed to stay on a long-term basis. Therefore, a socialist system by the mainland is the prerequisite and guarantee for Hong Kong's practicing capitalism and maintaining its stability and prosperity. For Hong Kong to retain its capitalist system and enjoy a high degree of autonomy with "Hong Kong people governing Hong Kong" according to the Basic Law, it must fully respect the socialist system practiced on the mainland in keeping with the "one country" principle and, in particular, the political system and other systems and principles in practice. The mainland should respect and tolerate the capitalism embraced by Hong Kong while upholding its socialist system, and draw on the successful experience of Hong Kong in economic development and social management. Only by respecting and learning from each other can the "two systems" in the "one country" coexist harmoniously and achieve common development'.

PRC in shaping the development of the legal system and the institutional setting without endangering the strongest unitary political control while, at the same time, preventing differences and diversities to fully display a rationale of their own and ultimately affect the condition of national uniformity.

As we have seen, acknowledgement of differences and diversities has indeed been introduced, as it was inevitable: on the one hand, national minorities and ethnic groups are recognised also through a distinctive mechanism of regional autonomy, although under strict political control, and, on the other, the advantages of allowing single parts of the territory to adopt a different speed on the way toward ongoing modernisation and economic development have gradually increased asymmetric forms of decentralisation. Socialist constitutionalism with Chinese characteristics has grown into a fairly polymorphic and multichromatic texture, many threads of different colour and thickness departing from one central knot; and yet the one central knot maintains the control of the whole texture. However, China increasingly seems to be in a transition that needs to be governed.

The main and, in fact, exclusive inspiration of modernising policies in the PRC couldn't be but strictly coherent with an inherently pragmatic vision – which, by the experimental practice of cherry-picking, has learned how to draw, separately and jointly, from whatever intellectual source (Marxism-Leninism, Western constitutionalism and rule of law, Japanese modernisation, Confucian ethics) appears to be more promising in ensuring the expected result, which may be identified mainly with economic power as the way of national(ist) assertion. The scale of the effort is huge, as firmness of the grip directing it must consequently be, and as unpredictable as the evolving and evolutionary dynamics of socialist constitutionalism with Chinese characteristic – among which a socialist market economy occupies a prominent role – have so far been (and, perhaps, as ever-more difficult managing the growing systemic contradictions is going to be).

It does not seem inappropriate to question the opportunity of new developments of constitutional policies and, more specifically, of such policies concerning nationalities and ethnic groups in the PRC, also with regard to the configuration of their respective regional autonomy which ought not to be further detached from their distinguishing world view and identity. In this direction, Asian and European models experiencing the combination of minorities' protection and regional self-government are useful references that provide important empirical evidence and technical know-how concerning the abstract feasibility and concrete practicability of such policies.

The perspectives of such compared references, nevertheless, are indeed more an intellectual and, ultimately, a cultural challenge to the Chinese constitutional order as they entail a radically different liberal founding paradigm, not compatible with Marxism-Leninism, even though re-elaborated with Chinese characteristics. Asian and European experiences may not be part of a process of imitation, or circulation, or even of adaptation to the Chinese context: the solutions that they offer need to be reshaped and reinvented, almost genetically.

The Tibetan quest for genuine autonomy – by its very nature and as articulated in the Memorandum – cannot be accommodated within any of the existing arrangements so far established in the PRC: not in the present form of National (or Ethnic) Autonomous Regions, nor in the form of Special Administrative Regions, the latter founded – as they are – on a thoroughly economic rationale, not because an economic rationale is wrong per se, but because it does not correspond to the Tibetan world view.

The SAR model safeguards – textually – the 'way of life', connected to the capitalist system, in Hong Kong (Article 5 of the Basic Law), but the question here is how to protect the 'way of life' in Tibet where the latter is not connected to a capitalist economy. Hence the suggestion for a *third* system within the one country.

The distinctiveness of Tibetan identity, Tibetan way of life, Tibetan spirituality, Tibetan understanding of the land and the environment, Tibetan social relations and institutions[65] – as compared to other minority cultures in China,[66] the principle of formal equality and the prohibition of discrimination among nationalities and ethnic groups not providing a persuasive ground for the denial of a proper constitutional status, inclusive of genuine autonomy – offers the objective rationale for engrafting a system of autonomy of its own on the generous perspectives disclosed by Article 31 of the PRC Constitution. Thus, a *third* system, within the one country.

The Tibetan Memorandum shows reliance on the PRC Constitution, and it could not do otherwise. But it reads the Constitution as if it were – or even might be – the source of a protected right of the Tibetan people to achieve a genuine autonomy in the regulation of a number of matters of vital importance for the preservation of their culture and identity. The PRC Constitution, because of its very nature, may only be the ground for the legitimate explanation of a politically discretionary decision by the PRC's authorities to experiment with – initially and, perhaps, consolidate at a later stage – yet another organisational and functional setting for the management of a problem which requires a durable solution.

Any political decision is adopted in order to achieve an advantage. Attributing some special forms of regional autonomy to some nationalities – under the influence of the Soviet Union's ways for coping with the pluralism of ethnicities – thus introducing exceptions to the general territorial organisation of governance, has been regarded as a political advantage, the alternative being sheer indifference to the reality of cultural diversities leading inevitably to their assimilation and ultimate disappearance.

65 It's noteworthy, for instance, that Buddhism has achieved 'some kind of political consensus' only in Tibet, as observed by GLENN, P. (2014), *Legal Traditions of the World*. 5th Edn. Oxford: Oxford University Press. p. 332.

66 The Islamic culture in Xinjang, of course, provides another situation to be considered in the same perspectives; see ISRAELI, R. (1978), *Muslims in China: A Study in Cultural Confrontation*. London and Malmö: Scandinavian Institute of Asian Studies Monograph Series No. 29.

Profiting from the advantages of 'capitalist' capitalism within a wider 'socialist' market economy (or 'socialist' capitalism *tout court*) has been regarded by the PRC's authorities as a proper justification for a provisional suspension of the Constitution insofar as it establishes and implements a socialist system, without giving up, of course, the sovereignty of the one country.

Only the Chinese authorities may be able to articulate a long-term vision of how and to what extent the PRC might profit from the advantages of a decision favourable to accommodating the Memorandum for Genuine Autonomy in Tibet and establishing a Special Cultural Region there. The creativity entailed by such an enterprise, even more so if experimented not only in Tibet, might give impulse to a new wave of constitutionalism in China, in which Chinese characteristics may cease to be added to a source of foreign inspiration, but may constitute the very core of a new trend of original and genuine Chinese constitutionalism.

Tibetans, for their part, drawing inspiration from both the 17-Point Agreement and the Memorandum, and considering – to the extent of their best and proper applicability – Asian and European experiences, ought to undertake writing a draft Basic Law for a Special Region of Tibet in which the institutional shape and functional consistency guarantees the cultural and spiritual heritage that is to be preserved, promoted and projected into the future. The Memorandum in fact does show full awareness of the need to shape the appropriate institutional setting for a genuine autonomy of Tibet within the PRC's sovereignty, although at the present stage it does not go into the necessary details of such an innovative structure of their regional self-government.[67]

Indeed, there is a conflict over the autonomy of Tibet.

In many parts of the world, we witness physiological tensions between central and sub-national governments and again even more so when the unitary and uniform policies of the former are exclusively reflective of the interests of an ethnic, ideological, linguistic majority rather than accommodating the interests of the diverse cultural minorities. Acknowledgement and reasonable regulation of diversities is the common understanding of the constitutional principle of equality.

Conflicts are physiological in all human affairs, but undoubtedly they are even more so when affecting cultural and identity issues, with symbolic underpinnings. Surely, conflicts are physiological but they turn into a pathology when there is no dialogue between the parties concerned and when the lack of dialogue is an indicator (if not the main effect) of the unwillingness of even just one of the parties to recognise the conflict and try to create a dialogue for managing it.

67 See, for instance, the Memorandum, where it acknowledges that 'the extent to which the right to self-government and self-administration can be exercised on the preceding subject matters largely determines the genuine character of Tibetan autonomy. The task at hand is therefore to look into the manner in which autonomy can be regulated and exercised for it to effectively respond to the unique situation and basic needs of the Tibetan nationality' (para. VI, on the 'nature and structure of the autonomy').

This seems to be the current condition of the Tibetan question: a conflict whose features are unfortunately well rooted in decades of denial of the conflict itself, on the ground that a solution to it – one's own unilateral solution – has been achieved already and historically established in a permanent way. The Tibetan question thus continues to be an unresolved pathological conflict precisely because of its alleged solution. Therefore, a new approach to the solution is needed, an approach – somehow suggested by the image of a Special Cultural Region as a Third System within the One Country – that should be peaceful, reasonable and founded on a trustworthy and reliable foundation, be it the law (as it would be in Western constitutionalism) or any other source of authority, as it might be consistent with Asian constitutional culture and traditional values.

Appendix

The 17-Point Agreement

1. The Tibetan people shall be united and drive out the imperialist aggressive forces from Tibet; that the Tibetan people shall return to the big family of the motherland – the People's Republic of China.
2. The Local Government of Tibet shall actively assist the People's Liberation Army to enter Tibet and consolidate the national defences.
3. In accordance with the policy towards nationalities laid down in the Common Programme of the Chinese People's Political Consultative Conference, the Tibetan people have the right of exercising national regional autonomy under the unified leadership of the Central People's Government.
4. The Central Authorities will not alter the existing political system in Tibet. The Central Authorities also will not alter the established status, functions and powers of the Dalai Lama. Officials of various ranks shall hold office as usual.
5. The established status, functions, and powers of the Panchen Ngoerhtehni shall be maintained.
6. By the established status, functions and powers of the Dalai Lama and of the Panchen Ngoerhtehni is meant the status, functions and powers of the 13th Dalai Lama and of the 9th Panchen Ngoerhtehni when they were in friendly and amicable relations with each other.
7. The policy of freedom of religious belief laid down in the Common Programme of the Chinese People's Political Consultative Conference will be protected. The Central Authorities will not affect any change in the income of the monasteries.
8. The Tibetan troops will be reorganised step by step into the People's Liberation Army, and become a part of the national defence forces of the Central People's Government.
9. The spoken and written language and school education of the Tibetan nationality will be developed step by step in accordance with the actual conditions in Tibet.
10. Tibetan agriculture, livestock raising, industry and commerce will be developed step by step, and the people's livelihood shall be improved step by step in accordance with the actual conditions in Tibet.

11. In matters related to various reforms in Tibet, there will be no compulsion on the part of the Central Authorities. The Local Government of Tibet should carry out reforms of its own accord, and when the people raise demands for reform, they must be settled through consultation with the leading personnel of Tibet.
12. In so far as former pro-imperialist and pro-KMT officials resolutely sever relations with imperialism and the KMT and do not engage in sabotage or resistance, they may continue to hold office irrespective of their past.
13. The People's Liberation Army entering Tibet will abide by the above-mentioned policies and will also be fair in all buying and selling and will not arbitrarily take even a needle or a thread from the people.
14. The Central People's Government will handle all external affairs of the area of Tibet; and there will be peaceful co-existence with neighbouring countries and the establishment and development of fair commercial and trading relations with them on the basis of equality, mutual benefit and mutual respect for territory and sovereignty.
15. In order to ensure the implementation of this agreement, the Central People's Government will set up a military and administrative committee and a military area headquarters in Tibet, and apart from the personnel sent there by the Central People's Government it will absorb as many local Tibetan personnel as possible to take part in the work. Local Tibetan personnel taking part in the military and administrative committee may include patriotic elements from the Local Government of Tibet, various district and various principal monasteries; the name list is to be prepared after consultation between the representatives designated by the Central People's Government and various quarters concerned, and is to be submitted to the Central People's Government for approval.
16. Funds needed by the military and administrative committee, the military area headquarters and the People's Liberation Army entering Tibet will be provided by the Central People's Government. The Local Government of Tibet should assist the People's Liberation Army in the purchases and transportation of food, fodder, and other daily necessities.
17. This agreement shall come into force immediately after signatures and seals are affixed to it.

Index